Lecture Notes in Artificial Intelligence 1400

Subseries of Lecture Notes in Computer Science
Edited by J. G. Carbonell and J. Siekmann

Lecture Notes in Computer Science
Edited by G. Goos, J. Hartmanis and J. van Leeuwen

Springer
Berlin
Heidelberg
New York
Barcelona
Budapest
Hong Kong
London
Milan
Paris
Santa Clara
Singapore
Tokyo

Mario Lenz Brigitte Bartsch-Spörl
Hans-Dieter Burkhard Stefan Wess (Eds.)

Case-Based Reasoning Technology

From Foundations to Applications

Springer

Series Editors
Jaime G. Carbonell, Carnegie Mellon University, Pittsburgh, PA, USA
Jörg Siekmann, University of Saarland, Saarbrücken, Germany

Volume Editors

Mario Lenz
Hans-Dieter Burkhard
Institut für Informatik, LFG für KI, Humboldt-Universität zu Berlin
Axel Springer Str. 54a, D-10117 Berlin, Germany
E-mail: {lenz, hdb}@informatik.hu-berlin.de

Brigitte Bartsch-Spörl
BSR Consulting GmbH
Wirtstr. 38, D-81539 München, Germany
E-mail: brigitte@bsr-consulting.de

Stefan Wess
TecInno GmbH
Sauerwiesen 2, D-67661 Kaiserslautern, Germany
E-mail: Wess@tecmath.de

Cataloging-in-Publication Data applied for

Die Deutsche Bibliothek - CIP-Einheitsaufnahme

Case based reasoning technology : from foundations to applications / Mario Lenz ... (ed.). - Berlin ; Heidelberg ; New York ; Barcelona ; Budapest ; Hong Kong ; London ; Milan ; Paris ; Santa Clara ; Singapore ; Tokyo : Springer, 1998
(Lecture notes in computer science ; Vol. 1400 : Lecture notes in artificial intelligence)
ISBN 3-540-64572-1

CR Subject Classification (1991): I.2, J.1, J.3

ISBN 3-540-64572-1 Springer-Verlag Berlin Heidelberg New York

Typesetting: Camera ready by author
SPIN 10637061 06/3142 – 5 4 3 2 1 0 Printed on acid-free paper

Preface

Human experts are not systems of rules, they are libraries of experiences.
Riesbeck and Schank (1989, p.15)

Broadly speaking, case-based reasoning (CBR) is concerned with solving new problems by adapting solutions that worked for similar problems in the past.

As with Artificial Intelligence in general, case-based reasoning deals with two different aspects of intelligence: A first motivation is to establish cognitive models in order to understand human thinking and behavior. A second motivation is to build systems which help to solve real-world problems. These two facets can be considered as two sides of the same coin. Traditionally, CBR research in Europe has concentrated very much on the second aspect, though, of course, successful projects are not possible without a sound theory.

The objective of this book is to summarize the results of recent years of research in CBR. A strong emphasis is put on projects performed and applications developed in Germany. However, research has not been performed in isolation. Rather, a large number of cooperations between research sites throughout the world have been established which provided a fertile ground for the community. Hence, it is only natural that work from colleagues from France, Ireland, the Netherlands, and the United States has been included in this volume.

This book is not intended to be a textbook giving a comprehensive overview of the field. Rather, the objective is to consider in detail different potential application areas, to work out the pros and cons of using CBR and to summarize the lessons learned from projects. For this, we assume that the reader already has at least a basic understanding of what case-based reasoning is all about.

In order to guarantee a high quality of the contributions, we appointed for every chapter authors who undoubtedly have a special competence in that particular area. It has been the responsibility of the authors to decide about the contents of their chapters and about further contributions from coauthors. After the first contributions had been collected, a revision process aimed at improving the quality of the chapters and giving the book a uniform look. Nevertheless, each chapter expresses the opinions of the author(s) and does not necessarily reflect the conceptions of the editors.

According to the objectives explained above, the structure of the book is as follows: In Chapter 1, Michael M. Richter gives a general introduction to the field. Here, the basic ideas of case-based reasoning are explained and important terms are defined. Following this, Chapter 2 suggests some new view points on CBR. The main part of the book, from Chapter 3 to Chapter 11, is concerned with several application areas that CBR has been successfully applied to. As these chapters show, a number of projects arose from the research activities and several systems have been implemented. Thus, CBR projects can no longer be performed in an ad hoc manner but need to be based upon a solid methodology; this is the topic of Chapter 12. Finally, related areas are discussed in Chapter 13.

As the list of contributors shows, in total 29 authors participated in writing this book. We want to thank all these authors for giving valuable insights in their domain of expertise. Particular thanks go to Michael Brown who took up the burden of reading a preliminary version of this book and correcting the usage of English.

Spring 1998

Mario Lenz
Brigitte Bartsch-Spörl
Hans-Dieter Burkhard
Stefan Wess

Table of Contents

List of Figures

List of Tables

List of Contributors

Klaus-Dieter Althoff
Fraunhofer Institute for Experimental Software Engineering (IESE)
Sauerwiesen 6
D-67661 Kaiserslautern
Germany
althoff@iese.fhg.de

Eric Auriol
AcknoSoft
58 rue du dessous des Berges
F-75013 Paris
France
auriol@ibpc.fr

Brigitte Bartsch-Spörl
BSR Consulting GmbH
Wirtstrasse 38
D-81539 Munich
Germany
brigitte@bsr-consulting.de

Ralph Bergmann
University of Kaiserslautern
Centre for Learning Systems and Applications (LSA)
P.O. Box 3049
D-67653 Kaiserslautern
Germany
bergmann@informatik.uni-kl.de

Andreas Birk
Fraunhofer Institute for Experimental Software Engineering (IESE)
Sauerwiesen 6
D-67661 Kaiserslautern
Germany
birk@iese.fhg.de

Katy Börner
University of Bielefeld
Faculty of Technology
P.O. Box 10 01 31
D-33501 Bielefeld
Germany
katy@TechFak.Uni-Bielefeld.DE

Mathias Bull
University of Rostock
Dept. for Medical Informatics and Biometry
Rembrandtstrasse 16/17
D-18055 Rostock
Germany
mathias.bull@medizin.uni-rostock.de

Hans-Dieter Burkhard
Humboldt University
Department of Computer Science
Unter den Linden 6
D-10099 Berlin
Germany
hdb@informatik.hu-berlin.de

Pádraig Cunningham
AI Group
Department of Computer Science
ORI.G.40, O'Reilly Building
Trinity College, Dublin 2
Ireland
Padraig.Cunningham@cs.tcd.ie

Lothar Gierl
University of Rostock
Dept. for Medical Informatics and Biometry
Rembrandtstrasse 16/17
D-18055 Rostock
Germany
lothar.gierl@medizin.uni-rostock.de

Christoph Globig
University of Kaiserslautern
Centre for Learning Systems and Applications (LSA)
P.O. Box 3049
D-67653 Kaiserslautern
Germany
globig@informatik.uni-kl.de

Christiane Gresse von Wangenheim
Universidade Federal de Santa Catarina - UFSC
Production Engineering
88049-000 Florianpolis , S.C.
Brazil
gresse@eps.ufsc.br

André Hübner
Humboldt University
Department of Computer Science
Unter den Linden 6
D-10099 Berlin
Germany
huebner@informatik.hu-berlin.de

Gerd Kamp
University of Hamburg
Computer Science Department
Vogt-Koelln-Str. 30
D-22527 Hamburg
Germany
kamp@informatik.uni-hamburg.de

Mirjam Kunze
Humboldt University
Department of Computer Science
Unter den Linden 6
D-10099 Berlin
Germany
kunze@informatik.hu-berlin.de

Steffen Lange
Universität Leipzig
Institut für Mathematik und Informatik
Augustplatz 10-11
04109 Leipzig
Germany
slange@informatik.uni-leipzig.de

Mario Lenz
Humboldt University
Department of Computer Science
Unter den Linden 6
D-10099 Berlin
Germany
lenz@informatik.hu-berlin.de

Michel Manago
AcknoSoft
58 rue du dessous des Berges
F-75013 Paris
France
manago@ibpc.fr

Erica Melis
University of Saarbrücken
Computer Science Department
D-66041 Saarbrücken
Germany
melis@ags.uni-sb.de

Héctor Muñoz-Avila
University of Kaiserslautern
Centre for Learning Systems and Applications (LSA)
P.O. Box 3049
D-67653 Kaiserslautern
Germany
munioz@informatik.uni-kl.de

Michael M. Richter
University of Kaiserslautern
Centre for Learning Systems and Applications (LSA)
P.O. Box 3049
D-67653 Kaiserslautern
Germany
richter@informatik.uni-kl.de

Rainer Schmidt
University of Rostock
Dept. for Medical Informatics and Biometry
Rembrandtstrasse 16/17
D-18055 Rostock
Germany
rainer.schmidt@medizin.uni-rostock.de

Thomas J. Schult
Redaktion c't
Helstorfer Str.7
D-30625 Hannover
Germany
ts@ct.heise.de

Barry Smyth
University College Dublin
Department of Computer Science
Belfield, Dublin 4
Ireland
Barry.Smyth@ucd.ie

Carsten Tautz
Fraunhofer Institute for Experimental Software Engineering (IESE)
Sauerwiesen 6
D-67661 Kaiserslautern
Germany
tautz@iese.fhg.de

Manuela Veloso
School of Computer Science
Carnegie Mellon University
Pittsburgh PA 15213-3891
USA
mmv@cs.cmu.edu

Gerhard Weber
Department of Psychology
University of Education Freiburg
Kunzenweg 21
D-79117 Freiburg
Germany
weber@cogpsy.uni-trier.de

Stefan Wess
TecInno GmbH
Sauerwiesen 2
D-67661 Kaiserslautern
Germany
wess@tecmath.de

Wolfgang Wilke
University of Kaiserslautern
Centre for Learning Systems and Applications (LSA)
P.O. Box 3049
D-67653 Kaiserslautern
Germany
wilke@informatik.uni-kl.de

1. Introduction

Michael M. Richter

1.1 Preliminaries

The purpose of this introduction is to provide the basic concepts of Case-Based Reasoning (CBR) underlying the chapters in this book in order to provide a unified terminology. It is not intended as an introductory text to a novice (this would, e.g., require the elaboration of examples and many more details) but rather to fix the language and to avoid unnecessary repetitions of elementary definitions in the following chapters. This introduction is split into sections dealing with

- knowledge representation in general
- specific terms in CBR
- the general structure of CBR-systems
- the main application areas of CBR.

The more technical terms are introduced in the first sections. The general structure of CBR-systems is discussed in Sections 1.3.7 and 1.3.8. In Section 1.3.8, we introduce the notion of a knowledge container which seems to be particularly suitable for the description of CBR systems. Some of the terms to be introduced have formal definitions while others are expressions of everyday language which are used in a specific way. For the latter, it is appropriate to provide explanations which paraphrase the meaning of the term in question in a sufficiently precise manner. Also, for the former, we will not use explicit formalisms; the intended meaning will become clear from the context. In all situations, the concept under consideration will be written in *italics*.

1.2 Some Aspects of Knowledge Representation

Knowledge in our context is to be understood as an informal notion describing something that a human, a formal system, or a machine can possibly use in order to perform a certain task or functionality, e.g., to solve a problem. In order to use some knowledge entity one has

a) to have access to it and
b) to know (i.e., to have instructions) how to apply it when the intended activity is performed.

The way the knowledge is expressed is the type of *knowledge representation*, which consists of certain data structures and additional *inference operations* that allow to change these data structures. A set of such data structures and inference operations is called a *knowledge base.* The representation may have specific structures available which are suitable for certain kinds of knowledge; these are called *knowledge containers* (see Section 1.3.8).

The instructions describing the intended use of the knowledge constitute the *semantics* of the represented knowledge; they tell how it is *interpreted.* If a system has access to the semantics, the knowledge representation is called *formal* for that system otherwise it is *informal.* An essential part of the system are strategies which organize the application of inference operations. A special case of informal knowledge for all machines is when only humans know the semantics.

In what follows, we will put our emphasis on those aspects of knowledge representation relevant to CBR.

1.2.1 Data Structures

One of the first questions to be handled in a knowledge representation system is which data structures are used to represent primitive notions. These may be, e.g., predicates, functions, or related constructs.

An important structure in CBR is the *attribute-value representation.* An *attribute* is given by:

- a name A
- a (usually) finite set $\mathcal{DOM}(A)$ called the domain of the attribute A or the set of values of A
- a variable x_A

Such a domain $\mathcal{DOM}(A)$ may carry an additional structure, e.g., a partial or total ordering. A is called *numeric* if $\mathcal{DOM}(A)$ consist of numbers (which are always ordered) and *symbolic* if it is an arbitrary finite set (with or without structure).

Attributes are often called *features.* For a finite set A_i, $1 \leq i \leq n$, of attributes an *attribute-value vector* is an n-tuple $(a_1, \ldots, a_n)$ such that $a_i \in \mathcal{DOM}(A_i)$.

If one wants to deal with incomplete knowledge one allows the entries of the vector to be variables which express "value unknown". In some applications, the set of attributes is fixed while others require an open world assumption with dynamic changes in the number of attributes as well as in the domains of the attributes. If nothing but the vectors are given, one calls this a *flat representation.* In a *structural representation*, it is equipped with additional structures reflecting, e.g., an object-oriented hierarchy. A way to achieve this is to group attributes together and to repeat this grouping on the higher levels (on groups of attributes etc.) and to supply an inheritance service. In CBR, cases are often represented using (flat or structured) attribute-value vectors.

Decision trees are data structures used, in particular, for classification tasks. Each non-leaf node represents an attribute and an edge starting from a node is labeled by some value of that attribute; the leaves represent classes. Hence, a path in the decision tree represents an implication saying that an object with specific feature values belongs to a certain class. Special techniques are used in order to minimize the number of attribute values to be determined in the classification task. Difficulties arise with missing values, i.e., with incomplete knowledge.

Constraints are n-ary predicates expressing certain required relations between the arguments which may be, e.g., attribute values or more general objects. *Hard constraints* have to be satisfied under any circumstances while *soft constrains* represent desires and can be violated. Soft constraints are mostly ordered by priorities and give rise to an optimization problem.

Another important notion is the rule concept. A *logical rule* is syntactically of the form: $A_1, A_2, \ldots, A_n \rightarrow B$ with the usual semantics of a logical implication; if variables occur, they are treated as universally quantified. A rule with variables is an example of abstract knowledge: It represents a possibly infinite set of instantiations for the variables. The *forward application* of the rule allows the addition of B to the knowledge if all premises A_i are true, requiring a possible unification or match. *Backward chaining* reduces the satisfaction of B to that of the premises. A major difference to the CBR approach is that only exact matches are admissible in order to achieve the conclusion B. A variation is when B is not a statement but an action to be performed; such an action may change the knowledge base.

Rules mainly occur in CBR in two ways: Firstly, cases can be considered as rules; their use is, however, very different from the use in rule-based systems. The main difference is that they are not combined in order to obtain longer chains of inferences. Secondly, rules are employed in the solution transformation (here as in rule-based systems).

Knowledge representation uses *abstraction* in various ways. The main types of abstraction are:

- replacing terms by variables
- omitting details
- introducing new abstract concepts

These types also occur in case descriptions. One usually distinguishes levels of abstraction with appropriate mappings between them (see Figure 1.1).

The mapping A performs an abstraction while the *refinement* R supplies the details. A and R are *compatible* if, for each abstract x, we have $A(R(x)) = x$. Abstraction is related to similarity because similar objects may be identified by some abstraction mapping.

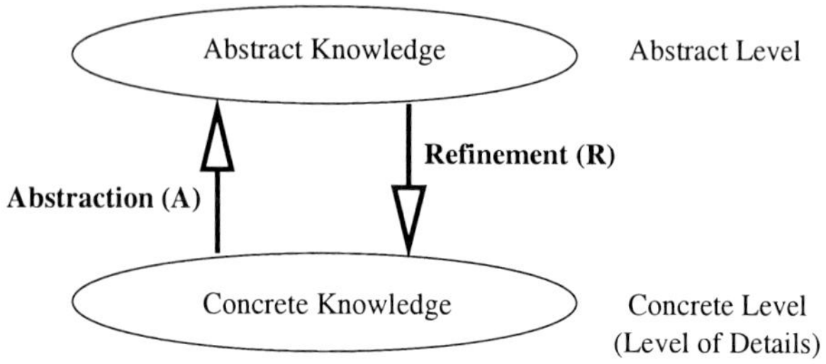

Fig. 1.1. The technique of abstraction and refinement.

Besides its data structures, a knowledge representation system is equipped with an inference engine. This allows the represented knowledge to be changed by adding, deleting or modifying knowledge entities (e.g., by applying rules). Inference, in the classical sense, occurs in CBR when cases are adapted.

1.2.2 The Use of Knowledge

Knowledge is necessary for all meaningful activities. The fact that (useful) knowledge is always interpreted implies that it is about something, namely the area of interest. In order to carry out some intended activities successfully, such areas have to be modeled, which results in certain pieces of knowledge.

The term *model* is very general and covers a great variety of intentions. A model can describe a machine or a more general artifact but also a process. *Model-based reasoning* tries to infer the solution of a problem (e.g. a fault diagnosis or a design) by inspecting the model description and drawing the necessary conclusions from it. CBR avoids this and makes use of experiences from previously solved problems instead.

There are also *domain models* which describe a larger area of interest. A *closed domain* is (nearly) completely described while *open domains* have only very incomplete descriptions. General and problem independent knowledge is called *background knowledge.* If the background knowledge describes a specific part of the domain it is also called *contextual knowledge.*

Some background knowledge is present in every knowledge based system, e.g., in the vocabulary. In a CBR-system, one can also find it in the similarity measure and in the solution transformation.

Episodic knowledge is of narrative character, it tells the story of something that happened in the past. Traditional expert systems have no place for it but CBR-systems employ it directly in the case base.

1.3 Basic CBR Concepts

CBR is a problem solving technology. In order to introduce the basic notions, we will first deal with some simplified situations. Although they will be of very different character, they all have in common that there is a *problem* and something called a *solution* to the problem. The basic scenario for CBR looks, from a naive point of view, as follows:

In order to find the solution to an actual problem one looks for a similar problem in an experience base, takes the solution from the past and uses it for a starting point to find a solution to the actual problem.

This requires the definitions of the following notions and the discussion of the following questions central to CBR:

- What are problems and how are they represented?
- What does it mean to say that something is *a solution to a problem*?
- How is *past experience* represented?
- What does it mean to say that something is *similar*?
- What does it mean to *look for a solution*?
- How to *use an old solution*?

1.3.1 Problems and Solutions

The concepts of problem and solution have no general definitions and vary from application to application. Both *problem* and *solution* may be, in fact, very general notions. In an abstract setting, there are just two sets $\mathcal{P}$ and $\mathcal{L}$ called problem set and solution set. The *problems* of interest come from an application area (see Section 1.4). They range from very specific tasks, such as classification, to quite general situations as in decision support. For the former, the notion of a *solution* is well defined while this is not the case for the latter. In classification, the solution is the class of an object, for a diagnostic problem it is a diagnosis. A solution may also be an action, a plan, or just a useful piece of information for the user.

For some problems, such as in classification, a notion of correctness of a solution is defined. Besides this, there may be some priority ordering on the set of solutions which then defines an optimization problem. In decision support, there are often no precise correctness conditions present and even the priorities are only informally defined.

Both problems and solutions are represented in some data structure, e.g., as attribute-value vectors (cf. Section 1.2.1). However, as in the case of document retrieval, data structures can also be just simple text files. In the problem as well as in the solution description, certain variables may occur which are instantiated for an actual situation. It is usually an important part of the problem to find appropriate variable instantiations for the solution description. This leads to the following distinction:

- A class of problems is of *rule type* if there is a partition of the variables into two sets of *problem* and *solution variables.*
- A class of problems is of *constraint type* if there is no such a priori separation of variables.

1.3.2 Experience and Cases

A general desire is to make use of past experience and every knowledge based system, and even each database, has a certain element or aspect for this purpose. An *experience* may be concerned with what was true or false, correct or incorrect, good or bad, more or less useful, etc. It can be represented by a rule, a constraint, some general law or advice, or simply by recording a past event. Experience is central to CBR, and CBR deals with experience in a way different from the classical techniques.

The idea of a *case* is to record an episode where a problem or problem situation was totally or partially solved. In its simplest form, a case is represented as an ordered pair

(problem, solution).

In order to establish such a case, it suffices that the corresponding episode happened in the past. The episode contains some decisions which the decision maker found useful. Of course, someone else may not be happy with such a case and neglect it. The experience recorded in such a case thus reflects just a single event; in the first place there are no steps like generalizations or incorporation of lessons learned from other events in the past. Also, there may be no explanations of how the solution was obtained and on which principles it was based; we are simply given the solution. However, the use of general or abstract cases is also typical.

A *case base* CB is a set of cases which, for retrieval purposes, is usually equipped with additional structures; structured case bases exist also under the name of *case memory*. Hence, a case base represents some class of past experiences. In order to make use of it, the case base has to be selected carefully, which leads to various notions of good, typical, important, misleading, or unnecessary cases. Often, case retrieval considers only the problem part of a case and, hence, a case is often identified with its problem part for retrieval purposes (cf. Section 1.3.4).

In certain situations, the solution may be an action with effects that are not a priori known and even not determined by the data given. This leads to an extension of the case concept to a triple:

(problem, solution, effects).

Here, the effects describe what happens when the actions that occur in the solution have been executed, see Gilboa and Schmeidler (1995). In this context, it is useful to have *multiple cases* in the case base because they indicate how likely certain effects are.

It is not wrong to regard cases as rules. In the same way as rules can be lifted to abstract rules, this can be done with cases too, using e.g., the abstraction techniques mentioned in Section 1.2.1; this leads to *abstract cases*, see Bergmann (1996). In rule-based systems, one may also derive completely new rules which represent, e.g., general insights into the area of interest and which can be employed in the problem solving process. This has no counterpart in the concept of a case. Such knowledge can, however, be stored in the similarity measure or in the solution transformation (two of the main knowledge containers of CBR).

Problems of constraint type create an additional difficulty in CBR. Suppose, e.g., that the task is to create an artifact which has to satisfy certain conditions and which gives rise to costs. One is tempted to represent a case simply by the artifact because it represents the solution. This neglects, however, that cost optimality is defined relative to the user wishes and these are partially reflected in the values of user selected variables (or in constraints on these values). The case representation should take into account these aspects.

In many applications, such as in diagnosis, one deals with problems with incomplete information. Both a problem in a recorded case as well as an actual problem may be incompletely described. In this context, one talks about *incomplete cases.* This is somewhat misleading because it is not the case in the case base but the actual problem description which has to be completed (as far as an identification of the solution is possible). From another point of view, the completion is the act which creates the case. The *case completion* is a task in itself which can again be performed using CBR (see Section 2.2). In diagnosis, the completion asks for a test selection (cf. Section 1.4.2) and the cases used for it are sometimes called *strategic cases.* We observe that, again, there is no clear distinction between problem and solution variables.

1.3.3 Similarity

In database systems, cases can only be used when the actual problem is exactly represented in the database, i.e., exact matches are required. The concept of *similarity* is the key notion to realize inexact matching. From a mathematical point of view, the notion of similarity is equivalent to the dual *distance concept.* However, both notions emphasize different aspects and have given rise to different computational approaches.

The basic difficulty involved looks like a kind of paradox: Two problems are similar if the (unknown) solutions are similar. The paradox is resolved by the observation that the similarity of solutions can be stated a priori; e.g., two solutions can be regarded as similar if they are equal or if the solution transformation is simple. A consequence is that similarity of situations or observations is not an absolute but a relative notion (relative to the problem or the problem class).

Similarity can be formalized in a relational and in a functional way. The relational approach uses a four-place relation $R(x, y, u, v)$ meaning "x and y are at least as similar as u and v are". This allows the definition of the *nearest neighbor* notion

$$NN(x, z) \Leftrightarrow (\forall_y) R(x, z, x, y)$$

meaning z is a nearest neighbor to x. If the nearest neighbor is unique, then NN is also used as a function symbol. A refinement is when k nearest neighbors are considered for some k ($k \geq 1$). In the relational approach, similarity is treated as a partial ordering. Such partial orderings can be realized by numerical functions which are called *similarity* (or dually *distance*) *measures* $\mathsf{sim}(a, b)$ or $d(a, b)$, resp. Both similarity measures sim and distance measures d induce four-place relations R_{sim} and R_d in an obvious way. If $R_{sim}(x, y, u, v) \Leftrightarrow R_d(x, y, u, v)$ holds, sim and d are called compatible. In order to reduce arbitrariness some assumptions are common:

(i) $0 \leq \mathsf{sim}(x, y) \leq 1$
(ii) $\mathsf{sim}(x, x) = 1$

The intention of (i) is normalization and (ii) implies that each object is itself its nearest neighbor. Although these conditions restrict, in principle, the expressiveness of case-based classifiers, they are generally assumed. This is less often the case for the following conditions:

(iii) $\mathsf{sim}(x, y) = \mathsf{sim}(y, x)$ (symmetry)
(iv) $d(x, z) \leq d(x, y) + d(y, z)$ (triangle inequality, in terms of distance measures).

The main reasons are that one has to deal with incompletely described objects and that the measures are restricted such that one argument comes from the case base:

$$\mathsf{sim} : U \times CB \rightarrow [0, 1]$$

which naturally introduces some asymmetry (here U refers to the *universe* of all objects while CB refers to the case base). The notion of a distance function $d(x, y)$ is dual; here, simply all orderings are reversed. For an attribute-value representation, a simple distance function is the Hamming distance. If problems are coded as n-dimensional real vectors, classical mathematical metrics like the Euclidean or the Manhattan distance are often used.

A similarity measure is a container which can store more or less sophisticated knowledge about a problem class. *Surface similarity* considers only syntactic properties of the representation. *Local similarity* deals with the values of a single attribute or feature.

Global similarity is what is finally used; it represents a holistic view of the cases. Global measures can be derived from local measures in various ways. The relative importance of attributes can be reflected by *weights* but also the relative position in a hierarchy, as well as general background knowledge, can be incorporated.

The term *structural similarity* is used in two distinct ways. On the one hand, it means to consider structural aspects of the problems or cases compared. On the other hand, it can also mean to consider the similarity of a whole set of cases.

1.3.4 Case Retrieval

Retrieval is a basic operation in databases and therefore in case bases, too. A query to a database retrieves some data by an exact match using a key. The question of efficient matching is called the *indexing* problem. A query to a CBR system presents a problem and retrieves a solution using inexact matches with the problems from the cases in the case base. As in databases, trees play a major role in structuring case bases for efficient retrieval.

An example of a frequently used tree structure is that of a kd-tree. In contrast to exact matches, such trees do not totally exclude certain branches of a tree because the region around the query described by some degree of similarity may intersect such branches, which gives rise to additional tests, such as ball-within-bounds or ball-overlaps-bounds test, which (in particular in a dynamic form) refine the classical tree techniques. In combination with decision tree methods, the kd-trees can play the role of decision trees, too. Other examples for retrieval structures are Case Retrieval Nets and discrimination nets (cf. Chapter 3 and Wess 1995).

1.3.5 Case Adaptation

The simplest way to use a retrieved case is simply to take the unchanged solution of that case as the solution to the actual problem. However, in many applications, like planning or configuration, even small differences between the actual and the case problem may require significant modifications to the solution. Making the appropriate changes of the case solution is called *case adaptation.* A natural demand is that the solution of a similar problem should be easily adapted to a solution of an actual problem.

In principle, this has a long history under the name *analogical reasoning*[1]. Today, analogy is mainly used to transfer solutions (or solution principles) from one domain to another one, like from the flow of fluids to the flow of heat. In contrast to this, CBR transfers solutions within in one domain. The adaptation requires additional (background) knowledge which can be represented by rules.

1.3.6 Learning

The task of *learning* (we use *machine learning* as a synonym) is to improve a certain performance using some experience or instructions. A very general type of learning appearing in various ways, is *inductive inference.* Here, examples for a problem together with their solutions are presented. The inductive

[1] The term *analogous* is of Greek origin and was introduced by mathematicians like Euclid in order to express relations of the form $a : b = c : d$; later on it became a term of everyday language (this seems to be the only case where a mathematical term entered common language; in all other cases it was the other way around).

step is to derive or improve a general solution method. An example is the generation of decision trees from classified examples. Here, and in related areas, techniques from statistics and information theory play a major role. Machine learning methods can be used in order to improve the knowledge containers of a CBR-system, in particular of the case base (adding, creating and deleting cases), of the similarity measure (e.g., adjusting weights) and of the solution transformation, for example, learning new adaptation rules.

1.3.7 Overall Structure of a CBR-System

A CBR system has not only to provide solutions to problems but to take care of other tasks occurring when it is used in practice. The main phases of the CBR activities are described in the *CBR-cycle* of Aamodt and Plaza (1994) (see Figure 1.2). *Retrieval* and *reuse* have been discussed above (the main part in the reuse phase is to transfer the solution after a possible adaptation). Because CBR, due to the inexact matching, only suggests solutions, there may be a need for a correctness proof or an external validation. The latter is the task of the *revise* phase. In the *retain* phase the "lessons learned" from the solution of a new problem and a possible revision shall be incorporated into the system. This can be achieved in different ways. The new case can simply be stored in the case base but the knowledge can also be extracted and enter the similarity measure or the adaptation rules. The latter is part of a learning process; in particular, if there are several new cases. It might also be decided that the new case contributes no additional insights and should be discarded.

1.3.8 Knowledge Containers

Next we will discuss the *knowledge containers of a CBR system* (cf. Richter 1995). The idea of a knowledge container is to be a structural element different from the traditional module concept in programming. In modules, certain subtasks (in the sense of subroutines) are performed; modules give a structure to the solution approach. But even small tasks require the participation of each container. A knowledge container does not complete a subtask but contains some knowledge relevant to many tasks; it gives, therefore, some structure to the knowledge. Prominent containers in rule-based systems are facts and rules.

In CBR we identify the following containers:

- the vocabulary used,
- the similarity measure,
- the case base,
- the solution transformation.

The knowledge for three containers is structured and used at compile time (or coding time) while the knowledge in the cases plays its role only at run

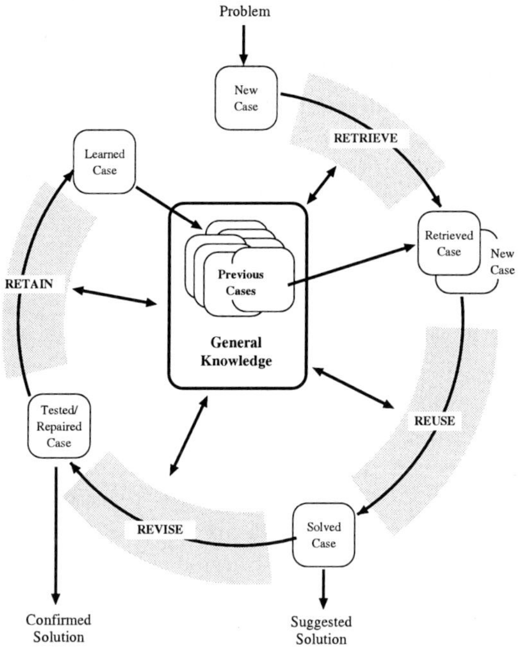

Fig. 1.2. The CBR-Cycle after Aamodt and Plaza (1994).

time. This is a major advantage of CBR because, in this way, the knowledge acquisition bottleneck is circumvented to a large degree. This is due to the fact that the acquisition of cases provides no or little additional work (provided that cases are present).

In principle, each container can carry almost all knowledge available. From a software engineering point of view there is another advantage of CBR, namely that the content of the containers can be changed locally, i.e., manipulations on one container have little consequences on the other ones. As a consequence, maintenance operations are easier to perform than on classical knowledge based systems. Such operations may react to changes of the context but also improve the performance of the system. Run time knowledge is easier to store but the compilation obtained by shifting knowledge from the case base to another container can significantly improve the system (see also Althoff et al. 1997).

CBR may be combined with other problem solving techniques, such as rule-based systems, statistical methods or machine learning approaches. Other systems incorporate CBR in a larger system or tool box for diagnosis, configuration or planning (see, e.g., Goos 1996). Such combinations run under the name *hybrid* or *integrated* systems.

With respect to the degree of integration, one may distinguish the following levels:

Toolbox level : A collection of more or less uncorrelated systems.
Workbench level : Communication between modules of the systems.
Seamless level : The user cannot distinguish any more between the different systems.

1.4 Types of Applications

One distinguishes between the *domain* and the *task type* of an application. The domain is, e.g., mechanical engineering, medicine, or business administration. Each domain has its own characteristics; in one domain, hierarchical structures may dominate while others can require flat structures, albeit structured by specific processes or user demands. The domain strongly influences the choice of data structure for the knowledge representation. A task type is, e.g., diagnosis, configuration or planning. This determines the type of the problems and solutions as well as the various activities a problem solver has to undertake. There is no one-to-one correspondence between domains and tasks but for each such pair specific expertise is required. In what follows, we will briefly describe the main task types. We also discuss why the concept of an application type is somewhat orthogonal to the concept of a problem type described in 1.3.1.

1.4.1 Classification

In classification one deals with a universe U and subsets $K_i \subseteq U, i \in I$, of U called classes. A classifier is a function

$$f : U \to I$$

such that $f(x) = i$ implies $x \in K_i$. In *cost sensitive classification*, with each wrong classification a certain cost is associated and hence not all errors are alike. This is of particular importance if the classification has an insecure base (as often in CBR).

Classifiers can be represented in different ways. A *case based classifier* is essentially of the form

$$(CB, \mathsf{sim})$$

where $CB \subseteq U$ is a case base and sim is a similarity measure on $U \times CB$. Thus, if the classes of the elements in CB are known, the class of $x \in U$ is now computed using sim, e.g., by

$$x \in K_i \Leftrightarrow NN(x) \in K_i$$

where $NN(x)$ is the nearest neighbor of x in CB. Of course, the nearest neighbor notion may be refined, e.g. by considering k nearest neighbors.

The classifier may, in addition to just providing the class of an element, also give additional pieces of information. If the objects of the universe are represented as attribute value vectors, these could contain the attributes which are responsible for a vector being close to its nearest neighbor.

In a more general form, a case-based classifier is of the form

$$(CB, \mathsf{sim}, T)$$

where T is a solution transformation. A typical situation where this occurs is when symmetries are present. Suppose we have left-right symmetries in the objects which are reflected in the classes, e.g., in the following naive way:

$$\text{if } x^{left} \text{ is in } K^{left} \text{ then } x^{right} \text{ is in } K^{right}.$$

If now $NN(z) = x^{right}$, x^{left} is not in CB but closer to z than x_i^{right} (because z is an object "of left type" then the solution transformation has to map $T(K_i^{right}) = K_i^{left}$.

1.4.2 Diagnosis

Diagnosis can essentially be considered as cost sensitive classification with incomplete information. This means that establishing the diagnosis is only the final step of a diagnostic process. This does not mean that this is the ultimate goal because it has to be followed by (or is even interleaved with) a subsequent therapy or repair operation.

The data on which the diagnosis is based are values of certain attributes (e.g., in a feature vector) which are acquired by observations, questions, or general tests. Hence, the diagnostic process splits into test selection and diagnosis (in the proper sense). Test selection is a problem in itself and can again be guided by cases (such cases are often called *strategic cases*), see Althoff (1992).

In addition, both the diagnostic as well as the strategic cases can provide additional information such as, e.g., explanations.

1.4.3 Configuration and Design

Configuration is generally understood as the construction of an artifact from a given set of components, such that certain conditions are satisfied. Hence, it can be considered as a constraint satisfaction problem.

Design introduces some degree of creativity because some components or even structural elements of the artifacts may not be presented a priori. Depending on the degree of creativity required, one distinguishes routine design, innovative design and creative design. In this area, the use of experience is of particular importance.

The solution to a configuration or design problem taken from a case base can almost never remain unmodified for an actual problem but has in general to be adapted. Another way to paraphrase this is that a previous solution is reused.

1.4.4 Planning

The term *planning* covers a great variety of tasks. We will restrict ourselves to *action planning*. The problem is to find a sequence of actions transforming a given initial situation into a desired goal situation. The size of the sequence is not restricted but the set of available actions is fixed. In *partially ordered* planning, the ordering of the actions is not total but only partial. This should not be confused with linear and nonlinear planning. *Linear planning* assumes that there is a total ordering on the goals of the goal situation, i.e., the goals do not interfere. Action planning in AI traditionally assumes complete knowledge which is, however, quite unrealistic for many applications.

For CBR, again the reuse aspect is important because the retrieved plans have to be adapted.

1.4.5 Decision Support

The role of *decision support* is to help the decision maker, rather than to replace them. In many situations, there is no precisely stated problem but rather a complex problem structure. The output of a support system is usually not a solution but rather an advice or a useful piece of information. An example is given by considering help desks. Experience, combined with the possibility of inexact matches, makes CBR an important technology in this field. This is a very wide area with many connections to other disciplines, last not least to cognitive sciences.

1.4.6 Information Retrieval

The task of *information retrieval* has changed over the years. Originally, *information retrieval* (or *text retrieval* as a synonym) was understood as the search for a particular document in a structured set of documents. Now the solution of problems is central and the retrieval of documents is considered as a useful step during the problem solution. There may be several such documents (or even none) and their relevant aspects may become known only in the retrieval process itself. Economically important examples are searches in the Internet where one looks for a certain product, a person, or an event. Here, e.g., some essential features of the product may not be known initially, what is known is just the intended use of the product.

Inexact matches are essential here and, therefore, CBR is a very natural problem solving technique. Because of the exponentially growing number of applications, Information Retrieval is a very promising field for CBR in the future, possibly connected with decision support.

1.5 Summary

In this introduction, we have provided the basic terms for the following chapters. We have also positioned CBR in the landscape of knowledge based systems. In our opinion, CBR is not a competitor which performs every task better than all previous approaches. It is, however, a technique which can do certain jobs better than other approaches. A good understanding of CBR would essentially include knowledge of when it should be applied and which other techniques it can be supported with or which it can support. We hope that this book will contribute new insights in this direction.

Acknowledgments

The author thanks Ralph Bergmann, Hans-Dieter Burkhard, Mario Lenz and Wolfgang Wilke for various improvements and corrections.

2. Extending some Concepts of CBR – Foundations of Case Retrieval Nets

Hans-Dieter Burkhard

2.1 Introduction

New research fields are developing on the foundations of well understood related areas. It is just like in case-based reasoning: Old experiences are reused for new problems. This has the advantage of solid starting points, but the disadvantage of dwelling on old ideas. Some of the adopted ideas need to be replaced by new ones as time goes on (consider the development of modern cars starting with a motor driven stagecoach).

It is necessary to reconsider critically the ongoing development from time to time. It is the aim of this chapter to reconsider and to extend some basic ideas of CBR. This may also help to clarify the special benefits of CBR. The investigations in this chapter can be considered as a theoretical foundation for the Case Retrieval Nets (CRN), which are discussed in Chapter 3.

CBR was developed in the context and in the neighborhood of problem solving methods (especially rule-based and model-based inferences), learning methods (Machine Learning, Statistics, Neural Networks), and retrieval methods (Data Bases, Information Retrieval). It has inherited the separation from "problem" and "solution" in the cases, and a notion of "similarity" based on distances.

Machine Learning, Statistics, and Neural Networks all look for the *common aspects* of the investigated examples (recently under the headline "Data Mining"). CBR can cover the orthogonal problems of the *extensional cases* (the knowledge of experts which goes behind the standard solutions of text books).

A basic idea in CBR is "to *remind* of useful cases". Reminding is related to *association*: Something (in the query) reminds of some memorized information (in the case). The Case Retrieval Nets (Chapter 3) implement remindings by association. The notions of "reminding" and "association" can guide a better understanding of the foundations of CBR (e.g., the basic asymmetry between queries and cases, which is often neglected in CBR).

We use the term *"acceptance"* instead of "similarity" (including similarity, but also other approaches related to "expected usefulness" in the sense of alternative possibilities, exchangeability, "reminds on" etc.).

We use the term *"Case Completion"* instead of "solution" (including solutions of problems, but also the proposal of intermediate problem solving steps).

We consider cases as sets of *"information entities"* instead of, e.g., vectors (whereby this approach includes vectors as well as textual descriptions).

Case Completion (Section 2.2) describes the completion of a task (of a "new case") in the real world, usually consisting of several steps. We consider the whole episode of task solving as a single case to be stored in the case memory. There, it has to be accessible by arbitrary subsets of its indexes (just like in a database, but additionally open to similarity matches). We do not actually need the distinction between "problem" and "solution" in a case. A case is more like a constraint than like a rule.

Information Entities are the atomic constituents of cases and queries (Section 2.3). Acceptance (Section 2.4) is locally defined for information entities and globally defined between cases and queries (Section 2.5). Section 2.6 discusses some new aspects of the notion "acceptance". The impacts on retrieval are investigated in Section 2.7. A general model for the computation of global acceptance for cases from local acceptance values of information entities is outlined in Section 2.8. Related implementation issues are discussed in Section 2.9.

The implementations by the *Case Retrieval Nets* (Chapter 3) have shown the efficiency of the approach. Successful applications are understood as a justification of the proposed extensions. Nevertheless, the extensions have to be evaluated by ongoing discussions and further applications.

2.2 Case Completion

2.2.1 Case = Problem + Solution ?

Case-based reasoning is considered as a problem solving method; given a problem we have to find a suitable solution. This leads to a view where cases are split into a problem and a solution part. Given a new problem we search for related problems in the case memory and adapt their solution for the new problem. However, problem solving usually does not start with a complete problem description which suffices for the identification of a final solution (cf. Section 1.3.1).

Nevertheless, the "new case" is often talked of as a given entity when only a first impression of the underlying task is given. Instead of this, we want to keep attention to the fact that the whole process of completing a task up to the final solution – and therewith the *resulting* "case" – is usually dependent on a number of decisions. These decisions are initially open; they depend on future (human) decisions. Depending on different possible decisions (e.g., in design), we can end up with different cases. Which one is addressed when talking about "the new case" from the very beginning?

Only in domains like classification, we could talk about a given new case when only the problem is known. A new case in classification is given by the description of an object ("problem"), and the goal is to *discover* the correct class ("solution") of this object. Because the class is uniquely determined for the object, the whole case ("problem" + "solution") is in fact completely determined by the problem.

Most practical tasks are performed as processes with a lot of intermediate steps (this book gives a lot of illustrations for such tasks). Each of these steps could be considered as a single new problem solving step. The question arises, as to whether we need different sets of cases to support each of these steps. This would mean splitting the whole story of the process into different cases for later usage by CBR. *Case Completion* is an attempt to avoid such an approach. A case should be the description of the whole performance of the task with all steps, and it should be useful for later tasks at intermediate situations too.

Before we go into the details, we take a closer look at stepwise problem solving processes.

2.2.2 Completing a Task

We restrict the usage of the notions "problem" and "solution" in the following, since these notions traditionally have a fixed (and as we feel restricting) meaning in the CBR literature. Instead, we talk about a "task" for more complex problem solving processes consisting of several steps.

We start with considering a task in the real world, which is to be managed by CBR-support. The task is specified in some way, but the specification is *incomplete*. This means that the known information is not sufficient for the successful *completion* of the task:

Diagnosis: First symptoms are given, but not enough to identify the malfunction and to propose the appropriate repair steps.
Design: First functional descriptions are given, but not enough to choose the appropriate parts and to fix their layout.
Consulting: First ideas of a customer are given, but not enough to make a clear specification and to propose a suitable offer.

As the completion of the task is going on, more and more information is collected and specified until the (hopefully) successful end. After completion, a new experience was learned and may be reused later for related tasks. The content of this experience is called a *case*. The *process* of elaborating the task under the aspect of collecting case relevant information is called *Case Completion*.

The underlying process usually includes several steps:

Diagnosis: Specify and perform further tests and (possibly experimental) steps of repair. The identification of the malfunction (classification) and/or the repair is only the final step in a chain of attempts (cf. Chapter 3).

Design: Perform a chain of design decisions (possibly with backtracking) up to a final layout (cf. Chapter 8).

Consulting: Discuss and specify the wishes of a customer under different aspects and available alternatives (cf. Chapter 4).

After each step, we have collected more information for the completion of the task. This information can be used for the next step (e.g. we may have identified a short circuit as the reason for missing power in our previous step, next we ask for the reason of that short).

2.2.3 Case Completion Supports Complex Tasks

The main idea behind Case Completion is not to distinguish between "problems" and "solutions" in the case descriptions. Our cases should be useful in each step (e.g., for the choice of a next test step as well as for a final identification of the diagnosis). This requires the treatment of different amounts of information; only few *information entities* are given at the start of a new task, and each step adds new pieces of information.

One could treat this situation by different case structures. If we consider cases as pairs of problems and solutions, then each set of given information entities defines a problem part, and the related proposal for a next step in our process defines a solution part. Thereby, an information entity may change its character during the process as follows:

Starting with the first symptom `missing power`, the information entity `short circuit` is a possible solution (which may be proposed by a related case). In the next step, the information entity `short circuit` is part of a problem description (which may be used to find cases which give hints to reasons of shorts). To follow this approach, we would need different cases; special cases with `short circuit` in the solution part, and other ones with `short circuit` in their problem parts. The original experiences concerning short circuits had to be split into such different cases. This seems to be unnatural with respect to the origin of the cases.

We propose to organize the CBR support according to process of *Case Completion.* The essence of Case Completion is the collection of further information. This information is obtained by the outcomes of our activities in the *real world.* CBR is not the source of this information, but it *can guide* our activity. Possible hypotheses for underlying (but still unknown) circumstances and possible outcomes of possible activities are checked on the base of former experiences, given by the cases: *CBR is a matter of proactivity.*

It is important to note that new information in the Case Completion process is given by decisions and results *from the real world.* Another viewpoint is discussed under the notion of *Information Completion* in Chapter 3, where new information is obtained only *from old cases.* Case Completion is considered as the collection of relevant information *while completing a task.* The completion of this task has to be done anyway, – in CBR we consider this process under the viewpoint of collecting and using experiences.

Case Completion is a general view to the process of CBR problem solving. A new case appears with incomplete and vague information. The process of problem solving is characterized by collecting new information while making decisions and acting in the real work until a satisfactory level is reached. CBR can guide this process by comparison with more complete cases from the past. Completed cases can be stored as new experiences for later reuse.

This means that CBR systems supporting such processes are designed as interactive systems. The users get information about complete cases, and they can choose the information they consider to be relevant from that cases. They can combine information from old cases to get new proposals as described in Chapter 7 for planning. Complete cases provide a good base for *argumentation* (e.g., in medicine and in jurisprudence).

The implementation of appropriate CBR systems is possible only with the handling of incomplete information. A case under the view point of Case Completion is more like a constraint than a rule. It connects items (information entities) which have appeared together in a problem solving process. Each subset of those items may appear in a query, and the related cases show possible completions (where existing constraints are satisfied because a case is an experience from reality).

A case under the view point of "case = problem + solution" is more like an instance of a related rule; the "problem" corresponds to the preconditions of the rule, while the "solution" corresponds to the postconditions or action part of the rule.

For Case Completion, a case can be *associated* (*reminded*) by certain differing indexes. This means that we have to build case memories where different (sub-)sets of input keys can be used for the retrieval of cases. As far as we have fixed structures (e.g., feature vectors), we can compare it with the access philosophy of databases; e.g., entries in a database of real estates can be accessed by their features, by their location, by their prices and so on.

However, while databases are build for exact matching, we want to use the case memory with inexact matching ("weak association"). A case memory of real estates could be used for the estimation of the price of a house with given features by looking for houses with only similar features. Now, the *same case memory* should also be useful for finding out the equipment of houses available for a given price in a special region. In a case memory designed by the principle of "problem + solution", we can only ask fixed kinds of questions, i.e. ask for the price ("solution") related to certain features ("problem"). We would need another case memory if we want to know certain features ("solution") related to a given price and given region ("problem").

In stepwise problem solving, we have the problem that certain indexes are not known at early states of the solution process. Moreover, there are often no fixed formats of the cases, as for example for diagnosis reports or design descriptions. Here we are closer to information retrieval – but again with the extended problem of inexact matching.

Having systems with such extended retrieval functions (inexact matching, treatment of missing values, intelligent information retrieval), we can use them in various ways as intelligent interfaces to stored information. CBR is going to capture new application fields like the sales scenario in Chapter 4.

The proposed way to build appropriate case memories is the consideration of the *information entities.*

2.3 Cases and Queries as Sets of Information Entities

2.3.1 Information Entities

We consider a case as the result of a case (task) completion process. Each step of that process adds some new *information entities.* The current situation during the elaboration of a task is described by the information entities known at the time point. The final case, as it later may appear in the case memory, is a completed set of information entities ("completed" refers to the state of information at the end of the task).

Some remarks are necessary at this point:

1. The collected information entities result from the real world (e.g., as the outcome of a test, a decision in an intermediate design step, or a specified customer requirement in consulting). They are not the direct result of a CBR process – CBR is used to *propose* the next step, e.g., the next test in diagnosis or the next design decision. The test outcome *might*, but need not, be the expected result according to former cases from the case memory, and we *might*, but need not, adapt the design proposal given by our CBR system.
2. The number of information entities in a case may be variable. It is up to a (human) decision at which time point the task is finished (e.g. the correct functioning of a device after replacing a special part may be sufficient without elaborating a detailed diagnosis based on a complete set of symptoms). It is usually not realistic to think about fixed formats of diagnosis reports in practice.
3. The information entities which are later used for retrieval (which appear as indexes in the case memory) may be only a subset of the information collected during Case Completion.

The "information entities" are considered as the atomic entities for the information processing during Case Completion. We can formulate:

1. Postulate:

A case is set of information entities.

During the process of Case Completion, the current situation is described by the set of known information entities. CBR is used to find former cases containing *hints for still missing information.* These cases should correspond to the recent situation; hence, we ask for cases which may be relevant to the already known information entities:

2. Postulate:

A query is set of information entities.

We have to choose an appropriate set of information entities for the design of a CBR system supporting Case Completion. The information entities must support reminding by comparison of information entities in queries and cases. We also have to choose an appropriate measurement of acceptance; i.e., which cases a users accept for their queries.

The related set of information entities is usually only a subset of all the information collected in the Case Completion process (Remark 3 above). In the following, we restrict the usage of the term "information entity" only to those information entities which are used in the case memory. These information entities serve as the *indexes* for retrieval. The case memory consists of cases which are sets of such information entities. These cases may then point to related complete descriptions in a collection of "full cases".

Following the postulates, we define:

Definition 2.3.1 (Cases and Queries Based on Information Entities). *We consider an* information entity *(IE) as an atomic part of a case or a query. The set of all (potential) information entities in a given domain is denoted by E.*

A case is a set of information entities: $c \subseteq E$.

The set of cases (in the case memory) is denoted by C, $C \subseteq \mathcal{P}(E)$.

A query is a set of information entities: $q \subseteq E$. □

2.3.2 Types of Information Entities

Information entities may be of various types. In many applications, the information entities are simply attribute-value pairs. This causes a structuring of the set E into disjoint sets E_A, where E_A contains all attribute-value pairs from E for a certain attribute A. If cases and queries are considered as attribute-value vectors over a finite set of attributes $A_1, \ldots, A_n$, then each case (query) may contain at most one information entity from each E_{A_i} ("at most" takes partial information into account). The description of cases by feature vectors is a specialization. We shall consider it for illustration purposes in Section 2.6.

Information entities may also explicitly express certain relations (structures) in the cases. This concerns the discussion about the treatment of relations between objects; a distinction is often made between "surface similarity" and "structural similarity" (cf. Gentner 1983). Surface similarity is usually defined in terms of similar feature values, while structure similarity is defined using corresponding relations (e.g. two buildings are similar because of similar arrangements of the rooms).

To evaluate structural similarity, we need access to the considered relations. These relations must be present, at least implicitly, in the descriptions of the cases. It is a question of (pre-)processing to make these relations explicit as special information entities. If the relations are known in advance, the processing might be performed already when preparing the case memory ("compilation").

We illustrate the problem for spatial arrangements of objects where information entities can describe the spatial relations between related objects. If we consider a fixed set of such objects and relations in our domain, then the cases and queries may be described simply by sets of related information entities (e.g., in the form `<relation, object-1, object-2`, where `relation` could be a spatial relation in ALLAN-style like `overlaps`, `meets`, etc.). Whether this approach is appropriate, depends on the complexity. We can also use graphs as more complex information entities, and graph similarity for comparison, – with severe efficiency problems as a consequence.

2.3.3 Case Completion Using Information Entities

Useful cases from the case memory must be provided for supporting Case Completion. Since usefulness is difficult to judge a priori, we ask for cases which the user would *accept* with respect to his query (cf. the discussion in Section 2.4.2).

The expected user *acceptance* of a case for a query is approximated by association of information entities. If a former case contains information entities which correspond to a great extend to the known information entities of a new situation, then the user is assumed to accept this case as a candidate for useful information (the information entities are used for "reminding"):

3. Postulate:

Useful information is expected from *the cases matching the query by related information entities.*

Corresponding information entities in the query and the selected cases may concern:

Diagnosis: Certain known symptoms, results of first attempts for repair.
Design: Certain desires for functionality, intermediate design steps and decisions.
Consulting: Certain specifications and further "vague ideas".

Useful hints for future steps are expected from the selected cases. This information may have the form of further information entities, or it may appear as additional information (e.g., pictures etc.) in the "full cases":

Diagnosis: Which further tests have been performed in former situations with what results? We can look for discrimination tests (differential diagnosis) if there remain several cases with different final diagnoses.

Design: Which further design steps may lead to what results? Are there risks for later conflicts w.r.t. to some constraints?

Consulting: Which further specifications meet the requests of the customer? Are there alternative offers?

Further information entities provided by the cases can be processed by the CBR system for adaptation purposes.

The technology of CBR applications is often described by the R^4 cycle (Aamodt and Plaza 1994 – cf. Chapter 1) with the phases Retrieve – Reuse – Revise – Retain. It starts with the input of a new "problem" and ends up with the integration of a new case (containing the problem description and its confirmed solution). The solution may have been proposed by the CBR system, and it could have been revised w.r.t. the practical results.

Case Completion differs from this picture since it covers several intermediate problem solving steps. These steps can be supported by cases from the CBR system (retrieve, reuse) and evaluated by reality (revise). After each intermediate step, the process continues for a next step, again with retrieve, reuse, revise. The supporting cases in the next step may be more or less different from the cases of the previous step. A related modified CBR-cycle is discussed in Chapter 4.

The "new case" is completed only if the whole task is completed, and then a single retain step can add this case to the case memory. Therefore the information entities must be identified which may be useful to remind the new case for later reuse. The new case and the new information entities (if any) have to be integrated into the case memory.

In the original R^4 model, each step of the completion process is treated as a single problem. The problem is matched in the retrieve phase with special cases having a solution part just for that step. After reuse and revise, the problem solving episode of that step is considered as a new case and added to the case memory in the retain phase.

In contrast, the whole story of completing a task is considered as a single case here. This case can be retrieved in future tasks in any situation described by information entities which are similar to some extent to certain information entities of the case (Postulate 3). Such a case can provide information not only related to a single next step of continuation, but to the whole process of all steps of a former task completion. The case can suggest a *complete plan* for solving the task. We can choose our next step according to such a plan. After performing this step, we can evaluate the results using the whole case memory again. If the old plan appears to still be an appropriate choice, then we can continue with its next step. Otherwise, we can react according to a new plan.

The modularization of the retrieval relevant parts of the cases into information entities is a useful way to organize the case memory. The idea of Case Completion can be the basis for a more natural and holistic treatment of cases.

2.4 Acceptance

2.4.1 Which Cases Are Acceptable?

We want to use the association of information entities for "reminding" cases with the expectation that these cases are useful for a given query. Usefulness of a case in the Case Completion process depends on real world circumstances which are not completely known at retrieval time. Cases are proactively used, as described in Section 2.2.3, for making proposals. The evaluation of those proposals is possible only after the response from reality to the user's activities (maybe even after completing the whole task). As widely discussed in the literature (cf. also Section 2.4.3 and Chapter 1), usefulness is only an *a posteriori* criterion.

The retrieval from case memory will be based on the (vague) matching of certain information entities, following Postulate 3 from above. Usefulness of former cases is not restricted to those cases which are similar to a given query for *all* information entities. Cases may contain information entities which have no counterpart in the recent query. It is also possible that some information entities of the query are not present in useful cases. Examples are:

Diagnosis: A query may ask only for the recently known symptoms, while the cases may contain complete information about solved tasks including all tests, experiments, knowledge about final diagnosis and repair.
A query may refer to a symptom which was not recorded in a previous case. It is even possible that the query and a useful case are different for some symptoms; e.g., the age of a patient may not be important for the diagnosis, but for the therapy.

Design: A query may ask for the layout of a certain detail, while the cases contain information about complete devices.
A query may contain a specification of the material, but some useful case giving a construction advice might refer to another material.

Consulting: A query may contain only some vague ideas of the customer, while a case contains completely specified offers.
A query may give limitations for the price, but under certain circumstances the customer accepts a more expensive offer.

The important point is that the cases in the case memory are indexed by all information entities which are *potentially* relevant for the retrieval. The features which are important for queries can not be fixed at design time. Moreover, the importance of an information entity may change from one query to another (i.e., the sex is important for some, but not for all diseases). *Compromises*, as in the consulting example above, may even relax special features *after* looking for available cases (cf. Section 2.6.6).

Common approaches using similarity for the retrieval of useful cases are too restrictive for such partial matchings. Hence, we propose to use the extended notion of acceptance which is formally introduced in Section 2.5.

We have also certain methodological aspects in mind: Acceptance looks more like a user dependent notion (and usability of a case dependents on the user too). Instead of this, similarity has the (questionable) flavor of an objective criterion. Backgrounds of CBR may become more transparent from the viewpoint of "acceptable cases which are reminded by related pieces of information".

Some special desirable properties for a general notion of acceptance are the following ones:

Property P1: A case might be acceptable for a query even if there exist some information entities which are not comparable (see the examples from above).

Property P2: A case might be unacceptable for a query if there exists an unacceptable information entity. (This is the counterpart to P1. Certain values are not subject to compromises: e.g., a fixed budget may forbid the acceptance of expensive offers).

Property P3: The same information entity may have different importance for different cases. For example, the attribute value pair `sex: male` rules out all cases of pregnancy, but it is of less importance for cases of influenza.

Property P4: The same information entity may have different importance for different queries according to the user's intentions. For instance, the material may have different priorities in design queries.

Property P5: Information entities may be not independent of each other. For example, fusing the lights causes the power to be lost. Statistical methods can be used to analyze such situations.

Before introducing acceptance functions, we give a short introduction to our understanding of some basic notions in CBR.

2.4.2 Preference

A central step in case based reasoning is the presentation of cases which are expected to be useful for a given query. Similarly to Section 1.3.3, we can think of a *preference relation* $\succeq_q$ over the set of all (potential) cases where

$$c' \succeq_q c'' \text{ if case } c' \text{ is preferable to case } c'' \text{ w.r.t. the query } q \;. \qquad (2.1)$$

The idea behind a preference relation is some criterion of *usefulness*: A case is preferable if it provides more useful information to an underlying task. There are some methodical problems; usefulness is a subjective assessment of the user, and it can be evaluated only *after* the task was completed. However, we need a preference criterion for the retrieval *before* usage and evaluation of the cases. Here the traditional basic hypothesis of CBR comes into play:

Similar problems have similar solutions. (2.2)

Similarity is considered as an *a priori* criterion to approximate the *a posteriori* criterion of usefulness:

A case is useful if it is similar to a query. (2.3)

2.4.3 Usefulness

Different users may have different thoughts about usability of cases at different times. It is difficult to maintain such subjective preferences by similarity (which is considered as a more objective criterion).

We may have several similar cases with the same outcome related to the "standard solution" of a problem. However, there may be also some cases which provide special solutions for related exceptional situations. The latter cases are related to the specific knowledge of experts, while the standard solutions correspond to the textbook knowledge.

Usability from the expert side could prefer the exceptional situations. A "normal" user might like to see one standard case (but not all) and additionally some exceptional cases. In a travel agency, for example, we are not interested in presenting all apartments in one hotel, but also some alternative offers. It seems to be difficult to regard this aspect of usefulness in any preference criterion, especially when using the notion of similarity. We have to be aware that the result of the retrieval must be further processed in order to select "interesting" cases (while not regarding maximal similarity).

Standard solutions might also be supported by related rules (cases may be used to extract those rules using machine learning tools). The exceptional cases are worthy of reminding since they cannot be covered by rules (as long as they refer to exceptional rare situations). The treatment of standard solutions in CBR is always in competition with other approaches from Statistics, Machine Learning, Neural Networks, etc. However, as long as there are not enough cases (examples) for generalization, CBR is the only solution.

2.4.4 Similarity

Similarity itself is not a fixed notion, it depends on the aspects under consideration:

Any two things which are from one point of view similar may be dissimilar from another point of view. (POPPER)

or as another quotation:

An essay is like a fish. (TVERSKY)
(Why: Both have head, body, tail etc.)

It is a central problem in the design and maintenance of CBR systems to adopt a notion of similarity such that the following assumptions are satisfied:

1. Similarity between a query and a case implies usefulness.
2. The similarity is based on a priori known facts.
3. As cases can be more or less useful for a query, similarity must provide a quantitative measurement.

Grounded on the basic hypothesis of CBR (cf. (2.3) from above), similarity of cases to a query can determine the preference relation:

$$c' \succeq_q c'' \text{ if } \mathsf{sim}(q, c') \geq \mathsf{sim}(q, c''), \tag{2.4}$$

where $\mathsf{sim}(q, c)$ is a quantitative (numerical) measure for the similarity of a case c to a query q. Similarity is often considered as a measure of "close neighborhood" for a related distance measure *dist* such that

$$c' \succeq_q c'' \text{ if } \mathsf{dist}(q, c') \leq \mathsf{dist}(q, c''). \tag{2.5}$$

As far as similarity is considered related to distances (cf. the discussion in Chapter 1), it may inherit properties of distances like maximal similarity in the case of identity, symmetry, triangle inequality.

These properties are useful in many domains, but they may also be misleading under certain circumstances. Symmetry is questionable if we make a strict distinction between queries and cases. Moreover, asymmetry occurs if a certain property covers another more specific property (see Chapter 4 for an example). The triangle inequality (in a related fashion for similarities) is not valid, e.g., for Tversky's contrast rule and for the simple matching coefficient.

Even maximal similarity for a case which is identical to the query may, in some situations, not lead to the maximal useful case. This occurs in practice, when a problem is solved over a longer period of steps and when intermediate steps are memorized as cases. A new problem in an early step of development is most similar to a related case reporting the solution process in that early stage. However, the greatest amount of useful knowledge is contained in a final report of the former problem solving process.

We have had serious problems with a customer in just such a situation (cf. Section 5.7). Thus, it might be better to replace the notion of similarity by another notion which expresses the subjective view point of expected usability in a more obvious way.

In this chapter, we will use the notion of *acceptance*. With this, we can go further than with the established usage of similarities and distances. The extended usage corresponds to the use of information entities supporting Case Completion. We want to meet the properties **P1** – **P4** from Section 2.4.1, which lie behind the common understanding of similarities and distances.

¿From a methodological viewpoint, the notion of acceptance makes a direct link to the (subjective) notion of usability, while similarity and distance are considered as objective notions. The latter can coincide with subjective notions of usefulness only to some extend, especially when different users may have different thoughts about usage of cases at different times.

2.5 Acceptance Functions

2.5.1 Global and Local Acceptance Functions

Acceptance is considered as a quantitative measure for pairs of queries and cases. Queries and cases are considered as sets of information entities according to Definition 2.3.1.

Definition 2.5.1 (Global Acceptance Function). *Acceptance between queries and cases is expressed by an* acceptance function

$$\mathsf{acc} : \mathcal{P}(E) \times \mathcal{P}(E) \to \mathcal{R}, \tag{2.6}$$

such that a higher value $\mathsf{acc}(q, c)$ *denotes a higher acceptance of the case* c *for the query* q*. The preference relation for cases induced by a query* q *is defined as follows:*

$$c' \succeq_q c'' \text{ iff } \mathsf{acc}(q, c') \geq \mathsf{acc}(q, c''). \tag{2.7}$$

□

The range of an acceptance function may include negative values to express unacceptability, and $\mathsf{acc}(q, c) = 0$ might be used to express neutrality (cf. the discussion in Section 2.6.2).

The computation of a global acceptance function should regard correspondences of information entities in the query and the cases. At a first glance, extended correspondences should enlarge the global acceptance. However, matching of information entities could be used for rejecting cases as well (example for a query: "we do not want a red car", example for a case: "don't present this case if the query asks for cheap offers").

Correspondences between information entities are defined by local acceptance functions. Global acceptance on the level of cases and queries is then computed from local acceptance values on the level of information entities.

Definition 2.5.2 (Local Acceptance Function). *The acceptance between information entities is described by a (possibly partial)* local acceptance function

$$\sigma : E \times E \to \mathcal{R}. \tag{2.8}$$

The acceptance $\sigma(e, e')$ is considered as a measure for the acceptance of an information entity e' in a case if the query asks for e. $\sigma(e, e')$ is undefined for information entities which are not comparable w.r.t. acceptance.

The set of all information entities e to which the information entity e' is comparable concerning acceptance is denoted by

$$E_{e'} := \{e \mid \sigma(e, e') \textit{ defined } \}, \tag{2.9}$$

and the set of all comparable information entities for a given information entity e is denoted by

$$E^{e} := \{e' \mid \sigma(e, e') \textit{ defined } \}, \tag{2.10}$$

respectively. □

2.5.2 Intuitive Meanings

We propose the composition of global acceptance functions by composition of the local acceptance values which are defined between information entities.

As already discussed, retrieval in CBR can be considered as a counterpart of the human process of reminding. Related pictures may be important for discussions with "naive" users of CBR systems.

The acceptance $\sigma(e, e')$ between information entities e, e' is regarded as the strength of reminding of an information entity e' when asking for e. The reason for reminding may be that e' describes *related circumstances* as e, that e' is an *alternative* for e, and so on. "Acceptance" can, therefore, cover other meanings than "similarity". This can be helpful for understanding CBR approaches by the naive users.

Because e in $\sigma(e, e')$ is related to a query, while e' is related to a case, σ needs *not* to be symmetrical (e.g., asking for "colored" devices should also remind cases with blue devices, but asking for "blue" devices should only remind blue devices). For that reason, the sets $E_{e'}$ and E^{e} in Definition 2.5.2 may be different.

We can implement vague notions using approaches from fuzzy theory. Thereby, the value $\sigma(e, e') = 0$ means that there is no indication by e to remind e' (cf. Section 2.6.2). Negative values of $\sigma(e, e')$ can intuitively indicate that e' (and in the consequence, a case containing e') should explicitly not be regarded if e is in the query. An appropriate *combination* is needed for the computation of a global acceptance value $\mathsf{acc}(q, c)$ from the local acceptance values $\sigma(e, e')$. An intuitive picture for that computation process is the "collection (accumulation) of arguments" for the acceptance of a case.

A commonly used intuitive form is the accumulation of local acceptance values by weighted sums. Weighted sums are known in the context of case descriptions by feature vectors, but often under the view point of accumulating local distances. Higher values of a distance are used to reject a case, while higher values of acceptance are used for preference of a case. It is helpful to analyze the difference in more detail (next section). We will come back to the general consideration of the computation of global acceptance values from local ones in Section 2.8.

2.6 Acceptance for Feature Vectors

2.6.1 Acceptance Functions for Feature Vectors

The information entities may have the form of attribute value pairs $< A, a >$ for some attribute A and a value a from the domain $dom(A)$ of A.

Attribute-value pairs over a fixed finite set of attributes are a convenient form of representation: Both the queries and the retrieval relevant parts of the cases are considered as *feature vectors* $(a_1, \ldots, a_n)$, where a_i specifies the value for the i-th attribute A_i. Formally, there is no difference between case vectors $c = (c_1, \ldots, c_n)$ and query vectors $q = (q_1, \ldots, q_n)$. Instead of the general Definitions 2.5.1 and 2.5.2 we can use the following more specific definitions:

Definition 2.6.1 (Global Acceptance Function for Feature Vectors). *Let $U := dom(A_1) \times \ldots \times dom(A_n)$ denote the set of all (potential) queries and cases, respectively. The acceptance of a case for a query is expressed by a* global acceptance function

$$\mathsf{acc} : U \times U \rightarrow \mathcal{R}, \tag{2.11}$$

such that a higher value $\mathsf{acc}(q, c)$ denotes a higher acceptance of the case c for the query q. The preference relation $\succeq_q \subseteq U \times U$ induced by a query $q \in U$ is defined by

$$c' \succeq_q c'' \text{ iff } \mathsf{acc}(q, c') \geq \mathsf{acc}(q, c''). \tag{2.12}$$

□

Local acceptance is defined separately for the attributes:

Definition 2.6.2 (Local Acceptance Functions for Attributes). *A* local acceptance function *σ_i for the attribute A_i is defined over the domain $dom(A_i)$:*

$$\sigma_i : dom(A_i) \times dom(A_i) \rightarrow \mathcal{R}, \tag{2.13}$$

such that a higher value $\sigma_i(q_i, c_i)$ denotes a higher acceptance of the value c_i (of a case c) for the value q_i (of a query q). □

Global acceptance functions can be composed from local acceptance functions by a related composition function as follows:

Definition 2.6.3 (Composite acceptance function). *A global acceptance function acc is called* composite *if it is composed by a* composition function $\phi : \mathcal{R} \times \ldots \times \mathcal{R} \rightarrow \mathcal{R}$ *from related local acceptance functions* σ_i*:*

$$\mathsf{acc}((q_1, \ldots, q_n), (c_1, \ldots, c_n)) = \phi(\sigma_1(q_1, c_1), \ldots, \sigma_n(q_n, c_n)). \quad (2.14)$$

We require that composition functions are monotonously increasing. □

An example for the composition of local acceptance values is given by a weighted sum (with only *positive* weights g_i because of monotonously increasing composition functions):

$$\mathsf{acc}((q_1, \ldots, q_n), (c_1, \ldots, c_n)) = \sum_i g_i \cdot \sigma_i(q_i, c_i) \qquad (g_i > 0). \quad (2.15)$$

Addition is widely used for the combination of local values not only in CBR. It has an intuitive interpretation concerning acceptance in the sense of "collecting arguments" in favor of something. Positive arguments have positive values, while negative arguments are expressed by negative values. The value "0" does not change the result, thus unimportant (or unknown values) can be treated as indifferent values by "0". Therefore, Properties **P1** and **P2** from Section 2.4.1 are satisfied. Different weights g_i can express different importance of a feature. However, this is possible only in a uniform way w.r.t. that feature, i.e. Property **P3** from Section 2.4.1 is not satisfiable. A more general combination is necessary to satisfy **P3** and **P4** (Section 2.8).

2.6.2 Local Acceptance Functions for Attributes

Local acceptance functions σ_i can have different forms according to the underlying domains $dom(A_i)$ which may be, e.g., symbolic, ordered, or numerical domains (cf. Wess 1995).

We consider numerical attributes in the following. The local acceptance $\sigma_i(q_i, c_i)$ is considered as a function of the difference between q_i and c_i. It holds by intuitive arguments:

The acceptance decreases as the difference grows. (2.16)

For a fixed query value q_i, we consider the local acceptance function σ_i as a function

$$\chi_{q_i}(c_i) := \sigma_i(q_i, c_i) \quad (2.17)$$

which depends only on the possible case values c_i. According to (2.16), this function has the maximum value in a region around $c_i = q_i$.

When asking for "July 1st" we mostly accept cases which are near to this date. A related function χ_{July_1st} for the fixed query value $q_i =$ "July 1st" and a variable date c_i is given in Figure 2.1.

Vague queries may ask for a date "during summer", or "during vacation", respectively. The related functions χ_{during_summer} and $\chi_{during\_vacation}$ are

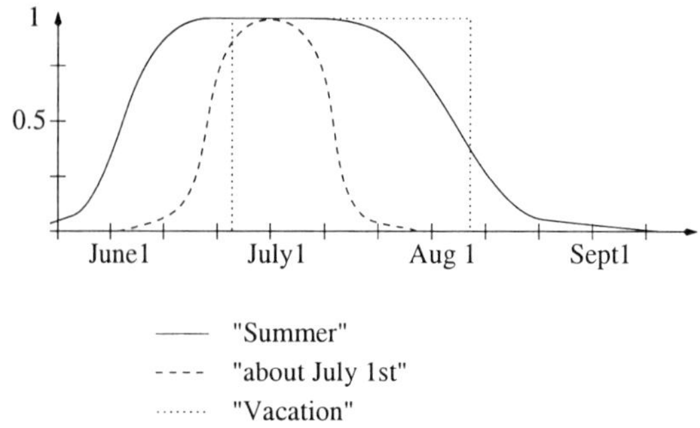

Fig. 2.1. Local acceptance functions (linguistic terms)

given in Figure 2.1 too. A concrete date c_i in a case fits more or less to such wishes: "during summer" (i.e., during hot season) permits different degrees of acceptance, while "during vacation" is true or not.

The functions χ_{q_i} in our examples range over $[0, 1]$, and they have the form of characteristic functions for linguistic terms in fuzzy theories. We can actually interpret $\sigma_i(q_i, x)$ for a fixed query q_i as the characteristic function χ_{q_i} of the linguistic term "about q_i" (cf. Burkhard 1998).

In this way, we can ask for cases "about July 1st", "during vacation", "during summer", respectively, where we treat the queries as linguistic terms over the domain of days in a year (Figure 2.1). The vague notions can be matched with concrete values c_i in the cases. We could also compare concrete values in a query with related vague notions in cases, or even vague notions in both the query and the cases, respectively. In the latter situation, the evaluation of matching could follow operations from fuzzy theory.

Characteristic functions of linguistic terms usually have a non-zero value only in a limited region of their domain. In contrast, similarity measures derived from distances, as for example by

$$\mathsf{sim}(x, y) := \frac{1}{1 + \mathsf{dist}(x, y)}, \tag{2.18}$$

result in non-zero values even for very great differences. Thus, "10 DM" is similar to "1 Million DM" to a very small, but non-zero amount. This may cause unnecessary effort during retrieval (cf. Section 2.7)

To express unacceptability we can use negative acceptance values. Using weighted sums as in (2.15), a negative local acceptance value $\mathsf{acc}(q_i, c_i)$ decreases the global acceptance of a case c for the query q. We can even assign a negative value to $\mathsf{acc}(q_i, c_i)$ that cannot be compensated by the acceptance values $\mathsf{acc}(q_j, c_j)$ of other attributes A_j. Such values can be viewed in two ways: One is the intuitive description of reasons for absolute rejection, the other is due to implementation issues of the retrieval (cf. Section 2.7). For example, using negative values for local acceptance functions in the domain of prices, a related function χ_{cheap} may have the form of Figure 2.2.

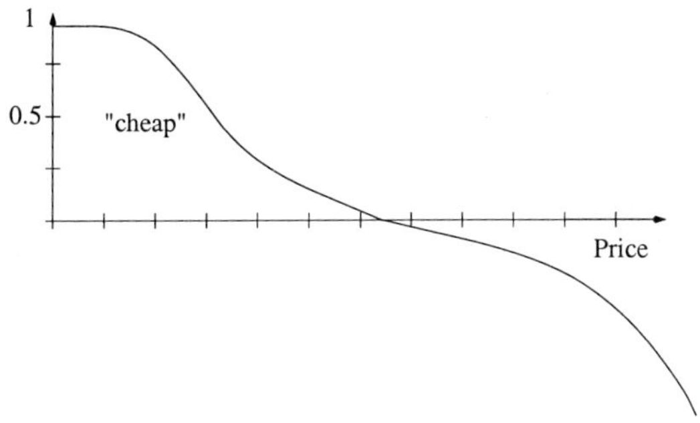

Fig. 2.2. Local acceptance with negative values

2.6.3 Accumulation for Acceptance and for Rejection

According to the intuitive meanings of the composite acceptance functions (Definition 2.6.3), the global acceptance is *accumulated* from local acceptance values by a monotonous function. Higher values indicate higher degrees of acceptance, i.e. *higher preferences* of cases.

In contrast, higher values of distances indicate *lower preferences* of cases. Similar to the consideration of composite acceptance functions we can consider *composite distance functions* $\mathsf{dist}((q_1,\ldots,q_n),(c_1,\ldots,c_n))$ which are composed from local distance functions dist_i by a *monotonous composition function* ψ such that

$$\mathsf{dist}((q_1,\ldots,q_n),(c_1,\ldots,c_n)) = \psi(\mathsf{dist}_1(q_1,c_1),\ldots,\mathsf{dist}_n(q_n,c_n)). \quad (2.19)$$

Weighted sums are widely used as the composition functions for distances, in an analogous way as for acceptances in (2.15):

$$\mathsf{dist}((q_1,\ldots,q_n),(c_1,\ldots,c_n)) = \sum_i g_i \cdot \mathsf{dist}_i(q_i,c_i) \qquad (g_i > 0). \quad (2.20)$$

As for acceptance, we can consider the computation of composite distance functions as a process where the global value is *accumulated* from local values. However, the intuitive goals behind accumulation are opposite; in the case of acceptance functions, we are looking for arguments of acceptability, while in the case of distances we are looking for arguments supporting rejection. For this reason, we refer to the first approach as *accumulation for acceptance*, while the second one is called *accumulation for rejection*. Composite distances are an example of the latter.

We have monotonous composition functions in both situations. The differences are determined by the interpretation of the local functions as acceptance functions (higher values indicate preference), or as distance functions (lower values indicate preference), respectively. Thus we have:

Accumulation is understood is as the combination of local functions by monotonously increasing combination functions. We talk about "accumulation for acceptance" if the local functions increase for decreasing differences between the local case value and the local query value. We talk about "accumulation for rejection" if the local functions increase with increasing differences. (2.21)

Because the combination functions are monotonously increasing, the resulting global functions are increasing when the local functions are increasing – and vice versa. The functions that increase with decreasing differences (accumulation for acceptance) are those functions which we consider as acceptance functions by the intuitive argument (2.16). The notion "differences" is used to express the more intuitive meaning. The absolute numerical difference is a related formal notion, but other distances could apply as well. Thus, accumulation for rejection is related to distances.

We have chosen the view point of positive numbers in the explanation of the forms of accumulation in (2.21). Acceptance functions may have positive values as well as negative values. The *negative* values are considered intuitively as arguments for rejection, thus we could explain accumulation for rejection in a related way for negatively increasing functions.

The *criterion* for acceptance (or rejection, respectively) of cases can have different forms:

- It may have the form of a fixed limit such that all cases with higher global acceptance values are accepted.
- It may be a criterion relative to a given set of cases such that the n "best" cases are accepted.

2.6.4 Differences Concerning Acceptance and Rejection

At a first glance, there seems to be no essential difference between the approaches of accumulation for acceptance and accumulation for rejection. Acceptance is a notion related to similarity, and similarity is often considered as an equivalent notion to distance (Chapter 1). However, both approaches may differ in important aspects, with essential impacts on useful retrieval algorithms (Section 2.7).

For illustration, we consider some simple local distance and acceptance functions over the real numbers which are all composed by addition.

In Figure 2.3 we consider the local distance functions (a) $\mathsf{dist}_i(q_i, c_i) = |q_i - c_i|$ and (b) $\mathsf{dist}_i(q_i, c_i) = (q_i - c_i)^2$. The left side presents the functions $f(x)$ for $x := q_i - c_i$, i.e., $f(x) = \mathsf{dist}_i(0, x)$. The corresponding righthand parts of the figure show some "characteristics" of the resulting global distance functions in a universe with dimension $n = 2$. All points $c = (c_1, \ldots, c_n)$ on a characteristic (equi-distance curve) have the same distance d from a given point $q = (q_1, \ldots, q_n)$. The characteristics have the form of cubes for

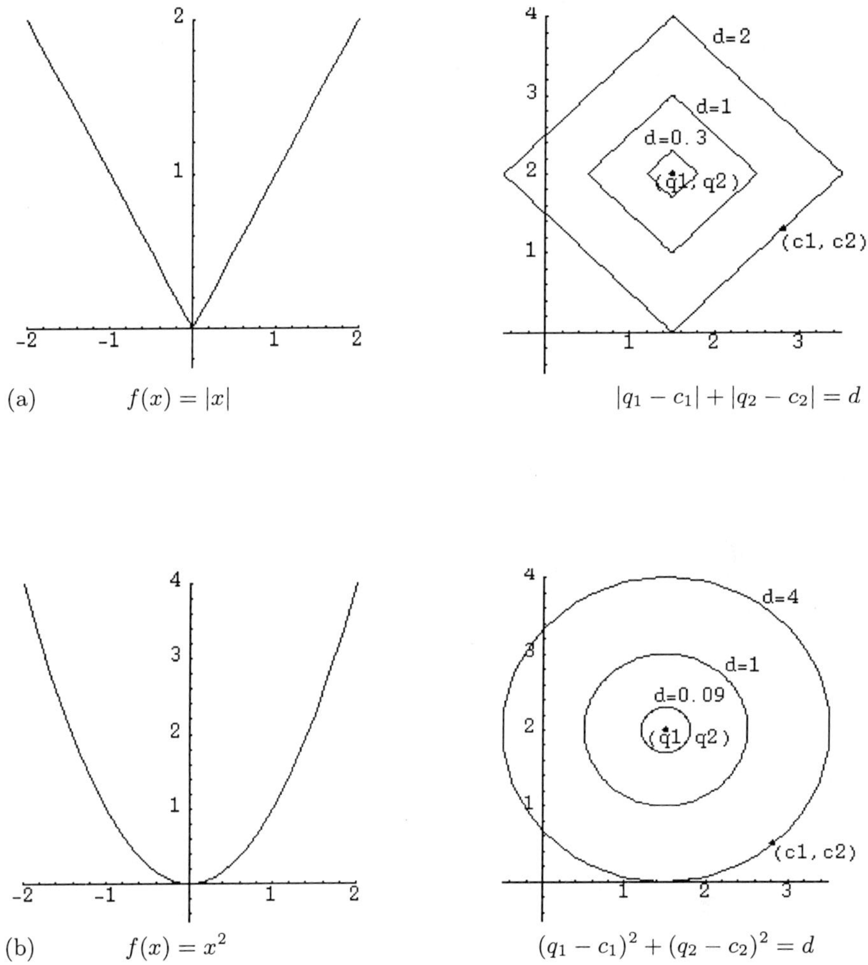

Fig. 2.3. Characteristics of Composite Distances

(a) (Manhattan distance), and the form of spheres for (b) (similar to the Euclidean distance).

In Figure 2.4 we consider the local acceptance functions (a) $\sigma_i(q_i, c_i) = 1/(1+|q_i - c_i|)$, (b) $\sigma_i(q_i, c_i) = Gauss(|q_i - c_i|)$, and (c) $\sigma_i(q_i, c_i) = 1 - |q_i - c_i|$. The left side presents the functions $f(x)$ for $x := q_i - c_i$, i.e., $f(x) = \sigma_i(0, x)$. Function (a) is the transformation of the distance $\mathsf{dist}_i(q_i, c_i) = |q_i - c_i|$ from Figure 2.3(a) to the similarity function $\sigma_i(q_i, c_i) = 1/(1+|q_i - c_i|)$ as given by (cf. (2.18)). Function (b) is intended to give an impression of fuzzy functions, while function (c) illustrates the usage of unlimited negative values.

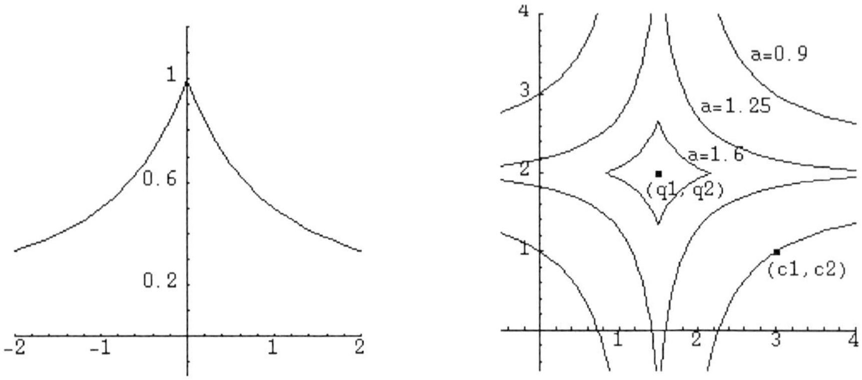

(a) $f(x) = 1/(1+|x|)$ $\quad$ $1/(1+|q_1 - c_1|) + 1/(1+|q_2 - c_2|) = a$

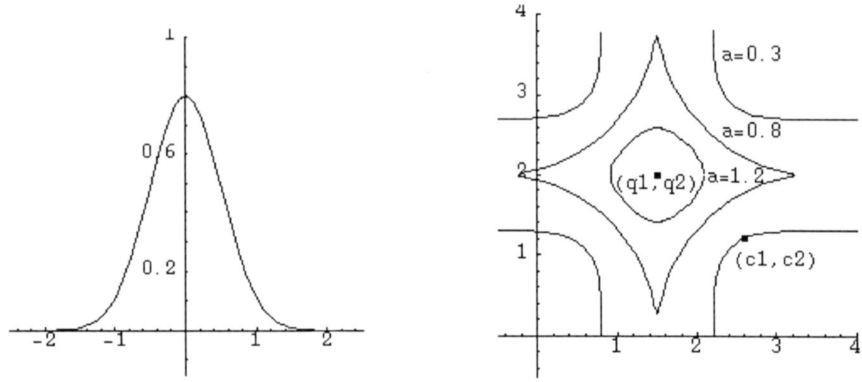

(b) $f(x) = Gauss(x, 0, 0.5)$ $\quad$ $Gauss(q_1 - c_1, 0, 0.5) + Gauss(q_2 - c_2, 0, 0.5) = a$

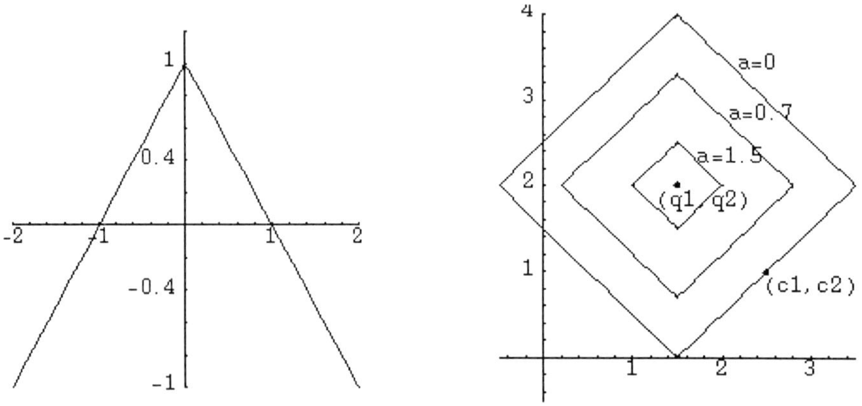

(c) $f(x) = 1 - |x|$ $\quad$ $(1 - |q_1 - c_1|) + (1 - |q_2 - c_2|) = a$

Fig. 2.4. Characteristics of Composite Acceptance Functions

The corresponding righthand parts of the figure show some characteristics of the resulting global acceptance functions in the two-dimensional universe. All points $c = (c_1, \ldots, c_n)$ on a characteristic (equi-acceptance curve) have the same acceptance a from a given point $q = (q_1, \ldots, q_n)$.

Functions (a) and (b) show great differences to the pictures seen before; for large values a we have closed characteristics, as before, but the characteristics are open for lower values a (the branches actually never meet each other). The reason is that a high local acceptance value of a single attribute is sufficient to reach a moderate global acceptance value independent of other attributes.

The situation changes if unlimited negative acceptance values are allowed as for function (c). Here we have a situation with a similar picture as in Figure 2.3 (a) with only closed characteristics. This corresponds to the usage of acceptance functions with unlimited negative values in a sense of "accumulation for rejection".

The inner characteristics have higher values a and lower values d, respectively. However, the *preference* of cases is higher on the inner characteristics anyway. The characteristics denote cases having equal preference according to (2.4), (2.5), and (2.7).

Thus, the difference between Figure 2.3(a) and 2.4(a) illustrates an essential difference between the distances $|q_i - c_i|$ and the related similarities $\sigma_i(q_i, c_i) = 1/(1 + |q_i - c_i|)$ which are derived according to (2.18).

2.6.5 Other Combination Functions

Weighted sums are intuitive means for the composition of local values. However, their results have different properties which depend on the interpretation of the underlying local functions as acceptance or as distance functions.

Acceptance concerning a single feature can be described in terms of fuzziness, as in Section 2.6.2. Global acceptance can be considered in the light of fuzziness too; the global value $\mathsf{acc}(q, c)$ can be interpreted as the measure for the linguistic term "*c is acceptable for q* ".

To be consistent with fuzzy theory, the combination function ϕ has to be considered as a fuzzy operator for the combination of the local fuzzy measures. The usage of a weighted sum as combination function for acceptance can be related to *disjunctions* in fuzzy logics. Thus we might interpret accumulation for acceptance in the sense of fuzzy disjunction.

Fuzzy conjunction looks more similar to the common usage of nearest neighbor approaches; a single "bad" feature value is sufficient for a "bad" global value. Such a conjunctive interpretation is given to distances when the close neighborhood depends on close distances in *all* features. Note that addition plays a different role here since higher values are used for rejection.

The relationship of CBR to fuzzy theory is an interesting point for further investigations. In particular, the combination of local values to global ones is interesting. Desirable properties of combinations for acceptance functions have been discussed in Section 2.4.1.

2.6.6 Compromises

Accumulation for acceptance can handle compromises. To be acceptable, it might be sufficient that a case is acceptable for *some*, but not necessarily for all features. We may accept for example

- an expensive offer for more satisfying properties, or
- the colour "red" instead of "blue" because the red cars are cheaper, or
- a house in a bad state because of its wonderful garden.

Sometimes, offers are formulated in a related style; "we are looking for people who are qualified in at least one of the following disciplines...". The examples given in the beginning of Section 2.4.1 are further illustrations for compromises, and the Sales Situation in Chapter 4 needs proposals for compromises, too.

Sometimes it is argued that the problem can be solved using different weights in a weighted sum. It is, in fact, possible to give some features a low priority (e.g., by low weights in a weighted sum). However, these priorities must be fixed *in advance*, while compromises are a matter of relaxing certain features *after* the presentation of cases. We do not know in advance that, e.g., the colour is the feature which corresponds to the cheaper offer. Thus we cannot say that the colour is an unimportant feature in general – but that is what a low weight in a weighted sum means. We would surely not agree to consider the price as unimportant in general, but we might, in some circumstances, accept a higher price after knowing all alternatives.

A real compromise c for a query q does not reach the highest values of the acceptance function $\mathsf{acc}(q, c)$. A compromise means to accept (at least) one feature with a greater difference to our query and, consequently, an only moderate global acceptance value. The characteristics of global acceptance functions for moderate values in Figure 2.4 (a) and (b) have open branches: The unmatched features correspond to "far points on open branches".

The open branches are the geometrical picture for compromises. A convex closed line indicates the necessity to be "near" to the query for *all* features. This means that distances as in Figure 2.3 are unsuitable for searching compromises.

Limitations of compromises (e.g., for too expensive offers) could be expressed using negative values for local acceptance functions (cf. Figure 2.2). In this way, we can "close" the open branches in the characteristics of global acceptance functions.

Compromises can also be seen under the view point of disjunction (alternatives) in fuzzy logics, while conjunction is related to strong constraints (cf. the discussion in Section 2.6.5).

To accept a compromise it must be clear that there are no better alternatives fitting in more features. For that reason, it is not possible to get related offers from a database using range queries. It is often argued that a database with range queries could serve as a case memory. This is only partially true.

Range queries search in a region which is bounded by a distance line; they produce the set of *all* matching answers in-between the fixed ranges. This set may be empty (then we need new ranges) or very large (then we need further processing to find the best cases).

This means that, under the view point of compromises, as in the case of a weighted sum, we have to decide in advance which features are less important (i.e., are asked for with a larger range). However, we are willing to give up certain aspects of an original query only when we know that there are no better alternatives. Which features we give up will depend on the available benefits in other features. If we ask with large ranges in all features, then we may obtain a lot of answers which actually have bad values in all features.

This aspect is problematic for many CBR systems too. It can be managed under the view point of accumulation for acceptance (Section 2.6.3). It is one of the great advantages of the Case Retrieval Nets (Chapter 3) that they can detect cases which provide compromises very efficiently.

2.7 Acceptance and Rejection in the Retrieval

Retrieval is a central part in CBR and has a great impact on the efficiency of a system. Traditional indexing techniques from databases are not sufficient for handling requirements of inexact matching.

The ideas behind *accumulation for acceptance* and *accumulation for rejection* can be exploited in different ways for efficient retrieval strategies. Both approaches are characterized by the combination of local measures to global measures by monotonously increasing combination functions. The computation of the global acceptance value can be considered as a (stepwise) accumulation process of local values. However, while the accumulation of a high value leads to the rejection of the case in the latter approach, it leads to acceptance in the former approach.

A great local distance $\mathsf{dist}_i(c_i, q_i)$ for a single attribute A_i is a k.o. criterion for the case c. In contrast, a related small amount of acceptance/similarity $\mathsf{sim}_i(c_i, q_i)$ (computed e.g. using (2.18)) has only marginal influence (if any) on the rejection or acceptance of that case.

The differences between both approaches become especially significant if fixed limits are used as criterion for acceptance (resp. rejection). This means that for distances, we search for all cases up to a certain *maximal* distance. The characteristics in Figure 2.3 mark such limits. If the accumulated local distances for some attributes already exceed that limit then the case can be excluded (it especially suffices to find a single attribute where the local distance exceeds a related value). Hence, pruning strategies over the case memory which exploit such a rejection criterion are useful.

In contrast, if a fixed limit is given for accumulation for acceptance, we search for all cases with at least a certain *minimal* acceptance. Here, we have to accept the cases exceeding the limit instead of excluding them. Hence, we do not have simple pruning strategies as above. Pruning is possible only as far as estimations can be given for remaining values; a case can be excluded if the amount of accumulated values together with the expected remaining amount is not sufficient to reach the given limit. The usage of very high negative acceptance values for rejection appears as a special case of this strategy.

Accumulation for rejection can be realized as a top down approach. The whole space U of potential cases is divided into different regions of cases which are near to each other. A new query is classified according to the region it belongs to. This can be implemented by a decision tree, and the resulting leaf of that tree can point to the matching cases in the related region. A related compilation process can optimize the regions and the search within a concrete case memory.

The boundaries of the regions (the test criteria in the decision tree) specify values which serve for excluding certain cases. Problems may occur if a query is near to that boundaries; in these situations, the necessary value for rejection is not really reached, and it may be necessary to search in several subtrees. Unknown values are also critical. Without any hypothesis about the underlying value, all related subtrees have to be considered. Detailed discussions of this approach including implementation issues can be found in Wess (1995).

Accumulation for acceptance can be implemented as a bottom up approach. The local acceptance values are accumulated for the cases. This can be implemented in a net like structure using spreading activation. Activation is initially put on the information entities of the query. It is then spread out according to local acceptance functions σ to further information entities. It is finally accumulated in the cases according to information entities which constitute a case (cf. Section 2.8). Chapter 3 discusses the implementation by Case Retrieval Nets.

Pruning at intermediate steps is more difficult in the case of accumulation for acceptance, because remaining attributes might add significant contributions to the global acceptance. Nevertheless, there are strategies to estimate the remaining contributions (according to given minimal global acceptance values, or in comparison with the "best" cases at an intermediate time point). Related discussions can be found in Lenz (1995) as well as Lenz and Burkhard (1996b).

The chances for an efficient spreading activation process in the bottom up approach are greater due to sparse connections in the net structure (cf. Section 2.9). Very small acceptance values (as they may appear by transforming distances into similarities using formulas like (2.18)) may cause unnecessary effort for retrieval. It is questionable if this effort is justified by the results, since CBR is an approximative approach in many applications. For the same reason, negative local acceptance values as means for rejection should be used only rarely in bottom up approaches.

2.8 The General Case

2.8.1 Local Accumulation

Using σ we can compute the acceptance of an information entity e' from a case for a single information entity e of a query. However, a query may contain several information entities e such that $\sigma(e, e')$ is defined for the single information entity e'. The question arises as to how these values can be combined to a single value for e' which expresses the resulting acceptance value of e' for that query. Such situations are related to property P5 from Section 2.4.1, and they may occur, e.g.:

- for queries with alternative wishes (e.g. a query for holidays "in `Cuba` or in `Trinidad`" where `Jamaica` counts as an alternative for `Cuba` as well as for `Trinidad`),
- for queries with information entities on different levels of abstraction (e.g., "in `Cuba`, preferably in `Havana`"),
- for (text) queries using related notions (e.g., a query asking for documents containing relevant information concerning "case based reasoning", "acting by experience", "machine learning", "analogical reasoning", where each notion should also point to the other ones).

Definition 2.8.1 (Local Accumulation Function). *Let $E_e = \{e_1, ..., e_n\}$ denote the set of all information entities to which the information entity e is comparable concerning acceptance (i.e. $E_e = \{e' \mid \sigma(e', e)$ is defined $\}$ as given in Definition 2.5.2).*

The local accumulation function π_e *for e is a function*

$$\pi_e : \underbrace{\mathcal{R} \times \ldots \times \mathcal{R}}_{n \text{ times}} \rightarrow \mathcal{R}, \tag{2.22}$$

such that $\pi_e(a_1, \ldots, a_n)$ denotes the accumulated acceptance in e. The values a_i denote the contributions of the information entities $e_i \in E_e$ according to their occurrence in the query q and their local acceptance computed by $\sigma(e_i, e)$.

The occurrence in the query is expressed by the characteristic function

$$\alpha_q(e) = \begin{cases} 1 & : \text{ if } e \in q \\ 0 & : \text{ otherwise} \end{cases} \tag{2.23}$$

and then the contributions are computed by a (universe) function

$$f : \mathcal{R} \times \mathcal{R} \rightarrow \mathcal{R}$$

such that

$$a_i = f(\alpha_q(e_i), \sigma(e_i, e)). \tag{2.24}$$

□

We can use simply the product for f, such that $a_i = \alpha_q(e_i) \cdot \sigma(e_i, e)$. This has the effect, that $a_i = 0$ if $\alpha_q(e_i) = 0$, or if $\sigma(e_i, e) = 0$. That means that the absence of e_i in the query has the same effect on e as the acceptance value $\sigma(e_i, e) = 0$. The usage of "0" as neutral element is usually consistent with such interpretations.

The more general definition using the function f permits other semantics too. Whatever the function used, one has to be aware of the consequences especially concerning unknown and unspecified values.

2.8.2 Relevance of Information Entities for Cases

We consider the retrieval of cases as a process of reminding. The indexing information entities are used for association concerning a given query. Reminding may be of different strength; cases are in competition for retrieval according to the query. The cases receiving more reminders of more strength are the winners.

It is possible to define for each $e \in E$ a *reminder value* for the cases (how much does `broken cable` remind of the defect case `number 1054`). The cases can then be compared according to the accumulation of reminder values from the information entities of a given query. The problem arises as to how the reminder values are computed. An individual assignment for all pairs $[e, c]$ of information entities $e \in E$ and cases $c \in C$ is inappropriate.

Reminding can be understood as an accumulation process performed over several stages. Cases $c = \{e_1, \ldots, e_n\}$ are directly accessed only by their constituting information entities $e_i \in c$. The reminding which leads from information entities of queries to the information entities of cases follows the local acceptance functions for information entities (Definition 2.5.2).

The strength (importance, relevance) of reminding for an information entity $c_i \in c$ is given by *relevance* values:

Definition 2.8.2 (Relevance function). *The relevance between information entities and cases is described by a partial* relevance function

$$\rho : E \times C \to \mathcal{R}. \tag{2.25}$$

The relevance $\rho(e, c)$ is considered as a measure for the relevance of e for the retrieval of a case c. Thereby, $\rho(e, c)$ is defined if and only if $e \in c$. □

Negative values $\rho(e, c)$ may be used in the meaning "do not retrieve the case c if one asks for the information entity e" (formally such an information entity e is considered as a part of the case c too).

The acceptance of a case c for a query q is accumulated from the contributions of the constituting case information entities $e \in c$ according to their relevances $\rho(e, c)$. The contributions p_e of the information entities are computed by their accumulation functions π_e as described above. For the accumulation at the cases, we need another kind of accumulation functions:

Definition 2.8.3 (Global accumulation function). *The* global accumulation function π_c *has the form*

$$\pi_c : \underbrace{\mathcal{R} \times \ldots \times \mathcal{R}}_{k \text{ times}} \rightarrow \mathcal{R}, \tag{2.26}$$

for $c = \{e_1, \ldots, e_k\}$. *The accumulated acceptance of the case* c *regarding its constituting information entities is then computed by* $\pi_c(p_1, \ldots, p_k)$, *where* p_i *is the contribution of the information entity* $e_i \in c$. *This contribution* p_i *depends on* $\rho(e_i, c)$ *and another real value* x_i *assigned to* e_i *(actually* x_i *is the accumulated local acceptance value computed by* $\pi_{e_i}(a_1, \ldots, a_n)$ *from Definition 2.5.1). The contributions* p_i *are computed by a function* $g : \mathcal{R} \times \mathcal{R} \rightarrow \mathcal{R}$ *such that*

$$p_i = g(x_i, \rho(e_i, c)). \tag{2.27}$$

□

The product can be a suitable choice for g such that $p_i = x_i \cdot \rho(e_i, c)$. But again, such an assignment may have further hidden consequences, as for the function f in the case of local accumulation functions. We shall discuss some special consequences later in Section 2.8.5.

2.8.3 Weighted Queries

Queries have been defined as sets of information entities. Hence, the computation of $\alpha_q(e)$ by the characteristic function as in Definition 2.8.1 is straight forward. We can generalize this definition in the following way:

Definition 2.8.4 (Weighted query). *A* weighted query *assigns an importance value to each information entity by a function*

$$\alpha_q : E \rightarrow \mathcal{R}, \tag{2.28}$$

where $\alpha_q(e)$ *denotes the importance of the information entity* e *for the query* q. □

High values indicate high importance, negative values indicate the rejection of related cases. The value 0 is used as a neutral element, i.e. $\alpha_q(e) = 0$ stands for "not mentioning e in the query". The "unweighted" form $q \subseteq E$ is available by α_q ranging over $\{0, 1\}$.

An implementation of the function f from Definition 2.8.1 by ordinary multiplication may now produce curious effects. The standard idea behind negative values is the rejection of related cases:

- a negative value of $\alpha_q(e)$ indicates that cases related to e should be rejected,
- a negative value of $\sigma(e, e')$ indicates that cases containing e' should be rejected when asking for e.

Multiplication leads now to the effect that two negative values $\alpha_q(e)$ and $\sigma(e, e')$ are combined to a positive contribution $a_i = \alpha_q(e) \cdot \sigma(e, e')$. They have the same impact on the final result as corresponding positive values $|\alpha_q(e)|$ and $|\sigma(e, e')|$. We shall come back to this point later on in Section 2.8.5.

2.8.4 Putting it all together

We have to extend the notion of global acceptance functions according to weighted queries:

Definition 2.8.5 (Extended acceptance function). *Acceptance between weighted queries and cases is expressed by an* extended acceptance function*:*

$$\mathsf{acc} : \mathcal{R}^E \times \mathcal{P}(E) \to \mathcal{R}. \tag{2.29}$$

□

The acceptance $\mathsf{acc}(\alpha_q, c)$ of a case c for a weighted query α_q can now be accumulated using the introduced functions:

$$\begin{aligned}
&\mathsf{acc}(\alpha_q, c) = \\
&\quad \pi_c(g(\pi_{e'_1}(f(\alpha_q(e_{11}), \sigma(e_{11}, e'_1)), \dots, f(\alpha_q(e_{1n_1}), \sigma(e_{1n_1}, e'_1)), \rho(e'_1, c)), \\
&\qquad\qquad \dots \\
&\quad\quad g(\pi_{e'_k}(f(\alpha_q(e_{k1}), \sigma(e_{k1}, e'_k)), \dots, f(\alpha_q(e_{kn_k}), \sigma(e_{kn_k}, e'_k)), \rho(e'_k, c))\ ) \\
&\quad \textit{with } c = \{e'_1, \dots, e'_k\} \textit{ and } E_{e'_i} = \{e_{i1}, \dots, e_{in_i}\} \textit{ for } i = 1, \dots, k.
\end{aligned} \tag{2.30}$$

For illustration we consider f and g as products, π_e and π_c as sums respectively. Then we get:

$$\mathsf{acc}(\alpha_q, c) = \sum_{e' \in c} \rho(e', c) \sum_{e \in E_{e'}} \sigma(e, e') \cdot \alpha_q(e). \tag{2.31}$$

Here, we meet the properties **P1**–**P4** from Section 2.4.1. **P1** and **P2** are already satisfiable by weighted sums as discussed in Section 2.6.1. Now we have:

- **P3**: Different importances of an information entity for different cases are expressed by different values $\rho(e', c)$.
- **P4**: Different importances in a query are expressed by $\alpha_q(e)$.

The treatment of dependencies (Property **P5**) needs appropriate functions f, g, π_e, and π_c.

We define the "reminder value" of an information entity e for a case c by

$$\mathsf{remind}(e, c) := \sum_{e' \in c} \rho(e', c) \cdot \sigma(e, e'). \tag{2.32}$$

Then, the acceptance can be computed by the weighted sum of all reminder values, where the weights denote the importance for the weighted query α_q:

$$\mathsf{acc}(\alpha_q, c) = \sum_{e \in E} \alpha_q(e) \cdot \mathsf{remind}(e, c) \tag{2.33}$$

2.8.5 Special Problems

Property **P2** from Section 2.4.1 can be implemented using negative local acceptance values in the sum formula (2.31). To express that an offer for `1 Million DM` is strictly unacceptable if a query asks for a price of `about 10 DM`, we can give a negative value to local acceptance value $\sigma(<\texttt{price}:10>,<\texttt{price}:1000000>)$. This negative value must result in a negative reminder value $\texttt{remind}(<\texttt{price}:10>,c)$ for all cases c to which the information entity `<price:1000000>` belongs to c. Moreover, $\texttt{remind}(<\texttt{price}:10>,c)$ should be low enough to keep the value $\texttt{acc}(\alpha_q,c)$ low even if all other summands in the sum (2.33) have good acceptance values. Therefore, we need a negative value $\sigma(<\texttt{price}:10>,<\texttt{price}:1000000>)$ with an amount of multiple order of the positive local acceptance values.

Alternatively, we may use other functions than the sum; e.g., for the function π_c such that negative reminder values are not treated as summands. Such an approach is necessary if negative values are used at different levels. We have permitted negative values:

- for the weights $\alpha(e)$ of a query to express that information entities related to e should not appear in an acceptable case,
- for the local acceptance $\sigma(e,e')$ to express that e' is not acceptable for e,
- for the relevance functions $\rho(e,c)$ to express that e gives the advice for not accepting c.

All these values appear as factors in formula (2.31). A reminder value will get a positive value if both $\sigma(e,e')$ and $\rho(e',c)$ are negative. Moreover, the negative values may have a great amount to compensate positive values in the sum. The reminder value will become very high under such circumstances, which is not the intent.

This shows that the multiple use of negative values at different levels can have undesired effects. However, related effects can be implemented in different ways such that the usage of negative values can be restricted. A more detailed investigation of useful replacements and of appropriate composition functions is still open.

2.9 Implementation Issues

Case memories based on acceptance functions can be implemented by net structures with information entity nodes for each information entity $e \in E$ and case nodes for each case (descriptor) $c \in C$. There exists an "acceptance" arc from the information entity node e to the information entity node e' if $\sigma(e,e')$ is defined, and it exists an "relevance" arc from the information entity node e to the case node c if $\rho(e,c)$ is defined. The arcs in the net are weighted by the values $\sigma(e,e')$ and $\rho(e',c)$, respectively.

It may be impossible in practice to include all (potential) information entities $e \in E$ in the net (there may be infinitely many information entities, e.g., for attributes with numerical ranges). It suffices to build a net from the information entities which occur in the cases from the case base only. Nevertheless, a query may ask for an information entity not occuring in a case from the case base. Special computation nodes can be used to deal with such situations (cf. Burkhard 1995a; Burkhard 1998).

Acceptance values are computed by a spreading activation process in the net as follows: Information entity nodes e are initially activated by $\alpha_q(e)$ according to the weighted query α_q. The computation is performed by propagating along the acceptance arcs to further information entity nodes e', and from these nodes over relevance arcs to case nodes c. This propagation process has some analogy to the propagation in Neural Networks. The functions $f/\pi_{e'}$ and g/π_c are responsible for the accumulation of activities at the information entity nodes and the case nodes, respectively. Negative values for $\sigma(e, e')$ and $\rho(e', c)$ can be interpreted as inhibitor arcs. The final activations at the case nodes c denote the acceptance value of c for the query α_q as given in (2.30).

Related implementations have been developed and investigated as *Case Retrieval Nets* (Chapter 3). They have been evaluated in several applications with up to 200,000 cases (with a retrieval time of about 1 second on a SPARC20).

The complexity of the computation process is estimated by the arcs in the net. $|E|$ is the number of information entities, and $|C|$ is the number of cases in the case memory, respectively. The relevance fan out of an information entity node e is given by the number of cases c where $\rho(e, c)$ is defined. The average relevance fan out is denoted by out_{EC}. Similarly, the acceptance fan out of an information entity node e is given by the number of information entities e' where $\sigma(e, e')$ is defined. The average acceptance fan out is denoted by out_{EE}.

We assume that each case consists of exactly n information entities (e.g., if each case is described by n attribute values). It follows that we have $n \cdot |C|$ relevance arcs in the net, and the average relevance fan out of the information entity nodes is given by $out_{EC} = \frac{n \cdot |C|}{|E|}$.

We assume that a query consists of n information entities too. Then an average propagation process from the initially activated information entity nodes e over the further information entity nodes e' to the case nodes c uses

$$n \cdot out_{EE} \cdot out_{EC} = n^2 \cdot out_{EE} \cdot \frac{|C|}{|E|} \tag{2.34}$$

arcs. If out_{EE} is proportional to $|E|$, then we obtain a complexity linear to $|C|$, i.e., some value $k \cdot |C|$ with $k = n^2 \cdot \frac{out_{EE}}{|E|}$. As far as we have a moderate connectivity between the information entities, the value $\frac{out_{EE}}{|E|}$ will be small, such that the factor k is small enough to provide very good answer times in practical applications.

We may even have a constant computational complexity if out_{EE} and $\frac{|C|}{|E|}$ can be considered as constants. This is the case if new information entities appear proportionally to new cases, and if the average acceptance fan out does not grow.

Further computational effort is needed for the computation of the preference relation. This means a sorting process according to the values of acceptance, but usually only the best cases have to be retrieved. This results in additional constant complexity.

2.10 Conclusion

Case Completion was discussed as an attempt to allow more flexible use of cases. Cases are not compared by their problem sections, but by the information available at certain stages of Case Completion. The indexes to the cases are given by information entities.

The whole Case Completion process is described by a single case, where we prefer the viewpoint of constraints (instead of rules). Old cases contain information about the handling of such constraints in earlier tasks. When enough cases are collected, other methods may discover the underlying constraints in a general form. CBR can be used to handle the remaining uncertain situations and the unexpected cases. Related cases give hints to the experts, they may be used for argumentation. Concepts, constraints, and rules might be integrated as "higher level" information entities and cases (Burkhard 1997).

CBR systems supporting Case Completion have to work as assistance systems in close interaction with the user. They need a very flexible handling of cases, where queries may become more and more specified during a session. It is not clear at design time, which indexes will be known at run time – hence arbitrary sets of indexes are allowed for queries.

The traditional correspondence of similarity and distance is critically reconsidered in the light of the differences between acceptance and distances (Section 2.6.4). The approach using acceptance can be seen under the aspect of accumulation for acceptance, while distances are more related to accumulation for rejection. Accumulation for acceptance provides a means to regard possible compromises in the retrieval and can go further than the established approaches based on distances.

The intuitive meaning of "acceptance" makes transparent the subjective criteria for the preferences for cases. This is important for the designer as well as for discussions with the user of a system: The system should be designed in a way that enables the user to understand why a special case is presented for a query. An on-line influence of the user to the preferences (the acceptances) is a matter for advanced systems. It can be implemented using Case Retrieval

Nets as far as the technical viewpoint is considered. The main problem is the appropriate user interface.

Local acceptance can implement fuzzy notions. Furthermore, we have proposed to use negative values for unacceptability, while the value "0" denotes the neutral situation. However, negative values with different sources may cause problems, which need another treatment (e.g. by inhibiting strategies). Further investigations are necessary.

The computations are implemented as a propagation process in a net; efficient implementations are realized by Case Retrieval Nets (Chapter 3). The propagation of activations can be interpreted as a successive discovery of "reminders" which lead to former episodes. Reminding is first pushed by some items (query information entities), then spread out to related items (acceptable information entities) and finally collected at cases, which provide additional items of interest. This corresponds to the idea of "remembering as reconstruction" (Bartlett 1932; (Burkhard 1995b). It is possible to consider more than two steps for the spreading activation process (i.e., further information entities may be activated if the first found cases are not satisfying).

The spreading activation in a Case Retrieval Net is similar to the computation process of Neural Networks. This permits a close coupling of symbolic and subsymbolic computations. Learning strategies known from Neural Networks can be used to tune the weights at the acceptance and relevance arcs in the Case Retrieval Net. These issues are covered in further ongoing work.

Acknowledgments

Special thanks are due to the colleagues from Humboldt University Berlin for a lot of fruitful discussions and for their work in implementations, especially to Mario Lenz, Miriam Kunze, and Andre Hübner.

3. Diagnosis and Decision Support

Mario Lenz, Eric Auriol, Michel Manago

In this chapter, we will focus on the utilization of Case-Based Reasoning for solving problems in the area of diagnosis and decision support. For this, we will first discuss different types of analytic problem solving, explain alternative approaches of coping with specific problems, and finally sketch a number of successful applications.

3.1 Aspects of Analytic Problem Solving

In the AI literature, a variety of approaches exist for establishing a taxonomy of problem solving methods (cf. Puppe (1993, Chapter 11) for a discussion of the most prominent work on this). A commonly accepted distinction is between *analytic* and *synthetic* problem solving. While Chapters 6 through 8 go into detail about the latter, we will consider the former type in this chapter.

Analytic problem solving means that the major task is to analyze, or interpret, a given solution and to drive inferences based on these interpretations. In most situations, a problem is solved as soon as an appropriate (similar) case has been found because the solution directly emerges from that case. An extensive process of really *constructing* a solution as, e.g., in planning or configuration, is rarely performed.

In general, analytic problem solving covers specific methods, such as classification, diagnosis, and decision support. The relationship between these three, however, varies from one author to another. Hence, we will clarify first what our understanding of these terms is and how they are related.

3.1.1 Characteristics of Classification

According to Puppe (1993), classification is a

> *"Problem solving type in which the solution is selected from a set of given solutions, ..."*

More precisely, the following properties are essential for classification:

1. The problem domain consists of two disjoint sets of domain objects, namely

   - a set of symptoms (or observations) and
   - a set of problem solutions (or classes).
2. A problem description is represented as a set of observations.
3. The solution of a problem (and thus the result of classification) is the selection of one or more classes.

To ease the understanding of the following discussion, let us recall the definition of classification from Chapter 1:

Definition 3.1.1 (Classification). *Let U be a universe of objects and let further subsets $K_i \subseteq U, i \in I$, of U be classes. A* classifier *is a function*

$$\mathsf{class} : U \rightarrow I$$

such that $\mathsf{class}(x) = i$ *implies* $x \in K_i$. □

To perform case-based classification, the central idea arising from Definition 3.1.1 is that cases have to be represented as tuples consisting of a problem description and the corresponding class. In slogan form:

case = problem + classification

Again using the notation of Chapter 1, classification clearly belongs to the class of problems which are of *rule type*: The fundamental assumption of case-based classification is that if two cases $c_1 = (x_1, \mathsf{class}(x_1))$ and $c_2 = (x_2, \mathsf{class}(x_2))$ have similar problem descriptions x_1 and x_2, then they will have similar or even the same classifications:

$$x_1 \approx x_2 \longrightarrow \mathsf{class}(x_1) \approx \mathsf{class}(x_2) \tag{3.1}$$

Given this, a query $q = (p_q, ?)$ can be classified by simply determining (q', i) where q' is the nearest neighbor of q in the case base and adopting i for the class of the query q. Alternatively, one could determine the k most similar cases (for a given k) and let these *vote* for the proper class (see Section 1.4). This approach has a long tradition in the area of *nearest neighbor classification* (cf. Dasarathy 1990), which represents domain objects as vectors in hyperspace and utilizes *clusters* of objects to determine classes.

Note that the reverse of implication (3.1) does not hold in general: Two defendants may well receive the same sentence although they have committed completely different crimes (cf. Chapters 1 and 2 for discussions on general aspects of similarity).

A major advantage of CBR is that learning can be integrated into case-based classification and hence an initially *approximate* classifier function appr_class where

$$\exists x \in U : \mathsf{appr\_class}(x) = i \land x \notin K_i$$

can be adjusted such that appr_class becomes a correct classifier over time.

There are several ways to realize learning within a case-based system, including insertion of cases into the case base and modification of the similarity measure (cf. Sections 1.3 and 13.6 for more details).

Example 3.1.1. Consider automatic quality control in manufacturing: A robot might monitor a production process and protocol important parameters of both the products and the machinery used (e.g., temperatures, pressures, noises, colors, etc.). At any time during the process, each produced item can be classified according to whether or not it is of sufficient quality.

3.1.2 Characteristics of Diagnosis

While Puppe (1993) uses the terms classification and diagnosis as synonyms, the latter usually includes a *process* of ascertaining (further) symptoms to improve the quality of problem solving. In contrast, all features are typically known at the beginning of a classification process.

To emphasize this distinction, Richter (1992b) introduces a third set of domain objects, namely tests which can be performed at any time during a diagnostic process in order to obtain knowledge about further symptoms. Furthermore, while the main objective remains finding diagnoses, subtasks may aim at identifying differences between sets of observations in order to determine which test should be performed next. This is usually referred to as *differential diagnosis.*

Another difference to classification is that in diagnosis very often the reverse of relationship (3.1) is assumed: It is quite natural to assume that, if similar diagnoses have been established in two situations, then similar symptoms should be observable too. Some diagnostic approaches heavily rely on this assumption, e.g. when using Bayes' theorem to derive a diagnosis for an observed set of symptoms given the knowledge about which symptoms are expected for certain diseases (Heckerman 1991; Pearl 1988).

Consequently, diagnosis can be considered as a generalization of classification in the sense that symptoms are not necessarily known at the beginning but have to be inferred in a diagnostic process. Apart from this, the same definitions as for classification may be applied. In particular, a diagnostic case clearly distinguishes between a problem description (the symptoms) and the solution of that problem (the diagnosis) in these approaches.

In reality, this description of diagnosis is often not sufficient:

- Firstly, diagnosis often includes features of case completion as described in Section 2.2. Given a first set of initial symptoms, it is most often impossible to diagnose a faulty component. Rather, a diagnostic process most often includes subtasks for identifying the next test to perform in order to obtain additional symptoms or to choose among various alternative solutions.
- Secondly, it is not always required that the faulty component is actually identified. In many situations it is sufficient that the machine works again or that it is not worth repairing it.

Example 3.1.2. Repair diagnostics: Given a set of complaints and observed malfunctions, a diagnostic system may search for probable reasons for these and suggest further tests to be performed in order to confirm or reject hypotheses. Finally, the faulty component should be identified.

3.1.3 Characteristics of Decision Support

Decision support is an even more general problem solving type. In particular, the distinction between symptoms and solutions of problems is not straightforward. Rather, it is often unclear in advance, which features of the domain will be used for describing future problems and which will be considered as solutions.

In the context of decision support, a problem is a representation of a situation with missing information. The objective is to complete the description of that situation during problem solving such that a certain demand for information can be satisfied (cf. Richter 1992b; Lenz et al. 1996b, as well as Chapter 2). In terms of Chapter 1, decision support clearly belongs to the class of problems which are of *constraint type.*

Furthermore, it is usually not possible to decide whether a solution (i.e., a piece of information) found by a decision support system (DSS) is *correct* or not. Rather, this information may be more or less useful, it may be better or worse than some other piece of information. This problem is due to the following domain characteristics:

- DSSs are most often applied in domains where the terminology is highly ambiguous.
- The interpretation of certain pieces of information is context-sensitive and depends on the intention of the human user.
- The existing domain knowledge is, in general too weak to allow for strong problem solving methods.

Problem areas in which most of these problems have to be coped with, are usually referred to as *weak-theory domains.*

Example 3.1.3. A vivid example for a decision support application will be given in Section 11.3.4 when the Icons system is described: Because of the enormous complexity of the problem space in medical domains and due to the many different aspects that have to be considered, Icons is restricted to providing information relevant for the current case. It is the human expert who finally has to come up with a decision and take the responsibility.

In addition to these features, Richter (1992b, p. 343) identifies four characteristic properties of decision support systems:

1. The amount of information that has to be coped with is too large to be handled by humans without support by an appropriate technical system.
2. Decisions have to be made rapidly.
3. Data has to be prepared in some way for decision making.
4. The process of decision making is highly complex.

Normative and Descriptive DSSs. For the design of decision support systems, two alternative approaches may be utilized: a *normative* and a *descriptive* one.

Normative approaches attempt to establish general rules for rational behavior in general and, in particular, for determining when a solution to a problem is better than another.

Descriptive approaches, on the other hand, do not rely so much on general principles but on examples of successful problem solving episodes. Such episodes are investigated to obtain knowledge about *how* the solution was derived – not primarily *why* this solution worked.

In terms of general reasoning techniques, normative and descriptive approaches perform deductive and inductive inference, respectively.

Case-based techniques clearly belong to the second category. However, case-based reasoning differs from traditional inductive reasoning / inductive learning in several respects. The relationship between the two will be explored in the following sections.

3.2 CBR and Inductive Learning

Case-based reasoning and inductive learning are different but complementary methods for utilizing past information in solving problems. When a new problem is encountered, CBR recalls similar cases and adapts the solutions that worked in the past for the current problem. Inductive learning (Quinlan 1983) creates a general description of past examples, and then applies this description to new data. The INRECA project (Baudin et al. 1996) demonstrated that the integration of inductive learning and CBR improves the capabilities of the resulting system (Althoff et al. 1995a; Auriol et al. 1995).

Recently, the number of applications in various domains has grown impressively (Auriol et al. 1994). The most convincing systems are fielded in help desk areas, particularly for diagnosing complex equipment. Troubleshooting of CFM 56 engines for Boeing 737 airplanes (Heider 1996; Heider et al. 1997) and the diagnosis of robots axis position faults developed by AcknoSoft for CFM International and SEPRO Robotique (Manago and Auriol 1996) are two examples of successful applications in this field. Both will be explored in some detail in Section 3.6.

3.2.1 Inductive Learning versus Case-Based Reasoning

In all its various guises, *inductive learning* or *induction* means reaching conclusions about a whole class of facts based on evidence on part of that class. Recorded cases, e.g., of equipment failure and repair, legal cases and their adjudication, or the credit records of debtors, represent a small part of the potential events in each of these areas. The original idea of what is called induction is to generalize the lessons of past cases into rules.

The inductive method presented here creates a decision tree from a history of cases and then uses this tree for problem solving. Inductive learning requires that the data is structured, for example, by using classes of objects with slots. A standard relational database schema can easily be mapped onto this object model. It allows to define the vocabulary used to describe the cases. For example, an error code on a control panel, the state of a pipe, etc.

A decision tree is built by recursively splitting the tree into subtrees. This is most effective if, at each node, splitting is performed according to the feature providing the highest amount of information with respect to the subtrees arising from this splitting. A widely accepted concept of information is the quantity that is transferred in the act of informing. By learning something not previously known, the recipient of information reduces uncertainty about the world. This is what Shannon (1948) formalized in information theory and what is used today to build decision trees. The question that, if answered, yields most information is the one that most reduces the uncertainty about final classification, as measured on the population of historical cases that match the answers already given.

We now briefly present the main ideas concerning the inductive technique, and the advantages and drawbacks of inductive learning.

Underlying Concepts of Induction. Induction is a technology that automatically extracts knowledge from training examples in a structured form, such as a decision tree or a set of rules. We will restrict ourselves to the former here. At each node in the decision tree, the inductive process evaluates a numeric measure, called the information gain, for all the relevant slots. It then picks the one that, if answered, yields the highest increase of the information gain measure. The process is iterated onto the child nodes, until some stopping criteria (defined by the user) are encountered.

Formally speaking, the uncertainty about the value of the classification target T is measured by its entropy, and the information gain of an attribute A is the reduction of the entropy of T due to knowing the value of A. If C is the current case base, and the k values of the target T occur with relative frequencies $p_1, ..., p_k$ in C, then the entropy of C with respect to T is:

$$E_T(C) = \sum_{i=1}^{k} -p_i \log_2 p_i \qquad (3.2)$$

If the values of A partition the case base C into l subsets $C_1, ..., C_l$, and, within subset C_j, the k values of T occur with relative frequencies $q_{1j}, ..., q_{kj}$, then the conditional entropy of C with respect to T when A is known is:

$$E_T(C/A) = \sum_{i=1}^{k} -p_i \sum_{j=1}^{l} q_{ij} \log_2 q_{ij} \qquad (3.3)$$

The information gain of A within C with respect to target T is:

$$IG_T(A, C) = E_T(C) - E_T(C/A) \tag{3.4}$$

When A is a numeric attribute, it does not generate directly a partition of the case base. In this case, A is turned into an ordered symbolic attribute by automatic thresholding. Another important refinement of the basic induction approach is to weight the attributes in the information gain calculation to take into account the time or cost to find its value.

The main advantages of induction can be summarized as follows:

- The building and the consultation of the tree are fast and efficient.
- The information gain measure is built on a sound basis. This insures the correctness and the effectiveness of the resulting tree with respect to the data used to build it.
- During consultation, only a few tests are necessary on average before a conclusion is reached.
- For industrial applications, the consultation system can be delivered as a runtime system.

Induction, however, also has its limitations:

- A decision tree is not incremental and the consultation system is static. A tree is built at a fixed date and cannot directly be modified in the runtime environment.
- An induction tree cannot handle unknown values in an optimal way during consultation.
- The inductive approach does not enable the distinction between various kinds of users. The tree consultation may not be adapted for all users. One always has to use an entire path of the tree before reaching a conclusion. This approach might be appropriate for a technician, but not for a skilled expert who wants to rush immediately to a specific level of detail.

In summary, one can state that the final system quickly delivers a diagnosis after a reduced subset of questions. On the other hand, the final user cannot modify the system behavior but has to follow exactly the set of questions produced by the tree. An underlying assumption is that the environment does not evolve too much over time. Of course, these are unrealistic assumptions in most applications. One is likely to use case-based reasoning for handling these kinds of applications. In the next section, we compare inductive learning and case-based reasoning approaches and show how case-based reasoning and induction technologies complement each other.

Underlying Concepts of CBR. Instead of building a generalization of a database as inductive learning approaches do, case-based reasoning directly looks for similar cases in the database, with respect to the requirements of the user. For applications where safety is important, the conclusions can be further confirmed, or refuted, by entering additional parameters that may modify the similarity values. CBR appeals to those professionals who solve problems by recalling what they did in similar situations. It works well even in domains that are poorly understood or where rules have many exceptions. Some of the characteristics that indicate whether CBR technology is suitable for a particular domain are:

- Experience is as valuable as textbook knowledge: CBR makes direct use of past experience.
- Historical cases are viewed as an asset that should be preserved and it is intuitively clear that remembering past experience is useful.
- Specialists talk about their domain by giving examples.

Case-based reasoning has some advantages compared to a pure inductive system:

- CBR can handle incomplete and noisy data at consultation time. Case-based reasoning is robust with respect to unknown values because it does not generalize the data. Instead of using a minimal set of questions (as an induction tree does), a case-based search makes use of all the knowledge specified by the user within the query. It returns the most similar cases and an associated degree of similarity.
- A case-based reasoning system may be more easily adapted to different users. For instance, an expert who consults the system can drive it by skipping some steps that are useless for him. The search for similar cases can be made directly based upon a subpart of the overall information. This approach may improve the user acceptance. It makes the consultation system more flexible.

Further characteristics of the CBR approach are:

- It performs no generalization of knowledge. Note that this is a major principle of the case-based reasoning paradigm. Thus, unlike induction, CBR avoids the danger that useful information might be forgotten.
- When not designed properly, a case-based reasoning system may have efficiency problems on big databases, or when access to the database is slow. This problem may result in a lack of efficiency of the consultation system.

The Need for Case-Based Reasoning. A key distinction between case-based reasoning and inductive learning is that induction first computes an abstraction of the case database (in the form of a decision tree or a set of production rules) and uses this general knowledge to do problem solving. During the problem solving stage, the system behaves as if the case database did not exist. This can result in a loss of useful information which was originally contained in the training cases. The following example demonstrates this side effect.

Example 3.2.1. Let us consider the case base and the decision tree that has been generated by induction on this case base, displayed in Figure 3.1 (this toy example is a subpart of a real case base that concerns the diagnosis of failures of a CNC-machine). When consulting the decision tree, the user may not be able to answer the first question (*What is the error code?*), for instance because of a deficiency of the monitor. When answering `Unknown`, one reaches on one branch the first conclusion `Tool Gripper`, associated to case $c3$, and on the second branch the question `IO state IN32`. When answering `low`, one reaches the second conclusion `Pipe System`, associated to case $c2$. The overall conclusion is therefore `Tool Gripper` or `Pipe System`, each with probability 0.5. However, if we look carefully at both, the decision tree and the case base, we can see that this conclusion is partially wrong: Case $c3$, which supports the conclusion `Tool Gripper`, contains the value `high` for attribute `IO state IN32`, whereas we said during consultation that the value was `low`.

CASE	Diagnosis	io state IN32	error code	cable	pipe(valve 5y2)	...
case 1	io card	high	I53	ok	dense	...
case 2	pipe system	low	I53	ok	leaking	...
case 3	tool gripper	high	none	?	?	...
...						

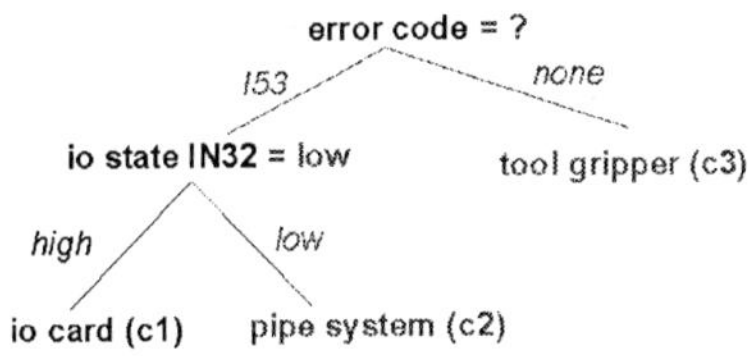

Fig. 3.1. A sample case base and the corresponding decision tree

Note that this problem is neither due to the formalism of the induction tree nor due to the information gain measure which has been used for building it. The problem is due to the approach of reasoning about a problem using abstract knowledge: The important information (the value of `IO state IN32` for case $c3$) has been generalized away and is no more available during consultation.

Hence, if the user who consults a decision tree cannot answer a question, the consultation mechanism spreads towards all the possibilities (i.e., all the possible values of the unknown slot). This has two undesirable effects:

- The solutions returned are less accurate because they are based on a subset of information that is not complete.
- The solutions may even be wrong, according to the features of the cases that are not used by the decision tree.

Comparison of Benefits of Inductive Learning and CBR. We summarize and compare the advantages of inductive learning and case-based reasoning in Table 3.1. Inductive learning performs several tasks that cannot be done by a case-based reasoning system. It builds a tree from the case database which can reveal inconsistencies among the cases. For instance, it can reveal that two (or more) cases belonging to different classes are located under the same leaf node of the tree.

Table 3.1. Comparison of inductive and case-based approaches

Case-based Reasoning	*Inductive learning*
CBR evolves over time and works incrementally.	Induction is non-incremental: Once a decision tree has been built, it can, in general, not be changed.
CBR reasons directly on the basis of the entire case base.	The decision tree can be compiled in a form that does not require the full environment to do diagnosis.
CBR does not perform any kind of generalization.	Induction extracts explicit knowledge from the data. This knowledge can be interpreted and understood.
CBR can handle missing values during consultation.	Induction may have problems with missing information.
CBR can react dynamically and the consultation is more flexible. The system can be driven by the user.	A decision tree is static and the expert can influence the way of consultation only by modifying the tree.

3.2.2 Integrating CBR and Induction within the INRECA Project

AcknoSoft, TecInno, IMS and the University of Kaiserslautern joined forces in 1992, with the help of the European Union's (EU) Esprit program, and started the INRECA project to:

(1) integrate the technologies of induction and case-based reasoning and
(2) apply the results to real industrial problems.

INRECA was successfully completed in Autumn 1995 and influenced largely the technical results and the software developed by the industrial partners of the consortium. INRECA allowed to depict the respective advantages and drawbacks of each technique (see below). It fully demonstrated the necessity and the usefulness of integrating both technologies and identified four levels of integration. Finally, INRECA was the starting point of six major applications in the domain of diagnosis and decision support areas. Whereas former sections presented both technical approaches together with their strengths and weaknesses, we want to outline in this section the four integration levels depicted in INRECA with practical usefulness. For this we will elaborate in more detail the integration levels mentioned in Section 1.3:

Toolbox: Separate inductive learning and case-based reasoning engines are accessible through a common user interface, for application to the same case base.

Cooperative: CBR and induction exchange results expressed in a common case representation language. The results of one extends the classification capabilities of the other.

Workbench: Individual modules of each technique collaborate.

Seamless: Both techniques are integrated within a single platform in such a way that the users are unaware of which technique is being used.

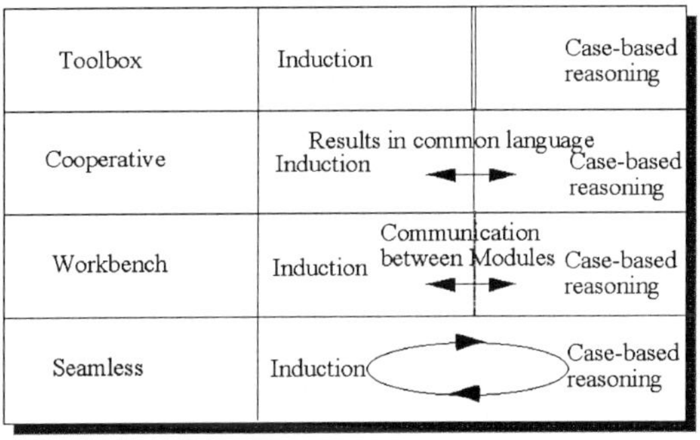

Fig. 3.2. Four integration levels of CBR and induction

The characteristics of the four levels of integration are summarized in Figure 3.2. Note that the goal of INRECA was not only to create a seamlessly integrated platform, but to define how the integration should take place. It is wrong to state that one approach is better than the other, or that a particular integration level is more suited than the other ones. The choice of an architecture depends on (1) the characteristics of the problem to be solved and (2) on the characteristics of the end-user who will use the resulting software. A good technical solution may not be appropriate because the habits of the user do not correspond to the proposed solution. For instance, a pure case-based reasoning approach may outperform a pure decision tree in domains where problems represent uncertainty. On the other hand, a decision tree will be more suited for the final *naive* users because they are used to troubleshooting manuals with strong guidelines.

In practice, most applications performed on the basis of the INRECA approach demonstrated that intermediary integration levels were appropriate. This gave rise to the following results.

The Toolbox Approach. It is always necessary to offer the choice of a particular technique to deal with a problem. This is not a real *integration* but one has to keep in mind the final goal of a decision support system: helping the user to solve problems. There are at least four reasons, mainly related to ergonomics, that may justify the toolbox approach:

1. Different consultation modes require different tools. For instance, if a set of features is already known before the beginning of the consultation, a case-based reasoning approach seems likely to be used instead of induction.

2. The users feel better when using a special investigation method. They understand the technical requirements, find it easier to handle the results produced, and will be able to explain their choice to peers. Prerelease validation is another consideration. For instance, in Cassiopée (see Section 3.6.2), CFM International wants to evaluate and control the tools they provide to the airlines.
3. Results are needed in a particular form. For instance, a decision tree can easily be handled by a low-level technician because he is guided step by step during the consultation. This is also the case for a robot that automatically runs all the tests listed in a path from the root to leaf in a tree. Experts will probably prefer a case-based reasoning method because it is more flexible and may provide shortcuts for them.
4. For some applications, the results of one of the techniques may be better w.r.t. to ergonomics, maintenance, etc. than a combination of two.

An integrated tool has to propose the separate use of inductive learning and case-based reasoning if the user wants it. Of course, both modules have to share a common description language at this level and have common features for input and output.

The Cooperative Approach. In the cooperative approach, the results of either technique are used to improve the other one. The individual algorithms do not have to be modified. For example, an induction tree allows the user to detect inconsistencies in a database before using it for CBR.

Questions and solutions arising from the cooperative approach are of interest to overcome some of the limitations inherent to each isolated method. Hence, a typical cooperative approach will take the following form:

1. Start the consultation of a decision tree for a given query.
2. Collect the cases which correspond to the leaves of the tree at the end of the consultation.
3. Switch to the case-based reasoning module.
4. Order these cases according to their similarity to the query.

A variant of this process is:

2a. When the answer to a question asked during the consultation of the decision tree is unknown, collect the cases found in the corresponding internal node.

The Workbench Approach. The workbench approach allows different inductive learning and case-based reasoning modules to collaborate with each other. Key components of inductive learning and CBR tools are the information gain measure and the similarity measure, respectively. The main difference between the two is that the information gain is an interclass measure (it computes the power of an attribute for separating two clusters) while the similarity measure is an intraclass measure (it compares how near two situations are). They may be combined in several ways in the decision support system at building time to produce a more accurate consultation system, or they may be used concurrently in the maintenance system to improve the results.

A typical example of a workbench approach is the following:

1. For a given query, retrieve a list of cases by using a similarity measure.
2. If the cases do not all belong to the same class, use the information gain to compute the ranked list of attributes to be answered.
3. Ask the user for the corresponding answers.
4. Continue with step 1 until a stop criterion is reached (all retrieved cases belong to the same class etc.)

A variant of this process is to use a decision tree for retrieving the first set of cases.

The Seamless Approach. Both induction and case-based reasoning techniques have pros and cons. Moreover, they are not redundant but complementary. The main goal of the INRECA project was to improve the two technologies by combing their advantages. This is achieved in the first three integration levels not by changing the algorithms, but by combing their inputs and outputs in the first two levels, and by exchanging the similarity and information gain modules in the third level.

At the seamless level, we are going a step deeper by looking at how the algorithms can be merged within a single tool: the INRECA tree. The INRECA tree is basically an extension of kd-trees: Originally, a kd-tree was an indexing structure to access multi-dimensional data (Friedman et al. 1977) which has been extended for CBR purposes to include a backtracking process in order to retrieve more accurately the cases indexed by the tree (Wess et al. 1993a). The INRECA tree combines induction and CBR methods in the following two ways:

1. It uses induction to optimize the weights given to attribute similarity measures when computing case similarity measures.
2. It uses induced knowledge to modify attribute similarity measures, to reduce backtracking in indexing trees.

The INRECA tree uses induction to partition the case base into classes and then computes optimal weights as a basis for case similarities within each of these classes. In the INRECA system, it is possible to define a weight vector for every class of cases. These weights play the following roles:

1. They express a significant part of the domain knowledge.
2. They influence the retrieval process.
3. They also influence tree building.

The user can define these weights or the system calculates them automatically. In the latter case, the INRECA tree computes optimal weights for each class, based on the normal difference between the inter- and intraclass similarity for each attribute (see Baudin et al. (1996) for details concerning these measures). The knowledge discovered in the INRECA tree about the class of each case is transferred to the case similarity assessment through the definition of the weights.

The second idea of the INRECA tree is to use the knowledge extracted by induction from the cases to adapt the attribute similarity measures themselves, by a process we call *learning preferences.* While the kd-tree is a powerful retrieval structure, it sometimes requires a high number of backtracking steps. These steps can be avoided during retrieval by building an indexing structure that can be used both as indexing tree and decision tree. We can use the latter for modifying the similarity measure. The basic similarity measure is weighted based on the knowledge extracted from the decision tree: it increases the similarity between the query and those cases that are reached when using the INRECA tree as a decision tree. Increasing this similarity decreases the diameter of the ball used in the backtracking test and consequently reduces backtracking. If all the attributes occurring in the cases are also used as branches in the INRECA tree, the case similarity will increase to 1. In this case, no backtracking in the retrieval process is required at all, because the ball used in the backtracking test has a diameter of 0. The introduced improvements support the implementation of a CBR system and an inductive learning system in the same structure. The integrated system combines these approaches in a seamless way - that is, invisibly to the end-user. The integrated system can evolve smoothly as the application grows, from a pure CBR approach, where each case is a piece of knowledge, to a more inductive approach where some subsets of the cases are generalized into abstract knowledge.

3.3 Problem Solving as Information Completion

As discussed in Section 3.1, decision support has to cope with ambiguous terms, vague and maybe inconsistent problem descriptions in highly complex domains. Because of these difficulties, it is hard, if not impossible, to build expert systems in the traditional sense, i.e., stand-alone AI systems that solve problems automatically.

As the term *decision support* already suggests, the requirements on such a system are weakened in the sense that an automatic problem solving capability is no longer the (unrealistic) ultimate goal. Rather, it is sufficient if a (human) user is *supported* in making better decisions.

For example, obtaining information about previous events can be extremely helpful for the user. Even if this information is provided *as it is*, i.e., without a further inference process, it may well give hints for the current problem at hand, such as ways to overcome the problem, obstacles to avoid, or undesired side effects.

However, it is not sufficient to recall just the outcome of the previous events (in the sense of classification) because this may hide the specific conditions that caused the outcome. Rather, the complete description of the episodes has to be available in order to allow for a detailed evaluation of applicability.

3.3.1 Remembering as Reconstruction

The required information is not normally accessed in a single step, but rather may involve a longer process of subsequently collecting more and more pieces (cf. also Section 2.2). This *remembering as reconstruction* has a long tradition in psychology (Bartlett 1932) and had already been employed in the dynamic memory model of early CBR systems (Kolodner 1983; Riesbeck and Schank 1989).

This recall of problem solving episodes is exactly what a case-based DSS can provide; that is, it can be considered as a tool for accessing information stored in a kind of *external memory* and for judging the relevance of the found information (Lenz et al. 1996b).

The realization of this idea is straightforward: Given a query, the case memory is searched for similar cases – or, more precisely, for cases having a similar description[1]. Components of these similar cases are candidates for completing the information contained in the query, i.e., they have to be checked for consistency with the already known pieces of information and can then be added to the query description. Alternatively, the additional information may not come directly from the most similar cases but these might suggest tests to be performed in order to obtain new information (cf. Chapter 2). Thus, information completion heavily relies on the retrieval phase of case-based reasoning during which a preference ordering of cases is established which will guide the process of information completion.

In contrast to, for example, the classification task, a formal definition of information completion is not straightforward. Rather, a number of domain- and application-specific criteria have to be considered, such as

- What similarity function will be used for establishing the preference ordering?
- Which cases will be selected: Does it make sense to accept the k most similar ones? Should exceptional cases be preferred, or a set of cases be selected which differ concerning important aspects?
- What does it mean to *complete* missing information? Can it be extracted directly from the retrieved cases or do these cases suggest tests to perform for obtaining new insights (such as in the process of *differential diagnosis*)?
- When will the desire for more information be satisfied, i.e., when can the problem initially represented by the query be considered as being solved?

[1] We adopt here the common notion of *similarity*, although Chapter 2 clarified some misconceptions in particular when considering similarity as a kind of inverse distance. To be more precise, we should use *acceptance* instead.

Nevertheless, we will try to give a fairly general definition of information completion in what follows. For a related discussion and the notion of *information entities*, see Chapter 2.

Definition 3.3.1 (Information Completion). *Let*

E *be the set of information entities in the representation of the domain;*
$\mathcal{C}$ *be the set of all cases* c_i *in the case base* C *where each* $c_i \in \mathcal{C}$ *is represented as a set of IEs* $c_i \subseteq E$*;*
q *be a* query *also represented as a set of IEs* $q \subseteq E$*;*
$\mathcal{R}$ *be the function*

$$\mathcal{R} : \mathcal{P}(E) \times \mathcal{C} \to \mathcal{C}^k$$

retrieving the k *most similar cases to a given set of IEs from* $\mathcal{C}$ *and providing a preference ordering of these;*
$\mathcal{S}$ *be some function*

$$\mathcal{S} : \mathcal{P}(E) \times \mathcal{C}^k \to \mathcal{P}(E)$$

which for a given set of IEs and the result of the retrieval function $\mathcal{R}$ *selects a new set of IEs with which to proceed.*

Given this, the information completion *process can be formalized as follows:*

Step 1 (Query posing) *Given a query* $q \subseteq E$*, let* $E_0 = q$ *and* $i = 0$.
Step 2 (Retrieval) *Determine the* k *most similar cases to the current set of known IEs (i.e., the preference ordering):*

$$[c_1, \ldots, c_k] = \mathcal{R}(E_i, \mathcal{C})$$

Step 3 (Selection) *From the retrieved cases, select appropriate pieces of information which are considered useful in the current situation* E_i*:*

$$E_{i+1} = \mathcal{S}(E_i, [c_1, \ldots, c_k])$$

Step 4 (Stop criterion) *Decide about the quality of* E_{i+1}
- *If* E_{i+1} *provides sufficient information to solve the problem represented by* q*,* `exit successfully`.
- *Otherwise, if* E_{i+1} *provides some new information, let* $i = i + 1$ *and continue with Step 2.*
- *Otherwise* `exit with failure`*, i.e., the problem expressed by* q *could not be solved.*

□

Even when finished successfully, the result of this process is not really a *solution* to the initial problem which may readily be applied to solve it. Rather, in DSSs the retrieved information can be used by a (human) expert in the decision making process.

The retrieval function $\mathcal{R}$ as well as the selection function $\mathcal{S}$ give rise to a number of different approaches to information completion. Traditionally,

$\mathcal{R}$ is applied to the query only and $\mathcal{S}$ selects just the most similar case(s). In contrast, the model of OCRNs applies the above scheme in that cases are used to collect further IEs (cf. Section 3.4.5).

Note that classification and diagnosis as defined in Section 3.1 are just special cases of information completion: For classification tasks, the symptoms are used for querying the case base, and the found class(es) complete the query. Additionally, tests for further symptoms can be derived for diagnostic tasks.

3.3.2 Problems with Top-Down Retrieval Techniques

In a very restricted sense, even the structures of dynamic memory can be considered to perform information completion as defined above: When searching in a hierarchy of *memory organization packets* (MOPs), for example, some information is known about the event right from the start. By traversing this hierarchy, questions are answered which guide the search through the entire graph – thus additional pieces of information are collected along the way until all the pieces fit together and describe the entire event (cf. Kolodner 1993, Chapter 4).

However, in contrast to Definition 3.3.1, missing information is completed according to the structure of memory (i.e., by traversing the MOP hierarchy) are based on inputs from the user. The stored cases are not directly utilized for this purpose. Consequently, to handle missing information, MOP hierarchies contain several paths leading from an initial description to the final case – each one for a specific subset of known features of the case.

To allow for a more efficient implementation, top-down memory models are often limited to decision trees and related structures as discussed in Section 3.2. These memory models have severe limitations: What happens if (while traversing the hierarchy) a decision is to be made for which insufficient information is available? For example, the value of certain parameters may be unknown, or the knowledge about these parameters might be too vague to really base a decision on it.

It turns out, that this is not merely a problem of decision trees but a principle disadvantage of memory models relying on a top-down search through case memory. In cognitive psychology, there has been some discussion about whether this kind of case retrieval is cognitively adequate (see, for example, Enzinger et al. 1994; Thagard and Holyoak 1989). But even when ignoring cognitive aspects for a moment, some features are inherent in top-down approaches to case retrieval:

- They support a structuring of the data by grouping together related objects (see Section 3.2.1).
- They support efficient retrieval by utilizing traditional tree search algorithms.

- Traversing a top-down memory structure is performed by answering questions in the internal nodes (as in decision trees, cf. Section 3.2.1) in order to come up with a decision about which path to follow. This implies that these questions have to be answered in a certain order and that incomplete information will result in a blind guess possibly leading into the wrong direction.
- Once a certain cluster of cases has been found, e.g., in the leaf of a tree, it is hard to access neighboring clusters containing similar cases.

There have been several attempts to overcome these problems, in particular the latter. One has been explored in Section 3.2.1, namely the combination of inductive and case-based techniques.

In Chapter 2, principle differences between these top-down retrieval methods (based on distances) and accumulation of similar cases (based on acceptance) have been explored. In the following, we will describe a memory model which is appropriate for the latter notion of retrieval. This model does not rely on a top-down search but instead tries to *re-construct* similar cases in a bottom-up fashion.

3.4 Case Retrieval Nets

In this section, we present *Case Retrieval Nets* (CRNs), a memory model that has been developed especially for being employed in the area of decision support. CRNs are able to deal with vague and ambiguous terms, they support the concept of information completion, and can handle case bases of reasonable size efficiently.

The problems discussed in the previous section served as a starting point in the development of CRNs. It seemed to be widely accepted that this kind of search is absolutely necessary for the retrieval of cases: *Artificial Intelligence just does not work without search.* However, when taking a look at other areas, alternative approaches become obvious: Neural network techniques as well as associative memory models, for example, do not perform a *search* in the traditional sense of Artificial Intelligence. Rather, they try to find an answer to a posed query in a bottom-up fashion.

Of course, case-based reasoning differs significantly from both, neural networks and associative memory models. Nevertheless, it is possible to borrow some of the ideas developed in these communities to come up with an alternative memory model: Instead of building a tree from the case base, a properly structured net might be constructed. In contrast to neural networks, however, all the nodes and arcs in that net should have a precise meaning, i.e. they should be interpretable in terms of the considered application domain. Given this kind of net, one can apply a spreading activation process in order to retrieve cases being similar to a posed query. This idea will be elaborated in the following.

3.4.1 Basic Ideas of Case Retrieval Nets

Basic ideas of Case Retrieval Nets have already been sketched in Section 2.9. Here, we will give a more formal description of that model.

The most fundamental item in the context of CRNs are so-called *Information Entities* (IEs, cf. also Chapter 2). These may represent any basic knowledge item, such as a particular attribute-value pair. A *case* then consists of a set of such IEs, and the *case memory* is a net with nodes for the IEs observed in the domain and additional nodes denoting the particular cases. IE nodes may be connected by *similarity arcs*, and a case node is reachable from its constituting IE nodes via *relevance arcs*. Different degrees of similarity and relevance may be expressed by varying arc weights.

Given this structure, case retrieval is performed by

1. activating the IEs given in the query,
2. propagating activation according to similarity through the net of IEs,
3. and collecting the achieved activation in the associated case nodes.

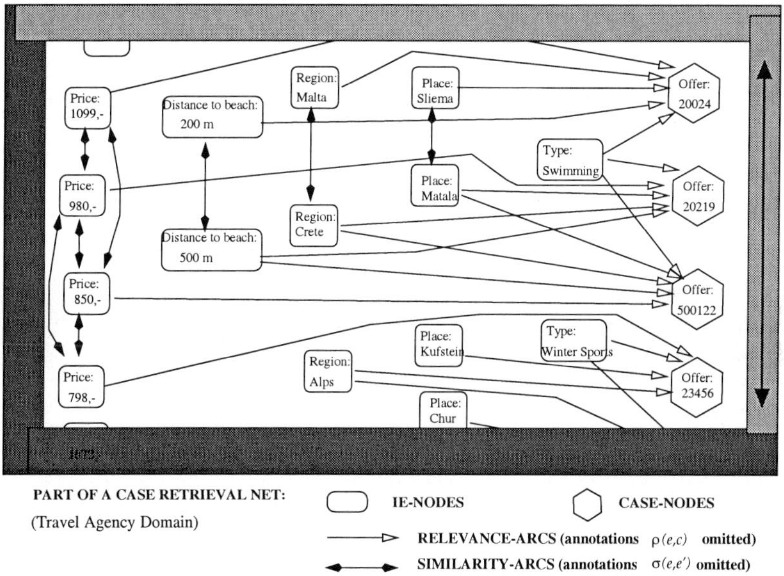

Fig. 3.3. Example of a CRN in the TRAVEL AGENCY domain

Example 3.4.1. The idea is illustrated for the TRAVEL AGENCY domain (cf. Section 3.6.4, Lenz 1994; Lenz 1996b) in Figure 3.3: A *case* is a special travel offer, denoted by a case descriptor, e.g. `<Offer 20219>`. It consists of a set of corresponding IEs giving the specification of that offer, in case of `<Offer 20219>` the IE nodes `<Type:Swimming>`, `<Price:980>`,

`<Place:Matala>`, `<Region:Crete>`, `<Distance to beach:500 m>` are associated to that case node. Asking for an offer in Crete for swimming and not too far from the beach, the IE nodes `<Type:Swimming>`, `<Distance to beach:200 m>` and `<Region:Crete>` are initially activated. By similarity, the IE nodes `<Region:Malta>` and `<Distance to beach:500 m>` will be activated in the next step, but the amount of activation depends on arc weights. Finally, the three offers `<Offer 20024>`, `<Offer 20219>`, `<Offer 500122>` will each get some activation depending on the incoming activations of IE nodes and their relevances. The highest activated cases may be collected and proposed to the customer. A first list of proposals might include alternative solutions which are pruned after the customer decided for either of them.

3.4.2 A Formal Model of Case Retrieval Nets

In this section we will give a formal description of Case Retrieval Nets in a basic (*flat*) version allowing for a detailed investigation of the approach.

Definition 3.4.1 (Information Entity). *An* Information Entity *(IE) is an atomic knowledge item in the domain, i.e., an IE represents the lowest granularity of knowledge representation for cases and queries, respectively.* □

For example, an IE may represent a particular attribute-value-pair.

Definition 3.4.2 (Case in a CRN). *A* case *consists of a unique case descriptor and a set of IEs. Similarly, a* query *is just a set of IEs.* □

Definition 3.4.3 (Basic Case Retrieval Net). *A* Basic Case Retrieval Net *(BCRN) is defined as a structure* $N = [E, C, \sigma, \rho, \Pi]$ *with*

E *is the finite set of* IE nodes*;*
C *is the finite set of* case nodes*;*
σ *is the* similarity function

$$\sigma : E \times E \to \mathcal{R}$$

which describes the similarity $\sigma(e_i, e_j)$ *between IEs* e_i, e_j*;*
ρ *is the* relevance function

$$\rho : E \times C \to \mathcal{R}$$

which describes the relevance $\rho(e, c)$ *of the IE* e *to the case node* c*;*
Π *is the set of* propagation functions

$$\pi_n : \mathcal{R}^E \to \mathcal{R}.$$

for each node $n \in E \cup C$.

□

The graphical description (cf. Figure 3.3) is given by a graph with nodes $E \cup C$ and directed arcs between them. The arc from $e_i \in E$ to $e_j \in E$ is labeled by $\sigma(e_i, e_j)$, the arc from $e \in E$ to $c \in C$ is labeled by $\rho(e, c)$ (arcs are omitted if they are labeled with zero). The functions π_n are annotations to the nodes n.

An IE e belongs to a case c (is *associated* to it) if $\rho(e, c) \neq 0$. Its relevance for case c is given by the value of $\rho(e, c)$ expressing the importance for refinding e in a retrieved case c. Similarity between IEs e_i, e_j is measured by $\sigma(e_i, e_j)$. The functions π_n are used to compute the new activation of node n depending on the incoming activations (a simple setting may use the sum of inputs as π_n).

Definition 3.4.4 (Activation of a BCRN). *An* activation *of a BCRN* $N = [E, C, \sigma, \rho, \Pi]$ *is a function*

$$\alpha : E \cup C \to \mathcal{R}$$

□

In the graphical notation, the activations $\alpha(n)$ are further annotations to the nodes $n \in E \cup C$. Informally, the activation $\alpha(e)$ of an IE e expresses the importance of that IE to the actual problem. The influence of an IE on case retrieval depends on that value and its relevances $\rho(e, c)$ for the cases c. Negative values can be used as an indicator for the rejection of cases containing that IE.

Formally, the propagation process for the basic model is given by:

Definition 3.4.5 (Propagation process in a BCRN). *Consider a BCRN* $N = [E, C, \sigma, \rho, \Pi]$ *with* $E = \{e_1, ..., e_s\}$ *and let* $\alpha_t : E \cup C \to \mathcal{R}$ *be the activation at time* t*. The* activation *of IE nodes* $e \in E$ *at time* $t + 1$ *is given by*

$$\alpha_{t+1}(e) = \pi_e(\sigma(e_1, e) \cdot \alpha_t(e_1), ..., \sigma(e_s, e) \cdot \alpha_t(e_s)),$$

and the activation *of case nodes* $c \in C$ *at time* $t + 1$ *is given by*

$$\alpha_{t+1}(c) = \pi_c(\rho(e_1, c) \cdot \alpha_t(e_1), ..., \rho(e_s, c) \cdot \alpha_t(e_s))$$

□

To pose a query, the activation of all IE nodes may start with

$$\alpha_0(e) = \begin{cases} 1 & : \quad \text{for the IE nodes } e \text{ describing the query} \\ 0 & : \quad \text{else} \end{cases}$$

For more subtle queries, α_0 might assign different weights to special IE nodes, and some *context* may be set as initial activation for further nodes.

Given α_0 and Definition 3.4.5, it is well-defined how the activation of each node $n \in C \cup E$ has to be computed at any time. In particular, case retrieval by propagation of activations is a three-step process:

Step 1 – Initial Activation:
Given the query, α_0 is determined for all IE nodes.
Step 2 – Similarity Propagation:
The activation α_0 is propagated to all IEs $e \in E$:

$$\alpha_1(e) = \pi_e(\sigma(e_1, e) \cdot \alpha_0(e_1), ..., \sigma(e_s, e) \cdot \alpha_0(e_s)) \tag{3.5}$$

Step 3 – Relevance Propagation:
The result of step 2 is propagated to the case nodes $c \in C$:

$$\alpha_2(c) = \pi_c(\rho(e_1, c) \cdot \alpha_1(e_1), ..., \rho(e_s, c) \cdot \alpha_1(e_s)) \tag{3.6}$$

Putting all the formulae together, we obtain the following result:

Proposition 3.4.1. *Consider a BCRN $N = [E, C, \sigma, \rho, \Pi]$ with the activation function α_t as defined in Definitions 3.4.4 and 3.4.5. The result of the case retrieval for a given query activation α_0 is the* preference ordering *of cases according to decreasing activations $\alpha_2(c)$ of case nodes $c \in C$.*

3.4.3 Advantages of Case Retrieval Nets

Representation of Composite Similarity Measures. In many applications, cases are represented using attribute vectors: $c = [c_1, ..., c_k]$. In these situations, similarity of cases is often computed on the basis of the case components, e.g. by using a weighted sum of the *local* similarities to come up with a *global* similarity (Goos 1994; Wess 1995). BCRNs can model any such *composite* similarity measure:

Definition 3.4.6 (Composite similarity measure). *A similarity measure* sim *is called* composite *if it is combined by a function $\phi : \mathcal{R}^k \rightarrow \mathcal{R}$ from feature similarity functions $\mathsf{sim}_i : W_i \times W_i \rightarrow \mathcal{R}$ such that*

$$\begin{aligned} \mathsf{sim}(x, y) &= \mathsf{sim}([x_1, ..., x_k], [y_1, ..., y_k]) \\ &= \phi(\mathsf{sim}_1(x_1, y_1), ..., \mathsf{sim}_k(x_k, y_k)) \end{aligned}$$

□

A simple example of an often used composite similarity function is given by the weighted sum of the feature similarities:

$$\mathsf{sim}([x_1, ..., x_k], [y_1, ..., y_k]) = \sum_{i=1,...,k} g_i \cdot \mathsf{sim}_i(x_i, y_i).$$

Proposition 3.4.2. *For any finite domain, every composite similarity function can be computed by a BCRN.*

Proof. Let sim be an arbitrary composite similarity measure with

$$\mathsf{sim}(x,y) = \phi(\mathsf{sim}_1(x_1,y_1),...,\mathsf{sim}_k(x_k,y_k))$$

Then we define a BCRN $N_{sim} = [E, C, \sigma, \rho, \Pi]$ with

- E is the set of all IEs occurring in the (finite) domain.
- C is the set of cases of the domain.
- For every pair x_i, y_i of IEs similarity will only be considered if both belong to the same attribute:

$$\sigma(x_i,y_j) = \begin{cases} 0 & : \quad i \neq j \\ \mathsf{sim}_i(x_i,y_i) & : \quad i = j \end{cases}$$

- For every IE e and case c

$$\rho(e,c) = \begin{cases} 0 & : \quad x \notin c \\ 1 & : \quad x \in c \end{cases}$$

- For every case node c

$$\pi_c(r_1,...,r_k) = \phi(r_1,...,r_k)$$

Given this definition, we can compute the similarity for a case c and a query q:

$$\begin{aligned} \alpha_2(c) &= \pi_c(\alpha_1(c_1),...,\alpha_k(c_k)) \\ &= \pi_c(\sigma(q_1,c_1),...,\sigma(q_k,c_k)) \\ &= \pi_c(\mathsf{sim}_1(q_1,c_1),...,\mathsf{sim}_k(q_k,c_k)) \\ &= \phi(\mathsf{sim}_1(q_1,c_1),...,\mathsf{sim}_k(q_k,c_k)) \\ &= \mathsf{sim}(q,c) \end{aligned}$$

◊

Proposition 3.4.2 not only shows that any composite similarity measure can be represented in a BCRN but also that retrieval in a CRN is *complete*: Any case node in the net will have an activation α_2 according to the similarity of the case to the query which caused the initial activation. Actually, this is true for any similarity measure represented in a CRN. However, for arbitrary similarity measures it may be more complicated to prove the equivalence of the similarity function encoded by means of the components of the CRN with the intended similarity measure.

If the domain is not finite, i.e., if the number of IEs is not bounded (note that the number of stored cases will always be finite in any CBR system), then a similar approach may be taken if *computational nodes* (Burkhard 1995b; Burkhard 1998) are inserted, for example to compute similarity between different values of numeric features.

Context-dependent Similarity Measures. In many applications, a global (composite) similarity function is not sufficient. For example, the weights in a weighted sum may have to be adapted to special "contexts". Usually, each different similarity function has to be computed separately. CRNs, on the contrary, provide mechanisms even for computing case-dependent similarity measures. By specifying appropriate propagation functions π_c for each case node $c \in C$, every such case node may even evaluate its input differently according to Equation 3.6 and thus assign other preferences and weights than other case nodes.

Efficient Retrieval. A theoretical evaluation of the retrieval effort appears to be difficult as this depends on a number of parameters (cf. Section 2.9). These include:

Size of the query: The more IEs have to be activated initially, the more has to be propagated through the net.

Degree of connectivity of IEs: The more non-zero similarity arcs exist, the more has to be done during similarity propagation.

Specifity of the IEs: The more cases are associated to the IEs, the more has to be done during relevance propagation.

Distribution of cases: If a large number of similar cases exists, many of these will become highly activated and thus retrieval effort will increase. Similarly, if only few similar cases exist, the scope of considered cases has to be extended until a sufficient number of cases has been found. Hence, a kind of *homogeneous distribution* might be desirable.

Desired number of cases: Recall that CRNs do not just retrieve cases but also provide a preference ordering. Hence, the more cases have to be retrieved, the more effort will be required even for sorting the retrieved cases.

A number of experiments have been performed to empirically test the efficiency of CRNs. The major problem in these experiments was to access sufficiently large case bases. In many case-based applications only relatively few cases have been used: In a comparative study of several retrieval methods (Auriol et al. 1994), the largest case base consisted of the 1,500 cases used in the CaBaTA prototype (cf. Section 3.6.4). Another study used up to 3,000 cases (Goos 1994).

In order to have much larger case bases accessible, we performed several experiments with data from the *UCI Machine Learning Repository* (Murphy and Aha 1992). Here, data sets with up to 65,000 cases have been encoded as cases and used for experiments. The results have been very promising, in that performance was similar to that of a commercial database system up to a certain number of cases when memory swapping occurred. More details can be found in Lenz (1996a). However, these tests did have a major drawback: The data sets used were not really case bases. In particular, fairly meaningless similarity measures were applied just to test retrieval efficiency. Whether the retrieved cases were actually similar did not matter. As mentioned above, the chosen similarity measure influences the structure of the CRN and thus the efficiency of retrieval. In real-world domains, for example, often a clustering of the data naturally arises. This will improve the retrieval behavior of CRNs. In the domains of the *UCI Repository* this did not happen due to the artificially constructed similarity measure.

Recently, the Last Minute Kiosks (cf. Section 4.4) provided a better means for testing the efficiency of CRNs. During peak season, up to 200,000 offers are stored in that case base and retrieval can be performed in about 1.3 seconds on a SPARCStation-20[2].

Flexibility of Representation and Retrieval. CRNs have a simple modular structure which is easy to understand, to implement and to modify. Extensions are possible at any time, especially the number of features/attributes is not fixed – new attributes may be introduced simply by related additional IE nodes. New cases are added by inserting new case nodes, additional IE nodes (as far as necessary) and specific labeled arcs. The complexity of this process depends mainly on the complexity of the new case – no rebuilding of the entire structure is required. Hence, CRNs can be updated incrementally without losing the benefits of the structure.

The similarity functions need not be symmetrical, but can be. Even the feature similarities need not be symmetrical. Variations of the query activation α_0 permit a finer tuning of queries.

Missing information does not increase the complexity of retrieval: Similarity computations in CRNs are *pessimistic* as long as unspecified IEs are not activated by the query activation. In this sense, missing values are treated as *don't know* values rather than *don't care*.

As with other net methods, the CRN approach has a great potential for parallel work. Moreover, CRNs may serve as a bridge between sub-symbolic (pattern driven) and symbolic (rule driven) inferences (cf. Section 3.5.2).

Finally, BCRNs offer the possibilities of extensions in various ways, some of these will be sketched in Section 3.4.5.

3.4.4 Limitations of CRNs

Lack of Adaptation Mechanism. CRNs do not support directly the integration of adaptation knowledge in the retrieval phase. As the name indicates, this memory model may be used to *retrieve* cases – what these case are used for is up to another system or the user. However, as for all retrieval methods, this may in some situations result in cases being retrieved which appear to be sub-optimal in the sense that the most *similar* cases are not necessarily

---

[2] This result is even more remarkable as the structure of the data shows some kind of *worst case* complexity, namely that every case will have a non-zero similarity to a given query. This is caused by the high *connectivity* of IEs resulting from the applied similarity measure.

the ones that are *easiest adaptable* to the current problem (cf. Smyth and Keane 1993).

Representation of Relationships. CRNs have been designed for finding cases with components similar to a query. In particular, CRNs inherit some ideas of a *distributed representation* as introduced by the *Parallel Distributed Processing* group (Rumelhart et al. 1986). This means that an IE node encoding a certain property of cases is present just once – no matter how many cases share this property.

Consequently, the encoding of cases within a CRN is crucial. More precisely, the representation of cases is critical because similarity will be assessed based on these representations. Hence, when designing a CBR system making use of CRNs, one should have in mind a certain *scenario*, i.e., what types of queries will the potential user of such a system enter, what might s/he consider as similar, etc. — or, terms of Chapter 2: What would the user *accept* as suitable cases?

For some applications, this may partially be avoided by extending the net with additional structures, such as in *Object-directed Case Retrieval Nets* (cf. Section 3.4.5). Here only a part of the entire inference process is performed inside the CRN while other parts are carried out in more structured memory models.

3.4.5 Extensions of Case Retrieval Nets

In Section 3.4.2, we presented a formal model of *Basic Case Retrieval Nets* which introduces the basic ideas and allows for a formal investigation. For practical applications, CRNs may be extended in a variety of ways:

Integration of Concept Nodes. The BCRN model implies that the set of IEs are maintained in a flat structure, i.e., IEs have been considered as *atomic*, non-decomposable entities. To improve structuring, the net model can be extended to incorporate *concept* or *microfeature* nodes to support context-dependent similarity assessment (Burkhard 1997; Lenz and Burkhard 1996a).

Example 3.4.2. In the travel agency domain, for instance, the IEs encoding the `destination` feature may be represented using microfeatures such as `location`, `climate`, `landscape`, etc. (Lenz and Burkhard 1996a).

Integration of Object Models. While microfeature nodes only influence the IE layer, CRNs may also be enhanced by entire object models. In *Object-directed Case Retrieval Nets* (OCRNs, Lenz et al. 1996a) knowledge about technical devices is put *on top* of the CRN as sketched in Figure 3.4.

This knowledge may be used to provide some useful guidance during case retrieval. Very briefly, retrieval in a OCRN is performed by:

1. Activating the IEs representing the observed symptoms
2. Spreading activation as in BCRNs to access a set of possible faults

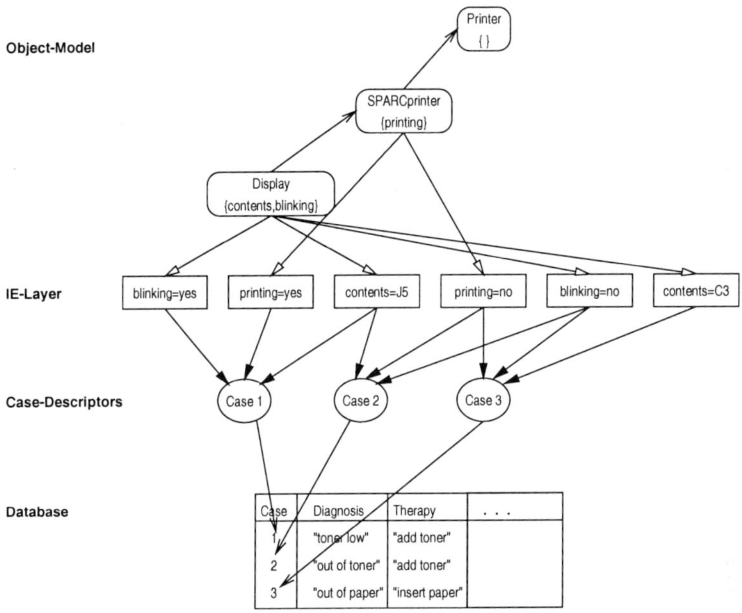

Fig. 3.4. An example OCRN for technical diagnosis: IEs represent symptoms and cases describe diagnostic episodes. A domain-specific object model is placed on top of the CRN

3. Selecting a set of *hypothetic* cases with associated diagnoses as indicated by the highest activated case nodes (if this allows for an unambiguous diagnosis, retrieval can be aborted)
4. Choosing additional IE nodes representing symptoms not yet determined and associated to at least one of the hypothetical cases
5. Performing a spreading activation process into the object model to access those object nodes, which contributed to the activation of the hypothetical cases and can provide further information about the symptoms selected in Step 4
6. Selecting the most specific object from the latter set
7. Determining the set of most *useful* symptoms (i.e., those symptoms which provide a maximum information to differentiate between the diagnoses of the hypothetical cases) and presenting them to the user
8. Using the obtained answers for activating further IEs and goto Step 2

Steps 1 through 3 correspond to the retrieval process as defined in Section 3.4.2. A more detailed description of OCRNs, including a formal model, can be found in Lenz et al. (1996a).

More Sophisticated Retrieval Procedures. As described in Section 3.4.2, retrieval in a BCRN is performed in 3 clearly separated steps:

1. Initial activation of IEs according to the query

2. Similarity propagation within the net of IEs
3. Relevance propagation to the case nodes

An alternative technique which interlocks Steps 2 and 3 and thus subsequently extends the scope of considered IEs and cases, is the *Lazy Spreading Activation* procedure (Lenz and Burkhard 1996b). This is best illustrated by an example:

Example 3.4.3. Imagine being in a foreign city, having a map, and looking for the nearest underground station. After having found the current location on the map (which is straightforward, e.g., by using the index of streets), one would probably search the region near the current location (e.g., the same quadrant on the map). If some stations are found one can compare them to select the nearest. Otherwise, i.e. if there was no station, one will extend the scope (that is, consider neighboring quadrants too) and continue until at least one station is contained in the considered region.

While this example only gives the basic idea, it can be shown that *Lazy Spreading Activation* may further reduce the retrieval effort (compared to BCRNs) without giving up the requirement of completeness. Furthermore, this technique provides a means for implementing *any time* retrieval algorithms.

3.5 Discussion

In Sections 3.2 through 3.4, two alternative methods for building diagnosis and decision support systems have been explored in some detail. In this section, we will briefly compare these to related work and show the advantages and disadvantages of the various approaches.

3.5.1 Relatives of INRECA

As mentioned in Section 3.2.2, the combinations of inductive and case-based reasoning utilize *k*d-trees, a classical memory structure ensuring efficient access of data (Friedman et al. 1977). These have been enhanced to cope with the ideas of case-based reasoning (Wess et al. 1993a). A major advantage of this combination is that it allows for precise statements about properties of the applied retrieval method, e.g., concerning efficiency, correctness, and completeness. A comprehensive discussion and evaluation can be found in Wess (1995). Finally, the INRECA tree is the latest offspring of this development. In addition to the functionality of case-based *k*d-trees, it also provides methods for adjusting weights and similarity measures.

In contrast to Case Retrieval Nets, *k*d-trees employ a pre-structuring of case memory into a decision tree like structure similarly to the top-down approaches discussed in Section 3.3.2. In order to overcome some of the limitations inherent to top-down techniques, *k*d-trees utilize the so-called BWB[3]- and BOB[4]-Tests (cf. Wess 1995) to access cases in neighboring leaf nodes and to assure completeness and correctness of retrieval.

3.5.2 Relatives of Case Retrieval Nets

Case Retrieval Nets inherit a number of techniques from other approaches to case retrieval and from completely different areas:

The similarity and propagation functions of Definition 3.4.3 indicate that CRNs share some ideas with recurrent Neural Networks. In particular, the computations performed locally in each node support this comparison. When allowing activation to be propagated also after step 3, the behavior of CRNs comes even closer to Neural Networks (Burkhard 1995c). However, in CRNs each node represents a particular symbol (IE or case), and it is the activation of single nodes that matters – not entire patterns of activation.

Similarly, the idea of using a spreading activation process to perform a kind of search is not a new one but dates back to the theory of *Semantic Memory* and systems like ACT (cf. Collins and Loftus (1988) and Anderson (1988), respectively). Compared to these, the notion of spreading activation is modified in Case Retrieval Nets in that not really a semantic inference is performed but similarity is propagated through the net.

The CRASH system (Brown 1993; Brown 1994) uses an activation passing scheme for case retrieval too. The major difference to CRNs is that in step 2 of retrieval, activation is propagated through a network of *world knowledge*. On the one hand, this allows for the integration of a deep background knowledge into the case retrieval system. On the other hand, it makes retrieval highly complex if this *world knowledge* is sufficiently broad. Also the acquisition of this knowledge may cause severe problems. In CRNs, on the contrary, the required memory structures automatically arise from the case descriptions in the form of IEs.

Knowledge-directed Spreading Activation (KDSA) (Wolverton and Hayes-Roth 1994; Wolverton 1995) is an improved variant of the basic spreading activation algorithms. In KDSA the spreading activation process is also performed in several steps. Each time an analogue has been retrieved from memory, the quality of it is evaluated by a heuristic mapping component. Based on the degree of usefulness determined by this mapping component, some

> "*... search control module modifies the direction of subsequent spreads of activation into more promising areas of the knowledge base*"
>
> (Wolverton 1995).

[3] Ball Within Bounds
[4] Ball Overlap Bounds

KDSA has been designed mainly for cross-domain analogies where the goal is to retrieve "*...semantically distant analogies*". This differs from our standpoint in so far as we assume that the goal of retrieval is to access previously encountered cases describing problem situations in the same domain. Given this assumption, the task of the heuristic mapping component of KDSA (namely to determine how close a retrieved case is to the query) can be fulfilled by simply assessing the similarity between the query and the retrieved case – that's exactly what Case Retrieval Nets do. Furthermore, if retrieval is performed by *Lazy Spreading Activation* (as described in Section 3.4.5), then retrieval in CRNs becomes similar to KDSA, in so far as the spread of activation is limited and hence blind and exhaustive search is avoided. In contrast to the heuristic KDSA approach, however, *Lazy Spreading Activation* has been shown to be *complete* in the sense that no similar case will be lost during retrieval.

Another retrieval approach, the *Fish & Shrink* algorithm has been developed within the FABEL project and is particularly suited for highly complex cases. In contrast to CRNs, however, *Fish & Shrink* relies on the assumption that the triangle inequality is valid for the similarity measure underlying the domain. This will explored in more detail in Section 8.5.

In the CONSYDERR system (Sun 1995) a formal approach to combine rule-based and similarity-based reasoning utilizing microfeatures is described. Similarly, microfeatures may be employed in CRNs. However, the integration of a formalism like the *Fuzzy Evidential Logic* developed for CONSYDERR has not yet been investigated.

3.6 Projects and Applications

In the remainder of this chapter, we will describe fielded applications that have been developed using the technologies introduced in previous sections.

3.6.1 Applicability of CBR Technology

"Data is a burden, knowledge is an asset".

Equipment manufacturers often collect a lot of data about the equipment they have to support (either internally or through their partners): Technical follow-up files, breakdown files, intervention reports, preventive maintenance reports and records of requests from their clients or distributors. Unfortunately, this information is usually not well exploited and corporate databases predominantly work in write-only mode:

1. The data is not used because it is so difficult to access, but no one invests in making it easy to retrieve because it is not used.
2. The data is not trusted, because many errors have been recorded, but no one cares to verify the accuracy of the data because it is not trusted.

This is sad because this material could often reveal strategic knowledge for the company; diagnoses of breakdowns, repair actions, the cost and duration of interventions, breakdown recurrence, etc. The collection and the exploitation of this information permits a notable improvement of the after sales service and maintenance of the equipment. The combination of case-based reasoning and inductive learning techniques is particularly efficient for troubleshooting complex equipment in these areas.

One active market for CBR technology is decision support software for help desks. A help desk is located in a call center, usually at the equipment manufacturer's site, to assist customers when they have problems with the equipments, such as failure of an equipment at the customer's site. One of the missions of the staff of the help desk is to troubleshoot the manufacturer's equipment and decide if the client can solve the problem by themselves. In this case, a list of spare parts that must be replaced on the equipment is identified. Otherwise, a field technician that belongs to the manufacturer must be sent to solve the problem on the customer's site (in which case, a decision about which spare parts have to be sent is also made).

Using AcknoSoft's KATE systems, a number of applications have been developed:

- to perform experience feedback in safety for nuclear power plants at the French Electricity company EDF;
- for troubleshooting large marine diesel engines at New Sulzer Diesel in Switzerland;
- for experience feedback in manufacturing and rapid assessment of production costs for a leading manufacturer of electrical supplies in France;
- for diagnosis of electronic boards at GICEP electronics;
- for train maintenance at Ansaldo Trasporti in Italy;
- for quality management of mission critical equipment in the oil industry at Schlumberger in Italy and Norsk Hydro in Norway;
- for reliability analysis of gas meters at French Gas GDF and German Gas Ruhrgas;
- in the aircraft industry at Aerospatiale in France, etc.

Here we will concentrate on two successful applications in this field: The first one, called Cassiopée, helps troubleshooting the CFM 56-3 engines of the Boeing 737. The second one, called LADI, is installed at the after-sale service of SEPRO Robotique, a French company that export plastic injection presses robots world-wide. LADI troubleshoots axis positioning defects for three axis robots. Both applications utilize a workbench integrated approach of CBR and inductive learning methods to help the end-user solving a diagnosis problem. Thus, they apply methods developed within the INRECA project (cf. Section 3.2).

3.6.2 Troubleshooting CFM 56-3 Engines

CFM-International has developed the CFM 56 engine family for Boeing and Airbus planes. CFM-International is a joint venture of General Electric aircraft engines and France's Snecma. One of the goals of CFM-International is to improve engine maintenance technology in order to reduce the cost of ownership of its engines for its customers. The Cassiopée project was launched in August 1993 to perform engine troubleshooting. The starting point was a reliability and maintainability database on an IBM mainframe from which 23,000 cases were extracted. Using a combination of inductive and case-based reasoning techniques, a decision support system for the technical maintenance of the CFM 56-3 aircraft engines was developed. All Boeing 737 aircrafts are equipped with CFM 56-3 engines.

The system assists CFM engineers in offering quicker and better advice to the maintenance crews of the airlines who perform on-line troubleshooting (i.e. when the airplane is at the departure gate). It is also being tested by several airlines including British Airways in the UK. The system was developed to:

- reduce downtime of the engines and avoid delays for the airlines;
- minimize the cost of diagnosis;
- reduce errors in diagnosis;
- record and document the experience of the most skilled maintenance specialists, in order to build a corporate memory and help transfer know-how from the expert to the novice.

The time required for diagnosis represents about 50% of downtime (the remaining time is used for repair). It is aimed to reduce this figure by a factor of two.

In order to build a decision support system from case history, one must first gather case data. The application data that was used originally came from the legacy database mentioned above. However, a lot of the information required to support the technical activity of maintenance was not formatted using fields of the database but was provided in free-text narratives. Because of the size of the database and in order to optimize the performance of the system in every day use, it was decided not to apply any text retrieval techniques. Instead, the *model* of the case databases was supplemented with the technical parameters and pre-processed the data (i.e., list of parameters used to describe a case). The pre-processing of the data was performed by a maintenance engineer who reviewed the cases at the rate of 15 cases per hour.

The consultation process runs as follows. New fault trees are generated by inductive learning. Unlike standard fault trees that are often built during the design stage and that are based on faults that should occur in theory, the fault trees are built automatically based on observed faults and can be updated as new faults appear. When browsing such a fault tree, the operator

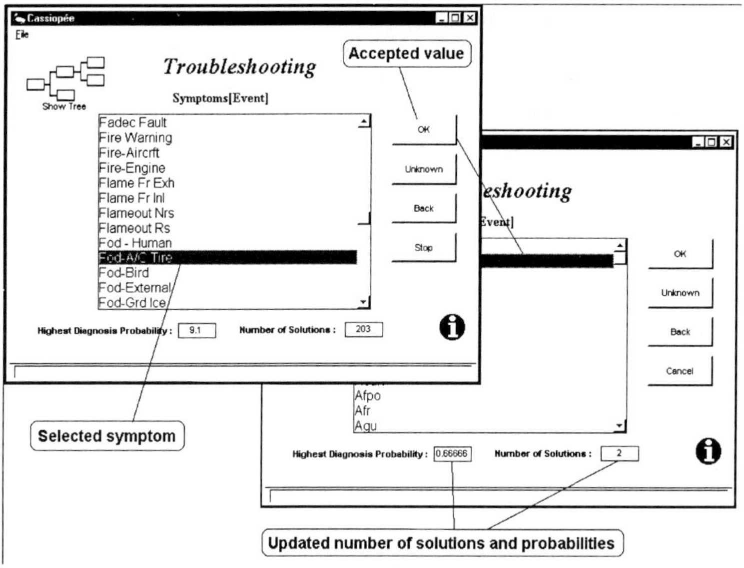

Fig. 3.5. Troubleshooting a CFM 56-3 engine

is requested to answer the questions that are in close relationship with the original trouble symptom (Figure 3.5). At the end of the consultation a list of possible solutions is proposed to the operator with their relative frequency. The procedure (test to perform on the engine), to confirm that the selected solution is the accurate one, is obtained by selecting that solution from the list. This is done to improve the accuracy of the system and not to replace the official maintenance documents (it is an add-on to the procedure that is certified by the authorities). The cases that support the conclusions are then retrieved and the user can browse them in order to confirm or refute the solution.

The system is fully integrated in the end-user environment. Thus, some important achievements are not directly tied to the technology per se: Link of the system with an Illustrated Part Catalogue (IPC) to take into account engine configuration evolution (Figure 3.6), interface the IPC with EXCEL to perform statistics on reliability and maintainability, support for electronic mail to collect events world-wide through the X400 network, etc.

The IPC makes extensive use of hypermedia facilities to navigate between the drawings of the parts and their nomenclature.

3.6.3 Troubleshooting Robots Axis

SEPRO Robotique is a French SME with more than 100 employees that has been manufacturing robots for plastic injection presses for over 10 years. SEPRO has sold over 2,600 such robots world-wide (over 65% of its production

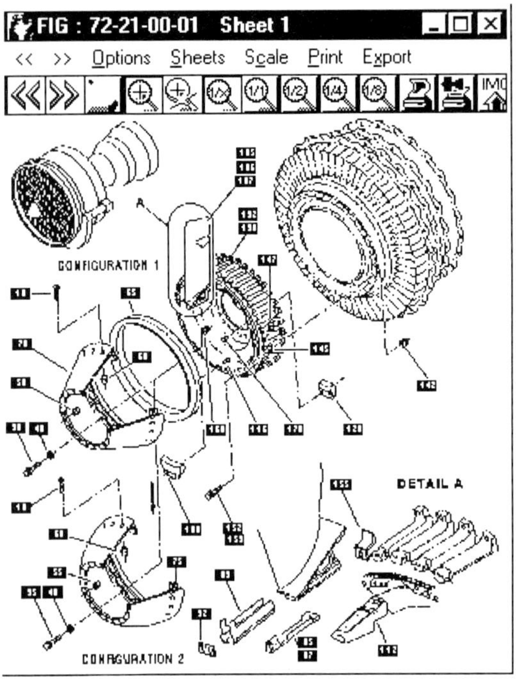

Fig. 3.6. The part nomenclature in Cassiopée is used graphically to indicate the faulty component

is now exported to foreign countries in Europe, Asia and in the US. The robots are heavy duty machines that automate the process of grabbing plastic parts from a plastic injection molding press and manipulate them in a variety of ways (place some inserts, load and unload peripheral devices, etc.).

Each robot is customized to meet the needs of specific clients and is made out of three main modules: The mechanical module, the motor, and the command and control box. Customer support engineers and field technicians at SEPRO Robotique often work by making correlation between the faults of these robots based on the generic modules. One difficulty is that plastic injection molding robots have a long life cycle. Robots installed ten years ago are still in operation and require support by SEPRO. New support technicians can no longer gain *in-house* experience with robots of the older families that are no longer manufactured by SEPRO and that are still in operation at the client's site as, for example, with SEPRO's ELEC 88-SZ family. As time goes, new technicians will have to support at the help desk more and more equipment for which they are not experienced. This is a general problem for all manufacturers of equipment that have a long life span. Thus, the customer support call center of SEPRO (four support technicians at the same time) has often problems troubleshooting this type of equipment when a technician with experience on these old robots is not on duty.

Because of the increasing cost of customer service, caused by their larger installation base, SEPRO has set a high priority on improving the efficiency of its after-sales division. In January 1995, SEPRO started to work jointly with AcknoSoft to install a CBR help desk. A help desk system, called LADI, troubleshoots axis positioning defects. A stand-alone prototype was first delivered in June 1995 and went live on a five user network in the after-sale division in Spring 1996.

Axis positioning defects represent about 20 to 30% of the problems that are the most difficult to solve. The system originally contained about 150 typical cases that have been reconstructed from the information available in the engineering department. The call tracking module that records incoming calls is shared on a network by the four support technicians. The case library is also shared on a local TCP/IP network of PCs. An internal organization (case steering committee) meets on a monthly base to monitor the quality of incoming cases before they are included in the reference case library. The case database is enriched at the rate of about 10 cases a month. The steering committee is also useful to provide better and quicker feedback to the R&D department to improve design. The system uses a combination of CBR and inductive learning in order to suit the technician *way of thought*. When a new call arrives at the after-sale service, it is pre-processed through an induction tree that has been previously built on the database, in order to eliminate the most common problems. 75% of the calls are solved at this stage. The size of the induction tree is intentionally left small (three to six questions) so that the call duration remains short.

If the problem is not solved, for instance, if there are still more than one diagnosis pending, the system automatically generates a list of relevant questions by *dynamic induction* (i.e., by using the same criterion as the inductive procedure – except that the list of questions is not static). A report containing the current conclusions and the list of questions is automatically generated and sent by Fax to the client site. The client is asked to answer them before calling back. As the system is connected to the Interleaf document databases on a SUN workstation, the support technician is able to access an illustrated parts catalogue, to cut and paste parts descriptions, and include troubleshooting reports in the Fax before sending it to his client. When the client calls back, his former problem is retrieved and missing information is completed with respect to the questions answered. The system performs then a nearest-neighbor search on the relevant cases and returns the most similar ones together with their associated diagnosis (Figure 3.7). The system:

- reduces the time required to solve problems that do require highly specialized technicians;
- reduces the number of wrong diagnosis done by the help desk which results in shipping the wrong spare parts and introduce additional delays when the field technician has to wait for the right spares to be shipped;
- increases the quality of service support and reduces the number of call backs to a client;

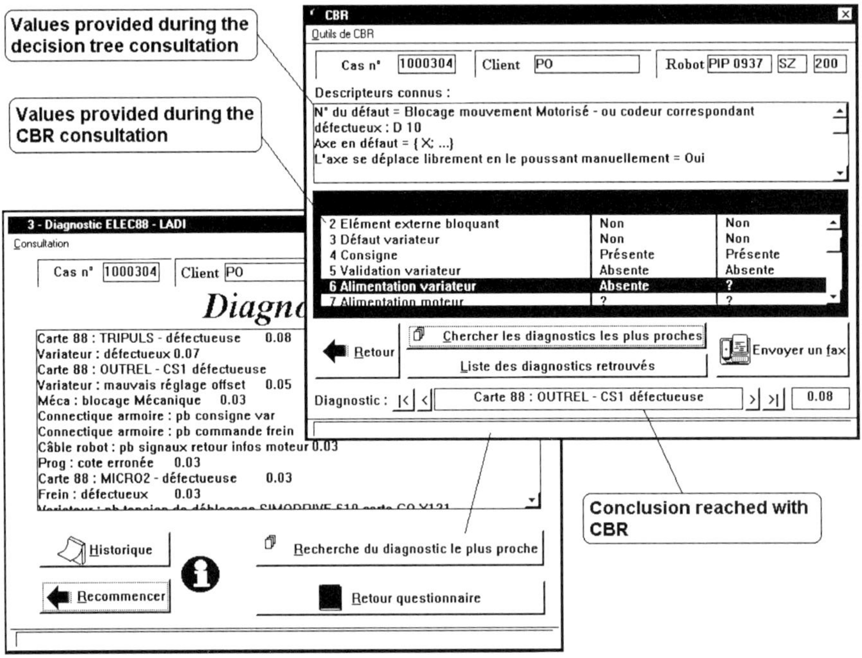

Fig. 3.7. Diagnosis of a robot axis fault

- formalizes the diagnosis process by choosing the most relevant tests in order to identify the fault (the training department of Sepro is actively involved in the project as well as the after sale support division);
- saves training costs by transferring experience from the specialists to the novice. This is becoming more and more important since old versions of their robots are no longer produced and new technicians cannot gain experience with these.

3.6.4 CaBaTA and Electronic Product Catalogues

CaBaTA[5] is a prototypical CBR system developed with the objective to give a vivid description of some fundamental ideas of CBR in an easy to understand domain. As became obvious later (cf. Section 4.4), the idea was highly realistic and could readily be applied in a commercial system.

Example 3.6.1. Imagine wanting to go on a vacation. Usually, you will have to go to a travel agent, express your (vague) intentions, and browse a stack of catalogues for an appropriate offer. You may have been lucky to find a quite nice hotel for a reasonable price – but when it comes to booking, this offer is already sold out!

[5] Case Based Travel Agency

A CBR system might be able to avoid both, browsing through masses of catalogues, as well as considering offers which are no longer available anyway. In particular, CABATA has been designed to:

- consider the set of all available offers as the relevant case base;
- interpret the desires and intentions of the traveler as a query;
- search for appropriate cases and establish a preference ordering based on the requirements expressed in the query;
- let the user browse through the best matching cases.

Integration of Other Knowledge Sources. In order to provide a more realistic behavior and to utilize existing domain knowledge, CABATA not only uses cases but also incorporates more general knowledge given as either rules or context graphs. The former allow for context-dependent similarity assessment and adaptation capabilities while the latter are used for encoding similarity relationships for certain features, such as `destination` or `season of travel`.

Features of CABATA. Even from this short description, two crucial properties of CABATA become obvious:

Firstly, CABATA is a true CBR system in that an ordering of the found offers (including alternatives) is established which allows the more suitable offers to be shown first.

Example 3.6.2. If, for instance, the customer expressed the intention to go to Crete, but all flights to that island are booked out, then it seems reasonable to suggest other Greek islands as alternatives. This is a feature which is not normally included in databases but can be achieved in CBR systems by considering similarity.

Secondly, CABATA *really* is a decision support system as discussed in Section 3.1. The task is more general than classification and diagnosis in the sense that it is not *a priori* known which features of a case will be part of the problem description and which will belong to the solution part. Rather, one query might express certain desires and ask for an appropriate destination while another one might ask for leisure time facilities in a specific region. And yet a third query might be highly specific about all query parameters. To cope with this, and to achieve short retrieval times, the model of Case Retrieval Nets (cf. Section 3.4) has been developed and implemented as part of the system.

Possible Extensions of CABATA. As described here, the system has been designed to search a set of tour packages for appropriate offers to a given query. By using specific rules, it can deal with adaptation to some extent (e.g., for adjusting the price for a varying number of participants). Currently, it *can not* deal with travel offers consisting of several packages, i.e., there is no planning component which can configure a complete offer given a flight, a hotel booking, a car rental, etc. This would require an additional planning module.

Electronic Product Catalogues. The case-based approach employed for CABATA, including major parts of the actual implementation, is not limited to the domain of traveling but rather can be adapted for *Electronic Product Catalogues* (EPC) in general. The CABATA system mainly stores a case base of offers and supports a search for similar offers to a given query – whether the offers are tour packages does not matter really. Prototypically, the system had been adapted for real-estate assessment (Lenz and Ladewig 1996) without major changes. This should be possible for any domain in which the offers are taken *as they are*, i.e., where adaptation, configuration, etc. are not essential. For such situations, the system had to be extended.

The Virtual Travel Agency on the WWW. As the World Wide Web is getting used more widely, Humboldt University started a cooperation with **check out**, a Berlin tourist office chain, in 1997. The objective of this cooperation was to build an online version of CABATA which would allow WWW users to search for appropriate *Last Minute* tour packages and book these online. Details on this will be given in Section 4.4.

3.7 Summary and Outlook

In this chapter, we have presented a broad overview on how state-of-the-art CBR technology may contribute to solving problems in the areas of classification, diagnosis, and decision support. As should be clear from the described projects, CBR is not just a research paradigm being applied to toy problems. Rather, it is a technology that is ready to be used in practical, large-scale applications.

Nevertheless, successful applications obviously require more than just a core technology. In the following, we will summarize some of the important aspects:

3.7.1 Integration Issues

A crucial issue in the development of successful applications is the integration of CBR within the existing industrial environment. This has two major consequences:

1. CBR should be a tool completely integrated with other IT components, such that it can be used in the sense of an external memory as discussed in Section 3.3. An example for this type of integration has been given with the Illustrated Part Catalogue in the Cassiopée project.
2. CBR should make use of other reasoning paradigms, whenever they are applicable, as explained in Section 3.2 for the inductive learning paradigm.

3.7.2 Maintenance Issues

A further problem that has to be solved for every specific application is maintenance. More specifically, questions that have to be answered in the context of CBR are:

Case Base Maintenance: How will the case base be maintained? How are cases inserted into the system? Who is allowed to add new cases? Is there some kind of *steering committee* caring about quality of cases? Will the case base shrink again, i.e. will cases be deleted?

Case Structure Maintenance: Will the structure of cases change over time? How will the indexing vocabulary as well as the retrieval structures be adapted?

Similarity Maintenance: Will the similarity measure be static over time or will it be adjusted? If the latter, will it be adapted automatically or manually? If manually, who is allowed to do so?

When addressing these questions, technical issues should not have too much priority. As shown throughout the book, a number of techniques exist for these tasks. Rather, a major focus should be on questions of business processes like:

- Who is allowed to change the system?
- What actions are required to perform these changes?
- When are these changes allowed and when will they become effective to the system?
- How can the entire CBR system be embedded within the existing business processes?

3.7.3 Outlook

Currently, we see two major streams of CBR technology in the area of decision support and information systems:

- Firstly, due to the growing availability of the World Wide Web, *Electronic Commerce* applications will become more and more important. In order to make these systems customer-friendly, however, new technologies are required which support the user in getting through the vast amount of information. As these applications have highly specific properties, Chapter 4 will address issues of *Electronic Commerce* in more detail.
- Secondly, a growing interest of both CBR researchers and potential users may be observed in using case-based technologies for handling of textual documents. The motivation behind this is obvious: CBR deals with storing and recalling experiences, but in many application areas experiential knowledge is contained in textual documents (be it manuals, documentations, FAQ collections, or the final report of physicians). How CBR can be used for this type of applications will be explored in Chapter 5.

Acknowledgments

Parts of the work described in this chapter have been funded by the European Commission as part of the INRECA project (RTD Esprit Project 6322), the APPLICUS project (Trial Application Esprit Project 20824) and the ESSI Software Best Practice initiative (Process Improvement Experiment Project 21522).

We would like to thank the INRECA team at IMS, TecInno and the University of Kaiserslautern, for their contributions to the development of technologies and methodologies implemented by AcknoSoft in these projects, and the APPLICUS partners at BSR-Consulting, and SEPRO Robotique and the ESSI leader CFM-International for their involvement in the projects LADI and Cassiopée.

Last but not least the authors want to thank Hans-Dieter Burkhard for lots of interesting discussions which lead to an improvement of this chapter.

4. Intelligent Sales Support with CBR

Wolfgang Wilke, Mario Lenz, Stefan Wess

"On the Internet Companies only have computers representing them. They better be Intelligent computers."
Chuck Wiliams CEO Brightware, San Francisco Examiner

4.1 Introduction

Electronic commerce applications are just about to leave their infancy. While electronic cash has been around for quite a few years, the amount of business carried out through the Internet is still relatively small compared to the potential of this young technology. There are plenty of reasons for this. Tennenbaum summarizes the barriers for using this medium today with the three words: *confidence*, *convenience*, and *content*. Customers must have confidence that their transactions are secure, their privacy is maintained, and they will not be subject to liability. It must be convenient, as simple to use as ATMs and as ubiquitous. Finally, there must be incentives to purchase goods via the Internet, be they a better price, service, or selection.

The goal of using CBR in electronic commerce situations is to support a customer with better services and selection facilities. As in every ordinary paper-based information source or product catalogue, it is often very difficult for customers to find the information or products they actually need. Today, searching for information or the selection of complex products on the World Wide Web is a painstaking task for consumers as well as for business partners. The main reason for this well-known deficit in electronic commerce is that, compared to usual business procedures, there is no intelligent support or assistance in the selection of products/services or navigation through complex spaces of available product information or product alternatives on the Internet. Current product-oriented database search facilities are widely used and recognized as being limited in capability for sales support.

So why should a customer searching for product information on the Web not be satisfied with a huge database of products and a database search engine on top of it? The most important answer to this question is: Because this system entirely fails to provide sales *support*. Imagine that a consumer is looking for a last-minute bargain for the summer season. They dial up their Internet provider and look for interesting web-sites, maybe by using one of the popular search-engines. After successfully reaching the homepage of a travel agency or a travel broker, they have to fill in their wishes into a predefined form. They have to choose between different locations, different duration, hotels with different quality standards and different dates to name a few. If the customer selects, for example, one of the Canary Islands as their favorite holiday destinations usually one of the following will happen:

- "Sorry, no match found !" - the customer has *over-specified* their ideal holidays and there is no current offer that fulfills all his demands.
- "100 matches found!" - the customer has just entered a destination and there are hundreds of different offers to choose from. They *under-specified* their demands.

To finally find a suitable trip the customer has to re-enter a slightly different query and repeat this approach several times until they are happy with the respective holiday package. If they now decide to visit another site to look for offers from a different provider, they have to start the whole process again. Most of the current sales systems follow this approach.

Imagine the real shop assistant acts like a database search engine. A customer enters a travel agency and the following dialog would take place:

Customer: Hello, I would like to go on vacation in mid July for two weeks. I want to go bathing in the Canary Islands. I want to travel with my wife and I want to spent less than 1500 Dollar.
Sales Agent: Sorry, we currently do not have such a vacation.
(No further explanation, no alternatives.)
Customer: Err, well, do you have such a vacation if we travel during the last two weeks in July?
Sales Agent: Sorry, we do not have such a vacation either.
(The Customer probably leaves the shop now, but let's see what happens if he doesn't.)
Customer: Well, do you have instead such a vacation, if we would travel to a region close by the Canary Islands.
Sales Agent: Can you please exactly state what you mean by saying 'close'? Can you specify a concrete location ?
Customer: (Sigh!), let's say a vacation at the Spanish coast.
Sales Agent: Sorry, but this is not close. This are over 700 miles away from the Canary Islands.
Customer: But the climate is quite similar and we can go bathing and ...
Sales Agent: Sorry, we do not have such a vacation.
Customer: *(Leaving frustrated, looking for another shop.)*

In this situation, the customers over-specify their query and there is no intelligent advice given by the sales agent helping the customers to find a vacation satisfying their demands. This also happens often during sale situations on the Internet.

If the customers under-specify their demands, they get also as a frustrating result too many vacations, and they have to select the best one by examining all offered vacations. Now, let's see how a real shop assistant would have managed the situation:

Customer: Hello, I would like to go on vacation in mid July for two weeks. I want to go bathing in the Canary Islands. I want to travel with my wife and I want to spent less than 1500 Dollar.
Sales Agent: Sorry, we currently do not have such a vacation. Did you ever visit the Spanish coast for bathing ?
Customer: Is there the same climate and can we go bathing ?
Sales Agent: Yes, and the flights are even cheaper
...
Customer: Okay, we would like to book the suggested vacation.

Finding the desired information or product online can be rather frustrating given the standard database implementations that are commonly used today. A customer using some kind of search facility to find a product in an online catalogue must fulfill certain requirements in order to have a chance to get usable results. In a simple database approach for sales support, the customers need to know all the products which are available and how they are described to formulate an appropriate query in such a way that they get a sufficient result.

The drawback of today's standard sales solutions on the Internet is that they cannot do *intelligent sales support*. This means that the customers must have an extensive knowledge about the field of products they are interested in. Therefore, it is very important to put the knowledge of the real shop assistant into the sales support system on the Internet. The system must have enough domain knowledge to be able to aid the customer's search. This would not only satisfy the customer, but it would also help the manufacturer or broker selling his information or products.

In this chapter, we will see how case-based reasoning can help to overcome these deficiencies. We will present three CBR solutions which are used during different electronic commerce situations on the Internet. Firstly, we will have a closer look at electronic commerce and we will informally introduce different selling situations, namely pre-sales, sales and after-sales. Also, we will present some new research projects which are currently trying to extend the already achieved results. We close with an outlook and some discussion.

4.2 What is Electronic Commerce?

Electronic Commerce (EC) can be defined many ways. In a broad sense, it is any electronic communication carried out in support of business initiatives. For the purposes of this chapter, we will define electronic commerce as: *the exchange of information, goods, or services through electronic networks.* In the real world arrangements among trading partners often contain elements of several kinds. This addresses the needs of organizations, merchants, and consumers to cut costs while improving the quality of goods and services and increasing the speed of service delivery. If we have a closer look at the sales process from a business perspective, we identify three typical sales situations (see Figure 4.1).

Fig. 4.1. The business processes of selling products

During *pre-sales* a potential customer is provided with all necessary information about products and services. In this situation, the customer has a demand for a product and/or service and the firm provides them with information about what they can offer. Today, this is realized on the World Wide Web by *electronic catalogues* or *product databases.* However, the only active part in this process today is the customer in contrast to the real business world where all kind of marketing techniques are used. The customers have to search for information on their own.

During *sales*, a customer and a sales agent are negotiating about products and services and their desired costs for the customer. The task is to discover the customer demands and to find an appropriate product or service for the customer. Compared to pre-sales, which is often a one-step or even one-way communication, sales is a complex process with many interactions between the seller and the buyer. Sales in electronic commerce is an iterative process where two parties bargain resources for an intended gain, using tools and techniques of electronic commerce solutions. Today, this is also only realized on the World Wide Web by electronic catalogues or product databases and the potential customer is left alone during the product selection. However, there are first research attempts where system architectures are being developed to support this process in an active way from the seller's side (see Section 4.5).

After-Sales happens in the situation where customers have already bought a product or service from a firm and they need additional support during the usage of the sold goods. Customer support (see Section 4.6) is normally located in call centers where help desk solutions provide product experts during supporting the customers over the phone.

Today, the widest spread of CBR applications are found in solving customer support tasks. Also on the WWW, many database approaches, FAQ-systems, etc., exist, which provide the customer with information after having bought a product. Here, a simple single search for information can take place but also a complex process with many interactions between after-sales employees or call center solutions on the Internet and the customers.

Corporate memory plays an important role during all these selling situations and CBR provides an interesting mechanism to support sellers and buyers in all three. The *know how* about products and services has to be stored, maintained and applied in these different situations and CBR is a technology which helps to overcome the difficulties in this *knowledge managing task.*

4.3 The Pre-Sales Situation

Brightware Inc. has conducted a survey on pre-sales support on the web and got, for example, the following quote:

> *"...they sure make it hard for one to navigate through the l-o-n-g string of serial questions leading to a quote for a particular car at a specific location on a certain date.... When I called, the price was different than from the web site, gladly cheaper. Oh, one more thing. No way to e-mail questions."*
>
> (frustrated unknown customer on the Internet)

For pre-sales, besides a lot of informative material about products and services, often online catalogues and product databases are used. Catalogue-based approaches are replications of their printed counterparts. They support the navigation in the electronic catalogue with an index or an ontology. The index is a hierarchy of descriptive features of the products in the catalogue and supports the user during the search. The second kind of approaches is *requirement based* navigation were a user enters his demands for a product and a database is searched for appropriate products. As already mentioned, pre-sales is often a one-step or even one-way communication until the customer is interested in buying a product. However, the borders between pre-sales and sales are weak. The customers first decide if a product is, in general, interesting in their situation and after a positive decision they start to negotiate and to discover their demands, a process which belongs to the sales situation (see Section 4.5.2).

4.3.1 An Example System: Analog Devices

We will now have a closer look at Analog Devices' online catalog[1] of operational amplifiers based on a CBR approach. First some background information is required: Analog Devices is one of the major manufacturers and sellers of electronic devices in the U.S. According to the company's annual report (Analog Devices 1995), the company has direct sales offices in 17 countries which also provide pre-sales support. Many of Analog Devices' customers are small electronic firms or electronic departments of larger firms. Analog Devices currently employs a number of engineers to provide central pre-sales support for their customers. The situation is as follows; the customer has designed an electronic circuit or a part of it and is now searching for a special integrated circuit which has a desired functionality. The circuit s/he is searching for has also to fit into the actual design and has to fulfill the constraints given by the actual design of the circuit.

There is an online catalog with certain standard search capabilities and selection trees for potential customers. Many people calling the hotline do so because they could not find a suitable match for their problem in the printed or online product catalog. Roughly half of the calls to the hotline support relate to product information during pre-sales. It is obvious that the number of calls to the selection support service could possibly be reduced significantly, if only the online catalog were able to provide intelligent pre-sales support. So, it has been decided to offer CBR-based search facilities in addition to the standard database interface. This solution was integrated into the actual environment of Analog Devices and the existing marketing material and existing technical product descriptions on the World Wide Web.

In a first stage, the application domain for this system was chosen to be Analog Devices' product family of operational amplifiers, but the system is currently being extended to cover at least three more product families. Their product catalog contains about 130 operational amplifiers suitable for a wide range of applications. In many cases, the new CBR system is able to provide customers with information about devices that satisfy their requirements. This reduces the number of calls to Analog Devices' pre-sales support line and enables some engineers to care about more advanced support problems that cannot be solved automatically.

Case Representation. The data sheet for an operational amplifier consists of about 40 parameters which can be logically structured into categories of parameters, such as electrical input and output specifications, functionality, dimensions, etc. Most of the parameter values are high exponent real numbers, but there are also symbolic and string parameters. No object decomposition or hierarchical representation has been used for this application.

[1] http://www.analog.com

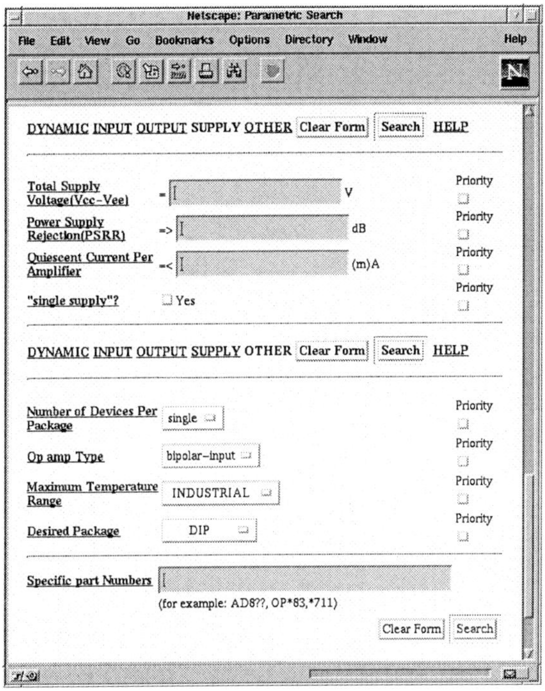

Fig. 4.2. Part of the Interface to Analog Devices' CBR server for operational amplifiers

The retrieval interface provides hyper-links to explanations of each of the 40 attributes (see Figure 4.2).

The Similarity Measure. To assess the similarity of two operational amplifiers, the similarities for all corresponding parameter values are calculated by applying local similarity functions to each pair of corresponding parameters. These local parameter similarities are then used to calculate an overall similarity value for the two devices. The overall similarity is computed as the weighted average of the individual similarities. The original weight factors have been suggested by experts in operational amplifiers but they can be influenced by the customer according to his priorities.

query \ case	com.	industr.	military	space
com.	1	1	1	1
industr.	0.6	1	1	1
military	0.4	0.6	1	1
space	0.1	0.4	0.6	1

Fig. 4.3. An example similarity function for discrete attribute values taken from Analog Devices' operational amplifier application

The local similarities for discrete and continuous values are calculated in different ways. Discrete similarity measures are defined by a table which explicitly lists the similarity values for all possible attribute combinations (Figure 4.3). This is the (simplified) similarity function for the parameter `maximum temperature range` of an operational amplifier. The symbols `commercial`, `industry`, `military`, and `space` describe temperature range standards of electronic devices. If, for example, the query specifies `industrial` standards, the CBR system regards `military` and `space` to fulfill the requirements, but `commercial` has a similarity of only 0.6. Note that the table is asymmetric: it makes a difference whether the query's attribute value is x and the case's value is y or vice versa. If, for example, the user asks for a device with industrial standard temperature specifications, s/he will be satisfied by a part that fulfills military requirements (provided that no other attributes, such as the price, stand against it). On the other hand, the request for `military` standards can not fully be satisfied by a part that only has `industrial` specifications. This situation is reflected by the asymmetry of the similarity table.

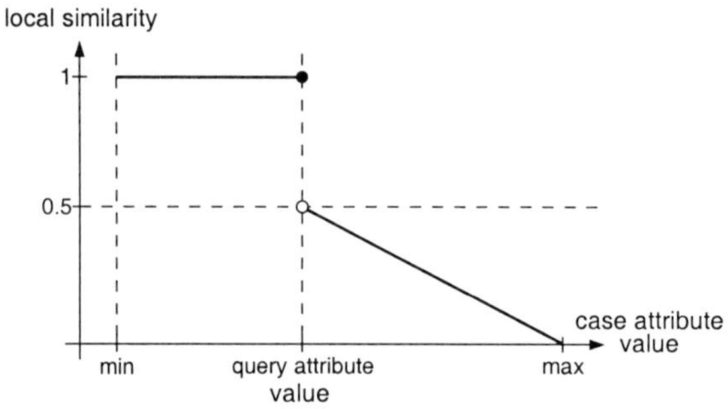

Fig. 4.4. Another example similarity function but for continuous attribute values

This principle also holds for most of the *continuous* attributes of an operational amplifier. The only difference is that their similarity measures cannot be as easily represented in a table, but must be formulated as a function. An example of one such similarity function is shown in Figure 4.4. The similarity function for the parameter "current noise density" of an operational amplifier is shown. The corresponding attribute of a product has similarity 1 if its value is less than or equal to the query's value. Otherwise the similarity is significantly smaller. This function assumes that there is a minimum and a maximum attribute value. If the case's attribute value is less than or equal to the query attribute's value their similarity is 1. Otherwise it is a value somewhere between 0 and 0.5. For certain other attributes the function must be reversed to return 1 for values greater than or equal to the query's value and 0 to 0.5 for smaller values.

This application does not use adaptation. This is because operational amplifiers are unchangeable parts that cannot be reconfigured to the customer's individual demands.

The Architecture. Figure 4.5 shows the functional units and data paths of Analog Devices' operational amplifier server: The parametric search server

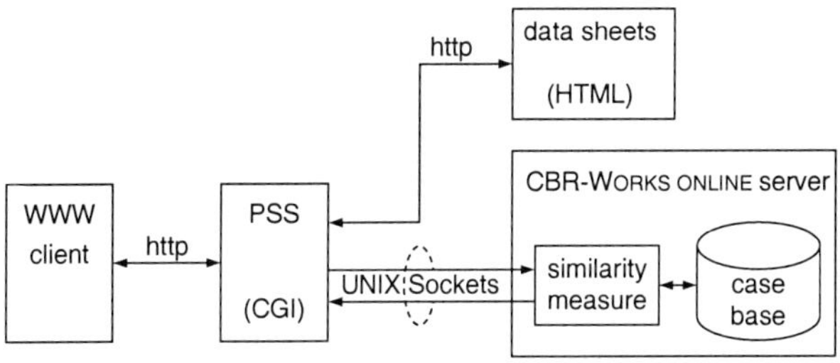

Fig. 4.5. The architecture of Analog Devices' CBR-based catalog of operational amplifiers

(PSS) generates the HTML representations of the query form and the search results. It provides links to explanations of the individual parameters of the operational amplifiers and to data sheets containing more detailed information about the products. Part of the HTML user interface is shown in Figure 4.2. The user has influence on the priority of every parameter value. The server always returns the ten best matches to the user's query.

The user's query is pre-processed by the PSS and forwarded to the CBR-WORKS ONLINE server[2]. The preprocessing stage, for example, normalizes numerical values with units, such as 5 mV, to scalar values like 0.005. CBR-WORKS ONLINE is a generic CBR Shell and retrieval server. The case base, similarity measure, retrieval mechanisms, and other domain dependent knowledge are maintained by this system. The communication between the PSS and the CBR-WORKS ONLINE server is established by UNIX-Sockets. They communicate in a protocol named Case Query Language (CQL) especially developed for distributed CBR applications.

A typical pre-sales support session runs as follows: The customer enters the parameter values s/he needs into the query form. The system will then retrieve the ten best matches to the request. If the results do not exactly fit the customer's needs, s/he will usually increase the priorities of the parameters that are most important to them. Again, the system displays the ten best matches to the refined query. If the results still do not satisfy the customer, s/he might fill more parameter slots that s/he left empty so far, thus further improving the quality of the returned results. When finally a suitable device has been found, the customer can link directly to its detailed data sheet. The detailed technical datasheets are annotations to the cases which provide customers with detailed technical parameters of the circuits and their layout.

[2] CBR-WORKS is a case-based reasoning product family from TecInno, Germany.

The CBR system has part of the product knowledge built into it. This knowledge is used to interpret the user's query and greatly enhances the quality of the retrieved data. Even the first request — typically formulated very vaguely — immediately produces usable results. Near misses, as they are typical for common data base queries, are avoided. If the system returns more than one answer, the results are ranked by their similarity to the query. This makes it easy for the user to refine his request until he is satisfied with the results.

But it is not only the customer who gains profits from this intelligent pre-sales supporting catalog. As this approach will be pursued further, in the future Analog Devices will be able to allow some of their engineers to spend more time addressing more complex pre-sales support for customers. Encouraged by the first success of the new CBR catalog, Analog Devices have decided to further extend the application of CBR technology to other product families.

4.3.2 Current Research

A new research project has started recently with the aim to further explore and integrate the possibilities of CBR-related techniques into product catalogs and reuse applications during pre-sales. The READEE[3] project applies CBR-techniques to the reuse of complete or partial electronic circuit designs. Reusing such designs, in general, can require solving very complex configuration tasks. The reuse assistant is meant to help electrical engineers in selecting and configuring third party intellectual property to fit their personal requirements. Making such a reuse tool available over the Inter-/Intranet can speed up the time-to-market of new electronic circuits significantly. Both the vendor and the consumer of the intellectual property benefit from this tool. However, the resulting system will support customers during pre-sales and also during sales.

4.4 The Virtual Travel Agency on the Internet

In this section, we will describe another application for *Electronic Commerce* which utilizes CBR technology during pre-sales and sales: The Virtual Travel Agency, which provides all the major services of a travel agent via WWW facilities.

4.4.1 Motivation and Objectives

After the prototypical CABATA system (cf. Section 3.6.4) had been in discussion for some years, Humboldt University started a cooperation with **check**

[3] Reuse Assistant for Designs in Electrical Engineering

out, a Berlin tourist office chain. From a research perspective, the objective of this cooperation was to get access to real data of major German travel agents and to apply the ideas developed within CaBaTA for building interactive World Wide Web-based kiosks. On the other hand, the goal of **check out** was to make use of WWW facilities for their daily business, i.e., to allow potential customers to browse their offers and perform online booking.

4.4.2 Components of the Virtual Travel Agency

Up to now, several applications evolved from this cooperation:

- An *Interactive Flight Kiosk* maintains a database of up to 100,000 flights, including online booking facilities.
- Two *Interactive Last Minute Kiosks* operate on the data of *Neckermann* respectively *Berliner Flugring* (BFR), two major German providers on the tourism market.
- A *Rent-A-Car* application provides access to a world-wide operating car rental agency.

The web site also contains a lot of useful information and services, such as descriptions of hotels and of specific regions, overviews over climate and culture, etc. Thus, the Virtual Travel Agency tries to cover all major aspects of this type of application.

For the flight database, CBR only plays a minor role, i.e., case-based techniques are being used for suggesting minor changes, e.g., when a minor date change or a neighboring destination airport would result in a cheaper flight. For the *Rent-A-Car* application CBR has not been used at all. Rather, this application provides convenient access to a traditional database system.

Special emphasis, however, has been put on the development of the *Last Minute* applications; this will be explored in the following.

4.4.3 Handling of *Last Minute* Offers

A special problem that travel agents have to deal with is the handling of so-called *Last Minute* offers, i.e., tour packages which come into sales just a couple of days before the date of departure. Traditionally, tour providers send several dozen sheets of papers to their agencies every day in order to inform them about available special offers. It is obvious that the vast amount of information that has to be handled this way can only be dealt with using appropriate tools. Consequently, there has been an urgent need for a system particularly focusing on *Last Minute* offers.

Specific features of the *Last Minute* domain are:

- Last minute offers (as provided by the tour providers) are tour packages: This means that the customer may accept an offer only as it is – there are no variations of it (except if it is stored as a separate offer). Consequently, there is no negotiation during the sales process.

- A regular (that is, at least daily) update is required. While online availability checking is in principle possible, we are currently not allowed to access the data pools of the providers online.
- During peak season, there are up to 200,000 offers, i.e. cases. Consequently, one has to come up with a highly efficient retrieval strategy in order to provide fast answers to user queries.

4.4.4 The Need for Intelligent Support

As already noted in the example in the introductory part of this chapter, simple database approaches would not be sufficient for this type of application as they cannot provide *intelligent* sales support. In particular, the following features are essential:

- The system has to be able to deal with vague as well as highly specific queries.
- The system has to be able to suggest appropriate alternatives if no offer completely fits the customers requirements.
- The system has to present the available offers to the customer in a reasonable manner. In particular, it should definitely avoid situations in which no offer is made to the customer (*no solution* situation) as well as those where the customer is left alone with pages and pages of possible offers (*100 solutions* situation).

As should be clear from the preceding chapters, CBR is a technology which satisfies all three criteria. More precisely, the requirements mentioned previously indicate that the ideas of CABATA (cf. Section 3.6.4) are indeed directly applicable, i.e. there is no need to implement, for example, an additional planning component for configuring an appropriate offer. Compared to CABATA, however, one has to deal with efficiency problems (due to the huge number of offers) and one has to provide solutions for the problems specific to the implementation of an online WWW systems, such as online booking, updates, etc.

The problems of efficiency have been solved by applying the Case Retrieval Net model as described in Section 3.4. For 200,000 offers approximately 1.3 seconds are required for retrieval – hence, in terms of the WWW, the result is available instantly.

4.4.5 Availability of the Virtual Travel Agency

The systems are accessible via the home pages of our project partners at http://www.reiseboerse.com respectively http://www.BFR-Reisen.com.

4.5 The Sales Situation

Recently, case-based reasoning was used to introduce intelligent support into electronic shopping solutions during the retrieval of appropriate products for the customer during the sales process (Wilke 1997). These applications sup-

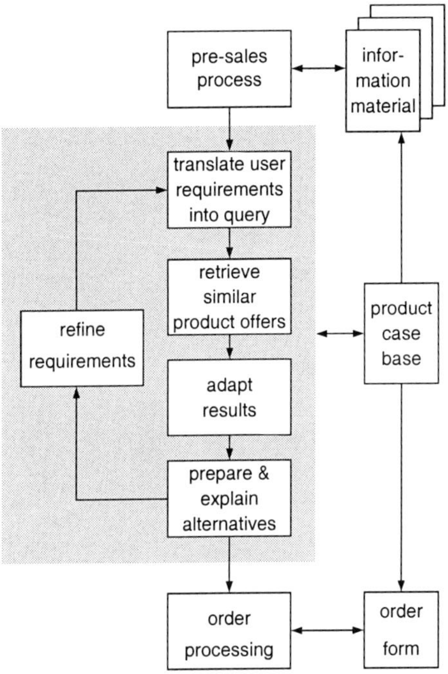

Fig. 4.6. The electronic sales process: Capabilities of existing intelligent CBR sales support applications

port the retrieval of products by a similarity based match. However, the whole CBR process can improve more than one step in the selling process via the Internet. We identify the following major steps during the selling process in our selling situation (see Figure 4.6): After the preliminary pre-sales process, the users have to turn their requirements into a description of the desired product during the "translate user requirements into query" phase. Next, the sales assistant retrieves appropriate product offers. During a possible adaptation of the retrieved products (synonymous to product configuration) the retrieved products are adapted to best fit the users' requirements, if necessary. The results are presented and alternatives are explained to the users. Successive refinement of requirements may lead to a cyclic sales process. If the users have obtained a satisfactory result, the overall business process can proceed to the processing of the order.

4.5.1 The CBR Cycle for Electronic Commerce

If we have in mind the sales process and take a look at the well established CBR-Cycle (Aamodt and Plaza 1994), we observe that this cycle is not directly applicable in our situation. Therefore, we suggest a modified cycle, shown in Figure 4.7, regarding the different situation in electronic sales support applications. First, the sales process starts with a set of initial demands

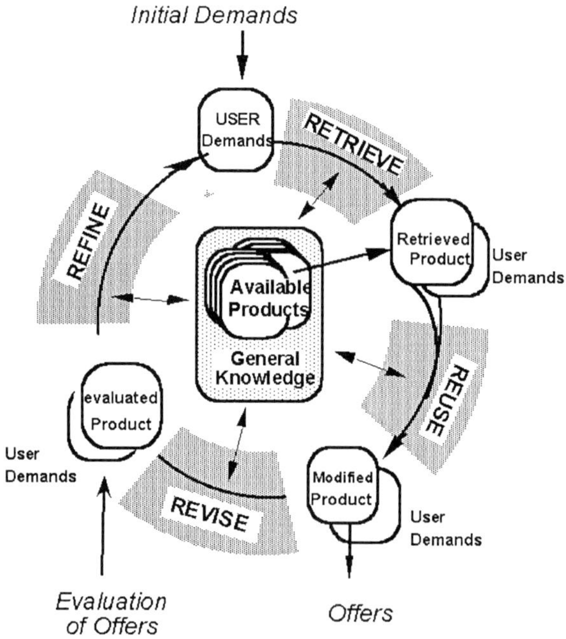

Fig. 4.7. The CBR-cycle for electronic sales support applications

stated by the user and a retrieval for similar products in the product base of all available products is performed. Next, the retrieved products may be reused in a product configuration phase. In this phase, the products are tailored to the specific demands of the user. These modified products are offered to the customer. The customer evaluates these offers during the revise phase, which results in a set of evaluated products. The customer can state that he accepts certain products or parts of the products or he may state that something is not appropriate. Next, a new step called refine is introduced. This step does not occur in the traditional CBR cycle. Here, the current user demands are refined based on the evaluations given by the customer. This is required if the current demands cannot be fulfilled on the basis of the available products. After this refine phase, the E-Commerce cycle is re-entered. Here, a retain phase must not take place because a successful selling of a product does not lead to an additional product in the product base. The user demands accompany the products from the product base during all phases. This cycle must possibly be re-entered several times until a sufficient negotiation result (meeting of demands and offered products) is achieved. In general, this cycle is applicable in all situations where an iterative retrieval in a decision support situation takes place. Unlike in traditional CBR, not only the case (product) is adapted, but also the query (demands).

4.5.2 Negotiation during Sales

As already stated, searching for and selecting complex products on the World Wide Web is a difficult task. This is particularly evident in the selection of products/services or when navigating through the complex space of available product information in an electronic mall. Therefore, there is a need for intelligent advise during the selling of products via the Internet. Like in the real world, an electronic *sales agent* is needed which is able to *negotiate* with the customers about their *demands* and to assist them during the search for an appropriate product.

Negotiation is an important part of the selling process via the Internet, and in order to support customers in a sufficient way, electronic commerce systems need the ability to negotiate. However, negotiation is a process with relatively little support to date. We define *negotiation* in electronic commerce as *a process were two parties bargain resources for an intended gain, using tools, and techniques of electronic commerce solutions.* The complexity of the negotiation process depends on the complexity of the product or service being negotiated.

4.5.3 Negotiation in Electronic Commerce

The underlying kinds of problem solving strategies divide different approaches for negotiation in electronic commerce into two classes: a *cooperative approach* and a *competitive approach*. However, both approaches present two extremes on a continuum of possible underlying problems. In existing research, negotiation during the search in an electronic catalogue is seen as a competitive approach (Beam and Segev 1996). It is assumed that a conflict is in the price of a good where all other attributes of the desired product are fixed. Competitive negotiation takes place if there is at least some conflict of interests between the buyer and the seller. Consequently, there will be not more collaboration than necessary between the buyer and the seller to solve the negotiation problem. Conversely, cooperative negotiation means that there is as much collaboration as possible between the two negotiation parties.

A second criterion to distinguish between different negotiation approaches is the underlying paradigm: the *human factor approach*, the *economics/game theory approach*, and the *computer science* approach. The human factor approach provides not much which is directly applicable to electronic negotiations. However, it defines the general objective of a satisfactory solution and should, therefore, be taken into account. The focus is to manage human factors, like pride, ego, or culture as well as possible, which leads to customer satisfaction if such criteria are fulfilled within a negotiation outcome. The fields of economics and game theory give some valuable insights into the problem. The approaches in the area of computer science are most applicable to product search and negotiations in electronic commerce. Research in the field of intelligent agents provides different approaches to the topic of electronic negotiations. A survey of these approaches has been given by Beam and Segev (1997).

We distinguish different approaches also by their underlying technology in the electronic shopping solution. Catalogue-based approaches have an index or an ontology which should help the customer finding relevant products. The index is a ontology of descriptive features of the products in the catalogue. The second kind of technological approaches are *requirement-based* navigation approaches where a users enter their demands for a product and a database is searched for appropriate products. Both approaches can be found, for example, in NETBUYER[4] were they are used to sell personal computers and computer components.

4.5.4 The Sales Agent

In this section, we have a closer look at the task of the sales agent supporting negotiation in an electronic commerce solution. Further, we provide some insights into what happens during the CBR process if the sales agent fulfils his task.

In electronic commerce solutions supporting sales, a case consists of a *problem description* which describes the demands of a customer in a specific situation together with a *product description* which satisfies these demands as a solution to the customer's problem. Modifying both descriptions is part of the negotiation between the customer and the electronic sales agent in the electronic shop, as shown in Figure 4.7. One step forward is the use of adaptation techniques during the product configuration phase (Schumacher et al. 1998) where the product is modified to satisfy the customer's needs. Product specific suggestions to the customer modify his problem description in a predefined way, which can lead to satisfying product search.

During the sales process, the customers are navigating through the available products and search for a products which meet their demands. Some demands are *known* in advance and additional ones may be *discovered* during the navigation in the product space. Some demands are *fixed* and must be fulfilled by the product and other demands are more or less *weak* and

[4] http://www.netbuyer.com

the sales agent can negotiate about them. The goal of the sales agent is to identify these demands in cooperation with the customers and to find a product which fulfils them. During negotiation in the selling situation, the agent might suggest or even add some new demands or modify some weak demands for the purpose of finding an appropriate product. For configurable products, it is also possible for the sales agent to modify existing products during adaptation to meet the customer's demands.

So the task for the sales agent during the negotiation process is *the iterative adaptation of user demands, by making proposals for adding or changing these demands, and the iterative adaptation of products by product configuration with the goal of finding an agreement point in the multidimensional demand/product space.*

4.5.5 Negotiation and the CBR Process

In general, the customer's satisfaction is maximal if the modification of his weak and hard demands is minimal and he finds his product as quickly as possible. There are several characteristics which describe a negotiation processes to meet the customer's demands.

Active or Passive Sales Agent. The Sales Agent is *active* if he explicitly suggests modifications of particular demands to the customer. This can be a suggestion to change one (or more) already specified demand(s) in a way or to specify new demands. The sales agent suggests the refinements of the customer demands and, after one or more iterations, the customer finally finds a satisfying product. *Passive* sales agents support the modification only by offering several techniques which may help the user to find out what demands he might have or which he is able to change. The decision what to do is left to the customer.

Modifications of Demands and/or the Product. Usually, during negotiation, the customer or the sales agent are allowed to modify the customer demands only. Compared to the situation with other CBR tasks, this is the normal situation were only the query may be modified. If products in the product base are configurable, it might also be possible to modify the products themselves and the demands during negotiation. Full-scale product configuration is not intended. In reality, it might be possible to refine the product during negotiation with a special "add-on". For example, a car dealer could offer a sliding roof for free during the negotiation or the price could simply be modified. The kind of allowed modifications must be described as a part of the general knowledge in the product base. One negotiation approach from the intelligent agents area is KASBAH[5] (Chavez and Maes 1996), where such modifications are described for every attribute in a function that determines the kind of allowed modification for every negotiation step (in our situation every iteration of the sales process).

[5] http://www.jeevies.media.mit.edu

Modification in Single or Multiple Dimensions. During one iteration in our electronic commerce cycle, it may be only possible to modify a *single* demand or a single attribute of the product. This means that, in the multidimensional demand/product space during one iteration, a movement in one dimension is allowed. This leads to a slower movement in the space but single actions are easy to survey. On the other hand, the customer or the sales agent are allowed to modify *multiple dimensions* during one iteration. This lead to a easier movement for the customer in the demand/product space.

Over- or Under-Specification of the Customer Demands. Depending on the current situation, the customer may have over-specified his demands (see Section 4.1). This leads to a situation where it is not possible to find an appropriate product in the product base. Therefore, the sales agent or the customer has to relax the demands to find an appropriate product. In the opposite situation, under-specific demands lead to too many possible products for the customer. As a result, he may get lost in the amount of offered products. Therefore, the current demands have to be further specified to come to an appropriate product.

4.5.6 An Example System: Used Cars

We will now illustrate the use of a sales agent in an example system which sells used cars in an electronic commerce solution. Figure 4.8 shows the system in an example session[6]. In our example, we are searching for a *BMW Coupe*

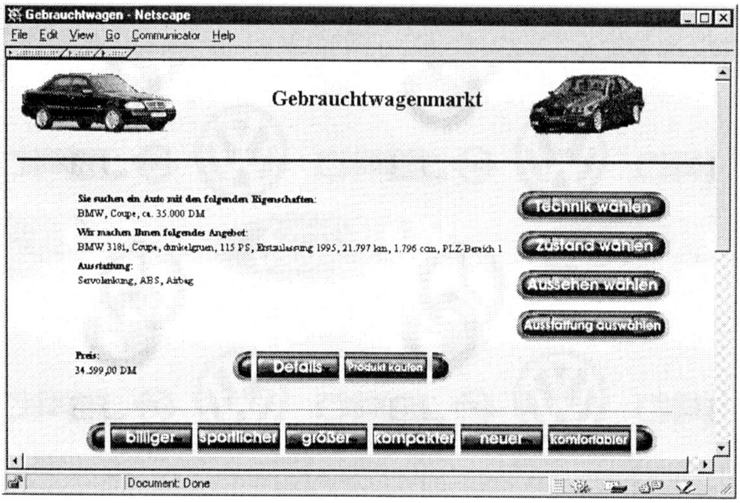

Fig. 4.8. The electronic sales agent during the refinement of the requirements

[6] http://minsk.informatik.uni-kl.de:8009/launch/PKWSalesAgent

and the price should be about 35,000 German Marks. After the retrieval, the sales agent suggests a *BMW-318i* with *115 hp, 1796 ccm cubic capacity* as the most similar car. The customer has now two different possibilities for negotiating:

Modification of Demands by Derived Attributes. At the bottom of the window in Figure 4.8, the sales agent offers several abstract aspects which modify the demands of the user. These are: *cheaper, more sporty, larger, more compact, newer, more comfortable*, respectively. Here, the sales agent allows the customer to modify the query in such a direction that these aspects are better fulfilled. This is realized by a modification of several demands in a way which move the query in the specified direction. Starting from our query's last result, we are searching for a more sporty car. Therefore, the value of the demand *horsepower* is raised and, additionally, the requirements for *cubic capacity* and a power assisted steering are added. As a result, a more sportive car, a *BMW-320* is offered which is more similar to the modified demands from the sales agent.

This approach is a passive approach because the customer has to choose the aspect to modify on his own. Only multiple demands are changed in this special application. Changing only single demands is possible in the generic architecture. This technique is normally used in a situation of over-specification, where the customer is not satisfied with the current retrieval result.

Case Focusing with Entropy. A second active approach for negotiation is realized in the car application. The customer gets suggestions for demands from the sales agent which he should specify. This approach is normally used in a situation where the actual demands are under-specified and the user gets too many product suggestions. Here, the goal is to focus faster on the relevant products. An entropy-based selection strategy is used to suggest a demand which is the most informative and which should therefore be specified by the customer. The selection strategy also incorporates the similarity measure. A determination of single or multiple attributes is possible during one iteration of the sales cycle.

CBR technology introduces intelligent sales support to electronic commerce applications. The deficits of standard database techniques are overcome by implementing expert knowledge into the retrieval system. CBR gets rid of the problem of near misses, the need of expert knowledge on the customer's side and resulting frustration. New solutions can be created by adapting old solutions. Finally, the vendor benefits from the ability to offer nearly optimal solutions and from satisfied customers that do not search for other vendors.

4.5.7 Summing Up and Future Research

Future improvements to intelligent sales support systems provide current research topics. The new technology can be expected to offer sophisticated adaptation and interactive configuration of complex products, interactive refinement of the customers requirements and explanation of results. As interactive electronic sales support becomes more common in future, interfaces for interactive adaptation and configuration will come into use. CBR-related techniques for indexing and clustering the case base can be used to help the customers refine their queries by a step-by-step analysis of their needs. By analyzing the structure of the case base, a CBR system can suggest which undefined parameters the user should define next in order to find a good solution as quickly as possible. It is also possible to *explain* to the customer the reasons why the retrieved results are suitable for his query.

Negotiation supports the customers in finding an appropriate product, depending on their demands. The ideas presented here are realized in a prototype for a sales agent. The research project WEBSELL, which has been started recently at the University of Kaiserslautern with several commercial partners, has the primary goal to explore techniques to support this sales process especially by employing CBR and related methods. In this project, the presented techniques will be enhanced, refined, further developed and, finally, used in an industrial setting by the participating commercial partners. However, concerning the weak border between pre-sales and sales, this technique seems usable in both situations.

4.6 The After-Sales Situation

After-sales support on the Internet has recently become a key application area. Industry, analysts and venture capital companies in the US seem to be convinced that after-sales support and sales automation on the WEB is the next emerging market for case-based reasoning applications. Researchers from the independent research firm Bruskin/Goldring conducted a US nationwide opinion survey. A general U.S. population sample was surveyed by telephone. 1017 interviews were completed during October 3-5, 1997.

Result: more than 70 percent of the Americans who currently use the Internet are interested in applying it to resolve customer service problems. This indicates a strong potential for acceptance of Web-based self-service systems that allow customers to help themselves at their convenience. Several US companies including *Compaq*, *3Com*, *Dell*, and *Gateway 2000* have started using CBR on their customer support Web-pages. During our survey, we found more than 50 articles in the recent press covering this issue.

The main motivation for firms to offer help desk systems on the Internet is a *call-avoidance* strategy. The goal is to reduce the permanently growing number of phone calls to the customer support center (see also the idea of the *Automatic Hotline* in Section 5.7.2). The support is shifted from the seller to the customer directly via the Internet. To assist the customer during problem solving on his own, he is supported with a case base of possible product problems and a query interface and similarity measures which should help him to find a similar problem.

Some examples of well-known CBR applications on the World Wide Web for trouble-shooting are:

GIZZMO TAPPER	Broderbund	http://seudo.broder.com
YODAS HELP-DESK	Lucas Arts	http://www.lucasarts.com/support
3COM ASSIST	3Com	http://infodeli.3com.com/wcp/

In these systems, CBR plays the role of a "background technology", that is, it has been seamlessly integrated within the existing applications. Customers actually are not aware of the fact that they are using CBR techniques.

We will now have a look at the customer support application GIZZMO TAPPER.

4.6.1 An Example System: GIZZMO TAPPER

Broderbound installed their online customer support solution in the Web in 1995. They use the same system which is also used by their operators on the internal hotline. *Broderbound* develop and distribute a lot off different computer games and other software products. The first system which was supported on the Internet was the computer game *Myst*. Figure 4.9 shows the entry screen to support system. The users can describe their problems as free text descriptions. In our example, the problem is a dark screen after the start of the game. After an initial search, the system asks the user a number of queries. There are questions about the used computer, installation details, error codes, and so forth. If the system finds an appropriate case in the case base, it is shown to the customer together with a solution also described in free text. After the successful launch of a CBR after-sales solution for this computer game, *Broderbound* extended the use of these kinds of solutions to thirty other products until the current date.

Beside the Internet, recently, also Intranets marched into larger firms. To support their own employees, they also have support centers which are used internally for maintenance of bought and used products from other vendors. Intranets enable these large firms to have their internal after-sales support available for all employees. One example of such a system is the HOMER system (Pantleon 1997). It is used at *Daimler-Benz* to support and maintain their internal CAD/CAM workstations in the case of hard- or software problems. They provide first and second level support for their used products via an internal customer support hotline. To have this support available in different locations across the firm, they also used a CBR solution implemented in Java which supports help desk operators over the Intranet. This enables *Daimler-Benz* to provide this service in different located service centers.

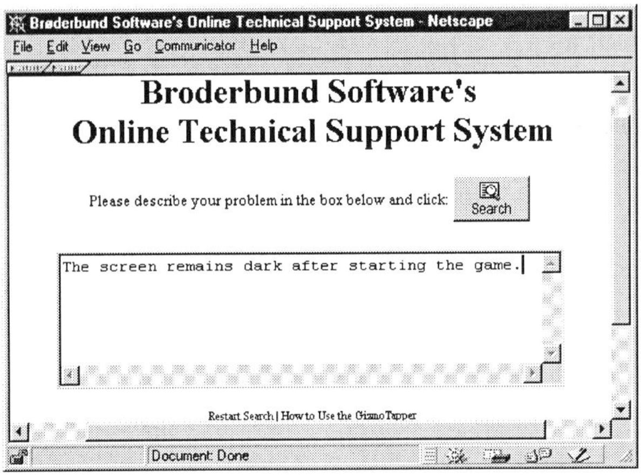

Fig. 4.9. The customer support system GIZZMO TAPPER from *Broderbound*

4.6.2 Current Research

Associated with the above mentioned HOMER application is the research project INRECA-II. One aim of the project is to develop a methodology (Bergmann et al. 1997a) for building CBR applications (see also Chapter 12). Building such a methodology for developing and maintaining CBR applications is an important goal currently addressed by CBR researchers and practitioners. Since CBR application development is a special kind of software development, building a CBR methodology can certainly be viewed as a software engineering research and development activity. One of the main driving forces behind the development and the use of a methodology relates to the need for quality in both the products and processes of the development of computer-based systems.

HOMER is one application of the project which delivers the input to the development of such a methodology. A second application is the ANALOG DEVICE scenario described in Section 4.3.

4.7 Discussion

Compared to other application areas of CBR, sales support solutions on the Internet are rather new. Until recently, there has been no integration of payment or other business processes into the existing applications. To build up a complete Electronic Commerce framework with a CBR engine as a Middleware is one of the future challenges in this area. Also, the seamless integration of the CBR process into the sales process is a promising investigation for the future. CBR is a technique to solve the knowledge management tasks in sale situations on electronic media's in the future.

Acknowledgements

Parts of the work described in this chapter have been funded by the European Commission as part of the INRECA-II project *Information and Knowledge Reengineering for Reasoning from Cases* (ESPRIT contract P22196). Partners are AcknoSoft (prime contractor, France), Daimler Benz (Germany), TecInno (Germany), Irish Medical Systems (Ireland) and the University of Kaiserslautern (Germany). For further information see also http://wwwagr.informatik.uni-kl.de/~lsa/CBR/INRECA-IIproject.html. Also, the WEBSELL project *Intelligent Sales Assistants for the World Wide Web* is funded by the Commission of the European Communities (ESPRIT contract P27068). Partners are TecInno (Germany, prime contractor), Adwired (Switzerland), EuroWEB (Germany), Irish Medical Systems (Ireland), Trinity College Dublin (Ireland) and the University of Kaiserslautern (Germany). See also http://wwwagr.informatik.uni-kl.de/~websell/. Finally, READEE is funded by the Foundation for Innovation of Rhineland-Palatinate and will last for a period of three years. See http://wwwagr.informatik.uni-kl.de/~readee/

5. Textual CBR

Mario Lenz, André Hübner, Mirjam Kunze

> *"All the evidence suggests that for end-user searching, the indexing language should be natural language, rather than controlled language oriented."* Lewis and Sparck Jones (1996)

In this chapter, we will explore a fairly new direction of research in the case-based reasoning community, namely the handling of textual documents. We will explain first why the ability to deal with natural language texts is crucial. We will then discuss more traditional methods for these tasks. Following this, we present the approach of Textual CBR and, in particular, the CBR-ANSWERS project.

5.1 Introduction

In recent years, case-based reasoning researchers have started to address tasks that have traditionally been coped with by the Information Retrieval community, namely the handling of textual documents.

When considering the roots of CBR, this development is not surprising at all: As discussed already in Chapter 1, the fundamental idea of this problem solving paradigm is to collect *experiences* from earlier problem solving episodes and to explicitly reuse these for dealing with new tasks. In real life, many of the most valuable experiences are stored as textual documents, such as:

- reports by physicians;
- documentations and manuals of technical equipment;
- Frequently Asked Question (FAQ) collections;
- informal notes and comments on specific functions and observed behavior.

Consequently, it is only natural to address the issue of textual documents from a CBR perspective.

In this chapter, we will demonstrate how CBR systems can be designed which are able to handle textual documents. We will discuss more traditional approaches to text retrieval, describe in detail some of the existing projects and what problems still need to be solved. Before this, an example application scenario shall clarify the goals of a Textual CBR system.

5.2 A Typical Application Area: Hotline Support

As pointed out earlier in Chapters 3 and 4, an efficient customer support is becoming more and more important in today's business world. Consequently, many companies establish so-called *help desks* and *hotlines* in addition to tools shipped together with the products (cf. Section 3.6). In case of a problem, the customer may contact these hotlines and will be given additional support. Generally, applications such as help desks and hotlines can be characterized as follows:

- A hotline will always focus on a specific domain, e.g., on some type of technical devices, on a set of software components, etc. This implies that no topics outside this domain will be dealt with and a *general world understanding* is not required.
- Because of the limitation to a specific domain, a number of highly specific terms will be used, such as names of components, functions, and modules.
- Naturally, a hotline will rely very much on textual documents such as FAQs, documentations, and error reports. Also, the customers' queries will be given in free text plus some additional information, such as names of hardware components, software release numbers, etc.
- The term *hotline* does not mean that customer enquiries have to be handled within seconds. Rather, finding the answers to problems usually involves a complex problem analysis and thus may take some time. Nevertheless, questions concerning problems that have been solved before should, of course, be answered rapidly.

Consequently, there is an urgent need for systems which can support the hotline staff in retrieving relevant documents in a specific problem context. For this, techniques are required which support the search for documents given a user's question; i.e., on the one hand they have to handle natural language texts, on the other hand these techniques must be flexible enough to cope with paraphrased documents which have essentially the same semantics (Lenz et al. 1998).

5.3 Basic Ideas of Information Retrieval

When trying to recall relevant textual documents in a problem situation, the technique that is traditionally applied is Information Retrieval (IR) (Rijsbergen 1979; Salton and McGill 1983). Despite the name, however, IR systems do not really retrieve information in the sense that they deliver facts satisfying an information need. Rather, they search for documents which are somehow related to the information need as expressed in a query:

> *"An information retrieval system does not inform ... the user on the subject of his inquiry. It merely informs on the existence ... of documents relating to his request."* (Rijsbergen 1979)

Consequently, a better name for this area would be *Document Retrieval.* However, *Information Retrieval* has now become a widely accepted term.

5.3.1 Fundamental Models of IR

Quite a number of successful IR systems now exist on the market, including search engines for the WWW. Most of these systems are based on either the *Vector Space Model*, the *Probabilistic Model*, or the *Inference Network Model* of IR. To ease the understanding of the differences compared to Textual CBR, we will sketch these models in the following. For a more detailed comparison see Lenz (1998).

In the *Vector Space Model* (Salton et al. 1975), documents are encoded by means of a very large vector, the elements of which represent the weight of a specific term of the index vocabulary for that document:

$$D_i = [d_{i1}, \ldots, d_{in}]$$

The weight d_{ij} of the jth index term is calculated on the basis of the frequency of that term in the considered document D_i as well as in the entire document collection. Once documents are represented this way, similarity of two documents may be assessed by comparing the corresponding vectors, e.g., by calculating the cosine measure.

In the *Probabilistic Model* (Fuhr 1989), too, documents are represented by means of term vectors:

$$D_i = [d_{i1}, \ldots, d_{in}]$$

However, D_i is now a binary vector, i.e. $d_{ij} = 0$ or $d_{ij} = 1$ depending on the presence of the jth term d_j in the D_i. In this model, the probability that a certain document D_i is relevant to a given request:

$$P(relevant|D_i) \tag{5.1}$$

is calculated, again, from the observed term frequencies where Bayes' Theorem is used to reformulate Equation (5.1).

Finally, in the *Inference Network* model (Turtle and Croft 1990; Turtle 1991), documents are represented by certain nodes in a graph which also contains nodes for index terms, query terms, etc. These nodes are connected via arcs which may be weighted according to observed probabilities in a document collection. Given a query representing an information need, the query network is built characterizing the dependence of that query on the document collection, i.e., a ranking may be performed based on the information encoded in the network.

5.3.2 Advantages of IR Models

A major advantage of these IR models is that they are domain-independent. All the information required for building such a system may be obtained from a given document collection, including the weighting of index terms. Thus, it is appropriate to consider IR systems as tools which may be easily applied to virtually any domain in which textual documents have to be handled.

Also, IR systems may handle large document collections, i.e., the number of documents that can be searched efficiently is, by far, larger than what has traditionally been the number of cases in a CBR system.

Finally, the IR community provided a number of valuable contributions concerning the evaluation of their systems. Using these evaluation methods, it is possible to compare various systems and estimate various performance parameters.

5.3.3 Limitations of IR Models

Assumption of Independence. All of the above IR models assume that the various index terms used for representing documents are, in some sense, independent of each other. For the *Probabilistic Model*, for example, an explicit assumption is that index terms are *stochastically independent* (Fuhr 1989).

A similar assumption underlies the *Vector Space Model*; if two documents contain disjoint sets of index terms, then the vectors representing these documents are orthogonal to each other and any reasonable measure should indicate that they have zero similarity to each other. If, however, two or more terms are synonymous to each other, then the two documents should have non-zero similarity. In fact, the assumption of independence of the two index terms is violated then.

Such problems often occur because in many situations terms are related to each other and during search one wants to consider these relationships.

Statistics Rather than Knowledge. As sketched above, all major IR models heavily make use of statistics, counting of index terms, etc.:

1. The index vocabulary is determined based on the given document collection and applying some statistics and heuristics. For example, terms that occur too often are considered to be useless — as are terms that occur too seldom.
2. The weight of index terms is again based on counting frequencies in a given document collection. Consequently, the similarity of documents is based on these frequencies, too.

In terms of the knowledge container model introduced in Section 1.3.8, this means that, in fact, only the document collection may contain meaningful knowledge — while both, index vocabulary and similarity measure are fixed for a given document set. Consequently, a number of problems arise when some kind of knowledge has to be integrated into an IR system to improve the problem solving behavior. In practice, this knowledge may contain both;

- descriptions of terms that are particularly relevant to a certain domain,
- specifications of relationships between different terms.

When attempting to work with textual documents without using any specific domain knowledge, one often has to struggle with the following two problems:

Ambiguity Problem: Although the sets of keywords in two compared documents may be similar, the actual meaning of both documents may differ significantly.

Paraphrase Problem: With natural language, the same meaning may be expressed using completely different expressions.

A further shortcoming of traditional IR methods is that they do not support the consideration of information that is represented in non-textual form, e.g. additional structured information, diagrams, etc.

5.3.4 An Even Simpler Approach: n-gram Matching

An alternative approach to the classical IR models has been implemented in some commercially available help desk systems as, for example, CBR EXPRESS from Inference Corp. Instead of representing documents as sets of index terms, CBR EXPRESS, uses an even simpler matching based on n-grams of common characters for comparing documents. More precisely, the text contained in a document is cut into sequences of n subsequent letters (most often $n = 3$) and the set of all the sequences is used as a representation of the original document.

Example 5.3.1. When using 3-gram matching, the textual description

`The new printer does not work.`

is represented in form of the following set of 3-grams:

{`the,new,pri,rin,int,nte,ter,doe,oes,not,wor,ork`}

Compared to the above models of IR, this is firstly less computationally expensive and secondly appears to be very robust against minor changes in the text as, for example, grammatical variations and misspellings.

As with the IR models, this kind of document matching does not permit the integration of additional knowledge sources, such as domain-specific thesauri, glossaries, etc. This is obvious from the fact that in the representation of a document not even the actual words occurring in that document are directly recognizable.

In a tool like CBR EXPRESS, however, such an approach is sufficient as the analysis of textual descriptions is intended to only give a first clue about which cases to focus on. A further refinement is then made by answering questions and evaluating the cases with respect to the obtained answers. As far as the underlying principles are concerned, this second step is equivalent to querying a decision tree as explained in Section 3.2, i.e., for this phase, a properly structured case memory is necessary which requires a careful knowledge engineering process.

In particular, a *case authoring* process must be performed during which the cases as they occur in the problem domain are encoded by means of the formalisms provided by the system. In particular, for larger applications, this case authoring process requires a lot of man power and skill. In contrast, the approach of Textual CBR, that will be explored in the following, directly utilizes the cases; i.e., the textual documents as they are available in the problem domain.

5.4 Textual CBR

As discussed above, reuse of information contained in documents, such as manuals and FAQ collections seems to be a straightforward task for a CBR system. However, until recently, CBR research mainly focussed on areas where a more structured case representation is applicable, i.e., where cases describe certain situations and events in some predefined format.

For building a CBR system handling textual documents, we have to solve a number of tasks as they occur in other application areas too, such as case representation, knowledge acquisition, etc. However, as we deal with natural language texts here, the emphasis is a bit different. Before going into the details about these issues, we will explain why we think it is worthwile to spend the additional effort required for Textual CBR.

5.4.1 The Knowledge of a CBR System

A crucial difference to the above sketched IR models is that CBR is a knowledge-based technique – hence any CBR system explicitly allows (*even:* requires) the integration of semantic knowledge. Consequently, during knowledge acquisition, a domain model has to be build which describes the essential properties of the domain, the entities which one is talking about, and their relationships (most importantly, similarity).

In terms of the knowledge container model (cf. Section 1.3.8), every piece of knowledge can be represented in one (or more) of the following categories:

(a) the collection of cases;
(b) the definition of an index vocabulary for cases;
(c) the construction of a similarity measure;
(d) the specification of adaptation knowledge.

For the purpose of this chapter, we will assume that (a) documents are available which can serve as the basis for a case base and (d) adaptation is of limited use only. Consequently, the most important knowledge containers are (b) the index vocabulary describing which term are used in the domain and (c) the similarity measure relating the various terms as well as queries and documents to each other. In particular, a *semantic* similarity measure of CBR systems will contain *additional* knowledge as a supplement to the other knowledge containers. This is possible because a Textual CBR system is built for a specific domain only:

1. By performing a careful knowledge acquisition, features important in that domain can be identified (e.g., based on keywords, terms, expressions etc.) and thus a *term dictionary* can be constructed which is not limited to statistic evaluations. Often, these features may cover more than a single keyword; an example might be the expression *Customer Administration Module* which represents a certain component in the FALLQ project (see below).
2. Additional knowledge may be represented by means of the *structure* of documents; for Textual CBR, a document is not merely a single text but may consist of several components. A FAQ, for example, would naturally contain (at least) two separate parts, a question and an answer.
3. Due to the limitation to a specific domain, the *Ambiguity Problem* is avoided to a great extend.
4. By carefully analyzing the domain under consideration, a similarity measure can be constructed which goes beyond statistical term weighting, e.g., by considering a domain-specific thesaurus, ontologies underlying the domain, etc.

With respect to the latter point, it is important to recognize the difference to IR systems; though some of these also use thesauri, it is much easier if domain-specific knowledge can be utilized. Also, terms which describe objects (such as names of devices, processes, etc.) do not normally occur in general-purpose thesauri but are available in a specific context.

It is obvious that the major advantage of Textual CBR is the ability to make use of domain-specific expertise in order to go beyond pure keyword matching and thus improve the problem solving behavior. However, this benefit is not for free; rather, a well-designed knowledge acquisition process is required in order to encode existing knowledge and make it available to the CBR system. While the non-textual information in these environments has to be dealt with as in other Artificial Intelligence approaches, handling of textual data is novel and, hence, requires additional effort.

5.4.2 Knowledge Acquisition for Textual CBR

In order to obtain cases to reason about from a given document collection, it is required to *extract* cases from the given text documents. Obviously, a first step towards this is to use keywords specific to a domain for building an appropriate index vocabulary. However, this allows only a rough estimation of the content of documents. If one wants to obtain a more meaningful representation of texts, Natural Language Processing (NLP) techniques are promising candidates.

In our projects, we experimented with a couple of NLP techniques to obtain a more sophisticated representation of textual documents. Unfortunately, most of the available NLP tools have a number of shortcomings when it comes to real-world texts:

- They are computationally expensive, i.e., the performance of the systems on larger text collections does not permit their integration into other systems.
- They only work with small dictionaries; even worse, they are not robust when unknown terms are encountered.

Besides these shortcomings, we experienced that sophisticated NLP is of limited use because in many situations, documents are in the form of short notes, remarks, etc. instead of properly structured sentences with correct grammar.

Consequently, we concentrated on so-called *shallow* NLP techniques, such as *Part-Of-Speech* tagging. These are both, efficient and robust as they do not attempt to build a highly structured representation of texts but merely *tag* each word with its probable class (i.e., whether it is a noun, a verb, etc.) and additional information such as the word stem.

For this purpose, we used the TREETAGGER[1] tool developed at the Institute of Natural Language Processing (IMS) at Stuttgart University and analyzed the result of tagging the document collection. In particular, the objective was to obtain both, lists of relevant keywords as well as stemming information.

More precisely, we applied the following procedure:

1. Let the NLP tool *tag* an example document collection.
2. *Normalize* the texts in the document collection by replacing particular words by their corresponding stems.
3. Obtain index terms by grouping together words with common stems.
4. Automatically classify the index terms on the documents as useful or useless according to the following heuristics:
   a) Mark a term as *useless* if it is a determiner, an auxiliary or modal verb, a preposition, a pronomen, etc.
   b) Mark a term as *useful* if it is an adverb, an adjective, a full verb, or a noun which is contained in the dictionary of the NLP tool.
   c) Otherwise, mark the term as *potentially useful*.
5. For the *useful* and *potentially useful* terms, determine how often these are present in the document collection and discard those which appear too seldom to be of interest (i.e. once or twice only).

[1] http://www.ims.uni-stuttgart.de/Tools/DecisionTreeTagger.html

6. Investigate the *useful* and *potentially useful* terms manually; in particular for those terms not present in the dictionary determine whether these are special terms of the domain or whether they are spelling errors, etc.

While the last step requires manual effort, this is limited to a relatively small set of terms. In the domain of SIMATIC customer support, for example, we had to manually investigate an index term list of less than 2,000 entries, which should be manageable in a few hours (cf. Section 5.7.2).

Concerning this procedure, the following issues are highly important:

1. Index term selection is not performed solely on the basis of statistics, keyword counting, etc. Rather, semantic information is used.
2. The above method only describes how index vocabulary can be obtained from a given document collection. It is, of course, possible to also utilize additional sources such as manuals, glossaries, etc. in which domain-specific terms are defined.
3. Every index term is not only classified according to its usefulness but also assigned a special tag indicating whether it represents a domain-specific or a general purpose term. In this way, development of index vocabulary for various domains is incremental in that the general purpose terms obtained from an analysis of one domain can be utilized without any further effort for another domain.

Information Extraction. While major parts of the contents of documents are given in plain text, some more structured information may be included in the documents too. In particular in technical domains, the text often contains expressions such as *"220 Volt"* or *"CPU 991-999"*. Obviously, a better representation for this kind of information is to use attribute-value pairs which, however, have to be obtained from the texts automatically.

For this, we applied techniques which originate in the area of *Information Extraction* (cf. Riloff and Lehnert (1994) for an overview). More precisely, we defined a number of *triggers* which indicate that a piece of text might contain an expression suitable for an attribute-value based representation.

As an example consider a phrase like

"The CPU 999 is constructed to work with 12 Volt instead of 8."

Obviously, both *CPU 999* and *12 Volt* should be considered as features of the corresponding case. To achieve this, physical units (such as *Volt*) as well as other names (such as *CPU*) have been defined as triggers. Additional information is provided for these triggers as constraints, for example that voltage should have a numerical value which is usually written in front of the *Volt* string. Once such a trigger is observed, a more complex sentence analysis starts, the objective of which is to *extract* the information associated with that trigger. As a result of this Information Extraction process, a case does not only contain the index terms present in the corresponding documents but also some more structured information in the form of attribute-value pairs.

Machine-Readable Thesauri. Obviously, similarity of documents should indicate similarity of contents of these documents. Because of the *Paraphrase Problem*, however, it is clear that similar contents may be expressed in various ways. Consequently, a thesaurus relating synonymous terms to each other is highly useful.

For English, WORDNET[2] is such a tool. It provides information about similar words, antonyms, etc., based on a solid linguistic ground. We utilized parts of WORDNET for some aspects of similarity assessment. Of course, such a tool can only cover general purpose terms while domain-specific expressions will not be related to each other. For the latter terms, we manually analyzed documentations, glossaries, etc. and encoded the obtained knowledge in terms of the similarity measure.

For the applications dealing with German texts (as the SIMATIC application described in Section 5.7.2) we had the problem that a tool like WORDNET is not available. Consequently, we had to build our own thesaurus which was, however, limited to the specific domain. To do so, we combined a manual knowledge engineering process with some heuristic procedures which could be performed automatically. For example, we utilized the fact that German texts make extensive use of compound nouns. To make use of this, we automatically derived similarities between words which are part of each other.

5.4.3 Requirements for Textual CBR

In Section 5.3, we mentioned that a major advantage of traditional IR techniques is that they can be applied to virtually any domain. The only requirement is that a document collection is available. Thus, all the information which is necessary to build a running IR system can be computed on the basis of this document collection.

Unfortunately, this is not the case for Textual CBR systems. In addition to the aspects of knowledge engineering discussed in Section 5.4.2, some further requirements have to be satisfied. In particular, the CBR-ANSWERS system, which will be described in detail in Section 5.5, is based on the following explicit assumptions:

Availability of Textual Documents. As with the more traditional IR models, a crucial requirement is that documents are available which can be utilized for building a case base. Note that, in contrast to the systems briefly described in Section 5.3.4, we do not attempt to perform a separate *case authoring* process but rather make direct use of available documents.

Availability of Knowledge. In order to really make use of the knowledge-based approach of Textual CBR, domain-specific knowledge has to be available from which information concerning index vocabulary, similarity assessment, etc. can be obtained. According to our experiences from projects, part

[2] http://www.cogsci.princeton.edu/~wn

of the required knowledge is readily available. For example, companies often maintain databases which contain descriptions of all their products, including names, components, etc. As with other knowledge-based approaches, the expertise required beyond this has to be obtained in a knowledge acquisition process. For this, domain experts have to be available.

Domain-specific Application. The previous requirement implicitly implies that a Textual CBR application is built with a specific domain in mind. As similarity knowledge is used to express relationships between the various entities in the domain, an implemented system will not be easiy protable to another problem domain.

Semi-structured Documents. A major advantage of Textual CBR is that it can handle *semi-structured* as well as unstructured documents. In our projects, we even assumed that, although all the major information is contained in the textual description, additional structured components are also available. It is even more beneficial if each particular document has a certain structure. This is the case, for example, with *Frequently Asked Questions*, where each document is, in fact, a question-answer pair. However, in other situations, there may even be more complex document structures.

5.5 The CBR-ANSWERS Project

As a result of our research activities in the area of Textual CBR, we have developed the CBR-ANSWERS system, a tool suitable for handling of knowledge contained in textual documents given the above requirements. In particular, CBR-ANSWERS addresses the hotline scenario sketched in Section 5.2. The system heavily relies on the model of Case Retrieval Nets as described in Section 3.4. In particular, concepts like *Information Entities* (IEs) will again be used here for describing the functionality of the system.

5.5.1 Overall Architecture of CBR-ANSWERS

Figure 5.1 gives an overview of the principle architecture of CBR-ANSWERS. The entire system is implemented in a Client-Server architecture. Using the system consists of two separate phases:

Off-line Preprocessing. During an off-line process, the textual documents are parsed in order to obtain an appropriate representation of the documents. Note, that *parsing* here refers to a much more sophisticated process than usually in IR systems (see below). The result of this process is a properly structured case memory in the form of a Case Retrieval Net which can be utilized by the *Retrieval Server*.

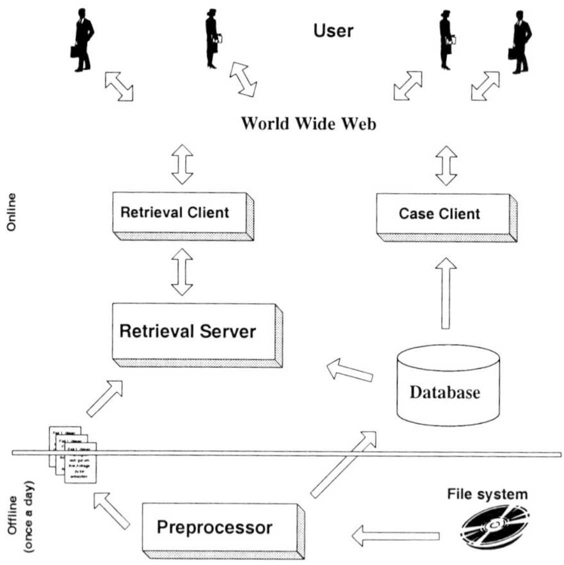

Fig. 5.1. Overall architecture of the CBR-ANSWERS system

Online Retrieval. For online retrieval, the *Retrieval Server* itself is permanently running. Users access the system, e.g., via the World Wide Web, and by submitting a query, the `httpd` server starts a *Retrieval Client* which is basically a CGI script[3]. This connects via TCP/IP sockets to the *Retrieval Server* to pose the query and receive the results. Finally, the *Retrieval Client* displays these results in an appropriate style (HTML, Java, etc.) to the user.

Besides the components required for the retrieval process itself, CBR-ANSWERS includes a number of additional modules. As an example, Figure 5.1 shows the *Case Client* which is utilized to display the documents which the user requested after having selected from the list of documents resulting from a retrieval process. This additional functionality has been implemented (a) to obtain a more modular structure of the system in which issues of retrieval are separated from displaying documents, and (b) to support situations in which the document collection used during preprocessing is different from the one used for displaying documents. The latter situation might occur, e.g., when CD-ROM catalogue are shipped to users; i.e., when preprocessing is probably based on company-internal documents while the customers should only see a public version of these.

5.5.2 Case Structure and Case Representation

In order to access the information contained in the textual documents, each document is *parsed* to obtain a properly structured case using the given IE

[3] Of course, the *Retrieval Client* may also be any other kind of program appropriate for communicating with the *Retrieval Server* and providing a GUI to the user.

dictionary. Note, however, that *parsing* here refers to a much more sophisticated process than usually in IR systems as this includes

- knowledge about the structure of the documents, e.g., that FAQs should be represented as question-answer pairs;
- a mapping from texts to sets of IEs where an IE may be more than just a *keyword* — the expression *Customer Administration Module* mentioned in Section 5.4 is an example;
- shallow NLP techniques (*Part-of-Speech* tagging) to identify basic linguistic structures in the given documents;
- some simple Information Extraction techniques to recognize structured items in the text, such as certain attribute-value pairs.

Another important issue is that an IE is a kind of symbol representing a specific meaning in the application domain. Consequently, a single IE represents a certain keyword or phrase, including grammatical variations, abbreviations, and even foreign language expressions. The set of all IEs may be further distinguished according to specific types, such as:

- keywords, such as *billing*;
- domain-specific expressions, such as *Customer Administration Module*, which would not normally be considered as a single keyword but have a specific meaning;
- special codes, numbers etc. which refer to a particular object in the domain;
- attribute-value pairs, like *Version=1.1*, which can be obtained by an Information Extraction process;
- further attributes required for domain modeling.

An important aspect of this *parsing* process is that it is performed automatically; i.e., no manual case authoring has to be performed.

5.5.3 Similarity and Retrieval

Once the documents have been converted into cases, the query can be handled in the same manner. Then, similarity of queries and cases is computed based on the similarity of the constituent IEs, i.e., the similarity of a case F to a query Q is defined as:

$$SIM(Q,C) = \sum_{e_i \in Q} \sum_{e_j \in C} \mathsf{sim}(e_i, e_j) \tag{5.2}$$

where e_i and e_j are the IEs used to represent the query Q and the case C, respectively. The function sim specifies the *local* similarity of any two IEs.

To get a better understanding of how the various types of IEs contribute to case similarity, it is helpful to sketch how the similarity function of Equation 5.2 is composed according to the types of IEs which really influence each other. In more detail, the overall similarity measure takes into account:

- similarity based on common IEs;
- similarity based on related (similar) IEs;
- similarity based on attribute values as specified in the documents;
- similarity based on attribute values obtained during automatic Information Extraction.

Note that the components of the similarity function become more and more knowledge-intensive in the order they are listed above. In Section 5.5.4, we will show how these components contribute to the overall performance of the system.

The retrieval process directly utilizes the IEs of cases and their similarity relationships as they are encoded by means of a Case Retrieval Net (cf. Section 3.4). In particular, efficiency and flexibility are valuable benefits of this model (Lenz and Burkhard 1996a).

5.5.4 Evaluation

Evaluation Methodology. Despite the users' acceptance of the systems implemented using CBR-ANSWERS (see Section 5.7), a theoretical evaluation is required to clearly show advantages and disadvantages of the approach. For this purpose, measures similar to those known from the IR community should obviously be used. However, there are some crucial differences with respect to the underlying assumptions:

Firstly, measures like *precision* and *recall* generally assume that relevance judgments are known for a set of test queries. In our projects, this appeared to be a major drawback as these projects were performed in highly specialized domains where relevance judgment is possible only by a domain expert. Furthermore, it is hard, if not impossible, to get these experts perform a task which is mainly interesting from an academic point of view.

Secondly, the original *recall* measures the percentage of the retrieved relevant documents with respect to all relevant ones. In the hotline scenario, however, the goal is not to retrieve *all* relevant items but rather to answer a query successfully. Hence, *one* relevant document is sufficient (for a similar discussion see Burke et al. 1997b).

Concerning the second problem, we modified the notion of *recall* such that for a single query *recall* is 1.0 if a relevant document has been retrieved, and 0 otherwise.

The first problem was harder to overcome. To construct a set of queries for evaluation, we utilized the observation that, while relevance judgments can only be given by a domain expert, virtually anyone can determine whether two queries have a similar semantics. Consequently, we randomly selected a set of FAQs and changed their question components in several steps, from minor grammatical variations to complete reformulations. In the latter case, we changed as many expressions as possible but kept the names of devices, modules, components, etc. An example of such a reformulation might be:

Original query: *In what modus do I have to shoot the 128 KByte EPROM for the CPU-944?*

Modified query: *How do I have to run the 944 CPU for shooting a 128 KB EPROM?*

As this example shows, the semantics of the query may change slightly. But the answer to the original query will still answer the modified one.

When applying this procedure, one knows which FAQs are relevant for each of the modified queries. In most situations it was just the original document, but in about 25 percent, a second relevant FAQ could be found as nearly exactly the same FAQ occurred in a different context again. Based on this, we built a set of test queries from the SIMATIC KNOWLEDGE MANAGER domain and used this test set for a number of performance tests. In particular, the ablation study described in the following provides useful insights into the behavior of the system.

Ablation Study. As described in Section 5.5.3, the similarity measure implemented in CBR-ANSWERS generally consists of several components with varying degree of knowledge contained. To determine the contribution of each component, we performed an ablation study by subsequently eliminating higher level components.

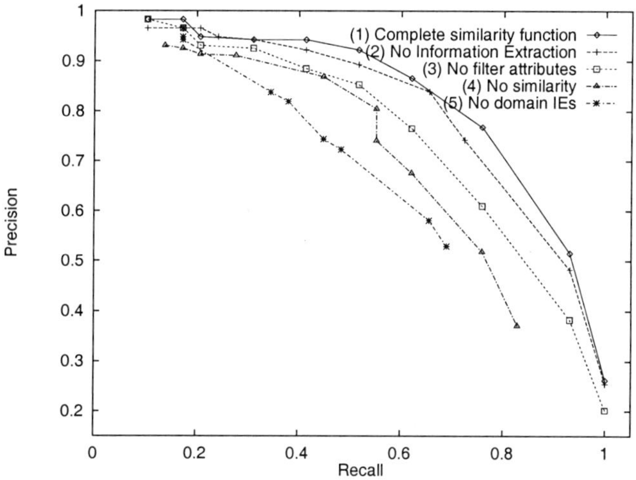

Fig. 5.2. Results of the CBR-ANSWERS ablation study

In Figure 5.2 some of the results obtained from evaluating the CBR-ANSWERS system with the SIMATIC domain (cf. Section 5.7.2) are shown. As the *precision–recall* curves show, the performance of the system degrades if less knowledge is integrated into the similarity measure. More precisely, the performance is degrading if more and more knowledge intensive components are eliminated:

- If no *Information Extraction* is performed, the system's performance degrades only slightly (curve 1 vs. curve 2).
- If the domain structure is not used to filter out similar documents from other areas[4], the same *recall* values are achieved at a lower level of *precision* (curve 1 vs. curve 3).
- Another step can be observed if structural information contained in the documents is not considered (curve not shown here).
- If the similarity of index terms is not considered and instead only exact matches are taken into account, the performance further degrades (curve 3 vs. curve 4).
- Finally, a major loss in performance results if the domain-specific terms are removed from the set of IEs (curve 4 vs. curve 5).

In fact, the performance of the system is as expected. Another observation which is not shown in Figure 5.2 was that performance further degrades if structural information, such as attribute-value pairs describing release numbers of devices etc., is not represented explicitly but handled as ordinary text.

The CBR-Answers system has been applied for several application projects which we will present briefly in Section 5.7. However, before this, we will discuss some related work in the area of Textual CBR.

5.6 Related Work

As mentioned in the introductory part of this chapter, some other projects addressed topics concerned with Textual CBR in recent years. In the following we discuss some of these.

5.6.1 FAQFinder

The FAQFinder project (Burke et al. 1997a; Burke et al. 1997b) also tries to apply CBR technology, in combination with other techniques, to document management. In particular, FAQFinder's goal is to answer natural language questions by retrieving these from frequently asked questions (FAQ) files from USENET news groups FAQs.

FAQFinder also uses a thesaurus (namely, WordNet) to base its reasoning on a semantic knowledge base and assumes that documents are given in a semi-structured format (namely, as questions-answer (QA) pairs).

FAQFinder differs from our projects in so far as it does not focus on a specific domain. Instead, it applies a two stage process:

[4] Note that in the SIMATIC Knowledge Manager application, documents may describe related observations – but as they apply to different components, such a document is of no use if it describes a behavior of a different component (cf. Page 134).

- In the first step, a shallow analysis, mainly of the keywords contained in the query, is used to infer the most likely news groups related to the request.
- After the user has decided on one of the presented news groups (i.e., after s/he selected a topic to focus on), a more sophisticated analysis of the related FAQ file starts to compare the contained QA pairs with the query entered by the user.

In some sense, this interactive scenario relates to the focus on a specific domain in that the user confirms the topic suggested by FAQFinder in the first stage. With the CRB-ANSWERS project, we have focussed still further on a specific domain in that each application has been designed specifically for a particular domain. For example, in technical areas, a lot of terms exist that would hardly be represented in general purpose thesauri, such as WORDNET. Also, a careful knowledge engineering process has been undertaken to employ domain-specific knowledge for similarity assessment. This would not be possible in the scenario of FAQFINDER, where the semantic base (i.e., WORDNET) is the same for all news group topics.

5.6.2 SPIRE

The SPIRE system introduced by Daniels and Rissland (1997) uses a completely different approach for dealing with textual cases. Based on the observation from the field of IR that people have problems in formulating *good queries* to IR systems, the idea behind SPIRE is to use a combination of CBR and IR technology:

- Given a user's request, a HYPO-style CBR module is used to analyze this request semantically and select a small number of relevant cases representing text documents.
- The most relevant cases from the first stage are then used to pose a query to the INQUERY retrieval engine.
- After having retrieved relevant documents, cases are used again to extract the most relevant passages from the documents.

Compared to the projects described in this chapter, this is a completely different approach in which CBR is in fact used as an interface to IR. Thus, the *Paraphrase Problem* can be overcome by letting the CBR module suggest alternative phrases. Whether the *Ambiguity Problem* can be solved, too, is still an open question. Furthermore, domain knowledge is limited to the cases suggesting good indices for the IR system. It cannot be used for similarity assessment, etc.

5.6.3 Automatic Index Assignment

Brüninghaus and Ashley (1997) address the handling of textual documents in yet another way than described so far. Here, the objective is to have a set of more abstract feature descriptions and utilize Machine Learning techniques in order to automatically assign these indices to textual cases.

In particular, the project builds upon the CATO project (Aleven and Ashley 1996), a CBR system in the domain of legal argument. More specifically, CATO uses so-called *factors*; a factor is a kind of fact pattern which describes a certain legal situation on a more abstract level.

Again, this is a completely different approach to the systems presented in this chapter. In particular, CATO assumes that a carefully selected set of factors (or even a factor hierarchy) is available. Nevertheless, ideas from this project might become useful if the functionality currently provided by the systems presented in Section 5.7 has to be extended in such a way that aspects of text classification become useful. For example, one could imagine that FAQs are classified according to whether they contain problem descriptions, requests for extended functionality, questions about available products, and so on. This information surely could provide further information and thus improve the performance of the systems.

5.7 Applications and Projects

Using CBR-ANSWERS as a common base, we performed several projects concerned with the application of CBR technology to document management tasks. Of course, each application had its own characteristics with respect to the particular application scenario, the application domain, available knowledge resources and so on. However, all applications followed more or less the hotline scenario of Section 5.2. In the following, we will sketch some of the specific properties of each application. Note, however, that most information used during application development has been confidential – so we are only able to give principle descriptions on how specific problems can be solved, i.e., without detailed examples.

5.7.1 The FALLQ Project

The FALLQ project has been performed in a cooperation between Humboldt University Berlin and LH Specifications (LHS), a market leader on the telecommunications software market (Lenz and Burkhard 1997a; Lenz and Burkhard 1997b). The primary objective of this project was to develop an information system that can be used for hotline support, e.g., for handling *Frequently Asked Questions*. As a result of the developed prototype, however, LHS realized that they may well utilize the same technology for maintaining various kinds of information within the company.

The Application Area. LHS is developing and selling a customer care and billing system for providers of telecommunications services. By spring 1997, this system had more than thirty projects and installations world-wide. Because of the dynamics of the telecommunications market, the complexity of the application software as well as the number of installations are steadily growing. To cope with this development, there is an urgent need for an information system which helps:

- keeping track of customers' enquiries;
- finding answers to problems that have already been solved before, either for another customer or by different staff members;
- maintaining information useful for internal purposes, e.g., descriptions of defects which might be useful for the system developers.

Within the company, information and knowledge are stored in many different places using various types of documents, such as:

- descriptions of *defects* and problems during the development of modules;
- specifications of modules summarizing the functionality provided;
- *Frequently Asked Questions*–like documents;
- documentations delivered with the products, training material, etc.

Last but not least, a wealth of knowledge is kept by the experienced staff members which have been developing the software for several years. Because of the rapid growth of the market, however, more and more new staff are employed who lack this historical knowledge.

Current State. As the application directly fits the hotline scenario, a version of CBR-ANSWERS, namely the FALLQ system, could be installed at LHS. FALLQ is specific in so far as it is integrated into the environment at LHS, and as knowledge specific to the application domain has been added to the system. By spring 1998, FALLQ manages approximately 45,000 documents of various types and is accessed by about 20 users a day. Currently, an extension of the system, MERLIN++, is being developed which will support more advanced functionalities and will be made accessible to a wider group of customers.

5.7.2 The SIMATIC Project

CBR-ANSWERS also serves as the basic model for a project being performed in cooperation with Siemens AG, in particular with the customer support group of *Automation & Drives*. Again the objective is similar to the hotline scenario described in Section 5.2, i.e., the goal is to answer questions posed by customers by reusing knowledge contained in FAQs and other types of documents.

In fact, when facing some problem customers of Siemens may already browse these documents which are provided at a particular web site[5]. CBR-ANSWERS provides a means of intelligently searching and analyzing these documents rather than browsing numerous directories.

[5] www.ad.siemens.de/support/html_00

The SIMATIC Knowledge Manager. An objective when developing the SIMATIC KNOWLEDGE MANAGER is that the hotline staff should be contacted only if a user's question can not be answered by showing them specific documents. This is related to the *call avoidance* strategy discussed in Section 4.6. More precisely, the process model of the SIMATIC KNOWLEDGE MANAGER (cf. Figure 5.3) is such that the customers use a specific WWW site to describe their problems in terms of a textual query, some information on the particular domain they are requesting help for, and possibly information on the devices involved. Given this, an available document collection is searched and the best matching documents are presented to the user, assuming that highly similar documents will very likely be helpful in answering the users' requests. Only if this does not yield a solution to the problem is the hotline staff contacted and asked for help. Finally, if the request is answered, this question-answer pair is added to the document collection and, thus, the SIMATIC KNOWLEDGE MANAGER automatically acquires new knowledge.

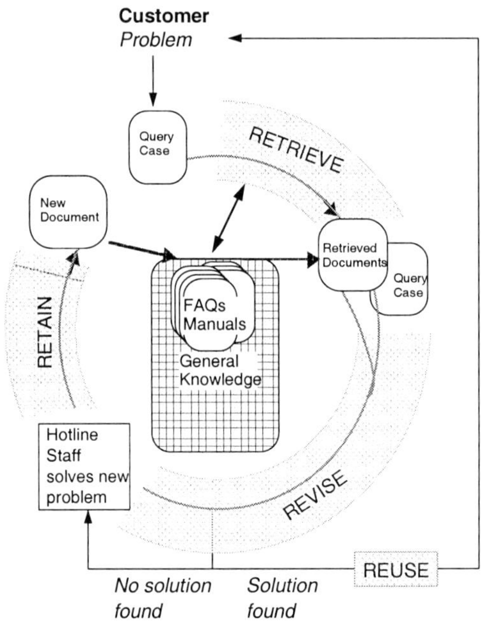

Fig. 5.3. Process model of the SIMATIC KNOWLEDGE MANAGER based on the R^4 model

The SIMATIC KNOWLEDGE MANAGER directly utilizes a number of document types which are available at Siemens. These include: the well-known FAQs, *Informal Notes* on recently observed problems as a simple textual description of these problems, and *User Information Notes*. While all three document types basically contain the same information, there is a difference in reliability. As the name indicates, *Informal Notes* are just draft notes which may give hints but are not trustworthy. On the other hand, FAQs express well-established knowledge resulting from frequent usage. *User Information Notes* lie somewhere in between these two extremes.

A key property distinguishing the SIMATIC KNOWLEDGE MANAGER from the FALLQ project is that several languages have to be supported by the system. In the first stage, a focus is set on German rather than English texts. This implies additional effort because German grammar is much more complicated and even more irregular than English. Later, English and other languages will be supported, too.

The approach of CBR-ANSWERS has the major advantage that textual documents are converted to cases represented by sets of IEs. These IEs are, in fact, a kind of *symbols* having a certain meaning in the real world. Consequently, it is possible to reuse exactly the same symbols including their similarity relationships for another language[6]. The only thing required is a description of how these symbols can be derived given the texts, that is a language-specific *parsing* method. Basically this should utilize a translation of the general purpose terms while specific terms, such as names of functions, devices, and modules, remain unchanged.

Current State. As a result of the project, a prototypical system was implemented which has been tested and evaluated by the SIMATIC hotline staff in a 3 weeks testing period. As with FALLQ, this system was intended to prove the applicability of the Textual CBR approach for the SIMATIC hotline. In particular, the system only worked with a subset of all available documents (about 500 only) and has not been integrated into the call tracking system running at the SIMATIC hotline. Nevertheless, with respect to the effort required to answer customer enquiries, savings of 10% to 30% have been estimated during the test period.

Figure 5.4 shows a snapshot of this application. Currently, the system is being extended in two directions:

- The SIMATIC KNOWLEDGE MANAGER scenario is being implemented for external customers. Besides the aspects of Textual CBR, issues of security etc. have to be considered for this.
- For *in-house* usage, the hotline application will be extended to cover the entire SIMATIC domain and will be integrated into the running call tracking system.

[6] Remember that CBR-ANSWERS is operating in a very specific domain only and that a general world understanding is not necessary.

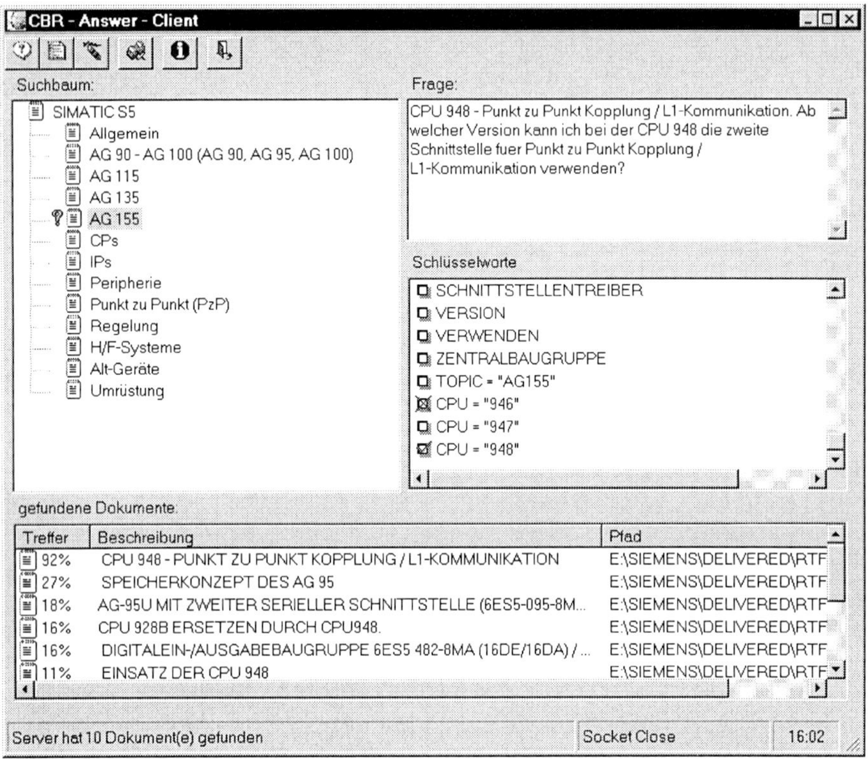

Fig. 5.4. Snapshot of the SIMATIC application working with German documents

– For external usage, a CD-ROM will be produced which is then shipped regularly to customers. Using a search engine based on CBR-ANSWERS, customers can browse this CD-ROM when facing a problem. Thus, only when this problem cannot be solved in this way, they will have to contact the SIMATIC hotline.

5.7.3 The EXPERIENCEBOOK Project

The EXPERIENCEBOOK (Kunze 1997) project differs from the above described applications in so far as it does not reside directly in an industrial setting. Rather, the objective was to provide the system administrators of the Department of Computer Science of Humboldt University with a tool for knowledge management.

System administrators need very detailed knowledge on a wide area of hard- and software systems. This is partly due to the very heterogeneous equipment used in our department. Even worse, the systems are changing fast and thus knowledge is changing rapidly.

Another specific property of the EXPERIENCEBOOK project is that the experts themselves are the users of the system; i.e., they query the system when facing problems and they provide some part of the input to the system by inserting new documents. Thus, the EXPERIENCEBOOK serves as an *external memory* as discussed in Section 3.3. That is, it provides content-oriented search for specific documents. Furthermore, the EXPERIENCEBOOK allows for the exchange of information and knowledge between the system administrators and, thus, helps maintaining a *Corporate Know How.*

To equip the system with a certain basic amount of knowledge, external knowledge sources such as manuals, newsgroup postings, etc. have been used to build an initial case base. For details, the reader is referred to the work described by Kunze (1997).

To make the manually inserted cases more useful, additional information may be added such as, for example, the author of a case, the specific reason of a problem, or the steps required to solve a problem. These additional sections are not considered during retrieval but may provide uaseful insights when reading the retrieved cases.

For historical reasons, the case base of the EXPERIENCEBOOK mainly consists of English case documents completed by some German ones. The preferred language for queries and new cases is English.

5.8 Summary

In this chapter, we have presented major results from the area of Textual CBR, a particular branch of research which deals with handling of textual documents using CBR technology. We have discussed traditional methods of Information Retrieval and why CBR can be a more powerful technique under certain conditions. Finally, we have presented an overview of the CBR-ANSWERS project and sketched some of the implemented systems which are now running at industrial partners.

6. Using Configuration Techniques for Adaptation

Wolfgang Wilke, Barry Smyth, Pádraig Cunningham

6.1 Introduction

Configuration is a design task that is the target of much AI research. It is a comparatively tractable design task and thus can be completely automated in a knowledge based system (KBS). Indeed the earliest commercially successful KBS was XCON, a rule-based system for configuring VAX computers developed by Digital Equipment Corporation.

KBS technology has moved on and the dominant techniques used in configuration now are constraint handling techniques. However expertise in configuration is evidently experience based and there has also been considerable research on using CBR for configuration. Normally, configuration problems are comparatively closed problems and so can be completely modeled in a KBS. For this reason, a CBR system for configuration can be a completely automated system rather than an interactive assistant, as is the case in more difficult open design tasks. It will be seen later in this chapter that this is a defining characteristic of CBR systems for configuration.

We believe that this characteristic of configuration, as a design problem that can be completely automated in CBR, tells us something about CBR. If we view adaptation as a configuration task then it too can be automated. We pursue this idea in the second part of this chapter where we analyze two case adaptation problems as configuration tasks. We show that this *adaptation-as-configuration* perspective provides insights into what can and cannot be achieved using automatic adaptation in CBR.

In the next section, we present an overview of configuration and CBR approaches to configuration problems. We present an in depth example of a CBR solution to a configuration problem that illustrates these approaches and we review three typical CBR configuration systems. With these examples, we establish the idea that configuration is a class of problems where case adaptation can be automated due to the closed nature of the problem. An overview of current adaptation practice is given. In Section 6.4.3, we introduce the configuration approach of *conceptual hierarchy oriented configuration* with configuration operators. In the remainder of the chapter, we apply a similar approach to the task of adaptation in CBR, which establishes the idea of adaptation-as-configuration. Next, the approach to adaptation using adaptation operators, inspired by the configuration operators, is introduced in detail. Further, we demonstrate the application of such an approach in two examples of different sorts of adaptation problems. We close with a summary and a detailed discussion about viewing adaptation as a configuration task in our presented framework.

6.2 Configuration in Context

6.2.1 The Configuration Task

Before we can proceed with a general description of configuration, we need to clear up some terminological variations. Configuration is a basic design task and much research on knowledge based configuration has gone under the name of design. In the next section, we will describe the accepted continuum of design tasks and identify where configuration fits into this structure. After that we will describe the components of the configuration process.

The Continuum of Design Tasks. The *continuum of design tasks* reflects the difficulty of the problem solving task being supported (see Figure 6.1). In design there is a broad acceptance that tasks can be partitioned into three

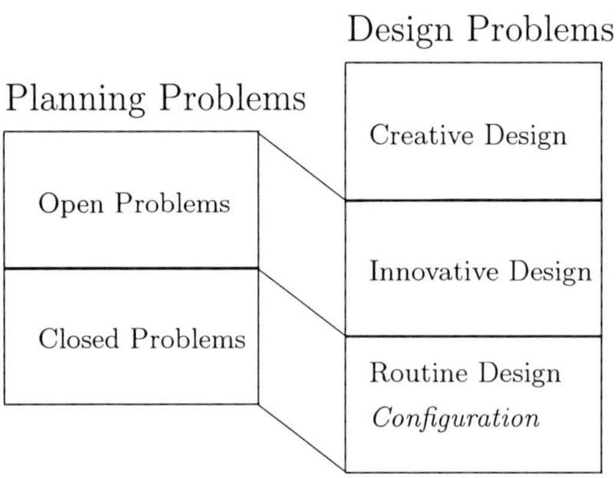

Fig. 6.1. The ordering of design tasks and the equivalence to planning problems.

categories (Brown and Chandrasekaran 1985; Gero 1990); these are as follows:

Routine Design: (a.k.a. Parametric Design) This is the simplest category of design tasks requiring knowledge based problem solving. The design process will follow well known procedures; new designs will be parametric variations or reorganizations of previous designs or parts of it.

Innovative Design: (a.k.a. Non-routine Design) Innovative design will produce an artifact significantly different from existing ones. Useful remindings in innovative design are likely to be abstract. CBR systems for this non-routine design task will be interactive systems that perhaps support remindings across sub-domains; i.e. case-based design assistants.

Creative Design: Creative design will produce a new type of artifact. This will create a new state space of designs. Evidently, this is qualitatively different from non-routine design as it expands or shifts the problem space.

In this scheme, *configuration* is a routine design task. The product will not be radically different from other designs but will be a working organization of a predefined set of components that meets a particular set of requirements. In Figure 6.1, we also show a categorization of *planning tasks.* Planning and design are related in that they both involve synthesis. We can talk about closed planning problems as problems that can be completely formalized in a knowledge based system (KBS). By contrast, an open planning problem cannot be completely captured in a KBS. We suggest that these closed planning problems are equivalent to routine design and open planning problems are equivalent to innovative design. In current planning research, there is no equivalent to creative design.

Configuration. Configuration can be defined as follows. Given

- the *user requirements* for a system,
- a set of *predefined components*, and
- the *knowledge of how components can be connected*;

the goal is to find the sets of components fulfilling the user-requirements and respecting all the compatibility constraints (Faltings and Weigel 1994). If all

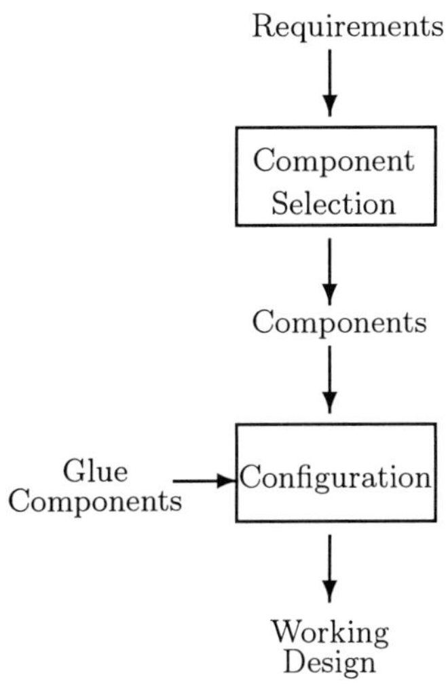

Fig. 6.2. The complete configuration process. The Component Selection stage take place outside the configuration system.

the knowledge of how the components can be connected can be formalized then this is a closed problem and can be completely solved in a knowledge based system. A key issue determining the complexity of a configuration task is the manner in which the task is specified. If the task is specified as a set of customer requirements, then it is more complex than a task specified as a set of components that must be configured into a working system. The first of these scenarios involves an extra component selection stage that has already been completed in the other situation (see Figure 6.2).

Perhaps the most famous configuration system is XCON (formerly known as R1) originally developed by John McDermott and used for over a decade by Digital Equipment Corporation (McDermott 1982; Hayes-Roth et al. 1983). XCON is a rule-based system for configuring VAX computers. The input to the system is a set of components that must be configured into a working system. During the configuration process extra "glue components" such as cables are selected to complete the system. Thus, the component selection task described in Figure 6.2 is performed outside XCON.

Since configuration problems are naturally viewed as a set of constraints that must be satisfied, it makes sense to consider configuration problems as constraint satisfaction problems (CSPs). Indeed, much research and development on configuration problems focuses on using dynamic CSP techniques (see Mittal and Falkenhainer 1990 for instance).

6.3 Configuration and CBR

6.3.1 A Complete Example

Now we will have a detailed look at a configuration problem and we will demonstrate how such a problem can be solved with a CBR system. After we have described our problem domain, we will solve a configuration problem in our domain with *compositional adaptation* and with *transformational adaptation* techniques[1].

The Problem Domain. The task is to configure an alarm system from a set of predefined components which will secure an apartment or private house. The problem description consists of the number of rooms, windows and doors for each floor of the house. Further, it is possible to install additional motion sensors in the rooms to enhance the security of the building or to incorporate a fire alarm. Figure 6.3 shows a simple example of such a problem description in an attribute value table together with the desired layout of the house. The number of windows, rooms, and external doors is described for every floor. Using a CBR approach to solve this configuration problem, a case consists of a problem description as shown in Figure 6.3, together with the description of a *valid solution* for the problem. The solution is a valid configuration of an alarm control unit, with the necessary sensors connected to different sensor

[1] For a detailed definition of these approaches see Section 6.4.2.

Attribute	Value
Doors	1
Rooms-1	2
Windows-1	2
Rooms-2	1
Windows-2	1
Fire Protection	false
Motion Protection	true

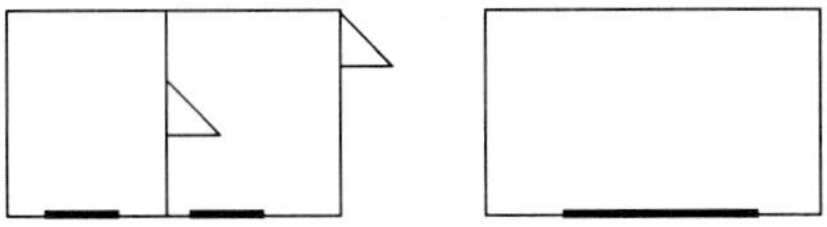

Fig. 6.3. A problem description and the associated real world problem

circuits and with an alarm circuit connected to the alarm unit[2]. The solution is modeled as objects where the five circuits are objects with placeholders for possible sensor or alarm units. Each unit consists of a description of the type of the unit and a price[3]. A solution is valid for a given problem if a set of properties holds for the solution; here are some examples:

- The maximum number of sensors connected to one circuit is limited to six.
- It is not allowed to mix motion or fire sensors with window or door sensors. So it is possible to enable/disable them separately.
- The resulting system has to secure the apartment as given in the problem description (e.g., if a fire alarm is needed, every room has to have a fire sensor in a valid solution).
- At least one door must have a door-delay sensor to ensure that the alarm system can be switched off as someone enters the house.
- Every system needs at least one sensor unit and an alarm unit.
- It is allowed to place fire and motion sensors of one floor into extra circuits of different floors. However this leads to a suboptimal solution and should be avoided. This is not allowed with door and window sensors.

A valid solution for our example problem is shown in Figure 6.4. It shows the central alarm unit with the sensor and alarm circuits. The windows are secured with window sensors (W), the door is secured with a door-delay sensor (DD) and every room is secured with an additional motion sensor (M). The alarm circuit is connected to an alarm unit with a bell and a strobe light. It is obvious that this is a valid solution for the problem.

Solving the configuration problem with CBR. The customer requirements are described by the problem description. The set of predefined components consists of: the alarm unit, the different types of sensors, and the different circuits. The knowledge of how the components can be connected

[2] We simply assume that every alarm control unit consists of four sensor circuits, two for each floor, where one contains the door and window sensors and the other one the sensors for the additional safety requirements, here the motion and/or fire sensors.

[3] We describe the representation of the solution in detail in Section 6.4.3.

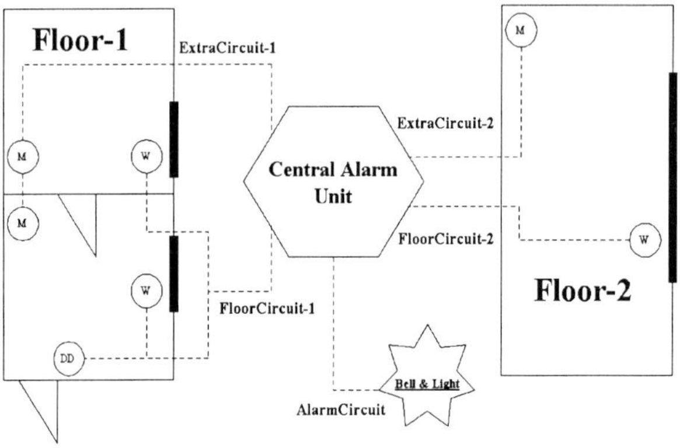

Fig. 6.4. A problem solution: A valid alarm control and the device units

is described by the constraints which define a valid solution. So, we have to solve a typical configuration problem (see Section 6.2.1).

A CBR approach involves using a case base containing known problem descriptions together with valid solutions. During problem solving, a problem description is given to the system and the most similar cases are retrieved. Normally, the solutions of the similar cases are not completely valid solutions for the entire problem. Therefore, these solutions have to be adapted to solve the new problem. In the next two sections, we describe two different approaches to adaptation which are known as compositional adaptation and transformational adaptation.

Compositional Adaptation. In Figure 6.5, we see a problem description together with the two most similar cases retrieved from the case base[4]. In

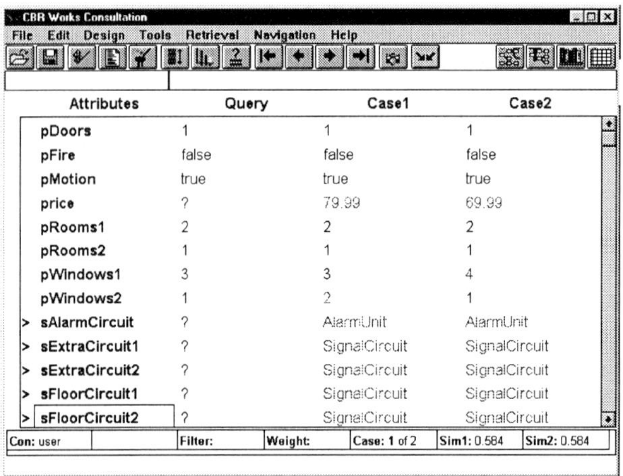

Attributes	Query	Case1	Case2
pDoors	1	1	1
pFire	false	false	false
pMotion	true	true	true
price	?	79.99	69.99
pRooms1	2	2	2
pRooms2	1	1	1
pWindows1	3	3	4
pWindows2	1	2	1
> sAlarmCircuit	?	AlarmUnit	AlarmUnit
> sExtraCircuit1	?	SignalCircuit	SignalCircuit
> sExtraCircuit2	?	SignalCircuit	SignalCircuit
> sFloorCircuit1	?	SignalCircuit	SignalCircuit
> sFloorCircuit2	?	SignalCircuit	SignalCircuit

Fig. 6.5. An example for solving the alarm system configuration task with Compositional Adaptation

[4] The problem description attributes are marked with p and the solution attributes with s.

the left column we see the entire problem description of the apartment which needs to be secured. The next two columns show the two most similar cases from the case base. The part of the first similar case describing the first floor is the same as the first floor description of the query. Therefore, the solution regarding the first floor can be obtained from this case. The second floor problem description is the same as the problem description of the second case retrieved from the case base. Therefore, the solution for the second floor could be copied from the second case. Also, the alarm circuit can be reused from either case, because it is independent from the other parts of the solution. This could be coded in a set of adaptation rules, where the preconditions check the equivalence of the problem description parts and the conclusions of the rule copy the desired solution chunks. So copying three different parts of the solution of similar cases without modification leads to a solution for the new problem. A simple composition of the solution is possible because the solutions for both floors and the alarm circuit are independent in this problem description.

Transformational Adaptation. Figure 6.6 shows a problem where compositional adaptation would not lead to a valid solution. Here the problem has

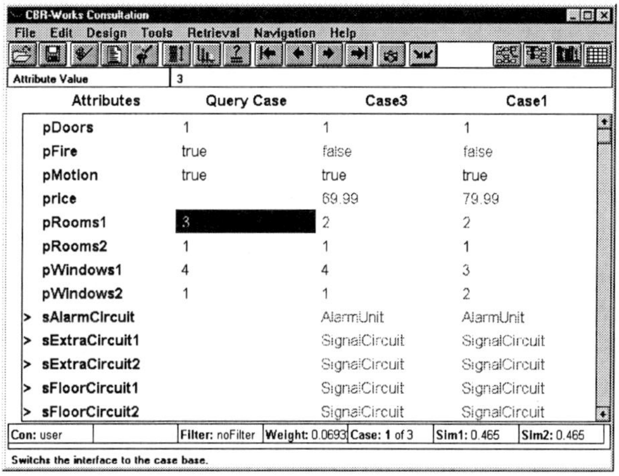

Fig. 6.6. An example for solving the alarm system configuration task with Transformational Adaptation

three rooms in the first floor and a fire and a motion protection is required. The similar cases have only two or less rooms and only a fire or a motion sensor. A valid solution which secures all rooms in the first floor needs at least six sensors, three for motion and also three for fire protection. Consequently, during adaptation, a modification of the solution of the similar cases is necessary to achieve a valid solution for the query. In our example, additional circuits for both floors have to be created and fire and motion sensor units have to be connected.

An adaptation rule which shows one piece of the described transformations of the solution is shown in Figure 6.7. The precondition of the rule tests

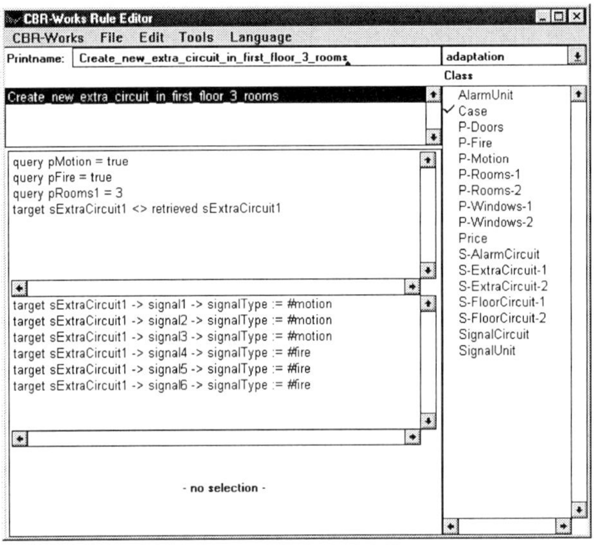

Fig. 6.7. An example for a Transformational Adaptation rule

if six sensors have to be installed in the first floor, i.e., the case that motion and fire sensors are required, and it was not possible to copy the solution from the case. Therefore, it is necessary to introduce a new extra circuit, which is needed for the sensors. This is shown in the conclusion of the rule where the extra circuit is created and appropriate sensor units are added. Furthermore, the price attributes of the sensors must also be set to the correct value. To perform the described adaptation task, many more rules are necessary just to cover the transformation requirements of this small example. Transformational Adaptation is, in general, more complex than Compositional Adaptation and consequently requires more adaptation knowledge.

6.3.2 Review of Typical CBR Configuration Systems

In Section 6.2.1, we described the general characteristics of configuration problems and in Section 6.3.1 we described the characteristics of CBR configuration systems. Configuration is a routine design problem that should be possible to model as a closed world. As such, it is possible for CBR systems for configuration to be complete systems where retrieval and adaptation are performed without user intervention. This contrasts with more difficult design tasks such as innovative design where the closed world assumption is not valid and current CBR solutions have to be interactive systems. In this section we review three prominent CBR configuration systems to present a flavor of some of the research in the area.

Clavier. CLAVIER is a CBR system for designing loads for an autoclave (Barletta and Hennessy 1989; Hennessy and Hinkle 1991). The autoclave loads are composed of composite materials, such as graphite or fiberglass, for aerospace applications.

This load planning problem is complex because the temperature profile of the autoclave is sensitive to the geometry of the objects being cured. In turn, the success of the curing process is sensitive to the temperature profile. Since the temperature behavior is not well understood and is difficult to model, this is a weak theory domain. Because of this, CLAVIER is not a typical configuration system as it does not conform to the closed world assumption.

CLAVIER operates as a load planning assistant by proposing solutions to the operator. It works by retrieving cases from the case-base and composing a solution for the target problem from these cases. It then performs substitutions on this solution to resolve any inconsistencies with the new problem description. The adaptation is compositional rather than rule or operator based and it is argued that this is more in keeping with the spirit of CBR. By this they mean that compositional adaptation avoids the need to model the interactions in the problem domain, as is needed when implementing adaptation using rules.

Compositional adaptation does have the risk that case components from different contexts will not produce good quality solutions when linked. This issue is addressed in CLAVIER by explicitly modeling context. This representation of context includes features such as the relative position of groups of parts in the oven and the material composition of other parts in the oven. Thus, CLAVIER is a fine example of a CBR configuration system that performs adaptation by composition and it is argued that this requires less knowledge engineering than the operator based alternative.

CLAVIER also supports learning by allowing solved problems to be added to the case base. This causes the competence of the system to increase over time.

Composer. Configuration is naturally viewed as a constraint satisfaction problem (CSP) so it makes sense to use CSP techniques to solve configuration problems. Since configuration problems, viewed as CSPs, are NP-hard it makes sense to use CBR to help in this search process. This is the logic underlying COMPOSER, a system that has been applied to configuration design and assembly sequence generation (Purvis and Pu 1995; Purvis and Pu 1996). COMPOSER has been used to plan the assembly sequence of electric motor assemblies and in the car configuration domain described in Mittal and Falkenhainer (1990).

There are two perspectives on how COMPOSER combines CBR and CSP. It can be viewed as a CSP system that uses retrieved cases to give the constraint satisfaction search a head start. Alternatively it can be viewed as a CBR system that uses a CSP engine to perform adaptation.

Since COMPOSER incorporates a CSP engine, it has the competence to solve problems from scratch without recourse to CBR indexing and retrieval. The case retrieval is included as a speedup mechanism because starting the CSP engine with an initial locally optimized solution will normally be quicker than working from scratch with CSP alone. Purvis and Pu point out that, in some circumstances, COMPOSER does not produce a speedup over from scratch reasoning. They identify that this happens when the edge variables of the case components are overly constrained. They argue that such a measure of *constrained-ness* of the boundaries of case components can be used to decide whether to reuse case components or not.

From the second CBR dominated perspective, the CBR system retrieves case components that can be assimilated into a single solution to the new problem. It is to be expected that there will be a problem assimilating these disparate components. COMPOSER uses a repair-based CSP algorithm to combine these components into a globally consistent solution for the new problem.

Bioprocess Planning. The final system that we review is described as a planning system rather than a configuration system. Nevertheless, it has all the defining characteristics of a configuration problem as described in section 6.2.1. This is because of the close correspondence between configuration tasks and closed world planning tasks already identified in section 6.2.1.

Aarts and Rousu have described a CBR system for developing recipes for the production of mash in brewing (Aarts and J. Rousu 1996; Rousu and Aarts 1996). The input to the system is a product specification, a product analysis, a list of ingredients, and a vessel. The product specification is a set of constraints that the product analysis must satisfy. Developing a recipe involves selecting ingredients and determining amounts, then planning actions, such as heating or cooking steps, and addition of ingredients. This conforms to our description of a configuration problem, except that the output looks more like a plan than a configuration. However, we saw with COMPOSER that there is not a clear demarcation between a configuration and a plan for producing that configuration.

This bioprocess planning system is completely automatic in that it retrieves and adapts cases. Adaptation is operator based and uses a qualitative model of the process to transform cases to meet the new specification.

6.3.3 Summing Up

We have emphasized that configuration is a problem with a level of complexity that allows for complete automation in a CBR system. This is because configuration is a comparatively simple design task that allows for a closed world assumption in KBS development.

If a CBR system for configuration is to work without user intervention, then it must be able to adapt retrieved cases. We have presented examples of CBR configuration systems that use the standard form of rule-based adaptation. However, the particular characteristics of configuration problems also suggest adaptation by composition of case components. This is because the solution to a configuration problem is a structure and a CBR system for configuration can work by assimilating parts of different cases to meet a new specification. These locally optimal parts may not compose well into a globally optimal whole, so it may be necessary to make repairs at the edges of these solution chunks so that they work together as a whole.

6.4 Adaptation within Configuration

6.4.1 Introduction

While the theory and practice of case-based reasoning has benefited greatly from recent advances in case representation, similarity assessment, and retrieval, there have been only modest advances in case adaptation and composition. The result has been a wide array of representations and techniques without any real agreement on a definite way forward. The working hypothesis for the remainder of this chapter is that there are benefits to be derived from taking a configuration perspective on adaptation tasks within the CBR cycle. This perspective will be appropriate for a restricted set of adaptation problems that have the same characteristics as configuration problems. In particular, this perspective will yield a uniformity of representational and algorithmic practice that will empower the development of an important class of practical adaptation and composition mechanisms.

Before we can proceed, however, we need to explicitly define a direct mapping between the configuration task and adaptation. By definition, configuration tasks involve organizing an identifiable and pre-defined set of components in order to satisfy some set of ordering constraints. Thus, in each configuration problem, we expect to find the following main constituents:

– a well defined set of (atomic) configurable components
– a set of ordering constraints that the final configuration must satisfy
– configuration operators that encode valid component configurations

After a closer inspection of the adaptation and composition sub-tasks of CBR it becomes clear that there is a direct mapping between these tasks and configuration (see Table 6.1). In particular, a common adaptation scenario involves using a set of adaptation operators to instantiate and re-order a set of pre-defined solution components (these components having been selected from the retrieved case) to meet the target specification goals. In turn, case composition is characterized by a collection of adapted cases which must be combined and arranged to satisfy target goals.

6.4.2 Current Models of Adaptation

From a case-based reasoning perspective, there is a relationship between the complexity of the problem solving task and the complexity of the CBR adap-

Table 6.1. Case composition and adaptation as configuration tasks

Classic Configuration	Case Composition	Case Adaptation
Configurable Components	Adapted Sub-Cases	Applicable Operators
Ordering Constraints	Target Composition Constraints	Target Adaptation Constraints
Configuration Knowledge	Hierarchical Case Structures	Adaptation Strategies

tation process. In particular, a *continuum of adaptation models* has been identified and exploited in recent research (see Figure 6.8).

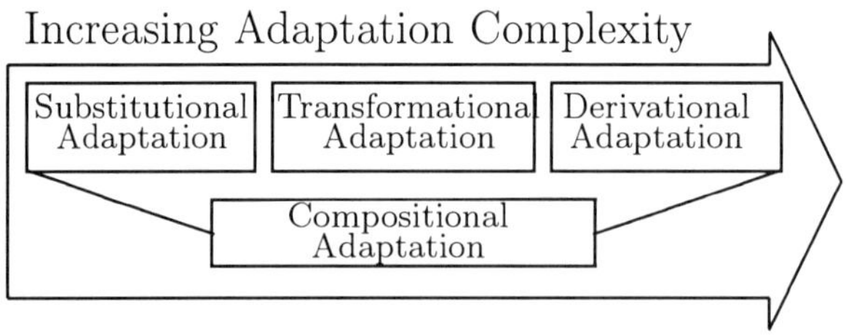

Fig. 6.8. The Adaptation Continuum

Substitutional Adaptation. CBR systems concerned with simple problem solving tasks will require simple, *substitutional adaptation*; the retrieved case will typically be very close to the target and consequently will require only very basic substitutional adaptation, where the details of existing solution elements maybe changed without the possibility of adding, deleting, or rearranging elements. Substitutional adaptation is most commonly found in systems performing identification and prediction tasks. Detailed descriptions of substitutional adaptation can be found in Bain (1986) and Sycara (1988).

Transformational Adaptation. With routine problem solving tasks, the retrieved case, while being similar to the target, will probably require more substantial modifications. *Transformational adaptation* (Goel and Chandrasekaran 1989; Hinrichs and Kolodner 1991; Smyth and Keane 1996) supports the reorganization of solution elements and permits the addition and deletion of these elements under certain conditions. Typically, transformational adaptation systems employ a fixed set of adaptation operators and transformation rules. For example, in DéJà Vu (Smyth and Cunningham 1992) , a collection of *adaptation specialists* encode common transformation operations in the plant-control domain and are used during adaptation to structurally modify the retrieved case's solution under the guidance of general *adaptation strategies*.

Derivational (Generative) Adaptation. With more complex, innovative problem solving tasks, extensive modifications are necessary during adaptation so interactions are unavoidable and difficult to resolve. To accommodate this level of adaptation complexity, it is generally necessary to augment cases with detailed knowledge, such as the reasoning trace structures of Derivational Analogy (Carbonell 1986), leading to *derivational adaptation*. Reasoning traces record information about the derivational process that lead to a particular solution, including decision information, justifications, and reasoning alternatives. During derivational adaptation, these traces are essentially replayed in the context of the new target problem, leading to a generative solution process. CBR systems using such an adaptation approach include PRODIGY/ANALOGY (Veloso 1994) and CAPLAN/CBC (Muñoz-Avila et al. 1994; Muñoz-Avila and Weberskirch 1996).

Compositional Adaptation. In addition to these three basic models of adaptation, recent research has demonstrated the power of delivering solutions through the retrieval, adaptation, and subsequent composition of multiple cases. This leads to a fourth model of adaptation, *compositional adaptation* (Redmond 1990; Sycara and Navinchandra 1991), in which newly adapted solution components from multiple cases are combined to produce a new composite solution. Compositional Adaptation is used for example in CADSYN (Maher and Zhang 1993), COMPOSER (Purvis and Pu 1995; Purvis and Pu 1996) or DéJà VU (Smyth and Cunningham 1992).

6.4.3 Adaptation from a Configuration Perspective

In this section, we introduce *conceptual hierarchy oriented configuration* using *configuration operators*. Inspired by this approach we will introduce *Operator Based Adaptation* as a domain independent and uniform adaptation technique. Further, we demonstrate the usefulness of the Adaptation Operators in our examples of Compositional Adaptation and Transformational Adaptation.

Conceptual Hierarchy Oriented Configuration. A successful technique in the area of configuration research is conceptual hierarchy oriented configuration. This approach was first used in PLAKON (Cunis et al. 1991), IDA-II (Kratz 1991), their consecutive systems KONWERK (Günter 1995) and IDAX (Paulokat 1995), and in several related systems such as AMOR (Tank 1991) and MOKON (Sommer 1993).

The configuration process is guided by a set of configuration operators which describe different single configuration steps. These configuration steps mainly modify the structure of the solution and also guide the specification of concrete solution attributes. The configuration process is explicitly represented along with all dependencies between single configuration steps. This leads to an effective control and management of decisions during the configuration. Furthermore, the configuration steps are guided by the object-oriented model of the solution. We will now informally describe a core selection of these operators with an example in the solution description of our configuration domain, given in Section 6.3.1.

The Object Oriented Model of a Solution in Our Problem Domain. The object-oriented model[5] of a solution in our domain consists of four *concept instances* for the different sensor circuits and a concept instance for the alarm circuit. A concept instance is a set of attributes in a concrete case. These attributes could contain *simple attributes*, like integers, symbols, Boolean, etc., or *complex attributes*, where the attribute represents an additional concept instance. In our example, the `Case`-concept which represents the complete alarm system is decomposed with a *has-part* relation into five different complex attributes for the circuits. Additionally, there is one parameter, the price. Four of the circuits are signal circuits (two circuits named `FloorCircuit-1/-2` for the door and window sensors, and two named `ExtraCircuit-1/-2` for the fire and motion sensors) with concept instances for up to 6 `SensorUnits`. An additional circuit describes the alarm circuit, which is represented by one instance of the concept `AlarmUnit`. A partial structure of the concept instances of a solution, here for the `Case`, is shown in Figure 6.9 (a).

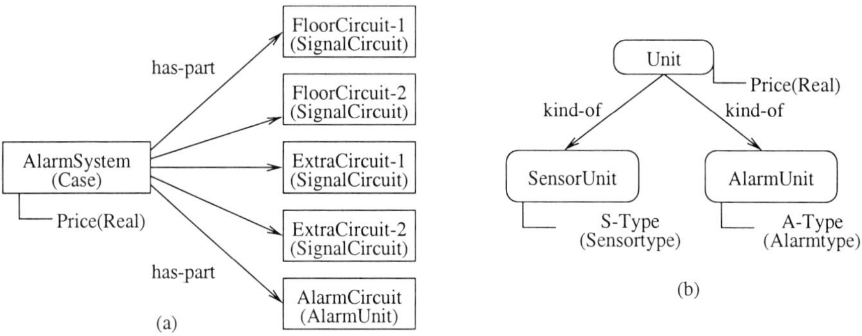

Fig. 6.9. A description of the concept instances of a solution in our example domain (a) and an example of a kind-of relation between concepts (b).

The *concepts* for the sensor and the alarm unit are derived from a concept for a general unit in the domain model. This is described by a *kind-of* relation between both subconcepts `AlarmUnit` and `SensorUnit` and their super-concept `Unit`, illustrated in Figure 6.9 (b). All subconcepts inherit the attributes of their super-concepts. In our example, the `AlarmUnit` and `SensorUnit` inherit the attribute `Price` from the concept `Unit`. Each concept like `SensorUnit` or `AlarmUnit` defines further parameters which more closely describe the type of the sensor, but none has any subcomponents. More specialized concepts, like `DoorSensor`, `DoorDelaySensor`, or `WindowSensor`, could also be derived from `SensorUnit`.

[5] A detailed description of the object-oriented modeling has been given by Booch (1991).

In general, the has-part relation decomposes a concept instance into subparts and the kind-of relation allows the object-oriented modeling of different concepts.

The Configuration Operators. The configuration process starts at the root node of the solution description with an initial operation, which performs the configuration of the whole solution structure. The application of a particular configuration operator can result in the instantiation of further configuration steps in order to completely configure the solution at hand. The operators describe what has to be done for a successful configuration and also determine the structure of the solution, excluding the concrete determination of all concrete parameters. Thus, the operators trace the solution-finding process and dependencies between decisions are made explicit. This leads to an effective management of the configuration process and results in an effective, guided search during problem solving. It should be noted that the operators supporting the configuration process are abstract operators and do not implement the concrete actions which have to be carried out to come to a final solution. The configuration operations which must be performed are managed in an agenda which holds all configuration steps needed to complete the solution configuration. We describe here a core subset of the operators, which are used in PLAKON and also in IDAX[6], namely:

Configure(`Object`): This operator initiates the configuration process for an object (either an attribute or a concept instance). Its effect is to generate and introduce the additional configuration operators, which ensure the remainder of the configuration.

Parameterize(`Attribute`): This operator specifies that the attribute has to be instantiated with a value. For example, Parameterize(`Price`) applied to the Attribute `Price` in the Concept `Sensor-6` would indicate that a real value for the price of the Sensor-6 has to be assigned.

Compose(`Concept`): This operator merges multiple concept instances which have already been configured, and assigns them as parts of the concept. The operator Compose(`ExtraCircuit-1`) indicates that the user must select necessary sensor units from the already configured sensor units and assign them as parts of the concept instance in the solution slot `ExtraCircuit-1`.

Decompose(`Concept`): This operator decomposes a concept instance into the desired subconcept instances, described by the has-part relation of the concept. Also the Configure operators for all subconcepts and the attributes of the concept are generated. For example, Decompose(`FloorCircuit-2`) decomposes the concept instance `FloorCircuit-2` into six

[6] IDAX uses a refinement of these kind of operators and distinguishes between the introduction of configuration tasks and configuration steps themselves. For our purpose, we concentrate on the common PLAKON and IDAX operators, enhanced by some techniques used in IDAX.

different instances of sensor units `Sensor-1` to `Sensor-6` which have to be configured.

Specialize(`Concept`): This operator specializes the concept of an object along an is-a relation to a subconcept. The operator Specialize(`Unit`) could specialize a concept instance of the concept `Unit` to a concept instance of `AlarmUnit` or `SensorUnit`.

The application of the operators is controlled by a rule-based system which can prefer operators that lead to an optimal solution and by a constraint system which prevents the user from using operators which would lead to an invalid solution. The main benefits of the operators are:

- The explicit representation of problem solving decisions and their dependencies.
- The support for withdrawing decisions during problem solving in an effective manner.
- Guiding the configuration along the object-oriented hierarchy in a data-driven manner to move from abstract decisions to more concrete decisions.
- The possibility of controlling the application of operators during problem solving with rules and constraints.

In this section, we have introduced the concept of operator based configuration. Next, we explain how adaptation could benefit from the configuration operator concept during solving an adaptation task.

6.4.4 Configuration Based Adaptation

Motivation. For most CBR systems, especially for domain independent commercial CBR Shells, adaptation is limited to simple substitutional techniques on atomic solution entities. However, recent complex case-based reasoning applications often require structured case and solution representations which necessarily implies a move away from simple substitutional methods towards more sophisticated transformational or even derivational approaches. There are a number of implications associated with this move to more structured case representations. First of all, there is typically a more complex relation between a case's descriptive features (as used in retrieval) and its solution features; contrast this to the more obvious relationship between case descriptive features and a single atomic solution feature. Secondly, it may be necessary to consider the composition of many case solutions during problem solving, rather than dealing with just a single case. Finally, due to the added complexity of transformational adaptation rules, it is no longer feasible to employ large unstructured rule bases.

The most immediate observation that one can make concerning the development of adaptation is that relatively little is known about the right way to structure adaptation knowledge. One of the more useful perspectives is the container-view of CBR knowledge (Richter 1995; Wilke et al. 1997), and while the structure of knowledge within the case, similarity, and domain containers is well understood, the adaptation knowledge container is conspicuous by its almost complete absence of useful structure. The motivation for this section is to present one way of structuring adaptation knowledge for more complex adaptation tasks. The remainder of this section will describe how a configuration perspective can provide insights about this structuring. In particular, we will describe how a simple form of compositional adaptation can be implemented and how object-oriented configuration knowledge and operators can guide transformational adaptation procedures.

The Adaptation Framework. One of the most immediate implications of the move towards more sophisticated structured case representations is that there needs to be an explicit relation between case description features and case solution features. Rather than associate individual features of the case description and solution, mapping knowledge is needed to express this relation by correlating groups of description features with groups of solution features (as shown in Figure 6.10). This mapping is necessary during case composition and transformational adaptation.

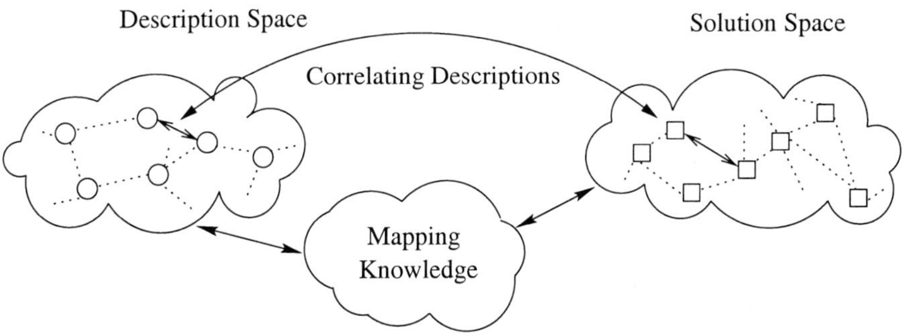

Fig. 6.10. Mapping between description and solution spaces

Of course, it is conceivable that there is no straightforward mapping between these two feature spaces (descriptive and solution) or that there are potential conflicts and interactions between the different relations that contribute to this mapping. This will obviously have ramifications for case composition and transformation and, indeed, it is our contention that a configuration-based approach to adaptation is only suitable when this mapping is well-behaved; that is, when there are little or no objectionable conflicts.

Figure 6.11 shows the basic idea of how to use adaptation operators and actions for the adaptation of complex and simple attributes. It displays some of the operators and actions which are used to adapt a concept with some simple and some complex attributes and the relations between the objects involved in the process. Each task which has to be solved for the adaptation

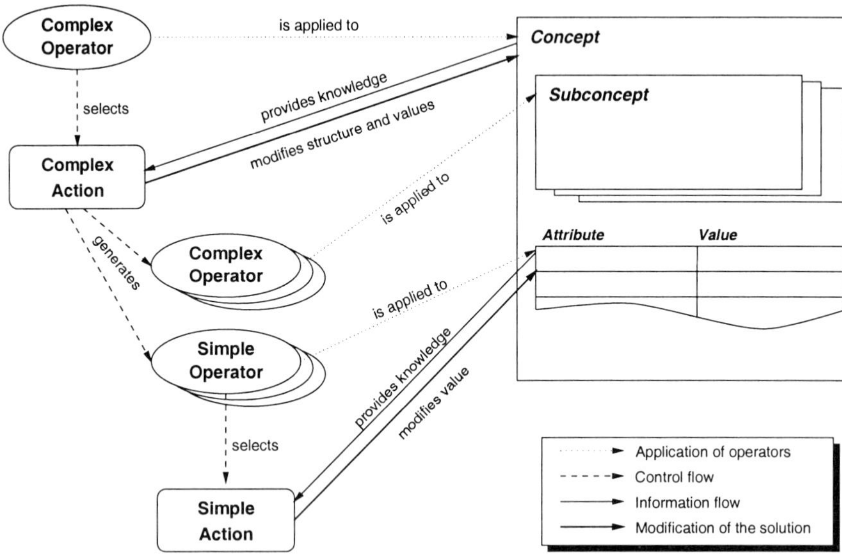

Fig. 6.11. Using adaptation operators and actions: the general idea

of the solution is modeled by an *adaptation operator*. An operator is applied to an attribute of the solution and is responsible for the adaptation of it. Because we have complex and simple attributes, we need one special operator for complex and another for simple attributes. To adapt the solution, an operator chooses one of several *adaptation actions* which implement the necessary functions to accomplish the modification of the solution: *Simple Actions* only define a function that determines a new value for the attribute, e.g., it calculates the value of a parameter or copies a concept from the similar cases. *Complex actions* can additionally generate consecutive adaptation operators which are needed to complete the adaptation of the attribute, e.g., if subconcepts were introduced by the action, further operators for these subconcepts can be generated if necessary. For adapting simple attributes, a simple action is sufficient while for the adaptation of a complex attributes always a complex action is needed because the complex action concentrates on determining the structure of the subconcept and not on assigning values for all simple attributes which belong to the subconcept.

Furthermore, in Figure 6.11 the sequence of the application is denoted by reading from top to bottom: The process starts with a complex operator applied to the root concept, which will eventually describe the complete solution. This operator selects an action which tries to develop some of the structure of the concept, by introducing subconcepts, and generates more operators for the attributes if necessary. After that, the new operators are executed in some order; in the example first the complex operators complete the determination of the solution's structure before the simple operators fill in the values for the simple attributes. Of course, other heuristics could be used if appropriate.

The knowledge needed by the adaptation actions to evaluate the new values is provided by rules, constraints, and functions which can be associated to each attribute of the solution concept. Rules can suggest preferences for the application, while constraints are used to exclude illegal solutions as well as the application of not permitted operators or actions. Functions can be used to express well defined dependencies between different parameters of the problem and solution description and their implications on the solution, so that they can be used to calculate new values for parameters. In the light of the design continuum, the formulation of the concrete adaptation operators and actions is possible because we deal with configuration tasks and the adaptation process can be completely defined according to the closed world assumption. Conversely, solving complex tasks, like innovative or creative design, during adaptation would not facilitate the formulation of the concrete adaptation knowledge.

The adaptation operators are scheduled on a *working agenda*, which represents adaptation operators which have to be applied. During adaptation, an adaptation operator is selected from the agenda and its application leads to an adaptation action. Already executed adaptation operators are stored in an hierarchical history used for backtracking. Thus, the application of such an operator results in the *execution* of a concrete adaptation action, which leads to a modification of the solution, and the *generation* of a set of new adaptation operators, which represent further tasks in the adaptation of a component. During the application of adaptation operators, the rules and constraints also restrict the possible outcomes of the application. For clarification, Figures 6.12 and 6.13 give an overview of the adaptation operators and their possible refinements to adaptation actions. In the following, we give detailed definitions of operators and actions.

Adaptation Operators. We define two kinds of adaptation operators: one for complex attributes and one for simple attributes. Adaptation operators applied to components are refined to complex adaptation actions while adaptation operators applied to parameters result in simple adaptation actions. Besides the necessary definitions for its execution, an adaptation operator contains slots to store information about what has already been tried to adapt the attribute which can be used for effective backtracking. In the following definitions, this knowledge of the dependencies necessary for backtracking is associated to the operators because, logically, it belongs to them. However, these slots and some of the algorithms described below, in fact, realize a Truth Maintenance System (TMS) (Doyle 1979). So, when using adaptation operators in an implementation an efficient TMS, like REDUX (Petrie 1991), should be used for storing and maintaining this information instead of implementing one with the operators.

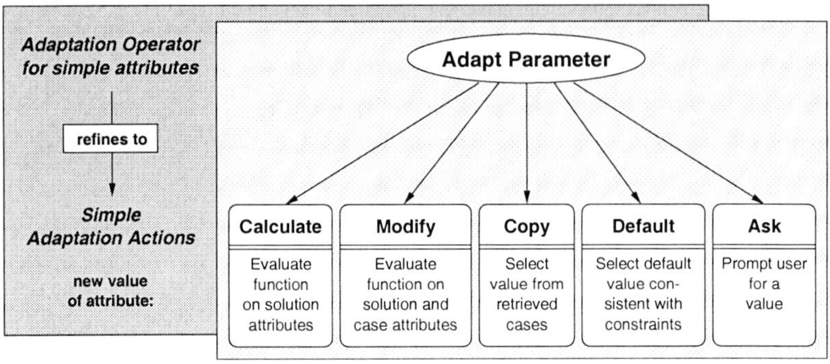

Fig. 6.12. The adaptation operator for simple attributes

First we define adaptation operators for parameters, for clarification the operator and the actions it can be refined to are shown in Figure 6.12.

Definition 6.4.1 (Adaptation operator for simple attributes). *An adaptation operator for simple attributes* SAO *is defined as*

$$\mathsf{SAO} = (\mathsf{attribute}, \mathsf{old} - \mathsf{value}, \mathsf{actions}, \mathsf{used} - \mathsf{values}, \mathsf{dependents})$$

where

- attribute *is the attribute which* SAO *is applied to.*
- old-value *is the value of the attribute when* SAO *was selected from the agenda. It is stored in the operator to restore during backtracking.*
- actions *is a set of adaptation actions which were already used on the attribute. If* SAO *is executed in backtracking, it uses this list to determine which alternatives are left.*
- used-values *is a set of values which already have been tried.*
- dependents *is a set of other operators which need to be re-executed if* SAO *changes the value of the attribute.*

□

When backtracking determines that an operator has to be re-executed, the old value of the attribute it restored using the old-value-slot. Then the next possible action can be determined by examining the already used ones stored in the actions-slot. Finally, the new action is executed. The repeated use of values is prevented by excluding those stored in the used-values-slot. We assume that, in a well defined domain, the set of possible values for an attribute is rather small. This can be achieved by defining constraints or using dependencies between attributes. Thus, the used-values-set will not get too large and this check is efficient.

If the value of the attribute is changed during the re-execution of the operator, all operators referenced in the dependents-slot must be marked to be re-executed, so that the values of their attributes can be kept correct.

If an operator is dependent in this way on another, it stores a reference to itself in the dependents-slot of the other. An operator does not change its own dependents-slot.

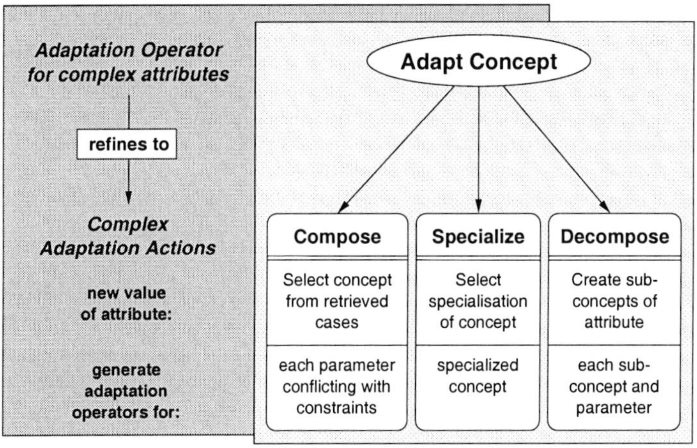

Fig. 6.13. The adaptation operator for complex attributes

The following definition of an adaptation operator for parameters CAO looks similar but it needs an additional slot. The possible refinements are shown in Figure 6.13.

Definition 6.4.2 (Adaptation operator for complex attributes). *An adaptation operator for a complex attribute* CAO *is defined as*

$$\mathsf{CAO} = (\mathsf{attribute}, \mathsf{old}-\mathsf{value}, \mathsf{actions}, \mathsf{used}-\mathsf{values}, \mathsf{operators}, \mathsf{dependents})$$

where

- attribute *is the attribute which* CAO *is applied to.*
- old-value *is the concept instance which was stored in the attribute when* CAO *was selected from the agenda.*
- actions *is a list of adaptation operators which have already been used on the attribute.*
- used-values *is the set of concepts which have already been used for the attribute.*
- dependents *is a set of other operators which need to be re-executed if* SAO *changes the value of the attribute.*
- operators *is a set of generated adaptation operators, after* CAO *has been performed. If* CAO *is on the agenda,* operators *is empty.*

□

Additional to the backtracking procedure described above, for complex attributes the operators in the operators-slot have to be retracted before the determination of a new value starts.

Now, we will have a closer look at the different adaptation actions.

Simple Adaptation Actions. If an adaptation operator is applied to a simple attribute, only a simple adaptation action is chosen to get a new value for the parameter. Complex actions are not necessary in this case because such a modification should not need to generate further adaptation operators. Instead if conflicts arise, backtracking will be necessary.

Definition 6.4.3 (Simple adaptation action). *A simple adaptation action* SAA *is a function which returns a new value for an attribute, given the attribute, the current solution, the query, the retrieved cases and optionally a list of values which are not permitted as results. If an action is not applicable to an attribute, it returns a* nil*-value.* □

Currently we use the following simple actions which were already shown above in Figure 6.12:

Calculate: If the attribute has functional dependencies on other attributes, a unique value can be calculated using this action. These functions describe general knowledge which is always true.

Modify: If a functional dependency exists between changes in description attributes and the current attribute, this action can be used to calculate a value from the attributes in the retrieved cases and the query (interpolation). The value calculated by such an interpolation function is not necessarily correct but is a good approximation for the correct value.

Copy: This action copies the most appropriate value from the attributes in the retrieved cases. To select a value, mapping knowledge is required.

Default: Otherwise, this action can calculate a default value, e.g., the minimum of the values consistent to the constraints.

Ask: Prompts the user for a value consistent with the constraints. If the domain can be modeled completely, this action is not necessary, but can be provided as a fallback.

The list of excluded values is necessary as an argument to the action if an action is used again after backtracking, e.g., if Copy is called the first time it should return the value from the most similar case. If called the second time on the same attribute it should use the value from the next similar case for the other values have been proven to be inappropriate.

The formulation of the adaptation actions should be possible, because we assume that the relation between problem description and solution is known in the problem domain and we have a closed world assumption. Otherwise the concrete adaptation action must be performed by a user.

Complex Adaptation Actions. The application of an adaptation operator to a component leads to the selection of a complex adaptation action. In contrast to simple actions, not only a new value is determined but additionally it is possible that a set of adaptation operators is generated which are necessary to achieve the remaining adaptation of the concept or the resolution of conflicts introduced by the execution of the action. Therefore, a complex action defines in addition to a simple action a function which is responsible for the generation of these operators. More formally, a complex adaptation operator is defined as follows:

Definition 6.4.4 (Complex adaptation action). *A complex adaptation action* CAA *is defined as* CAA = (action,effects)*, where*

- action *is a simple adaptation action performed by this operator. The action describes the changes done to the solution when this operator is used.*
- effects *is a function which generates the necessary adaptation operators after the execution of* action*. It describes what has to be done to complete the adaptation of the concept the action is applied to.*

□

There are three possible complex adaptation actions which can be used to adapt complex attributes. Each is defined by a simple adaptation action and a set of operators which are generated, as shown in Figure 6.13:

Compose: This complex action copies a concept from a similar case into the target problem solution. The copying process is guided by the similarities between the target specification and the retrieved cases, and by the mapping between the descriptive and solution features described in Figure 6.10.
  Action: Select the most appropriate concept instance from the retrieved cases. If called again, select the next appropriate concept, if any more are available.
  Effects: Generate adaptation operators for all parameters of the selected concept which are not consistent to the constraints.

Specialize: This complex action specializes the concept of a component along an is-a relation to a subconcept. This leads to a refinement of objects during adaptation according to the domain model of the cases.
  Action: Substitute the current concept instance stored in the attribute with a specialization.
  Effects: An adaptation operator for the specialized concept is generated.

Decompose: This complex action decomposes a concept instance into the desired subconcept instances, described by the has-part relation of the concept of the attribute.
  Action: Introduce empty concept instances for all parts of the attribute to adapt. The new instances can be specializations of the concepts defined for the attributes.

Effects: Generate adaptation operators for all new concepts and parameters and add them to the agenda.

Now that our framework is described, we want to give some more details on the algorithm which is used to control the application of adaptation operators.

If an attribute is complex ...

1. Store current value of the complex attribute in the old-value-slot.
2. Select applicable complex action. Add it to the actions-list.
3. Execute simple adaptation action of the chosen complex action and set attribute value. Add concept to the used-values-set.
4. Generate the new adaptation operators. Store the result in the operators-set and add the returned operators to the agenda.
5. If no executable operator could be found, trigger backtracking.

else (attribute is simple) ...

1. Store current value of the simple attribute in the value-slot.
2. Evaluate actions until one returns an attribute value which satisfies the constraints.
3. Add the action to the actions-list and the new value to the used-values-list. Store the new value in the attribute.
4. If no value is consistent, trigger backtracking.

Fig. 6.14. The application of the adaptation operators and adaptation actions

Application of Adaptation Operators. Figure 6.14 gives an overview over the adaptation algorithm. The following steps can be recognized: If executed, an adaptation operator for components searches for an action which could be applied to the attribute. A heuristics for the application of the operators is: First an operator tries to use Compose, then Specialize, and at last Decompose. This expresses that it should be best to reuse old cases, when they can be used completely without much adaptation. If this is not possible, the specialization is used to further determine the structure of the concept and, therefore, reduce the search space. At last, if the concept cannot be treated as a whole, it is necessary to decompose the concept and work on the parts of it.

The actions used for implementing adaptation operators for parameters are evaluated in a certain order, e.g., first Calculate, then Modify and Copy, and at last Default or Ask. The underlying heuristics is that if the correct value can be calculated this should be done. The second best case is that a value can be approximated from the cases, this should always result in a better solution than a simple copy of a value in the cases. If no such knowledge is available, a default value must be selected from the set allowed by the constraints or the user must be asked.

If an action is not applicable for an attribute, e.g., when there is no calculation function or no appropriate attributes are found in the cases for interpolation or copying, an action returns an `nil`-value which is inconsistent to any constraint and therefore leads to the execution of the next available action.

The backtracking procedure determines an operator in the history which must be re-executed to solve the conflict. When backtracking is performed, first the old value of the attribute is restored and all adaptation operators generated by it are deleted, then the last action stored in the actions-list of this operator is executed again. In general, one action can produce different results if called more than once. If no new result is produced, the next available action is chosen. If no applicable actions are available, further backtracking becomes necessary.

The Knowledge Needed for Adaptation. Some of the above actions need knowledge describing dependencies between the description and solution space or between parameters of the query, the solution, and the cases. Now that we have defined our basic set of actions, we describe more details about the contents of this knowledge: By analyzing the actions, we can identify what kind of knowledge is needed.

Compose and Copy: Compose needs two kinds of knowledge: Mainly, there can be constraints which determine which case components can be chosen for constructing the solution. These constraints describe relations between the description attributes in the query and a case. If these are fulfilled, then the component in question is allowed for use in the solution. Additionally, there can be a special similarity measure, other than the one used for retrieval, to determine the most appropriate component from the set of those that fulfill the constraints. The knowledge needed for the application of Copy is essentially the same.

Specialize: Specialize may choose a specialization dependent of values of concepts stored in other attributes. This can be expressed by a rule which allows a specialization to be chosen if the condition is fulfilled. The conditions do not need to be disjunct because different specializations are allowed.

Decompose: To choose a specialization of the attribute's concept similar rules as defined for Specialize can be used, but now they are associated to the component decomposed instead of the one specialized. To determine for which components adaptation actions are necessary, a predicate can be defined for each component. If it evaluates to true an adaptation operator is generated.

Calculate and Modify: In this case, the knowledge consists mainly of the function which calculates the new value. The function for Calculate considers only attributes of the solution, while the interpolation-function for Modify uses attributes of the retrieved cases too. For Modify there can be an additional constraint determining if a case is appropriate to be used in interpolation.

Having described our basic adaptation framework we will now illustrate the application of our framework in our two already presented examples.

Compositional Adaptation with Adaptation Operators. To demonstrate the adaptation process in our framework, we want to focus here on the adaptation of the four different sensor circuits which describe the input for the alarm system. We can identify the following mapping relations between the problem description and the solution, shown in Table 6.2, together with the concrete instances of the query and the two similar cases:

Table 6.2. The relation between the problem description and the solution

Probl. Descr.	Query	Case-1	Case-2	Related Solution Part
Doors	**1**	**1**	1	FloorCircuit-1
Window-1	**3**	**3**	4	FloorCircuit-1
Window-2	**1**	2	**1**	FloorCircuit-2
Fire	**false**	**false**	**false**	ExtraCircuit-1/-2
Motion	**true**	**true**	**true**	ExtraCircuit-1/-2
Room-1	**2**	**2**	**2**	ExtraCircuit-1/(-2)
Room-2	**1**	**1**	**1**	ExtraCircuit-2/(-1)

The table represents the mapping knowledge together with the instances from our example for compositional adaptation. We observe, that the attributes `Doors`, `Window-1` affect only the concept instance `FloorCircuit-1` of the solution, while `Window-2` only influences the concept instance `Floor-Circuit-2`. This results from the fact, that in the alarm domain it is not permitted to connect a sensor to a circuit which does not belong to a particular floor. The remaining attributes can affect two circuits.

The table describes the relation between the problem description features and the solution. We observe that the solution consists of the four concept instances in the last column of the table, together with the alarm circuit and the price.

Therefore, we can formulate a set of constraints which allow to copy a component from the cases into the solution as shown in Table 6.3. In this table, references to the query are denoted with Q, while C references the current retrieved case. Additionally, the complete case can be copied if all problem description attributes are the same in case and query and the alarm circuit can always be copied. A more complex example is the constraint defined for the extra circuits; it describes the fact that an extra circuit can be copied if either all room numbers are the same or no sensors from one floor have to be connected to the circuit of the other floor.

Table 6.3. The constraints for Compose, describing whether a concept can be reused from a case.

Concept	Constraint
FloorCircuit-1	Q.Doors = C.Doors ∧ Q.Windows-1 = C.Windows-1
FloorCircuit-2	Q.Windows-2 = C.Windows-2
ExtraCircuit-1	Q.Fire = C.Fire ∧ Q.Motion = C.Motion ∧ Q.Rooms-1 = C.Rooms-1 ∧ (Q.Rooms-2 = C.Rooms-2 ∨ Q.Rooms-2 ≤ 3 ∧ C.Rooms-2 ≤ 3 ∨ ¬(Q.Fire ∧ Q.Motion) ∧ Q.Rooms-2 ≤ 6 ∧ C.Rooms-2 ≤ 6)
ExtraCircuit-2	Q.Fire = C.Fire ∧ Q.Motion = C.Motion ∧ Q.Rooms-2 = C.Rooms-2 ∧ (Q.Rooms-1 = C.Rooms-1 ∨ Q.Rooms-1 ≤ 3 ∧ C.Rooms-1 ≤ 3 ∨ ¬(Q.Fire ∧ Q.Motion) ∧ Q.Rooms-1 ≤ 6 ∧ C.Rooms-1 ≤ 6)

The first adaptation operator on the agenda is AdaptConcept(`Case`). Neither Compose nor Specialize is applicable, hence Decompose will be used. In turn, this action adds the Adaptation Operators[7] AdaptConcept(`F-1`), AdaptConcept(`E-1`), AdaptConcept(`F-2`), AdaptConcept(`E-2`), AdaptConcept(`A`), and AdaptParameter(`Price`) to the agenda. Next, the first four operators try to apply Compose to their components, which, indeed, succeeds, as each constraint can be satisfied by one of the two cases. We find that a new solution is constructed by composing the solution features of case 1 for floor 1 and the floor 2 solution features of case 2. All Adapt operators for the circuits can therefore be refined to Compose, which copies the solution for floor 1 from the first case and the solution for floor 2 from the second case. The `E-1/-2` can also be composed in the same way; both cases fulfill the constraints and so the ready configured extra circuits can be copied from the cases into the solution. As we have not defined an additional similarity measure to select a component, both extra circuits are copied from case 1. After that, the alarm circuit can be configured in a similar way and the price of the whole system can be calculated from the prices of the single circuits.

Transformational Adaptation with Adaptation Operators. Now we want to have a closer look at solving a transformational adaptation task with our adaptation operators. In Table 6.4, we also show the problem description of the query from the example transformational adaptation in section 6.3.1,

[7] We abbreviate in the following examples the `FloorCircuits` with a `F`, `ExtraCircuits` with an `E`, `AlarmCircuits` with an `A` and `Sensors` with a `S`.

along with the problem description of the similar retrieved case and the mapping information about which problem description parts effect which part of the solution.

Table 6.4. The Relation between the problem description and the solution

Problem Description	**Query**	**Similar Case**	Related Solution Part
Doors	1	1	FloorCircuit-1
Window-1	4	4	FloorCircuit-1
Window-2	1	1	FloorCircuit-2
Fire	true	false	ExtraCircuit-1/-2
Motion	**true**	**true**	ExtraCircuit-1/-2
Room-1	3	2	ExtraCircuit-1/(-2)
Room-2	1	1	ExtraCircuit-2/(-1)

The adaptation process starts with the adaptation operators for the five circuits and the price, as in the first example. This time, a compositional adaptation is only possible for the `FloorCircuits-1/-2`. This works the same way as in the first example. As a specialization is not possible for the `E-1/-2`, the adaptation actions Decompose(`E-1`) and Decompose(`E-2`) are selected to refine the adaptation operators for these components. As there are three rooms on floor 1 and the user wants both fire and motion sensors, the result of Decompose(`E-1`) is that three fire and three motion sensors are added to `E-1` (as specializations of the six sensor units which can be connected to `E-1`) and adaptation operators are generated for all these sensors. Which sensors are generated must be described by rules. The retrieved case already contains motion sensor units connected to the first extra circuit. They can be copied by the operators for the motion sensors units of `E-1` of the solution. Therefore, these three operators are refined to Compose actions which each copy one sensor unit. However, as there are no fire sensor units in the case, the fire sensor units of `E-1` have to be configured from scratch. To achieve this, the operators for the fire sensor units are refined to Decompose(`E-2`) actions which introduce operators for the single parameters of the sensor unit. Following this, the operators for all parameters except of the price can be refined to Default or Ask, so that one value is selected of the set which the constraints allow. The operator for the price is then refined to a Calculate which evaluates a function which describes how the price depends on the other attributes of a sensor unit. The adaptation of `E-2` works in a similar way; this time Decompose(`E-2`) introduces one fire and one motion sensor unit and one adaptation operator for each of them. Again, the motion sensor unit can be copied from the case while the fire sensor unit has to be configured from scratch. Eventually, the alarm circuit will be copied from the case and the price can be calculated using a function which adds the prices of the single units.

6.5 Discussion and Summary

This chapter began with a characterization of the different types of design and planning tasks and we identified configuration as a design problem at the easy end of the spectrum. Many configuration problems are such that a closed world assumption is appropriate in KBS development. This means that a CBR system for configuration can operate without user assistance. This in turn means that automatic adaptation is possible in CBR configuration systems where it would not be in more complex design or planning tasks. We believe that this characterization of configuration as a task where automated adaptation is possible offers an important insight into adaptation in general.

From the spectrum of design tasks, configuration is one that can be automated. From the spectrum of adaptation methods - if we concentrate on techniques that operate as configuration does - these too can be automated.

In the last section of the chapter, we demonstrated an example of how configuration techniques could be used to improve current adaptation practice. The adaptation described is also possible with a powerful rule system. However, using configuration techniques is the natural progression of the current *from scratch* problem solving for adaptation tasks. This is also reflected in the grading of different levels of challenges by such tasks, like routine, innovative, and creative design in section 6.2.1. In addition, this configuration perspective offers a number of significant advantages over more traditional adaptation techniques such as rule-based methods:

Firstly, the necessary knowledge to perform the adaptation task is divided into small knowledge chunks which are easy to maintain and largely independent. Structural changes are carried out by the adaptation operators while the changes to the solution itself are performed by the adaptation actions. The adaptation actions are connected as well as the control knowledge for structural changes, the rules and the constraints, to the desired concepts of the solution model. Therefore, modeling and maintaining adaptation knowledge is easier, or even becomes possible, for larger adaptation tasks. The distribution of knowledge across different objects has also been successfully applied in the INRECA system (Wilke and Bergmann 1996b).

Secondly, the data-driven approach facilitates a natural way of making decisions from an abstract to a concrete level and supports an efficient backtracking mechanism. This is a result of the structure of the decisions which make dependencies between adaptation operators explicit.

Thirdly, we have a uniform and domain independent approach to model and apply adaptation knowledge for configuration tasks during adaptation. Furthermore, rules and constraints related to the concepts can be used to express a preference of optimal solutions against sub-optimal solutions. So, the fulfillment of an optimization criterion for adaptation tasks is realizable which is often not addressed in current systems.

However, these benefits do not come for free. Knowledge must be acquired for the constraints and rules. But this knowledge has to be coded for other approaches too, if they are to solve the same task.

The presented approach is not a proposal to use more adaptation during CBR. Nevertheless, it provides adaptation problem solving methods for tasks where powerful adaptation is required.

7. CBR Applied to Planning

Ralph Bergmann, Héctor Muñoz-Avila, Manuela Veloso, and Erica Melis

7.1 Introduction

Planning means constructing a course of actions to achieve a specified set of goals, starting from an initial situation. For example, determining a sequence of actions (a plan) for transporting goods from an initial location to some destination is a typical planning problem in the transportation domain. Many planning problems are of practical interest.

The classical generative planning process consists mainly of a search through the space of possible operators to solve a given problem. For most practical problems, this search is intractable. Therefore, case-based reasoning can be a useful idea because it transfers previous solutions rather than searching *from scratch*.

Since the space of possible plans is typically vast, it is extremely unlikely that a case base contains a plan that can be reused without any modification. Modification has been addressed in CHEF (Hammond 1986), one of the first case-based planners. It retrieves cooking recipes and adapts them to the new problem by using domain specific knowledge. As experience has shown, however, this kind of adaptation in realistic domains requires a large amount of very specific domain knowledge and lacks flexibility.

Given that classical generative planning may involve a very great search effort and pure case-based planning may encounter insurmountable modification needs, several researchers have pursued a *synergistic* approach of generative and case-based planning. In a nutshell, the case-based planner provides plans previously generated for similar situations and the generative planner is used as a source of modification. In this paper, we present four systems that integrate generative and case-based planning: PRODIGY/ANALOGY developed at the CMU, CAPLAN/CBC and PARIS developed at the University of Kaiserslautern, and ABALONE developed at the Universities of Saarbrücken and Edinburgh. These systems are domain-independent case-based planners that accumulate and use planning cases to control the search. In these systems, cases encode knowledge of which operators were used for solving problems and why. In our synergistic systems, the workload imposed on the generative planner depends on the amount of modification that is required to completely adapt a retrieved case.

7.2 Generative Planning

Since the presented case-based planners are built on top of generative planners, we briefly introduce generative planning here.

Together, the *initial state* and a set of *goals* form a *planning problem.* A planning task consists of finding a *plan*, which is a sequence of actions that transform the initial state, into a *final state* in which the goals hold. The plan is a solution of the planning problem. Usually, a state is represented by a finite collection of logical clauses. Actions are described by so-called *operators.* Following the STRIPS representation of Fikes and Nilsson (1971), operators are data structures that consist of preconditions and effects. A precondition is a conjunctive formula that must hold in a current state for the operator to be applicable. The effects describe how the state changes when the operator is applied. For more detailed introduction to planning; see e.g., Russell and Norvig (1995).

7.2.1 The Logistics Transportation Domain

Let us illustrate these notions by an example from the logistics transportation domain (Veloso 1994). In this domain, there are different sorts of locations and means of transportation (see Figure 7.1). The initial state of a problem describes a certain configuration of objects, locations, and transportation means and a goal is to place certain objects at target locations. Figure 7.1 (a) shows an example of an initial state. There is a post office, `p4`, and an airport `a12`. There are two transportation means: a truck, `tr2`, located at `p4` and an airplane, `p15`, located at `a12`. Finally, there are two packages, `ob3` and `ob8`. The first one is loaded in `tr2` and the second one is located at `p4`. The final state consist of two goals: `ob3` must be located in `p12` and `ob8` must be loaded in `tr2`

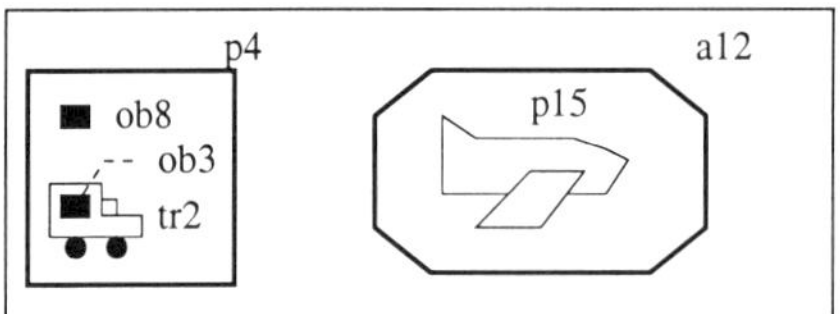

(a) Initial State

Operator: *load-truck*
Parameters:
(<obj> OBJECT)
(<tr> TRUCK)
(<loc> LOCATION)
Preconditions:
at-obj(<obj> <loc>)
at-truck(<tr> <loc>)
Effects:
add: in-truck(<obj> <tr>)
del: at-obj(<obj> <loc>)

(b) An operator

Fig. 7.1. Initial state of a problem and an operator in the logistics transportation domain

Figure 7.1 (b) shows an example of an operator, `load-truck`, loading the object <`obj`> in <`tr`>. The preconditions state that <`obj`> and <`tr`> must be in the same location, <`loc`>. Effects are divided into `add` and `del` lists indicating literals added to and deleted from the state of the world, respectively. Figure 7.2 shows a plan achieving the two goals. Initially, as both `ob8` and `tr2` are located at `p4`, the preconditions of `load-truck` are met and this operator is applied. `tr2` is then moved to `a12`, where `ob3` is unloaded and loaded into `p12`. After performing this plan, both goals are met.

load-truck(ob8,tr2)—move-truck(tr2,p4,a12)—unload-truck(ob3,tr2)—load-plane(ob8,p15)

Fig. 7.2. A plan consisting of four actions

7.2.2 Why is Planning Difficult ?

Although the previous example may seem simple, in fact, planning is a very difficult task. There may be several actions that can change the state of world. In the state illustrated in Figure 7.1 (a), dropping `ob3` in `p4` would have been a valid action, but it does not contribute to achieving the goals because an airplane cannot be moved to a post office. Typically, at any time of the planning process, there are several applicable operators but only few will lead to a solution. Even worse, it can happen that none of them are useful. In this situation, a state will be achieved in which no action can be taken and backtracking is necessary to revise the actions taken previously. In terms of computational complexity theory, the problem of finding a correct plan for a given planning problem is an NP-complete problem (Bylander 1991). This shows the intractability of the search involved in planning and calls for ways to restrict the search space.

7.2.3 Approaches to Planning

Several approaches to planning have been developed since the early days of STRIPS. Basically, all planners perform some kind of search; they differ, however, in the space they are searching and in the search strategy they use. The two dominant approaches search the *state space* and the *plan space*, respectively.

Figure 7.3 (a) illustrates the search space in state-space planning. The nodes represent the states of the world and the edges represent valid actions transforming states of the world. That is, actions transform states into states. From this point of view, the initial and final state are two nodes in the search space and a solution is a directed path from the initial to the final state.

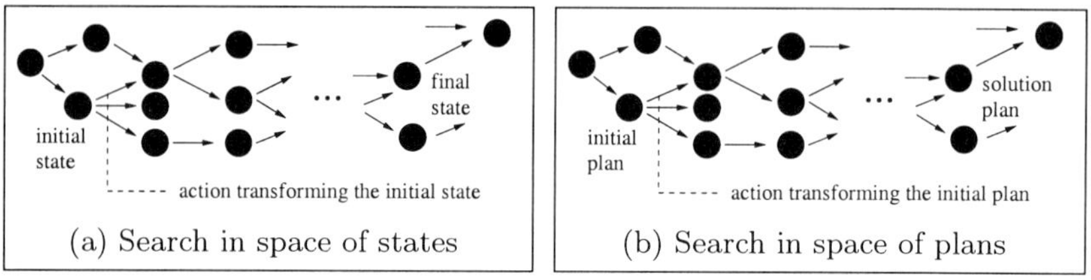

Fig. 7.3. Search in the space of states and in the state of plans

In plan-space planning, operations transform partially ordered plans into partially ordered plans as illustrated in Figure 7.3 (b). The *initial plan* is a partially ordered plan representing the problem. This plan must be transformed into a *solution plan*. There are two types of operations transforming plans: operations achieving goals and operations solving conflicts. To achieve a goal, an action is introduced into the current partial plan. Actions are partially ordered according to whether an action achieves a precondition of the other action. Conflicts may occur due to the partial order between the plan steps which can be solved by introducing additional ordering constraints into the current plan. For example, in the logistics transportation domain different steps may require a truck to be available. A conflict occurs when there are not enough trucks available. To solve this conflict, some of the steps must be ordered to ensure that every truck is used one at the time. In so-called least-commitment planners, an ordering between actions is introduced into the plan only when necessary. This is advantageous because additional ordering constraints can be introduced during planning.

Several studies have been made for indicating in which situations it is better to search in the space of plans rather than in the space of states and vice versa (Kambhampati et al. 1996; Veloso and Blythe 1994; Barrett and Weld 1994). Independent of the planning approach used, guidance is still needed to navigate through the exponential search space. We will now see, how case-based reasoning can provide this guidance.

7.3 Case-Based Planning

We now describe a general framework for case-based planning based on the CBR process model by Aamodt and Plaza (1994). This covers most case-based planning systems including those approaches developed at the CMU as well as at the Universities of Kaiserslautern, Saarbrücken and Edinburgh.

7.3.1 Retrieval and Organization of the Case-Base

A case in case-based planning consists of a problem (initial and goals) and its plan. Given a new problem, the objective of the retrieval phase is to select a case from the case base whose problem description is most similar to the description of the new problem. Because of the usually needed adaptation in case-based planning, the retrieval should select adaptable cases (Smyth and Keane 1993). More precisely, the main goal of the similarity assessment is to predict the effort required for reusing the solution to solve the new problem. Therefore, a case should be considered very similar to the new problem, if only little effort is required for adapting its solution to the needs of the target and less similar if the adaptation is computationally expensive. In case-based planning, the reusability of a case is strongly determined by the solution contained in the case and not only by the problem description. Therefore, the similarity assessment refers to the fragments of the problem description which are relevant for successfully reusing the plan. One way to extract the fragments is to compute the weakest preconditions of the plan. This computation employs the domain knowledge about the available operators that ensures that the plan can be successfully applied. The similarity will then be assessed based on the fragment of the conditions that are satisfied in the current problem to be solved.

As in case-based reasoning in general, computing the similarity assessment may become very expensive when the case base has reached a considerable size. In this case, a trade-off between the objective of finding the best case and the objective of minimizing the retrieval time exists, as depicted in Figure 7.4. As the number of cases visited during retrieval increases, more time must be spent for retrieval (see curve 2) but better cases (resulting in a shorter adaptation time) will be found (see curve 1). Up to a certain point (optimal point), the total case-based planning time (retrieval+reuse, see curve 3) decreases when more cases are visited during retrieval. However, beyond this point the total planning time increases again if more cases are visited, because the possible gain through finding better cases does not outweigh the effort of finding them.

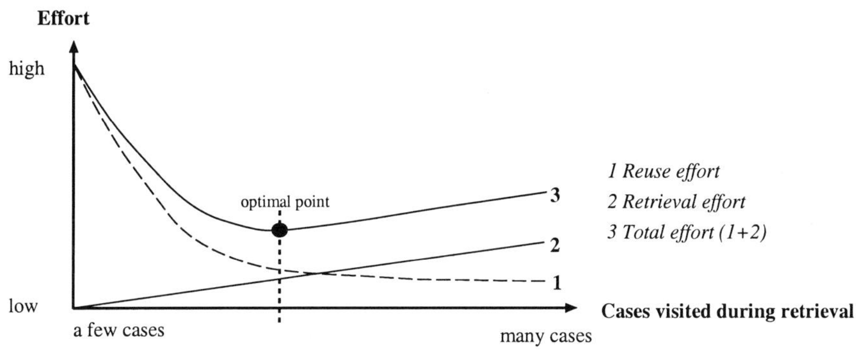

Fig. 7.4. Trade-off between retrieval effort and reuse effort (adapted from Veloso)

7.3.2 Reusing Previous Solutions

In case-based reasoning, at least two different kinds of approaches to reuse can be distinguished: *transformational adaptation* and *generative adaptation* (Carbonell 1983a; Carbonell 1986). Transformational adaptation methods usually consist of a set of domain-dependent knowledge which directly modify the solution contained in the retrieved case, based on the difference between the problem descriptions in the case and of the current problem. While in early case-based planning systems (e.g., CHEF, Hammond 1986) only transformational adaptation was used, most recent systems use generative adaptation. For generative adaptation, the integration of a case-based problem solving strategy and a generative problem solver is central. The retrieved solution is not modified directly, but is used to *guide* the generative problem solver to find a solution. A basic principle is the replay of *decisions* that were made during the process of solving the problem recorded in the case. When replaying the solution trace of a previous case, some decisions can be reused, while the remaining decisions are taken by replaying another case or by using a generative planner. The result of this reuse phase is either a correct solution (w.r.t. the domain model) or the indication of a failure in case the problem could not be solved with allocated time resources. In different case-based planners, the particular guidance that a case provides depends on the type of generative problem solver that is used.

7.3.3 Revision of Solutions

The goal of the revision phase is to validate the computed solution in the real world or in a simulation of it. Due to the correctness of the reuse-phase, the resulting solutions are known to be correct w.r.t. the domain model. Consequently, the simulation of the solution cannot contribute to an additional validation. Therefore, the solution must be validated in the real world. However, no methodological support of this kind is provided by today's case-based planning systems.

7.3.4 Retaining New Cases

In case-based planning, storing a new case in the case base requires far more effort than in the situation of analytic case-based reasoning tasks. While the latter simply stores a new case *as it is*, case-based planning requires determining the *right* goals to index the cases. Roughly speaking, the goals used for indexing are those goals that are required for or affected by the taken decisions stored in the case. Furthermore, the decisions taken by the generative problem solver must be captured in stored cases.

7.4 PRODIGY/ANALOGY

PRODIGY/ANALOGY was the first system that achieved a complete synergy between generative and case-based planning (Veloso 1994) and used for the first time a full automation of the complete CBR-cycle. PRODIGY/ANALOGY has been developed within the PRODIGY planning and learning architecture (Carbonell et al. 1991). The generative planner is a means-ends analysis, backward-chaining, nonlinear planner, performing state-space search. The integration is based on the derivational analogy method (Carbonell 1986). This is a *reconstructive* method by which *lines of reasoning* are transferred and adapted to a new problem, as opposed to transformational methods that directly adapt final solutions. PRODIGY/ANALOGY was and continues to be demonstrated in a variety of domains.

7.4.1 Retain: Generation of Planning Cases

A planning case to be stored consists of the successful solution trace augmented with justifications, that is, the derivational trace. The base-level PRODIGY4.0 reasons about multiple goals and multiple alternative operators relevant to achieving the goals. This choice of operators amounts to multiple ways of trying to achieve the same goal. PRODIGY/ANALOGY provides a *language* to capture three kinds of justifications for the decisions made during problem solving; links among choices capturing the goal dependencies, records of failed explored alternatives, and pointers to any external used guidance. We discovered in PRODIGY/ANALOGY that the key feature of this language is that it needs to be re-interpretable at planning replay time.

Automatic generation of the derivational planning episodes occurs by extending the base-level generative planner with the ability to examine its internal decision cycle, recording the justifications for each decision during its search process.

7.4.2 Indexing and Retrieval of Cases

From the exploration of the search space and by following the subgoal links in the derivational trace of the plan generated (Carbonell 1986), the system identifies, for each goal, the set of *weakest preconditions* necessary to achieve that goal. The so called *foot-print* of a goal conjunct of the problem is recursively created by doing goal regression, i.e., projecting back its weakest preconditions into the literals in the initial state (Waldinger 1977). Goal regression acts as an explanation of the successful path. The literals in the initial state are therefore *categorized* according to the goal conjunct that employed them in its solution.

The system automatically identifies the sets of interacting goals of a plan by partially ordering the totally ordered solution found. The connected components of the partially ordered plan determine the independent fragments of the case each corresponding to a set of interacting goals. Each case is multiply indexed by these different sets of interacting goals.

When a new problem is presented to the system, the retrieval procedure must match the new initial state and the goal statement against the indices of the cases in the case library.

The retrieval algorithm focuses on retrieving past cases where the planner experienced equivalent goal interactions and has a reasonable match between initial states. This maximizes the chance to achieve a large reduction in the new planning search effort.

7.4.3 Reuse: Replay of Multiple Planning Episodes

PRODIGY/ANALOGY can construct a new solution from a set of guiding cases as opposed to a single past case. Complex problems may be solved by resolving minor interactions among simpler past cases.

Consider the logistics transportation domain. In this domain packages are to be moved among different places by trucks and airplanes. The example below is simplified for the sake of a clear illustration of the replay procedure. Extensive empirical results on PRODIGY/ANALOGY have shown that the system scales well in problem complexity (Veloso 1994).

Figure 7.5 shows a new problem and two past cases selected for replay. The cases are partially instantiated to match the new situation. Further instantiations occur while replaying.

Past cases	*New problem*
(goal (inside-airplane ob3 pl5)) *(relevant-state* (at-obj ob3 <ap3>) (at-airplane pl5 a12)) *(goal* (inside-truck ob8 tr2)) *(relevant-state* (at-obj ob8 p4) (at-truck tr2 <ap7>))	*(goal* (inside-airplane ob3 pl5) (inside-truck ob8 tr2)) *(initial-state* (inside-truck ob3 tr2) (at-truck tr2 p4) (at-airplane pl5 a12) (at-obj ob8 p4))

Fig. 7.5. Instantiated past cases cover the new goal and partially match the new initial state. Some of the case variables are not bound by the match of the goals and state.

Figure 7.6 shows the replay episode to generate a solution to the new problem. The new situation is shown on the right side of the figure and the two past guiding cases on the left.

The transfer occurs by interleaving the two guiding cases, performing any additional work needed to accomplish remaining subgoals, and skipping past work that does not need to be done. In particular, the case nodes `cn3'` through `cn5'` are not reused, as there is a truck already at the post office in the new problem. The nodes `n9-14` correspond to unguided additional

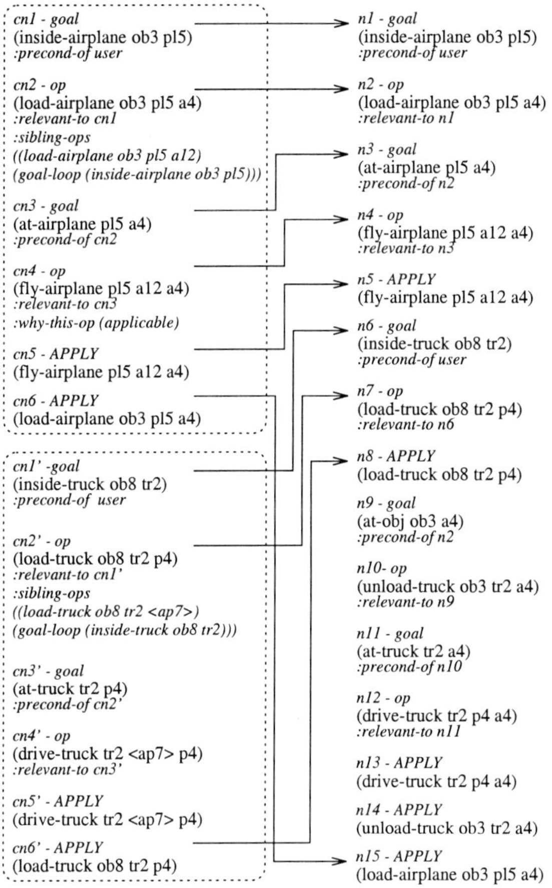

Fig. 7.6. Derivational replay of multiple cases

planning done in the new episode.[1] At node `n7`, PRODIGY/ANALOGY prunes out an alternative operator; namely, to load the truck at any airport, because of the recorded past failure at the guiding node `cn2'`. The recorded reason for that failure, namely a goal-loop with the `(inside-truck ob8 tr2)`, is validated in the new situation at node `n6`, as that goal is in the current set of open goals. Note also that, in general, two cases are merged with a bias towards postponing any additionally required planning. Different merges are possible.

[1] Note that extra steps may be inserted at any point, interrupting and interleaving the past cases, and not just at the end of the cases.

7.5 CAPLAN/CBC: Plan Reuse in the Space of Plans

CAPLAN/CBC (Muñoz-Avila et al. 1994) is a generic case-based reasoning system built on top of CAPLAN (Weberskirch 1995), a plan-space planner (McAllester and Rosenblitt 1991). CAPLAN/CBC is motivated in developing techniques for case-based planning in complex domains such as the domain of process planning for manufacturing workpieces. CAPLAN/CBC focuses on developing techniques for retrieval in technical domains and for reuse in plan-space planners.

7.5.1 Process Planning for Manufacturing Mechanical Workpieces

At the beginning of the manufacturing process a piece of raw material and the description of a workpiece are given. Descriptions of the cutting tools and clamping material available are given as well. The problem is to remove layers of raw material in order to obtain the workpiece. Typically, the piece of raw material is clamped on a lathe machine that rotates at a very high speed. A cutting tool is used to remove layers of raw material. The process proceeds by replacing the cutting tool or changing the clamping position to process areas of the workpiece. Figure 7.7 shows an intermediate stage during this process. The grid area corresponds to the portion of raw material that still needs to be removed. The parts presented, correspond to the two sides of a workpiece, two ascending outlines and a so-called undercut.

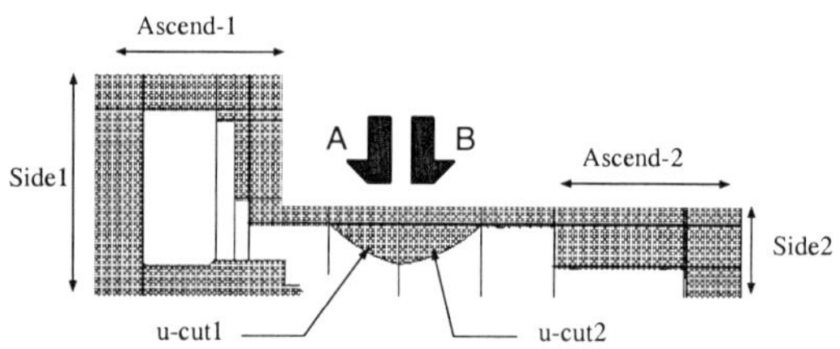

Fig. 7.7. Half display of a workpiece and two cutting tools.

Each goal of a problem corresponds to machining an area of a given workpiece. The initial state is a symbolic description of the geometry of the processing areas, the cutting tools, and the clamping material available. There are different types of areas. For each type, there is at least one operator indicating the conditions that must be met to machine it. Typically, a clamping position on the workpiece must be determined. Also, according to the clamping position and the type of area, a certain kind of cutting tool must be held. Other operators represent different clamping operations and regulate the use of the cutting tools. A basic restriction regarding the clamping and holding operations is that, at any time of the machining process, the workpiece is clamped from at most one position and a limited number of cutting tools is being held.

7.5.2 Dependency-Driven Case Retrieval

In the domain of process planning, it is possible to *predetermine* restrictions on the order for manufacturing certain parts of the workpiece. These ordering restrictions are determined based on the geometry of the workpiece and are independent of the cutting tools available. For example, at the beginning of the manufacturing process of the workpiece depicted in Figure 7.7, the undercut was covered by the area *intermediate* (not shown in Figure 7.7). Clearly, the area *intermediate* must be processed before the undercut. Thus, for any plan manufacturing this workpiece, the goal corresponding to processing *intermediate* is achieved before the goal achieving the undercut. In CAPLAN/CBC, these ordering restrictions are computed by a geometrical reasoner (Muñoz-Avila and Hüllen 1995; Muñoz-Avila and Weberskirch 1996a). In a more general context there are three possible sources for these ordering restrictions, which we denote by $\prec$:

- *A domain specific reasoner.* A typical example is the geometrical reasoner.
- *The user.* The user may specify additional restrictions because of quality considerations that are not explicitly represented in the domain theory.
- *Static analysis.* In principle, the domain theory can be analyzed to predetermine some ordering restrictions (Etzioni 1993).

Any solution plan induces ordering restrictions in which the goals are achieved. These ordering restrictions are called *dependencies* between the goals. The name *dependency* is motivated by a particularity of the domain of process planning; namely, the way an area is processed *depends* on the way other areas were previously processed. The initial situation, the goals, and the ordering restrictions form *extended problem descriptions* (Muñoz-Avila and Hüllen 1995; Muñoz-Avila and Weberskirch 1996a). For a case to be retrieved, the dependencies in the case (i.e., the order in which the goals are achieved), denoted by $\rightarrow$, must be consistent with the ordering restrictions of the problem. That is to say, if two goals in the new problem g_1, g_2 have the ordering restriction $g_1 \prec g_2$, then, for the corresponding goals in the source case, g'_1, g'_2, the relation $g'_2 \rightarrow g'_1$ must *not* hold. An architecture of the case memory has been developed that allows cases whose dependencies are consistent with the ordering restrictions of new problem to be found in an efficient way. The dependencies are the main criterion for discriminating between cases in the case base. We called this retrieval strategy *dependency-driven* as a clear contrast to other case-based planners where cases are retrieved based on the goals that they achieved (i.e., goal-driven). The dependency-driven retrieval strategy is adequate for domains in which a partial order between the goals can be predetermined, see Muñoz-Avila and Hüllen (1995) for further details.

7.5.3 Adaptation with Complete Decision Replay

The adaptation method conceived and implemented in CAPLAN/CBC is called *complete decision replay.* This method is fundamented on the way the base-level planner CAPLAN is built (Weberskirch 1995). To represent knowledge about plans and contingencies that occur during planning, CAPLAN is built on the generic REDUX architecture (Petrie 1991). The REDUX architecture represents relations between goals and operators and between operators and subgoals. In the parlance of REDUX, a *decision* is made when an operator is applied to achieve a goal. Decisions are represented as a subtree in the *goal graph.* It represents basic dependencies between goals and subgoals as well as between subgoals and decisions. A key aspect in CAPLAN is that the *justifications* of all decisions (valid and not valid) are always maintained. A justification has the form $\{a_1, a_2, ..., a_n\}$, where a_i is a ordering or a variable constraint. For example, consider a decision corresponding to the application of an operator that requires $X = Y$ to be true, where X and Y are variables. If the decision is valid, an example of a possible justification is $\{X = 1, Y = 1\}$. An example of a justification if the decision is invalid is $\{X = 1, Y = 0\}$.

The complete decision replay method consists of reconstructing the goal graph relative to the new situation. The validity of a decision (i.e., if the decision failed or not) is stated if its justifications can be reconstructed relative to the new situation. The partial solution represented in the reconstructed goal graph is then completed by first principles planning. Three major advantages can be observed as a result of this process:

1. The user may interact during the completion process. The user may prune parts of the replayed case or neglect the validity of certain problem conditions. Because CAPLAN/CBC reconstructs the goal graph, the functionality of the base-level planner CAPLAN is preserved. Thus, a plan can be generated by modifying the current plan without having to plan from the scratch.
2. Powerful backtracking methods can be used. CAPLAN performs dependency-directed backtracking based on the goal graph reconstructed by CAPLAN/CBC.
3. CAPLAN does not explore failed attempts. Having found that the justifications for a failed decision can be reconstructed in the new situation, CAPLAN/CBC prunes completion possibilities that otherwise could have been explored during the completion process.

The principle of considering the failed attempts during reuse is illustrated by continuing with the example depicted in Figure 7.7. This figure depicts an intermediate stage during the process, in which the undercut has not been processed. Undercuts always can be decomposed in two parts (labeled `u-cut1` and `u-cut2`). In this figure, left and right cutting tools are also shown, labeled `A` and `B` respectively. For manufacturing the undercut, the workpiece needs to be clamped from an ascending outline, for example `Ascend-1`. The left tool is used for removing the left part (i.e., `u-cut1`). For removing the right part (i.e., `u-cut2`) there are three possibilities: (1) to use the right tool, (2) to clamp the workpiece from the outline `Ascend-2` and use the same left tool again, or (3) to clamp the workpiece from `Side2` and use the left tool. The last possibility requires that there is a perforation on `Side2`. Since, in the example, there is only a perforation on *Side1*, it will be discarded if considered by the planner.

The left side of Figure 7.8 outlines a plan for manufacturing the workpiece shown in Figure 7.7, under the supposition that there is a left and a right cutting-tools available. Dashed boxes represent plan-steps and the arcs pointing downwards indicate the partial-order for performing them. This plan states that, for removing `u-cut1`, the workpiece must be clamped from `Ascend-1` and the left tool must be used. After that, `u-cut2` is removed by using the right tool. This plan contains also the information that clamping from `Side2` failed because it does not have any perforation (node labeled `R`).

Suppose that a new problem is given that consists of the same workpiece, but this time there is only a left tool available. For solving this problem the plan obtained with the two tools will be reused, as illustrated in Figure 7.8. The horizontal arrows show the decisions of the case that are replayed in the new situation. Particularly, the decisions concerning the manufacturing of `u-cut1` can be replayed in the new situation. However, the decision concerning the manufacturing of `u-cut2` cannot be replayed, since, in the new situation, there is no right tool available. As a result, a rejected decision is created (node labeled `S`). The rejection of the operator `clamping from Side-2` is replayed (node labeled `R'`), as in the new situation `Side-2` has no perforation.

Once the replay of cases is finished, the remaining goals need to be solved by the generative planner. As stated before, the key issue is that the generative planner (CAPLAN) will avoid performing unnecessary backtracking. Particularly, for solving the goal corresponding to manufacturing `u-cut2`, CAPLAN will not pursue the use of the right tool, nor to clamp from `Side2`. Instead, it will select to clamp the workpiece from `Ascend-2` (arc labeled `P`), which is the right choice.

7.6 Summary of Theoretical and Experimental Results

CAPLAN/CBC has been evaluated in the domain of process planning as defined in Muñoz-Avila and Weberskirch (1996b). This specification consists of 33 types of objects and 27 operators. Muñoz-Avila and Weberskirch (1996b) formally prove that this specification meets the conditions stated in Kambhampati et al. (1996) and Barrett and Weld (1994). These conditions state situations in which using a plan-space planner is better than a state-space planner. As a result, we conclude that planning with this specification is

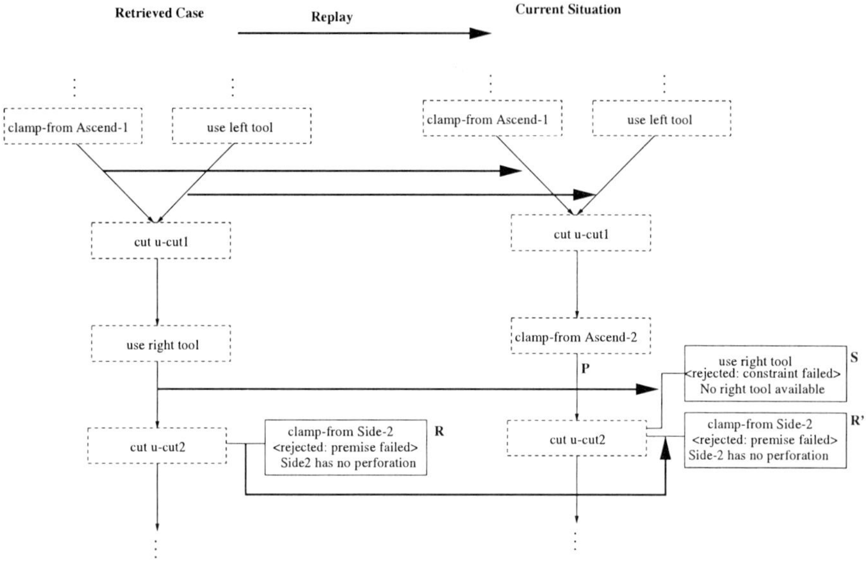

Fig. 7.8. Example of replay in CAPLAN/CBC.

more adequate with a plan-space planner like CAPLAN. Given that the first-principles planner plays an important role with reuse by complete decision replay, this result supports the use of case-based planning in CAPLAN.

Experiments suggest that dependency-driven retrieval increase the accuracy of the retrieval (Muñoz-Avila and Hüllen 1995) and reduce the effort of the first-principles planner to complete the partial solution obtained after replay. As a result, the performance of the overall case-based planning process is increased (Muñoz-Avila and Weberskirch 1996a).

Finally, the experiments performed show that the time taken by the first-principles planner to complete the partial solution obtained after replay is reduced when performing complete decision replay (Muñoz-Avila and Weberskirch 1996a).

7.7 PARIS: Flexible Reuse of Cases at Different Levels of Abstraction

Traditionally, case-based reasoning approaches retrieve, reuse, and retain cases given in a single, concrete representation. PARIS[2] (Bergmann 1996; Bergmann and Wilke 1995a) is a domain independent case-based planning system that differs from this traditional approach in that it introduces abstraction techniques into the case-based reasoning process. PARIS retrieves, reuses and retains cases at different (higher) levels of abstraction.

[2] Plan Abstraction and Refinement in an Integrated System

In a nutshell, PARIS works as follows. Available planning cases, given at the concrete level, are abstracted to several levels of abstraction which leads to a set of *abstract cases* that are stored in the case-base. Case abstraction is done automatically in the retain phase of the CBR-cycle. When a new problem must be solved, an abstract case is retrieved whose abstract problem description matches the current problem at an abstract level. In the subsequent reuse phase, the abstract solution is refined; i.e., the details that are not contained in the abstract case are added to achieve a complete solution of the problem. This refinement is done by a generative planner that performs a forward directed state space search. Figure 7.9 shows an overview of the whole system and its components. Besides case abstraction and refinement, PARIS also includes an explanation-based approach for *generalizing cases* during learning and for *specializing* them during problem solving. This technique allows to further increase the flexibility of reuse.

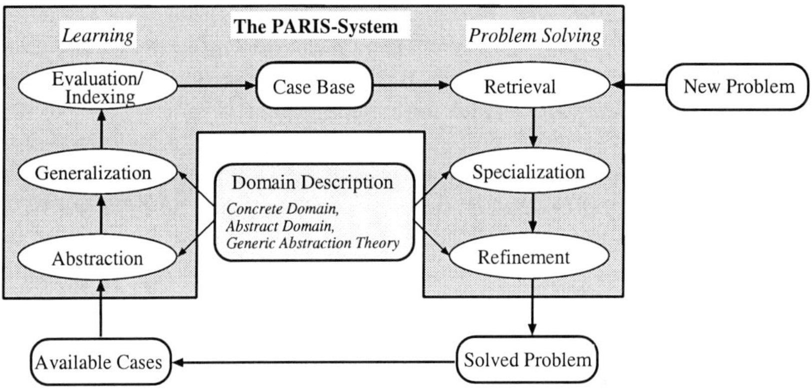

Fig. 7.9. Architecture of the PARIS system

The PARIS system benefits from using abstract cases in several ways (Bergmann and Wilke 1996):

- Abstraction reduces the complexity of a case, i.e., it simplifies its representation, e.g., by reducing the number of predicates, relations, constraints, operators, etc.
- Cases at higher levels of abstraction can be used as a kind of prototype, which can be used as indexes to a larger set of related, more detailed cases.
- Cases at higher levels of abstraction can be used as a substitute for a set of concrete cases, thereby reducing the size of the case base.
- Abstraction increases the flexibility of reuse. Adapting abstract solutions contained in cases at higher levels of abstraction leads to abstract solutions suitable for a large spectrum of concrete problems.
- Abstraction and refinement, on their own, can be used as a method for solution adaptation.

These advantages are particularly valuable in case-based planning. Since usually a large number of complex cases must be considered, the similarity assessment is very expensive. In addition, since flexible adaptation is required because of the vast solution space.

We now explain the approach followed in PARIS in more detail.

7.7.1 Different Levels of Abstraction and Abstract Cases

While cases are usually represented and reused on a single level, abstraction techniques enable a CBR system to reason with cases at several levels of abstraction. Each level of abstraction allows the representation of problems, solutions, and cases as well as the representation of general knowledge that might be required in addition to the cases. Usually, levels of abstraction are ordered (totally or partially) through an abstraction-relation, i.e., one level is called *more abstract* than another level.

A more abstract level is characterized through a reduced level of detail in the representation, i.e., it usually consists of less features, relations, constraints, operators, etc. Moreover, abstract levels model the world in a less precise way, but still capture certain important properties.

In traditional hierarchical problem solving (e.g., ABSTRIPS Sacerdoti 1974), abstraction levels are constructed by simply dropping certain features of the more concrete representation levels. However, it has been shown that this view of abstraction is too restrictive and representation dependent to make full use of the abstraction idea (Bergmann and Wilke 1995b; Holte et al. 1995). Therefore, PARIS enables different levels of abstraction to have different representation languages. That is, abstract properties can be expressed in completely different terms than concrete properties which enables the representation of meaningful abstractions in planning domains. Therefore, PARIS assumes that, in addition to the concrete planning domain, an *abstract planning domain* composed of *abstract operators* is part of the general knowledge. The general knowledge also contains a set of *abstraction rules* that describe different ways of abstracting concrete states. For example, in the domain of planning rotary symmetric workpieces, the concrete domain contains operators and predicates to describe the detailed contour of workpieces and individual cut operations that must be performed. The abstract domain abstracts from the detailed contour and represents larger units, called complex processing areas, together with the status of their processing (see also Figure 7.10).

Based on the level of abstraction, we can distinguish between two kinds of cases: *concrete cases* and *abstract cases.* A *concrete case* is a case located at the lowest available level of abstraction. An *abstract case* is a case represented at a higher level of abstraction.

7.7.2 Case Abstraction

Case abstraction means reducing the level of detail contained in the problem description and in the solution of a case, i.e., an abstract case contains less operators and less states than the concrete case. Furthermore, abstract operators and states are described using more abstract terms which typically require a reduced number of predicates.

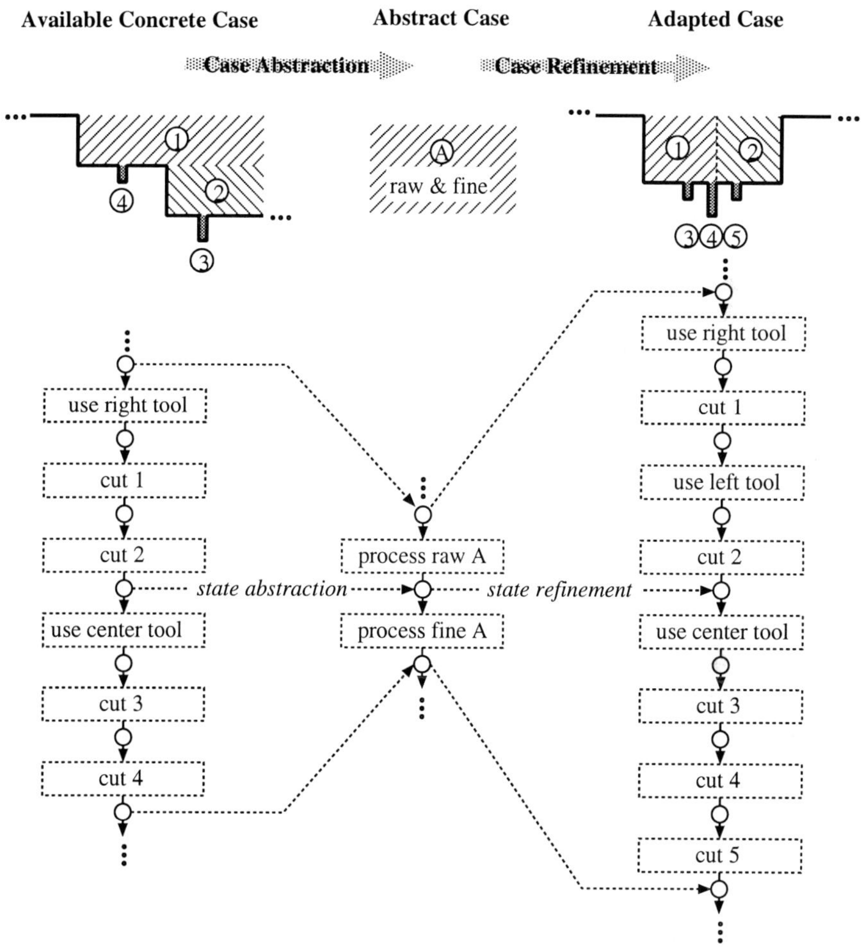

Fig. 7.10. Example of generating and refining abstract cases.

Figure 7.10 presents an example of the relationship between a concrete case and an abstract case. The left side shows a section of a concrete case, depicting how a step-like contour with two grooves is manufactured by a sub-plan consisting of 6 steps. The abstract case, shown in the middle of this figure, abstracts from the detailed contour and just represents a complex processing area named A that includes raw and fine elements. The corresponding abstract plan contains 2 abstract steps: processing in a raw manner and processing in a fine manner. The arrows between the concrete and the abstract case show how concrete and abstract states correspond. Each abstract state is derived from one of the existing concrete states (state abstraction). However, not all concrete states are abstracted. Some concrete states are skipped because they are considered to be irrelevant details. As a byproduct of this state abstraction, a sequence of concrete operators is abstracted to a single abstract operator. Note that the above explained kind of case abstraction is performed by an automatic procedure in PARIS, as part of the retain-phase of the CBR-cycle (see Bergmann and Wilke (1995a); Bergmann and Wilke (1995b) for details). Abstract and concrete cases are then stored in the case base for reuse.

7.7.3 Reuse of Abstract Cases

When a new problem must be solved, an abstract (or concrete) case is selected which matches the current problem at the respective level. If several matching cases are contained in the case-base, the retrieval procedure selects the case that is located at the lowest level of abstraction. The motivation for this preference is that, for more concrete cases, less effort has to be spent during refinement to achieve a complete solution. This corresponds to a similarity measure that ranks two cases more similar, the lower the level of abstraction for the identical parts of the problems (Bergmann et al. 1993).

During the reuse phase, the abstract solution contained in the retrieved case must be refined to become a fully detailed complete solution. The right side of Figure 7.10 shows an example of such a refinement. While the contour of the two workpieces differs drastically at the concrete level, the abstract problem matches exactly, because the 5 atomic contour elements in the new problem can be abstracted to a complex processing area with raw and fine elements. The abstract operators of the abstract case are then used to guide the state space planner to find a refined solution to the problem. Each abstract state is used as a sub-goal in the planning process. In the portion of the case shown in Figure 7.10, the abstract operator *process raw A* is refined to a sequence of four concrete steps which manufacture area 1 and 2. The next abstract operator is refined to a four-step sequence which manufactures the grooves 3, 4, and 5.

Note that PARIS allows the reuse of problem decompositions at different levels of abstraction. Abstract plans decompose the original problem into a set of much smaller subproblems. These subproblems are solved by a search-based problem solver. The problem decomposition leads to a significant reduction of the overall search that must be performed to solve the problem. With pure search the worst-case time complexity for finding the required solution by search is $O(b^n)$, where n is the length of the solution and b is the average branching factor. If the problem is decomposed by an abstract solution into k subproblems, each of which requires a solution of length $n_1, \ldots, n_k$, respectively, with $n_1 + n_2 + \cdots + n_k = n$, the worst-case time complexity for finding the complete solution is $O(b^{n_1} + b^{n_2} + \cdots + b^{n_k})$ which is $O(b^{max(n_1, n_2, \ldots, n_k)})$. So, if the sub-problems are small enough and mostly independent from each other, the underlying planner is able to solve them without stepping into the intractability problem.

7.7.4 Organization of the Case Base

As introduced in Section 7.3.1, the organization of the case base plays an important role in case-based planning. In PARIS abstract cases located at different levels of abstraction are used as hierarchical indexes to those concrete (or abstract) cases that contain the same kind of information but at a more detailed level. For this purpose, an *abstraction hierarchy* is constructed during the retain phase, in which abstract cases at higher levels of abstraction are located above abstract cases at lower levels. The leaf nodes of this hierarchy contain concrete cases (see Figure 7.11). During retrieval, this hierarchy is traversed top-down, following only those branches in which abstract cases are sufficiently similar to the current problem. This kind of memory organization is similar to the *memory organization packets* (MOPs) of Schank (1982).

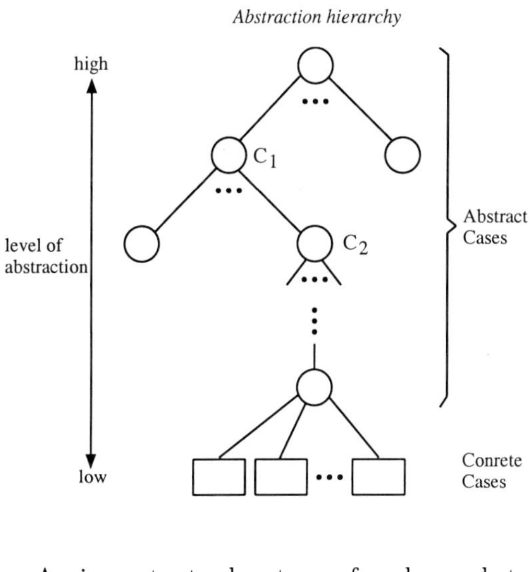

Fig. 7.11. Abstraction hierarchy for indexing cases.

An important advantage of such an abstraction hierarchy is that it provides a frame for realizing case deletion policies (Smyth and Keane 1995).

Cases deletion is particularly important to avoid the utility problem[3] (Tambe and Newell 1988; Francis and Ram 1993) that occurs when case bases grow very large. When reusing abstract cases for indexing and reuse, case deletion can be efficiently realized through a pruning of the abstraction hierarchy, i.e., deleting some branches of the tree. If a certain branch of the tree is removed (together with the respective concrete and possibly abstract cases) the abstract cases that remain accessible can still cover the set of target problems previously covered by the deleted case. However, not all details are present any more. During reuse, they must, therefore, be reconstructed by the generative planner. Consequently, pruning of the abstraction hierarchy has two contrary effects on the overall problem solving time:

- Since the detailed parts of the solution are not available any more, the *reuse effort increases* because these details must be reconstructed by the planner.
- Since the number of cases that must be inspected during retrieval is reduced, the *retrieval effort is reduced.*

The PARIS system makes use of an elaborated cost model for determining the expected cost or benefit (retrieval effort + reuse effort) of removing certain parts of the abstraction hierarchy (and the case base) (Bergmann 1996). Based on this model, an optimization algorithm computes a pruned abstraction hierarchy and thereby the related fragment of the case base that leads to the lowest expected overall cost for solving a new planning problem.

7.7.5 Summary of Experimental Results

The PARIS system was evaluated in extensive empirical studies using the domain of manufacturing planning. A detailed description of this domain can be found in Bergmann and Wilke (1995a); empirical results are presented in (Bergmann 1996; Bergmann and Wilke 1995b; Bergmann and Wilke 1995a; Bergmann and Wilke 1996). The most important results of these studies can be summarized as follows. For the used domain representation and case base it could be shown that:

- The case-based planning approach followed in PARIS leads to significantly shorter problem solving time than a pure generative planner.
- The reuse of abstract cases leads to a significant increase in the flexibility of reuse (number of new problems for which a case can be efficiently reused).
- Organizing the case-base using an abstraction hierarchy leads to a significant reduction of the retrieval time compared to a linear retrieval approach.
- The case deletion policy (pruning of the abstraction hierarchy) leads to a significant reduction of the overall problem solving time.

[3] The utility problem in CBR is also called swamping problem by Francis and Ram (1993).

7.8 ABALONE: Analogy in Proof Planning

Proof planning is an alternative to traditional methods in theorem proving that employs operators that represent chunks of a proof rather than low-level inference steps, such as resolution. Proof planning is AI-planning in a rather complicated domain, in which goals and state descriptions consist of complicated first-order or even higher-order sequents (axioms, lemmata, theorems, proof conjectures) rather than literals. In this domain, the enormous search spaces can be handled only by user-interaction or by very elaborated control knowledge. Often, control knowledge that avoids extensive search is not available, and therefore, case-based planning is a possible strategy to overcome the control problems.

The proof planner *CIAM* (Bundy et al. 1991), on top of which the analogy procedure ABALONE is implemented, has successfully been applied to theorem proving by induction. As known from Peano induction for natural numbers, inductive proofs have base-case and step-case subproofs. The latter has the subgoal $(IH \rightarrow IC)$ for an induction hypothesis IH and an induction conclusion IC and this subproof aims at rewriting the induction conclusion until the induction hypothesis is applicable.

For instance, in planning the theorem[4]

$$\texttt{lenapp} : \forall a, b.\ len(app(a,b)) = len(app(b,a))$$

the operator INDUCTION computes the induction schema (here, induction on lists[5]) and outputs the base-case and the step-case subgoal $(IH \vdash IC)$ for the induction hypothesis IH

$$len(app(a,b)) = len(app(b,a)) \tag{7.1}$$

and the induction conclusion IC

$$len(app(\underline{::(h,}a),b)) = len(app(b,\underline{::(h,}a))) \tag{7.2}$$

which is depicted as a tree in Figure 7.12(A)[6]. The operator WAVE applies rewrite-rules to subgoals, and three applications of WAVE reduce the goal $IH \vdash IC$ to

$$IH \vdash \underline{s}(len(app(a,b))) = \underline{s}(len(app(b,a))). \tag{7.3}$$

This subgoal is represented by a tree in Figure 7.12(B). The operator FERTILIZE uses the induction hypothesis to rewrite the current goal. Hence, FERTILIZE reduces the subgoal (7.3) to the subgoal

$$H \vdash \underline{s}(len(app(b,a))) = \underline{s}(len(app(b,a))) \tag{7.4}$$

---

[4] $app, len, ::$ denote the list functions *append*, *length*, *cons*. s is the successor function on natural numbers.

[5] with the successor $::(h,x)$ of x,

[6] The underlines mark the differences between IC and IH (*contexts*) that are shown as circles in the figure.

which can be removed by the operator ELEMENTARY. The whole step-case proof plan of `lenapp` is depicted in the lefthand sideof Figure 7.13.

The control in *CLAM* bases on the *rippling* heuristic that guides the rewriting of the induction conclusion in a systematic way that reduces the differences (context) between IC and IH. From an abstract point of view, rippling removes contexts or moves them to the top of the theorem tree (the term tree representation of a theorem) as shown in Figure 7.12, where the bold paths are those on which the contexts are moved. As soon as the contexts sit in the top position, FERTILIZE can be applied. Rippling is a powerful search heuris-

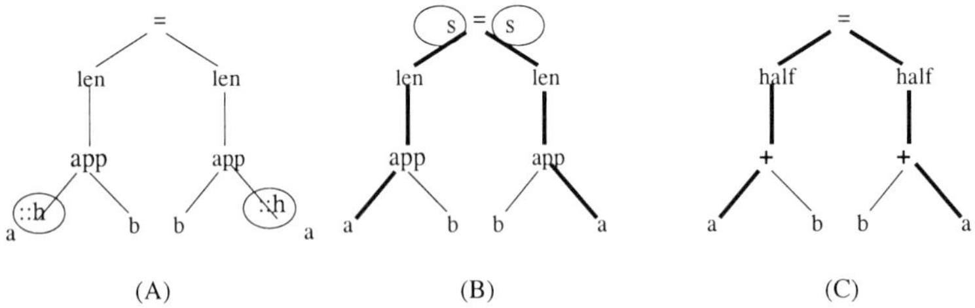

Fig. 7.12. Term trees (A) of the induction hypothesis of `lenapp`, (B) of the solved `lenapp`, and (C) of `halfplus` – with rippling paths in bold and ovals for contexts (omitted in C)

tic; but, even with such a heuristic, fully automated proof planning can fail because the control heuristics can be too restrictive, the default set of operators can be too restrictive, or the search for lemmata that are missing in the target becomes intractable. Using analogy as a control strategy in proof planning can help in these situations, see (Melis and Whittle 1997a). It can replay existing proof plans with the purpose of

- suggesting operators rather than searching for them,
- overriding the default control and default configurations,
- replacing search-intensive subtasks (such as finding an induction schema),
- suggesting target lemmata, and
- avoiding user interaction.

7.8.1 Analogy-Driven Proof Plan Construction

In accordance with the model of analogy-driven proof plan construction by Melis (1995), which is supported by empirical observations on human theorem proving (Melis 1994), ABALONE works at the proof plan level. Analogically replaying high-level plans is more robust than analogically replaying, e.g., resolution steps because the replay of higher-level proof plan operators may succeed while for many problems the exact replay of resolution steps fails. ABALONE analogically transfers a source plan produced by *CLAM* to a plan for the target problem. The transfer is done on the basis of second-order mappings, presented in the following subsection, that can map function and relation symbols. The replay of the source plan is made node by node. As in PRODIGY/ANALOGY, at each node in the source plan, justifications are stored and during the replay, these justifications are reinterpreted as described below. Of course, the actual justifications are specific for theorem proving; e.g., capturing the existence of a lemma needed in the proof or the identity of function occurrences in a formula. A source node is only replayed if its justifications still hold in the target or if the justification can be established. This serves two purposes. Firstly, it guarantees the correctness of target operator applications. Secondly, it provides a way of transferring only part of the source plan in some cases: if justifications cannot be established in the target, a *gap* is left in the target plan. In this way, it is only this part of the source that is not transferred, whereas the replay of the rest of the source plan can still be attempted.

Sometimes a node by node replay, as described above, is insufficient because the source and target plans differ in a significant respect. An example might be if the source and target plans have different induction schemes or operators have to be duplicated or replaced. Rather than failing, ABALONE is equipped with a number of *reformulations* introduced by Melis (1995) and Melis and Whittle (1997b), which make additional changes in the target plan. These reformulations are triggered by peculiarities of the mappings and justifications and are applied before the replay. Figure 7.13 shows an example of an analogical replay. The equations displayed in the source plan are justifications explained in section 7.8.3.

The main steps in the analogy-driven proof plan construction (Melis 1995) can be summarized as:

1. Retrieve a source problem.
2. Find a second-order mapping m_b from the source theorem to the target theorem.
3. Extend m_b to a mapping m_e from source rules to target rules.
4. Decide about the reformulations to be applied. The need for a reformulation is triggered by patterns in m_b or m_e.
5. Following the source plan, analogically replay the operators:
   - Apply reformulations
   - **if** operator justifications hold, **then** apply operator in target, **else** try to establish justification.
   - **if** justification cannot be established, **then** leave gap in target plan.

Second-order mappings and matching are those that can bind function symbols to function terms. Pure object-level syntactic similarity measures do not work for the retrieval and the mapping of proof plans because small changes of the problems can cause tremendous changes in proof plans. Therefore, ABALONE employs proof-relevant LF-abstractions, explained below, to restrict the retrieval, mapping, and adaptation. The restrictions derived from

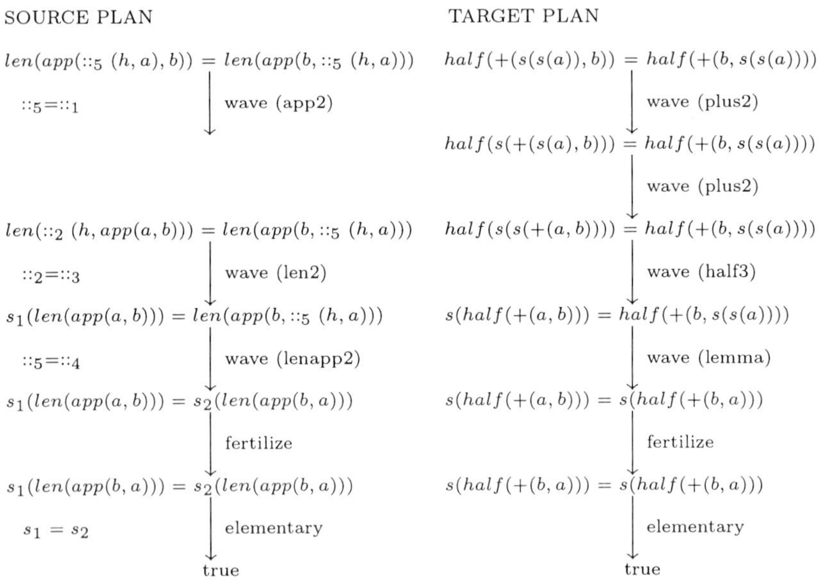

Fig. 7.13. Step-case replay

the abstractions guarantee the replayed (step-case) plan to be a correct plan for the target problem.

7.8.2 Retrieving Adaptable Cases

In the retrieval, second-order mappings are used to map the source theorem to the target theorem and source rules to target rules. Firstly, a *constrained* basic mapping m_b is constructed that maps the source theorem with indexed function symbols to the given target theorem. Secondly, m_b is augmented by an extended mapping m_e, which maps the source to the target rewrite-rules. m_b is restricted to essentially preserve the abstractions explained next. This constraint guarantees a successful step-case target plan.

Labeled fragments (LFs), introduced in Hutter (1994), are an abstraction of annotated rewrite-rules obtained by removing the structure of the contexts and those parts of the rules not affected by contexts. For each function/relation symbol occurring in the source and target theorems LFs corresponding to the rewrite-rules that belong to the source and target problem, respectively, are automatically computed. Take, for instance, the rewrite-rule

$$\mathsf{app2} : app(\underline{::\ (X,}Y), Z) \Rightarrow \underline{::\ (X,}(app(Y,Z)))$$

Note that in the lefthand sideof app2 the context is situated at the left argument of *app* and how it moves to the top of *app* in the righthand side of app2. This situation is reflected in the furthest right labeled fragment of *app* as shown in Figure 7.14.

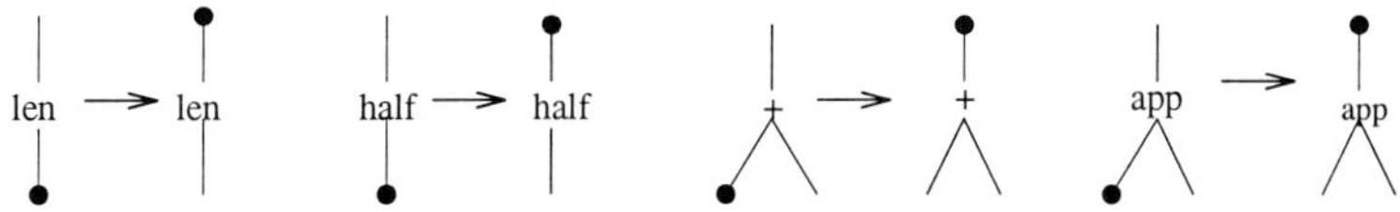

Fig. 7.14. Labeled fragments

The rippling paths in a theorem tree abstractly encode the step-case proof, in particular, the consecutive application of the WAVE operator in proof plans. In turn, the LFs determine the rippling paths. Therefore, LFs provide a *proof-relevant abstraction* of problems to be proved by induction. In the example, the WAVE operators (Figure 7.13) apply rewrite-rules, such as app2, that move the context as abstractly shown in Figure 7.14. First WAVE(app2) is applied and then WAVE(len2) which corresponds to the (abstract) rippling path of lenapp in Figure 7.12(B) which, in turn, is determined by the LFs in Figure 7.14. Based on corresponding LFs (Figure 7.14), the rippling path of lenapp equal those of halfplus in Figure 7.12(C) and hence the proof plan will be very similar.

With the help of LFs, the case base can be pre-structured into classes of cases. The elements of a class can be further distinguished by their rewrite-rules. This makes the retrieval a *two-stage* process with a first cheap step that retrieves the source class and a second, more expensive step that tries to second-order map the rewrite-rules of each case of that class rewrite-rules of the target problem. A class of source cases contains all cases with identical rippling paths. A class is represented by a theorem tree whose nodes on the rippling paths are annotated with the common LFs. The nodes occurring outside of rippling paths in any of the cases are abstracted to meta-variables in the class representation, because they are irrelevant for the abstraction. The first stage tries to approximately match the target theorem with one of the class representatives and checks the LFs in this process as well. It chooses the class with the fewest differences in rippling paths that are predefined by the available reformulations.

The second stage chooses the best case from the retrieved class by trying to second-order map the target-rules (lemmata) with the rules of the cases in the retrieved class. Second-order mapping is decidable but can be expensive, in particular when many rules are involved. The heuristics in Whittle (1995) support choosing reasonable mappings.

7.8.3 Analogical Replay

During the planning of the source theorem, justifications, (i.e., reasons for the application of an operator) are stored at each source plan node. As opposed to PRODIGY/ANALOGY, ABALONE's justifications consist of certain operator preconditions and of *C-equations*. For example, such a precondition of the WAVE operator is the existence of a rewrite-rule that matches the current goal. *C(onstraint)-equations* are justifications that are due to the use of indexed functions. ABALONE is able to map a function symbol at different positions in the source to different target images. For this reason, source function symbols at different positions are differentiated by indices. During the source planning, constraints of the form $f_i = f_j$, called C-equations, may be placed on these functions. In Figure 7.13,[7] for instance, $::_2 = ::_3$ states that the function $::_2$ in the subgoal is equal to the function $::_3$ in the rewrite-rule `len2` employed by WAVE in the source. In the target, this justification requires the identity of the images of mapping $::_2$ and $::_3$ to target functions. Note how the C-equations in Figure 7.13 arise in the source: When WAVE(`app2`) is applied, the lefthand sideof `app2` matches with the lefthand sideof the current goal – i.e., $app(\underline{::_1\ (X,Y)}, Z)$ matches with $app(\overline{::_5\ (h,a)}, b)$ which requires that $::_5 = ::_1$. These C-equations form an additional source justification the image of which must be satisfied in the target for a successful replay.

Deviations from a Simple Replay. As already described briefly, the main body of the analogical procedure replays the source plan, node by node, checking justifications at each stage. There are three occasions when ABALONE deviates from this simple node by node replay and performs different types of adaptation:
Firstly, peculiarities of the mappings trigger reformulations (Melis 1995) of the source plan. These reformulations are needed because sometimes the mappings alone are not sufficient to produce a correct plan proving the target theorem. Reformulations do more than just map symbols. In general, reformulations may insert, replace or delete operators or may change operators, sequents and justifications of proof plan nodes in a substantiated, rather than in an ad hoc, way. In the example, a reformulation duplicates the WAVE (`app2`) before actually replaying it to WAVE(`plus2`) because a C-equation failed in a particular way.

Secondly, in the situation that a justification does not hold in the target, ABALONE will try to establish the justification. Its exact action will depend on the type of justification:

- If the failed justification is associated with WAVE, and the situation is such that a source rewrite-rule has no corresponding rule in the target, then ABALONE speculates a target rewrite-rule. It does this by applying m_b, m_e, and C-equations to the source rewrite-rule. In the example in Figure 7.13, the justification at the WAVE(lenapp2) node fails because there is no target image for the source rewrite-rules `lenapp2`. The appropriate action is to suggest a target rewrite-rule `lemma` by using the mappings

[7] We have omitted some irrelevant indices from Figure 7.13 for the sake of clarity. In general, however, all function symbols are indexed.

and the C-equations to suggest a target rule. In the example, it uses the mappings $s_1 \mapsto s(w_1)$, $::_5 \mapsto s(s(w_2))$, and the C-equations $s_2 = s_1$ and $::_4 = ::_5$ to come up with the target rewrite-rule `lemma`: $half(X+s(s(Z))) \Rightarrow s(half(X+Z))$.
– A justification may fail because some side-condition does not hold. Whereas the side-condition may trivially hold in the source, the mapped version in the target may not hold trivially. Hence, ABALONE will set up the target side-condition as a lemma.

If a justification does not hold and cannot be established, then ABALONE produces a target plan node that has an empty operator slot and a subgoal that contains *gap variables* $?_i$. The gap variable is a place holder for the unknown subexpression of the sequent in the (current) target node that corresponds to the source subexpression that was changed by the source operator which could not be transferred.

Thirdly, after the replay, open goals are treated by the generative proof planner *CLAM*.

7.8.4 Summary and Results

ABALONE replays source *decisions*, among them decisions as difficult as the choice of induction schemes and induction variables for the INDUCTION operator. By replaying justifications, the system is flexible enough to suggest lemmata, override heuristics, and to override the default configuration of the generative planner.

ABALONE is implemented in Quintus Prolog as an extension to *CLAM*. It has been tested on a wide range of examples. It can plan several theorems that could not otherwise be planned in *CLAM*, or in other provers, fully automatically, see e.g., Melis and Whittle (1997b).

Analogy-driven proof plan construction uses an extended derivational analogy and, in this sense, is similar to Prodigy/Analogy and PARIS. ABALONE's use of abstraction differs from other systems. It uses abstractions at the meta-level only (Melis 1997). That is, the abstraction is used to restrict choices in the analogy process, and the retrieved cases are not abstracted, whereas in PARIS abstract cases are stored, retrieved and refined. As opposed to most CBR systems, ABALONE uses reformulations that are determined during the retrieval.

7.9 Summary and Related Work

On the one hand, the four systems presented in this chapter have in common the synergistic integration of planning from first principles with a case-based reasoner. On the other hand, they differ in many respects because of different motivations and mechanism.

7.9.1 Retain

Once a plan has been generated, each system performs different steps during the storage phase. In Prodigy/Analogy, an analysis of the solution is made relative to the problem description. Based on the partially ordered solution plan, connected components are determined and the corresponding interacting goals are identified to index independent subparts of the case. In addition, a goal regression process is performed to discriminate the initial state features relevant to the particular plan found. This process, known as the foot-printing process, ensures that only relevant features of the state cases are taken into account during retrieval. In Prodigy/Analogy, a case consists of a compression of the planning search episode. The case includes justifications of failed decisions taken during problem solving.

CAPlan/CbC computes the dependencies of the obtained solution. That is, the partial order in which the goals were achieved relative to the particular solution are computed and used as the main indexing criteria of the new case. In addition, the complete goal graph structure is stored including valid and invalid decisions and their justifications.

Paris computes several abstractions of the found solution. These abstractions are stored as cases in the case base. The rationale behind storing several abstractions of the same solution is based on two facts: firstly, an abstracted solution at a higher level represents more concrete solutions than an abstracted solution at a lower level. Secondly, refining an abstract solution is more expensive the higher the level of the abstract solution. By storing several abstractions of the same solution Paris finds a balance between these two opposite facts.

In Abalone, the proof of a theorem is stored together with a description of the theorem, which is abstracted to rippling paths representing a class of theorems having similar proofs.

7.9.2 Retrieval

Prodigy/Analogy supports multi-case retrieval; cases covering disjoint subsets of the goals of the new problem are retrieved. The structure of the case-base in Prodigy/Analogy reflects this principle by discriminating cases with respect to interacting top-level goals. When matching the initial states of the candidate cases and the problem, only relevant features are taken into account. That is, only features that contribute to the particular solution of the case are considered, as the relevance of a feature depends on the particular solution found. Retrieval is bounded to finding a case with a *reasonable* partial match.

In CAPlan/CbC, a dependency-driven retrieval strategy is performed. The idea is to consider interactions between the goals of the new problem, called dependencies. CAPlan/CbC retrieves cases by considering the dependencies between the goals first. This is reflected in the structure of the case base, as cases are discriminated by their dependencies at the top level. This strategy is adequate for domains, like process planning, in which interactions between the goals can be predetermined.

In PARIS, a case corresponding to an abstract plan is retrieved. This plan solves the abstracted problem description of the current problem. The structure of the case base allows PARIS to find an appropriate abstract case at the lowest possible level of abstraction. In this way, the adaptation costs are considered during retrieval because, the lower the level is, the less effort is required for the refinement of the abstract case. Furthermore, PARIS makes use of a case deletion policy in order to avoid swamping of the case base.

In ABALONE, retrieval is a two-stage process. In the first stage, the abstraction of source theorems is matched with the target theorem. An abstraction represents a whole class of theorems. In the second stage, an element is retrieved from the class selected in stage one. This is done by searching for a second-order match between rules of the target problem with rules of source problems from the class. The search is supported by heuristic preference criteria. The second stage is comparable to searching for a case by matching the initial states.

7.9.3 Adaptation

PRODIGY/ANALOGY annotates the derivational trace of the cases with justifications. During replay, these justifications are verified in the new situation. In this way, the first-principles reasoner will not make decisions known from the case to be wrong. The justifications are expressed in a language describing situations occurring in state-space planning. A similar principle is followed in CAPLAN/CBC and ABALONE. However, given that their first-principles planners are different, the way the justifications are expressed and handled is different.

A case in CAPLAN/CBC contains the goal graph expressing the relations between goals and decisions (valid and invalid). Justifications are expressed in these graphs and can be interpreted in terms of plan-space planning. When the goal graph is reconstructed relative to the new situation, the justifications are checked. The result, as in PRODIGY/ANALOGY, is that decisions known to be invalid from the case are not explored. However, by reconstructing the goal graph, CAPLAN/CBC enables the user to interact with the first-principles planner CAPLAN after replay has taken place.

ABALONE's justifications formalize concepts in theorem proving, such as identity of sorts, identity of function occurrences, and the existence of lemmata to be used. A singularity of the justifications in ABALONE is that the validity of a justification can be achieved by reformulations or by introducing new subgoals (lemmata). This is different from PRODIGY/ANALOGY and CAPLAN/CBC, where their justifications are matched directly in the current situation. Another unique ingredient of analogy-driven proof plan construction are reformulations that can be applied to enable a match of problems in the first place. These reformulations change a problem and its proof plan at the same time.

A case in PARIS is an abstraction of a plan. As a result, there are no justifications because the search space of cases are expressed from the search space of the first-principles planners. In this context, adaptation refines the retrieved abstract case to a solution at the concrete planning level.

7.9.4 Revise

Another common characteristic of the four case-based reasoners presented in this chapter is that they are based on a first-principles reasoner that ensures that the plans obtained are always correct with respect to the domain theory. This contrasts to, say, CHEF were the obtained solutions need to be revised as there is no guarantee of their validity.

7.9.5 Related Case-Based Planning Systems

Several other case-based planning systems have been developed in the USA and in Europe.

PRIAR (Kambhampati 1994) reuses plans produced by a generative, non-linear, hierarchical planner. Following the derivational analogy philosophy, PRIAR uses the *validation structure* of a plan, which represents the dependencies among the plan steps, for retrieval and reuse of planning cases. However, PRIAR additionally employs domain independent strategies for plan adaptation. However, PRIAR does not address the problem of how to organize a case base efficiently.

Within a deductive framework for planning, Köhler (1996) developed an approach to reuse plans. Her work concentrates on the retrieval process and used description logics as query languages for the plan library. In contrast to the systems presented here, her MRL system requires the domain to be represented in formal logic. Further, for indexing the cases a formalization in terminological logic is also required.

The adaptation approaches described by Smyth and Keane (1993) and Lieber and Napoli (1996) are similar to the use of reformulations in ABALONE. The closest related system in theorem proving, PLAGIATOR (Kolbe and Walther 1995), differs from ABALONE in many respects. Its pure transformational reuse produces a set of target assumptions rather than a target proof plan. For additional discussion of the differences see Melis and Whittle (1997b).

MPA is a case-based planner performing multi-plan adaptation of partial-order plans (Francis and Ram 1995). Adaptation is made by transforming the derivational trace of the retrieved cases with a generic procedure instead of a generic planner as in the systems presented here. This procedure, however, is based on a careful study of the way the first-principles planner SNLP works. Thus, the procedure subsumes the work done by the generic planner.

7.10 Conclusion and Future Tasks

Several case-based planning systems (including the ones reported here) address important problems that occur in real planning applications. Experimental investigations have shown a drastic speedup (factor 1000 and more) of problem solving through case-based planning compared to pure generative planning approaches in many domains. However, several important questions have to be investigated in the future:

- knowledge engineering for case-based planning,
- user interaction, particularly during the reuse phase,
- maintaining the quality of plans (e.g., the cost and resource usage during plan execution) during reuse, and, finally,
- the integration of a case-based planner into an industrial environment.

We think that further, basic research in the area of case-based planning should try to overcome the following limiting assumptions because, in most real world applications, they do not hold.

- All required knowledge (e.g., operators, problem description, ...) is available prior to the planning process.
- Planning and execution are separated, i.e., first a plan is constructed and then the plan is executed.

Consider, for example, the task of planning an information gathering process from different sources. In this situation, several actions (e.g., operators for obtaining some information) must be executed prior to completing the plan. That is, it is necessary to produce a preliminary partial plan before all required information is available and to execute parts of the plan in order to get the information for completing the plan. First steps towards a model of planning of this type can be found in (Etzioni and Weld 1994; Knoblock 1996).

Acknowledgments

This work was supported by the NATO grant CRG.950405 and by the Deutsche Forschungsgemeinschaft SFB 378. This work was also supported by the Commission of European Communities (ESPRIT contract No. 22196, the INRECA II project, *Information and Knowledge Reengineering for Reasoning from Cases*). The partners of INRECA II are AcknoSoft (prime contractor, France), Daimler-Benz (Germany), TecInno (Germany), Irish Multimedia Systems (Ireland), and University of Kaiserslautern (Germany).

8. CBR for Design

Katy Börner

8.1 Introduction

Design research has a number of goals, including a better understanding of design, the development of tools to aid human designers, and the potential automation of some design tasks. Computer-aided design is concerned with using computers to assist in the design process to produce better designs in shorter time. The reuse of well-tested and optimized designs is an important aspect for decreasing design times, increasing design quality, and improving the predictability of designs.

This chapter summarizes the main results of applying CBR to support human problem solving in design. Its special focus is on research carried out in Europe and in particular in Germany. We start by providing a general characterization of design tasks. An overview of applicable reasoning methods, as well as a survey of case-based systems for design assistance, will be provided in Section 8.3. Following this, Section 8.4 discusses characteristics of case-based design (CBD) using the domain of architectural design for illustration. Reoccurring problems in CBD are listed. Sections 8.5 and 8.6 describe a number of methods that have been developed to handle the complexity of design tasks. Section 8.5 introduces an algorithm for flexible case retrieval that allows for the combination of several similarity measures at query time dynamically. In Section 8.6 three approaches to structural similarity assessment and adaptation are presented and discussed. Section 8.7 introduces EADOCS, a multi-level and hybrid expert system for conceptual design tasks that achieves structural adaptation by case combination. To conclude, approaches for automating configuration tasks, as introduced in Chapter 6, are contrasted with approaches aimed at the assistant-like support of *design* tasks and directions for future research are pointed out.

Rather than preparing new descriptions of the Fish & Shrink algorithm (Section 8.5) and the EADOCS system (Section 8.7), collaborative participation was solicited from the original authors *Jörg W. Schaaf* and *Bart Netten*, respectively.

8.2 The Design Task

Design is concerned with the construction of an artifact from single parts that may be either known and given or newly created for this particular artifact. Constraints on the artifact may be rigidly or informally defined.

Routine, Innovative, and Creative Design. There is a general acceptance of the classification of design tasks into *routine*, *innovative*, and *creative* that has proved to be useful (Coyne et al. 1987; Gero 1990).

Routine design can be defined as design that proceeds within a well-defined state space of potential designs. That is, all the variables and their application ranges, as well as the knowledge to compute their values, are directly derivable from existing designs.

Innovative design can be defined as non-routine design that proceeds within a well-defined state space of potential designs. In contrast to routine design, the applicable ranges for values of variables may change. What results is a design with a familiar structure but novel appearance because the values of the defining variables (and their combinations) are unfamiliar.

Creative design can be defined as non-routine design that introduces new variables and, as a result, extends or moves the state space of potential designs.

The development of knowledge-based systems has concentrated on routine design tasks (also called configuration tasks, see Chapter 6), i.e., tasks that involve a well understood problem solving space where all decision points and outcomes are known *a priori*. Routine design problems are typically represented by a well defined set of configurable components, a set of constraints that the final design must satisfy, and operators that encode valid component configurations (cf. Section 6.4). There is a rich set of approaches that can be used to efficiently control the search for solutions. Configuration can be seen as a comparatively tractable design task that allows for a closed world assumption in knowledge-based systems development and can be completely automated.

Innovative and creative design tasks are usually described by incomplete knowledge about the number and type of components to arrange. Often, a complete set of constraints that the final design must satisfy is not available. The problem solution may correspond to a set of design solutions that can be ordered corresponding to preference criteria. Knowledge about the validity of solutions is not available in general. Often the complexity of this reasoning process requires an iterative process in which the level of abstraction is incrementally refined to establish the solution. That is, each solution reduces the design space and serves as a starting point for local search at a more concrete level.

8.3 Design Assistance

In recognition of the open ended nature of the input data and the lack of formal methods, approaches to innovative and creative design support have aimed at *assisting* the user rather than automating the architectural programming process. Usually, design systems work as interactive assistants employing user intervention whenever needed to generate or evaluate a proper solution.

In order to built assistance systems that are effective and can easily be integrated into the daily working environment, adequate user interfaces must be provided (Pearce et al. 1992). If drawings are the central medium for the communication (e.g., in architectural designs), then a design support system should offer a graphical, CAD-like user interface. Adequate user interfaces are an indispensable requirement to enable high interactivity. This is needed for two reasons. Firstly, the huge amount of knowledge necessary to support complex design tasks requires partially automatic knowledge acquisition; i.e., without bothering the user to answer thousands of questions. Systems that require an immense effort for knowledge elicitation will rarely if ever succeed. Filling in large forms to label and save each possibly useful experience is very difficult to integrate into the workflow of potential users. Secondly, the complexity of such design processes needs to be communicated in an appropriate, domain specific way. Highly user-interactive frameworks, which manage knowledge elicitation during the system usage, are a real challenge to enable efficient computer-aided support in design.

The more complex the real-world applications, the higher the need for having deeply integrated system architectures. Knowledge acquisition, learning, and problem solving are advantageously viewed as constructive and cooperative processes, in which the user is an integrated part (Aamodt 1991; Veloso 1994). Ideally, the system works as a *learning apprentice* (Mitchell et al. 1985) improving reasoning performance continually by requiring a user to accept, correct, or refuse solutions or to provide solutions for problems. The knowledge is integrated into the knowledge base, compiled, and exploited during continuous problem solving. By this close linkage of knowledge acquisition and problem solving, the system is able to provide incrementally increasing support that is adaptable to the user and the peculiarities of the chosen domain. However, the integration of problem solving and learning in a single system still demands progress in both fields. This is especially true for systems that aim at the support of design tasks.

8.3.1 Reasoning Methods

There are several approaches which have been proposed to handle design tasks. Among them are formulae (Coyne 1988), constraints (Thagard et al. 1990), rules and grammars (Fu 1974; Gonzalez and Thomason 1978), autonomous agents (Morgenstern 1993; Bhat 1995), case-based reasoning (Goel

1989; Domeshek and Kolodner 1992; Hinrichs 1992a), and prototype-based reasoning (Gero 1990).

Formulae, grammars, or complete and consistent sets of constraints can only be defined for *routine design* tasks. They are often constructed based on the a priori knowledge available to the designers and their experiences. In order to support *innovative design* tasks, classical AI problem solving methods are not applicable, in general. Here, the use of experience is of particular importance and case-based reasoning comes into play. In order to support *creative design* tasks, the application of analogical problem solving is advantageous. It allows for the transfer of knowledge across different domains with special emphasis put on structural dependencies. This chapter concentrates on the application of case-based reasoning to support *innovative* and *creative* design tasks.

8.3.2 Case-Based Design Systems

There are many case-based design systems described in the literature. They have been proposed for a variety of domains that range from well-structured domains, such as the design of mechanical devices, to largely informal domains, such as architectural design. For example, Cyclops (Navinchandra 1988) does landscape design. Archie, Archie-II (Domeshek and Kolodner 1992; Domeshek and Kolodner 1997), Seed (Flemming et al. 1997), Janus (Fisher et al. 1989), Cadre (Hua et al. 1993) and Fabel (Voß 1997) support architectural design. Kritik (Goel 1989) and Kritik-II (Bhatta 1995; Goel et al. 1997) combine case-based with model-based reasoning for the design of physical devices. Software interface design is supported by AskJef (Barber et al. 1992), Asp-II and Benton (Tsatsoulis and Alexander 1997). Cadsyn (Maher and Zhang 1991; Maher and Zhang 1993; Maher et al. 1996) solves structural design tasks. Cadet is a case-based design tool that aids the conceptual design of electro-mechanical devices (Sycara et al. 1992; Narashiman et al. 1997). Detailed descriptions of many of these systems can be found in (Maher et al. 1996; Maher and Pu 1997).

Every application domain requires special considerations about the knowledge representation used and the retrieval, solution adaptation, and solution verification applied. Many systems support architectural design tasks. Therefore, this domain is used in Section 8.4 to illustrate a number of reoccurring problems that have to be addressed by every implemented system that aims at the support of design tasks.

Focusing on research pursued in Europe, Sections 8.5 and 8.6 describe research results achieved in Fabel, a major research project in Germany (Voß 1997). The aim of Fabel was to investigate ways of supporting design tasks by case-based and model-based methods, thus bridging the gap between case-based systems (which so far did little more than presenting former cases to the user) and expert systems, which embody theories and heuristics. Fabel has been a research project with a strong application orientation. In the Fabel prototype, diverse approaches and tools to case retrieval and case adaptation have been developed (see (Voß 1994) and (Börner 1995c) for surveys). While the tools are rather independent, they have comparable user interfaces and work together according to the paradigm of a virtual construction site (Hovestadt and Schmidt-Belz 1995). Section 8.7 introduces EADOCS, a system that applies *structural adaptation by case combination* for the expert assisted design of composite sandwich panels (Netten et al. 1995).

8.4 Characteristics of Case-Based Design

Maher and Gomez de Silva Garza (1997) list three reoccurring themes in the implementation of case-based design systems; the need to represent and to manage *complex design cases*, the need to augment cases with *generalized design knowledge*, and the need to *formalize a typically informal body of knowledge*:

Complex Cases. According to Gebhardt et al. (1997) *complex cases* can be characterized as case which:

- may have to be cut out of large data models (such as CAD plans representing entire buildings);
- may not be described sufficiently in terms of attributes but have to be represented structurally (e.g., by graphs);
- contains variables that do not statically describe a problem or a solution. Instead these variables dynamically take the role of, e.g., problem variables if they match the query;
- may be useful in multiple ways and allow for more than one interpretation;
- may have to be composed and adapted to solve a problem.

The need for complex case representations has several implications. Among them are:

- Often, a new problem has to be reinterpreted or reformulated to be comparable with past experiences.
- Without distinguished problem and solution parts, the overlapping parts of a problem and past case(s) have to be identified and case parts for transfer and combination must be chosen.
- Multiple case interpretations require a flexible combination of several similarity functions. Similarity assessment has to proceed over complex structures.
- Different aspects of a case (e.g., pragmatic features, the structure of cases) may have to be jointly considered for retrieval, match, and adaptation.

Taken together, complex case representations cause increased computational expense in the retrieval, matching and adaptation of cases. To guarantee answer times that are acceptable for real world applications, efficient memory organizations directly tailored to the applied reasoning mechanisms are essential. Problems that relate to the amount and the structural complexity of the knowledge have to be addressed.

Generalized design knowledge. Design knowledge may include causal models, state interactions, heuristic models, heuristic rules, and geometric constraints. Often, this knowledge is not available for *innovative* and *creative* design tasks.

Lack of formal knowledge. In situations where only an informal body of knowledge is available, this may result in case representations that are suited to *support* human problem solving rather than automated reasoning or by focusing on tasks that can be formalized. However, this chapter concentrates on approaches that assist design tasks despite the informal character of the given knowledge.

8.4.1 Case-Based Architectural Design

Much work in CBD has been carried out in the domain of architectural design. Reasons for this may be the centrality of past experiences and the economical impact of design support. Both aspects are outlined in what follows.

In architectural design, prior experiences, typically represented by CAD-layouts, constitute the main source of knowledge. These layouts are used to inspire, guide, and communicate architectural work. By applying CBR, annotated layouts are employed directly in the case base. During problem solving, cases serve as a first guess to shortcut reasoning from first principles. Conversely, cases allow architects to refine, supplement, and qualify the rules of thumb, principles, and theories architects learned at school or university. The continuously increasing amount of electronically available data, the electronical connection of architectural bureaus, and the continuing standardization ease the access and reuse of this huge amount of design knowledge. The centrality of layouts directly suggests an application of case-based approaches to support design tasks.

Additionally, architectural design is one of the keystones to economic competitiveness. Each country spents about 30 percent of it gross national product (i.e., the annual total value of goods produced and services provided) for housing. In the modern competitive world, designers are under a constant pressure to turn out new and innovative products quickly. As a consequence, computational models for architectural design are important research topics and the development of computational models founded *Artificial Intelligence* paradigms has provided an impetus for much of current research in this direction (Coyne et al. 1988; Gero and Sudweeks 1994). For of all these reasons, the domain of architectural design was selected for illustration purposes here.

8.4.2 Knowledge Representation and Reasoning

As introduced in Section 1.3.8, four knowledge containers of a CBR system are distinguished; the *vocabulary used*, the *similarity measure*, the *case base*, and the *solution transformation*. We assume that the knowledge required to evaluate solutions is included in the container for *solution transformation*. While the content of the containers can be changed locally, the knowledge contained in these containers has to supplement each other. That is, the similarity measure has to be defined in such a way that it allows the comparison of queries and cases in their corresponding representations and to derive some degree of similarity from this comparison, for example, as a numerical value in the interval $[0, 1]$. The cases, the similarity measure, and the solution transformations will define the space of possible solutions.

Vocabulary. The selection of an appropriate vocabulary is to a great extend task and domain dependent. The vocabulary should be able to capture all the salient features of the design that are relevant to support problem solving in the selected domain.

Cases. Examining the way architects work reveals a wide variety of what should constitute a design case: the size varies from few design objects to a whole storey or even an entire building; the case layout could be a simple list of some properties or a complex structure involving many types of relations between components with composite attributes.

Among the major considerations in representing past design experience by cases are the *usage*, the *granularity*, the *level of abstraction,* and the *perspective* cases should have:

Usage: There are two ways cases can be used. On the one hand, cases may represent abnormal situations or exceptions while rules are applied to capture norms and regular situations. On the other hand, cases may successfully be used to capture regular or normal situations in a more natural way (especially if other knowledge is not available). Another decision refers to the use of positive *good* cases or the incorporation of negative cases helping to anticipate and thus avoid mistakes made in the past.

Granularity: In architecture, complete buildings have been taken as cases (Goel 1989; Domeshek and Kolodner 1992; Hinrichs 1992b). Other approaches promoted user-defined cases which are marked in an overall project in a creative way that is hardly definable and repeatable (Voß 1994). Aiming at a task-oriented user support, the grain size of cases matches the grain size of decisions the architect needs to make. A uniform, task-oriented methodology to derive cases out of CAD layouts representing entire projects was proposed by Janetzko et al. (1994).

Level of abstraction: Corresponding to their level of abstraction, Riesbeck and Schank (1989, p.12) distinguish *ossified cases*, *paradigmatic cases*, and *stories. Ossified cases* are like general rules of thumb and independent of the events they were originally derived from. They tend to be relevant in only the areas for which they were originally intended and form the basis for making everyday decisions. *Paradigmatic cases* represent the one experience that was in any way relevant to what you are now experiencing and the task left is to find where the current situation differs in order to adapt the case to solve the new situation. They form the base of expertise that a person accumulates beyond the textbook rules that s/he has been taught. *Stories* relate by virtue of their complexity and myriad aspects to a large variety of possible circumstances. They can be indexed and, later, accessed in multiple ways. Creativity depends on the ability to analyze stories effectively and under various poin ts of view.

Perspective: Cases may be acquired according to a *state-oriented* perspective or a *solution-path* perspective. While state-oriented cases represent essentially the problem and its solution, solution-path cases refer to the process or operator that derives the solution from the problem description.

Similarity Measure and Case Retrieval. Basically, there are two different approaches to similarity assessment in CBR. The *computational approach* (Tversky 1977; Stanfill and Waltz 1986; Aha 1991), which is based on computing an explicit similarity function for all cases in the case base, and the *representational approach*, proposed by (Kolodner 1980; Kolodner 1984) using a structured memory of cases. Some techniques, such as kd-trees and CRNs (both introduced in Chapter 3), attempt to combine these two fundamental approaches.

Similarity approach. Case sets are stored in an unstructured way. Retrieval is performed on the basis of a similarity measure[1]. Most approaches to similarity assessment in CBR estimate the usefulness of cases, based on the presence or absence of certain features (cf. Domeshek and Kolodner 1992; Richter 1992a). The features are pre-classified as important with respect to retrieval. Similarity is assessed by a numeric computation and results in a single number which is intended to reflect all aspects of the similarity.

To reduce the complexity of structural comparisons, two-stage models have been proposed in the literature, e.g., the MAC/FAC model (Gentner and Forbus 1991). In the first stage, Many cases Are Called using a computationally cheap filter. Here, flat vector representations of a past case and a problem representing the predicates are matched to identify a number of possible candidate cases; information about the inter-relating structure between these predicates is not considered. In the second stage, Few of these possible candidates Are Chosen by carrying out a structure mapping between the problem and each candidate resulting in useful, structurally sound matches. In such a way, the complexity of phenomena in similarity-based access can be reduced.

[1] See also memory-based reasoning (Stanfill and Waltz 1986) or instance-based learning (Aha 1991; Aha et al. 1991)

Representational approach. For representational approaches, the case base is pre-structured. Retrieval proceeds by traversing the index structure, e.g., *memory organization packets* (Schank 1982; Kolodner 1984). Cases that are neighbors according to the index structure are assumed to be similar. Constraints on a problem serve as indices into the memory. Probing the memory, returns cases that provide a solution, some of the context as well as feedback for external evaluation. This information is used to determine how applicable the case is, how to adapt it, and how to avoid repeating previous failures.

If case-based reasoning is applied to support *innovative* and *creative* design tasks, then case retrieval requires:

Flexible case retrieval: The need to exploit different views on single cases requires a method for so-called flexible case retrieval. Given a large case base, a problem, and a number of aspects that are relevant for similarity assessment, a set of cases have to be retrieved which show similar aspects as in the actual problem. Be aware that the importance of certain aspects for similarity assessment is not known at memory organization time. That is, different similarity measures, each determining the similarity of a case and a query under a certain point of view have to be dynamically composed during retrieval. Approaches, such as *k*d-trees (Wess 1995) or Case Retrieval Nets (cf. Chapter 3), allow for dynamic weighting of certain features to be considered during similarity assessment but apply exactly one similarity measure.

Structural similarity assessment: In order to consider the structure of cases during retrieval, similarity assessment has to process structural case representations in which variables dynamically take the role of problem or solution variables.

Similarity assessment in terms of adaptability: Conventional CBR systems treat retrieval, matching (or justification), and adaptation separately and sequentially. Recent work, however, shows that the integration of these stages, especially retrieval in terms of adaptability, improves the suitability and performance of CBR significantly (Smyth and Keane 1993). A more general notion of case usability (instead of similarity) is required (Paulokat et al. 1992). Ideally, similarity should imply adaptability. That is, retrieved cases should be adaptable to correctly solve a current problem. Existing techniques for so called *adaptation-guided retrieval*, such as implemented in DéJà VU(Smyth and Cunningham 1992; Smyth and Keane 1993) try to determine similarity without actually performing the computationally expensive adaptations.

Solution Transformation and Case Adaptation. In design, new situations rarely match old ones exactly. Even small differences between the actual problem and the most similar case may require significant adaptations. Adaptation plays a central role and comprises the selection of the parts of the past solution(s) that need(s) to be adapted, as well as the adaptation itself. Cunningham and Slattery (1993) distinguish three general kinds of adaptation:

(i) *Parametric adaptation* corresponds to the substitution, instantiation or adjustment of parameters.
(ii) *Structural adaptation*, as done by *transformational analogy* (Carbonell 1983b) or approaches that use grammars (Fu and Bhargava 1973), retrieves stored solutions and revises them by applying adaptation operators (or grammar rules) to solve a new problem.
(iii) *Generative adaptation*, such as *derivational analogy* (Carbonell 1986), reuses and adapts problem-solving episodes by replaying their derivation.

Given that architectural design is a weak theory domain, hardly any information about the relevance of features guiding the selection of similar (i.e., *adaptable*) cases is available. Often, the adaptation of prior layouts mainly corresponds to adding, eliminating, or substituting physical objects. Because of the variety and the possible high number of combinations of these modifications, adaptation knowledge is difficult to acquire by hand. Here, *structural adaptation* (as introduced in Sections 8.6.2 to 8.6.4) or *adaptation by case combination* (see Section 8.7) may provide a better approach.

8.5 Fish & Shrink Algorithm for Flexible Case Retrieval

This section proposes an algorithm for flexible case retrieval, named *Fish & Shrink*, that is able to search quickly through the case base, even if the aspects that define usefulness are spontaneously combined at query time.

8.5.1 Required Functionality

Given rich and complex cases, as in the design domain, it is reasonable to use them in different contexts by regarding different aspects. For example, if an engineer and an interior decorator both try to solve a problem, they can use the same case base if each one gets result cases selected with focus on their own special needs. To exhaust the full potential of inherent solutions of cases, we suggest to represent cases with respect to as many different aspects as reasonable. Regarding different aspects leads to different representations of cases, each trying to catch a very specific view of them.

We do not have any formal definition of what an aspect is. Nevertheless the idea of regarding aspects leads to some formal constructs. We use the name of an aspect to identify a point of view and to index a pair of functions. Firstly, α_{name} denotes a *representation function.* As input, α_{name} takes the original representation of a case and as output it produces a representation in the aspect representation space Ω_{name} which emphasizes features important to the aspect idea and which is usually condensed. Secondly, the distance function δ_{name} takes two representations (from Ω_{name}) and calculates the distance of two cases with regard to this particular aspect. Fulfillment of the triangle inequality is recommended but not postulated. How the presented approach handles violations of the triangle inequality is presented in Schaaf (1998).

As a result, a case base can be seen as a multiply linked set of polyhedrons (Figure 8.1(a)). Each polyhedron (representing a case) consists of several aspect representations linked to corresponding aspect representations of other cases by edges. These edges are labeled with the calculated distance between cases concerning one particular aspect.

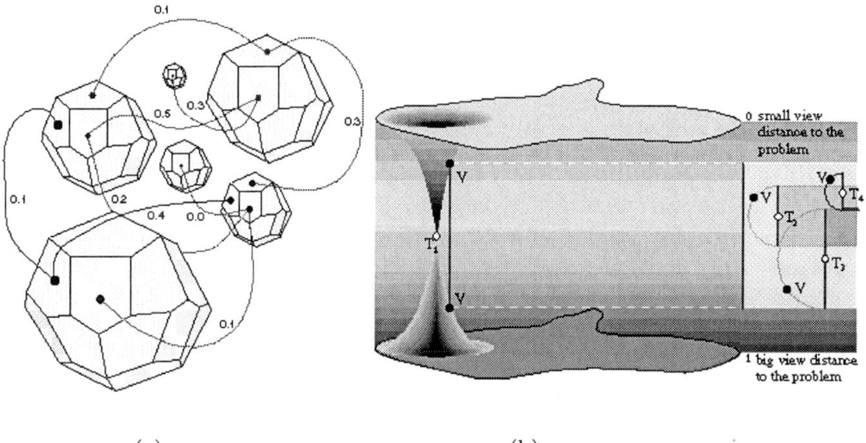

Fig. 8.1. Illustration of Fish & Shrink: (a) The case base as a network of cases. (b) The retrieval metaphor of sinking cases being dragged down by others

Up to this point, most standard approaches towards case base organization are very similar. Each network concerning one aspect can be seen as a separate case base with its own search structure. Problems arise in these standard approaches if *ad hoc* combinations (for example, a weighted combination) of several aspects should be allowed.

To describe a new approach, called the *Fish & Shrink* method, we first introduce the term *view distance SD* defined between two cases; the customized distance based on predefined aspect distances δ_i. As an example, the view distance may be the result of the function

$$SD(F_x, F_y, \mathbf{W}) = \sum_{i=1}^{n} w_i \delta_i(F_x, F_y)$$

where two cases F_x and F_y and a weight vector $\mathbf{W} = (w_1 ... w_n)$ serve as input. The weight vector holds an importance value for each aspect and can be manipulated in an *ad hoc* way; i.e., before each search request. Experts in case-based reasoning and domain experts are invited to invent more sophisticated view distance functions. They can be integrated online and tested.

Each view distance function ought to fulfill the triangle inequality. Violation can be detected while running the algorithm. Schaaf (1998) suggests a fault compensation based on empirical data.

8.5.2 Fish & Shrink

Given reasonable aspects, the corresponding representation functions, proper aspect distance functions, and a collection of view distance functions, we now define an anytime algorithm to search the case base.

The metaphor which led to the Fish & Shrink algorithm is sketched in Figure 8.1(b). Imagine cases being positioned in a continuous space. The closer a case (represented by a small circle or dot) is positioned to the top region of this space the smaller is its distance to the problem. While running, the Fish & Shrink algorithm successively picks up and directly tests cases from the *surface* which is represented as a plain. Each direct test has two effects: Firstly, the tested case sinks to a position according to its view distance to the problem. Secondly, cases in its neighborhood disappear from the surface and from the bottom. This effect is represented by two craters with the tested case at their joint peak. The craters indicate that cases in the nearby neighborhood of sunk test cases are dragged down deeper than cases afar. Closeness to the surface recommends cases to further examination.

Figure 8.1(b) shows what happens while the series of cases $(T_1, ..., T_4)$ is being directly compared to the problem. Firstly, T_1 sinks according to its view distance to the problem. A case labeled V in the neighborhood of T_1 becomes part of the two craters. Using the triangle inequality, minimum and maximum distance between V and the problem are computed. Both distances are represented by the position of V within the craters of test case T_1. The remaining interval of possible distances between V and the problem (represented by a line) is called the *uncertainty interval* of V. Further direct tests of cases from the surface can only shrink this interval. This is what happens to the uncertainty interval of V while testing cases $(T_2, ..., T_4)$. To simplify illustration of these tests, only the uncertainty intervals and case positions are pictured. If no case is left upon the surface, the surface level starts to sink and cases which have been sunk earlier reappear.

The main idea represented in Figure 8.1(b) is that it should be more efficient to avoid searching in the nearby neighborhood of cases which have already been found to be inappropriate. Inappropriateness is seen and treated as a gradual statement and depends on how close the neighborhood was.

Thus, the fundamental concept of the formal Fish & Shrink algorithm is the *uncertainty interval* which is applied to each case. Initially (when a new retrieval task starts), it is set to $[0, 1]$. The initial value represents the fact that we do not know anything about the distance between the case and the user's problem. The Fish & Shrink algorithm tries to position the uncertainty interval and minimize its length. Both increase knowledge about the corresponding case. The target of Fish & Shrink is to maximize the number of shrunk uncertainty intervals and the amount of shrinking in each step without losing reliability. Between two shrinking loops, the algorithm tries to interpret the position and length of uncertainty intervals to find whether user demands have already been fulfilled or not. The algorithm conceptually performs the steps depicted in Figure 8.2.

Input: The case base CB, the problem A, a vector of aspect weights $\mathbf{W}$ and the actual view distance function SD.
Output: A sequence of cases with increasing distance to the problem.

1. Represent problem A in all aspects with corresp. field in $\mathbf{W} \neq 0$.
2. Set uncertainty interval for each case to $[0,1]$.
3. Set precision line to 0.
4. While user demands not fulfilled and not interrupted:
   a) Move precision line according to prescription and present all cases that have been passed.
   b) Select (fish) a test case T depending on the position of the precision line.
   c) Calculate actual $SD(A,T,\mathbf{W})$ (direct test).
   d) $\forall$ view neighbors V of T do (indirect test):
      i. Minimum distance between V and A := $Max\Big(|SD(A,T) - SD(T,V)|,\ minimum\ distance\Big)$;
      ii. Maximum distance between V and A := $Min\Big(SD(A,T) + SD(T,V),\ maximum\ distance\Big)$;
   e) Recalculation of view neighbors finished.

Fig. 8.2. A sketch of the Fish & Shrink algorithm

To follow the steps of the algorithm, some more terms need to be explained. Firstly, in line 3, the *precision line* is set to zero. The precision line is a concept corresponding to the idea of having a surface level. Its task is to mark the smallest minimum distance of all uncertainty intervals (with length > 0) during retrieval. If an uncertainty interval (even with length > 0) is passed by the line, the corresponding case belongs to the output stream. A predefined movement prescription of the precision line determines the behavior of the algorithm. By using special prescriptions, answers to the following questions are possible:

- Which cases are better than a threshold?
- Which are the k best cases without ranking?
- Which are the k best cases with ranking?
- Which are the k best cases with ranking and their exact distances to a given problem?

The biggest challenge in developing precision line prescriptions is to avoid over-answering a user demand. For example, if a user wants to know the k

best cases, there is possibly no interest in getting a ranking of them. Leaving unasked questions unanswered can help to save time.

Each case V with $SD(T,V) \geq 0$ is called a *view neighbor* of T. The loop starting in line 4d examines the view neighbors of a test case T. The uncertainty interval of each view neighbor of T is recalculated in that loop. Recalculation of the uncertainty intervals is done by using three interpretations of the triangle inequality.

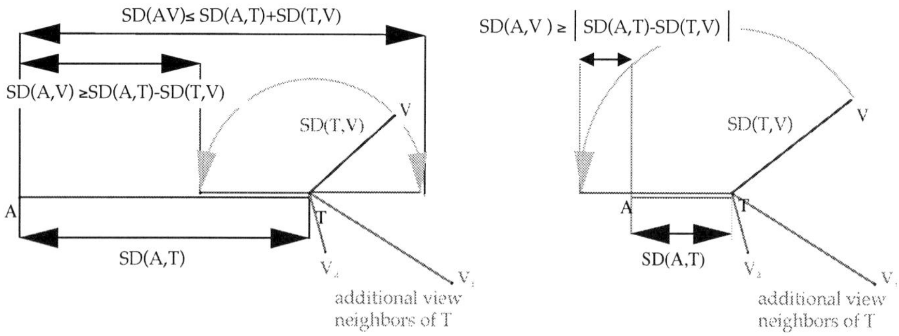

Fig. 8.3. Three interpretations of the triangle inequality to shrink uncertainty intervals of view neighbors of directly tested cases

Two interpretations, shown in Figure 8.3, maximize the lower limit (minimum distance). One interpretation minimizes the upper limit (maximum distance) - compare lines 4di and 4dii of Figure 8.2. As mentioned, recalculation can only shrink intervals. Because every direct test (line 4c) shrinks at least one interval to zero, Fish & Shrink definitely terminates. It can stop before having tested all cases if an interrupt condition becomes true. The interrupt condition depends on the user demand and is usually described within the precision line prescription.

The Fish & Shrink algorithm delivers the correct and complete set of result cases if the triangle inequality holds for distance functions. In contrast to most competitors in the field of retrieval algorithms for case based reasoning, Fish & Shrink does not make the *closed world assumption* that undocumented similarity automatically means implicit dissimilarity.

Fish & Shrink normally comes up with the requested results without searching the whole case base. Up to now, we have not been able to give exact information about the theoretical complexity. Some empirical tests have shown a positive behavior (Schaaf 1998). Systematic tests to confirm the evident performance of Fish & Shrink and the applicability of the presented approach have still to be performed.

To summarize, the Fish & Shrink algorithm enables the efficient exploitation of the different views on single cases. While in most CBR approaches to retrieval exactly one (sometimes dynamically weighted) similarity measure is used, Fish & Shrink combines different similarity measures dynamically at retrieval time time, thus, achieving flexible case retrieval.

8.6 Approaches to Structural Similarity Assessment and Adaptation

As stressed in Section 8.4, case retrieval for *innovative* and *creative* design tasks requires structural similarity assessment in terms of adaptability, as well as structural adaptation. This section introduces approaches that define the *structural similarity* (cf. Section 1.3.3) between structured case representations, i.e. graphs, via their *maximal common subgraph* (*mcs*) (Börner 1993; Jantke 1994). Given a new problem, the structurally most similar case(s) are retrieved. One out of several *mcs* is transferred and the remaining case parts are transferred as needed. Additionally, the *mcs* may be used to represent and access classes of structurally similar cases in an efficient manner. The remaining case parts can be seen as proper instantiations of *mcs*, i.e., as a special kind of adaptation knowledge that allows the adaptation of past cases to solve new problems. In such a way, structural case representations and limited domain knowledge is explored to support design tasks. The approaches have been exemplarily instantiated in three modules of the design assistant system FABEL-Idea that generates adapted design solutions on the basis of prior CAD layouts. For more details see Börner et al. (1996).

8.6.1 Required Functionality

The application domain used for motivation, illustration, and evaluation is architectural design. In particular we are concerned with supporting the *spatial layout*[2] of rooms and pipe systems in rectangular buildings.

Past experiences, stored as cases, correspond to arrangements of physical objects represented by CAD layouts and refer to parts in real buildings. Each object is represented by a set of attributes describing its geometry (i.e., position and extent in three dimensions) and its type (e.g., fresh air connection pipe). Concentrating on the design of complex installation infrastructures for industrial buildings, cases correspond to pipe systems that connect a given set of outlets to the main access. Pipe systems for fresh and return air, electrical circuits, computer networks, phone cables, etc., are numerous and show varied topological structures. For the retrieval, transfer, and adaptation of past cases to new problems not the geometry and type of single objects but their topological relations are important.

Because of the above, objects and their (topological) relations need to be represented and considered during reasoning. Therefore, a compile function

[2] *Spatial layout* can be seen as a representative of design tasks in general (Coyne 1988).

is used to translate attribute value representations of objects and their relations into graphs. In general, objects are represented by vertices and relations between objects are represented by edges. Reasoning, i.e., structural retrieval and adaptation, proceeds via graph-based representations. A recompile function translates the graph-based solution into its attribute-based representation that may be depicted graphically to the user. Concentrating on different aspects of structural similarity assessment and adaptation, different compile functions are appropriate, resulting in different graph representations of cases with their corresponding expressive power and reasoning complexity. They are explained in detail in Sections 8.6.2 to 8.6.4.

Figure 8.4 shows a design problem and its solution. Spatial relations (touches, overlaps, is_close_to) that can be used to represent cases structurally are visualized by arrows in the figures.

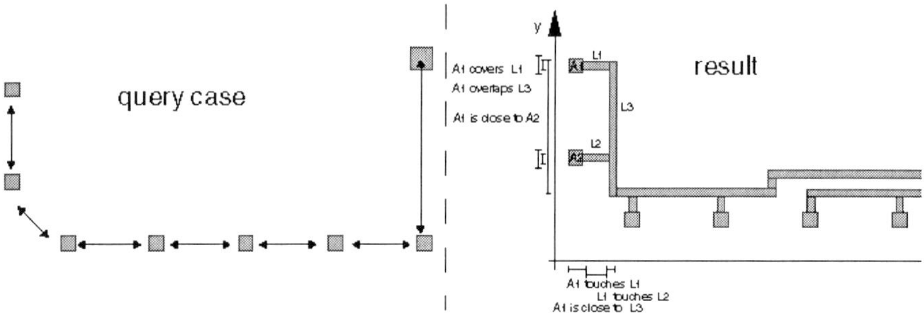

Fig. 8.4. Domain example: A problem and its solution

Given a base of cases represented by graphs and a structurally represented problem, reasoning proceeds as follows: Firstly, one or a set of cases that show a high *structural similarity* to the problem is/are retrieved. Here, structural similarity is defined via the maximal common subgraph (*mcs*) of a case and a problem. Assuming that cases and problem share more in common than their maximal common subgraph, *structural adaptation* proceeds by transferring and combining case parts that connect unconnected problem objects to the *mcs*.

In the following, we define the functionality of *structural similarity assessment and adaptation* by the mappings required to transfer a set of cases and a problem into exactly one solution or a set of problem solutions.

We give some basic notations first. A graph $g = (V^g, E^g)$ is an ordered pair of vertices V^g and edges E^g with $E^g \subseteq V^g \times V^g$. Let $mcs(G)$ denote the set of all maximal common subgraphs of a set of graphs G, with respect to some criteria. If there is no danger of misunderstanding, the argument of *mcs* will be omitted. Let Γ be the set of all graphs, and O be a finite set of objects represented by attribute values for geometry and type. $\mathcal{P}(\Gamma)$ denotes the power set of Γ; that is, the set of all subsets of Γ.

The mappings needed to accomplish the required functionality are depicted in Figure 8.5. Knowledge is denoted by circles and boxes denote functions. The indices _a and _g refer to attribute-value and graph representations, respectively. Arrows denote the sequence of mappings. The double arrow refers to the interaction between the compile and recompile function applied.

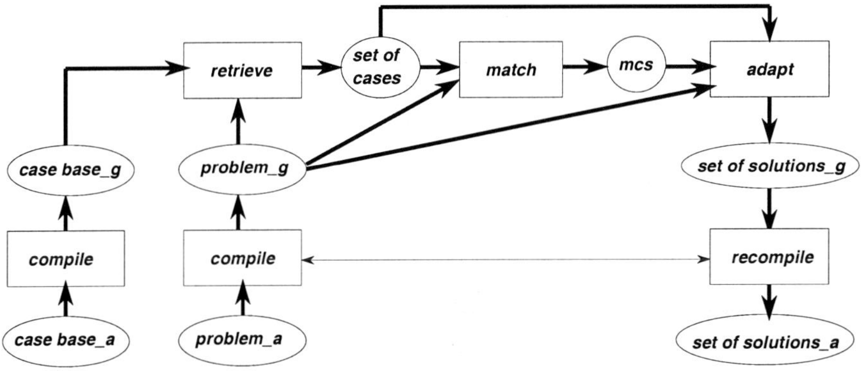

Fig. 8.5. Mappings required to accomplish the desired functionality

In order to access and interact via CAD layouts (that are represented by attribute values of their constituting objects) but to reason via their topological structure, there must be a way of translating attribute value representations of cases into graph representations and vice versa. Therefore, a compile function has to be defined that maps the attribute value representation of a set of objects representing a case or a problem into its structural representation:

$$\mathsf{compile} : \mathcal{P}(O) \rightarrow \Gamma$$

Inversely, the function recompile maps the graph representation of a set of objects denoting a solution into their attribute value representation:

$$\mathsf{recompile} : \Gamma \rightarrow \mathcal{P}(O)$$

The concept of structural similarity allows the selection of one or more cases, that are suitable for solving a problem. It is used by the function retrieve, that maps a set of cases (i.e. the case base) and a problem into a set of candidate cases that are applicable to solve the problem:

$$\mathsf{retrieve} : \mathcal{P}(\Gamma) \times \Gamma \rightarrow \mathcal{P}(\Gamma)$$

The retrieve function uses (sometimes repeatedly) a function named match that maps two graphs into their maximal common subgraph(s) *mcs*:

$$\mathsf{match} : \Gamma \times \Gamma \rightarrow \mathcal{P}(\Gamma)$$

As for adaptation, a mcs is selected and transferred to the problem. If needed, vertices and edges of the selected set of candidate cases are combined to complement the problem resulting in a set of solutions:

$$\mathsf{adapt} : \mathcal{P}(\Gamma) \times \Gamma \times \Gamma \rightarrow \mathcal{P}(\Gamma)$$

Given a finite object set and a compile function, we can restrict the last four mappings to finite domains, i.e., Γ may be replaced by $\mathsf{compile}(\mathcal{P}(O))$.

In the following, three approaches are presented that provide the defined functionality. The approaches differ in the compile and recompile functions applied, the graph representations (trees or arbitrary graphs) used, the memory organization applied and the retrieval and adaptation strategies proposed.

8.6.2 TOPO

TOPO (Coulon 1995) is a module that considers geometric neighborhoods as well as structural similarity to support the case-based extension and correction of three-dimensional rectangular layouts.

Compile and Recompile. The compile function used by TOPO detects binary topological relations of various types. The type of a relation is determined by the application dependent attributes of involved objects and their 3-dimensional spatial relations. TOPO's compile function projects each layout to the three geometric dimensions. For each projection, 8 different directed relations (similar to the temporal relations of Allen 1984) and several classes of disjoint intervals can be detected. Thus, a given object may be in one of 16 relationships for each dimension leading to $16^3 = 4096$ different 3-dimensional relationships (Coulon 1995).

Retrieval. TOPO uses the retrieval algorithm Fish & Shrink (see Section 8.5) and an attribute-value based similarity function to retrieve a case that shows a high similarity to the problem at hand. Subsequently, a match function is applied to determine the maximal common subgraph of the graph-based represented case and the problem. Finding matching subgraphs is known to be a NP-complete problem (Babel and Tinhofer 1990). Instead of searching for a common subgraph of two graphs, TOPO searches for a maximal clique in one graph representing all possible matches between the two graphs, called their *combination graph.*

Building the Combination Graph. Using the transformation given in Barrow and Burstall (1976), the vertices in the combination graph represent all matchings of compatible vertices in the graphs. Figure 8.6 shows an example. The graphs f and g contain objects of type a and b connected by directed relations. The type of a relation is defined by the types of its objects. Two vertices are connected in the combination graph if and only if the matchings represented by the vertices do not contradict one another. The matchings

($R_2(a,b) \Leftrightarrow R_8(a,b)$) and ($R_5(b,b) \Leftrightarrow R_{10}(b,b)$) are connected because both relations occur in both graphs in the same context. Both are connected by a shared object of type b. ($R_2(a,b) \Leftrightarrow R_8(a,b)$) and ($R_1(b,a) \Leftrightarrow R_6(b,a)$) are not connected because the matched relations share an object of type a in graph f but do not share any object in graph g.

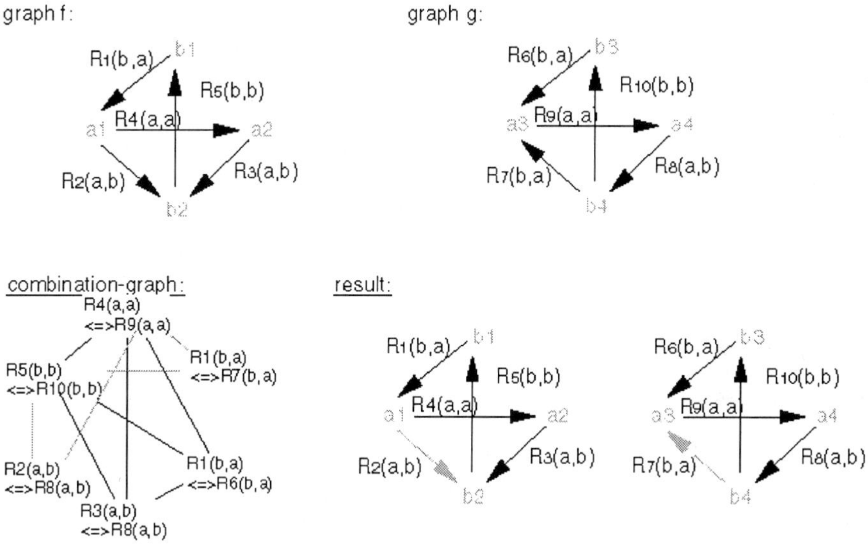

Fig. 8.6. Transformation of the problem of finding the maximal common subgraph to the problem of finding a maximal clique in a graph. The maximal clique and the corresponding matching are marked in black

A General Maximal Clique Algorithm. The algorithm of Bron and Kerbosch (1973), called *max-clique*$_{BK}$, finds all cliques in a graph by enumerating and extending all complete subgraphs. It extends complete subgraphs of size k to complete subgraphs of size $k+1$ by adding (iteratively) vertices which are connected to all vertices of the complete subgraph.

Given two graphs, the first similarity function returns the size of the maximal common subgraph relative to the minimum size of both graphs. Because a maximal common subgraph cannot be larger than the smaller of both graphs, the result is always a rational number between 0 and 1. In order to avoid the NP-complete search for the maximum common subgraphs, a second similarity function is defined. It compares the sets of relations occurring in both graphs. The result is the number of compatible relations relative to the minimum number of detected relations of both graphs, leading to a result which is also between 0 and 1. The second similarity function obviously returns an upper bound of the first similarity function, but has no NP-complexity.

Adaptation. TOPO extends, refines, and corrects layouts by case adaptation. Given that case parts can take the role of a problem or a solution,

TOPO uses the heuristics that every object of the case which is not found in the problem might be part of the solution. After determining the common subgraph of a case and a problem, TOPO transfers those case objects to the problem that are connected to the common subgraph by a path of topological relations. The user may influence this process by selecting types of objects to transfer.

During transfer, TOPO may change the size of transferred objects to preserve topological relations. For example, a window is resized in order to touch both sides of a room. To avoid geometries which are impossible for an object, TOPO limits the resizing to geometries which occurred in the case base. Additionally, statistics about the frequency of topological relations occurring in the case base for each type of objects supports the evaluation of solutions.

8.6.3 MACS

MACS extends the approach of structural similarity and adaptation to arbitrary graphs. Clumping techniques are applied in order to reduce the number of NP-complete matches during retrieval.

Compile and Recompile. The function compile guarantees the transformation of an attribute value represented case or problem into its graph representation. The graph representation should reflect the structure of the domain objects. In the selected domain, this can be achieved by representing all objects of a case as vertices and representing the topological relations between neighboring vertices by edges. Vertices may be labeled by the type of the object or by additional qualitative and quantitative attributes. Edges can be labeled with a type name of the topological relationship together with additional attributes. If the layout contains a certain number of spanning objects, such as pipes or beams, then it is more suitable to represent the spanning objects as edges and the remaining objects as vertices and, if necessary, to label them with their type name and necessary additional attributes.

The function recompile transforms vertices and edges of a graph-based solution into objects and relations of a concrete layout. In case of labeled graphs, this mapping is unique. Otherwise, the problem of non-unique mappings has to be solved. See Bartsch-Spörl and Tammer (1994) for examples.

Organization of the Case Base. In this approach, we consider arbitrary graphs which may be either directed or undirected and labeled or unlabeled. Computing structural similarity equates to the computation of the maximal common isomorphic subgraph(s). MACS applies a backtracking algorithm that realizes the function match to compute maximal common subgraphs of two arbitrary graphs (Tammer et al. 1995). In general, the maximal common subgraph of a set of graphs is not unique. For any collection of graphs $C \in \mathcal{P}(\Gamma)$, we use $mcs(C)$ to denote the set of maximal common subgraphs of all graphs in C with respect to counting vertices and edges. In order to determine a unique representative $\Theta \in mcs(C)$ for each class C, we introduce some *selection operator* $E : \mathcal{P}(\Gamma) \rightarrow \Gamma$.

Usually, the peculiarities of the application domain lead to a number of preferable selection operators:

- *other similarity concepts* based on labels of vertices or edges of graphs within $mcs(C)$ may be applied or
- *graph–theoretic properties* which characterize structures preferred in the domain can be exploited.

Given $mcs(C)$ and E, the *structural similarity* of any class C of graphs is denoted by $\sigma(C) = E(mcs(C))$ in the sense of Börner et al. (1993).

In order to reduce the number of NP-complete mappings during retrieval, cases are organized and indexed corresponding to their structural similarity. Applying clumping techniques, a case base CB is partitioned into a finite number of case classes. Each class consists of a set of graph-represented cases and is indexed by $E(mcs(C))$, called its *representative*.

Retrieval from a Structured Case Base. Assuming that a case base CB with $N = |CB|$ is partitioned into $k = \lfloor\sqrt{N}\rfloor$ case classes $CC_i, i = 1, \ldots, k$ each represented by its unique representative $E(mcs(C_i))$, retrieval proceeds in two steps:

1. Determine the maximal similar representative to the given problem g as well as the corresponding case class.
2. Determine the most similar case in the selected case class.

The retrieval result is a set of cases denoted by $S_{i^*} \subseteq CB_{i^*}$ were, for all cases $g_{i^*}^j \in S_{i^*}$, $mcs(\{g_{i^*}^j, g\}) = \mathsf{match}(g_{i^*}^j, g)$ holds. That is, the number of vertices and edges shared by a graph in S_{i^*} and the problem g are identical.

In such a way, the number N of comparisons can be reduced to $2\sqrt{N}$ matches in the best case. Note that the maximal similar representative/case determined in the first and the second retrieval step may not be unique. An appropriate *selection operator* has to be applied or user interaction is required to come up with a candidate case that can be used for adaptation.

Adaptation. The selected cases are proposed one after the other to a selection algorithm, or to the user, who selects the most suitable one.

In general, the number of vertices and edges constituting a problem is smaller than those representing a solution. Hence, a selected case may correspond to the problem solution itself. However, in building design, solutions are hardly ever identical and the selected case has to be adapted to solve the problem. Due to the lack of appropriate adaptation transformations, MACS realizes adaptation by transferring case structure resulting in a supplemented problem; i.e. a solution. The function adapt for a problem g and a selected case, $g'_{i^*} \in S_{i^*}$, uses the result of $h = \mathsf{match}(g, g'_{i^*})$; i.e., the list of matching vertices of g and g'_{i^*}. The *adapted graph* (solution) is generated from graph g by adding all walks in g'_{i^*}, which do not have an isomorphic mapping in g

but which begin and end with vertices of h. These walks may be sequences of edges which are incident with vertices not corresponding to a vertex of g excluding the begin and end vertices.

8.6.4 CA/SYN

Conceptual analogy (CA) is a general approach that relies on conceptual clustering to facilitate the efficient use of past cases in analogous situations (Börner 1995a). CA divides the overall design task into *memory organization* and *analogical reasoning*, both processing structural case representations. In order to ground both processes on attribute value representations of cases, a compile and a recompile function need to be defined.

Compile and Recompile. The function compile guarantees the uniform transformation of an attribute value represented case into its structural normal form; i.e. a tree. Especially suited for the design of pipelines, compile maps outlets into vertices and pipes into edges. Inversely, recompile maps vertices and edges into outlets and pipes. Geometrical transformations, such as translation and rotation, are considered. Representing the main access by a square, outlets by circles, interconnecting points by circles of smaller size, and pipes by line segments, Figure 8.7 (left bottom) illustrates six cases representing pipe systems. Each of them shows a tree like structure. The main access corresponds to the root R, outlets correspond to leaves L. Cross-points of pipes or connections of pipe segments are represented by internal vertices I. Pipes correspond to edges. Each object is placed on the intersecting points of a fixed grid (not shown here) and can be uniquely identified by its x and y coordinates and its *type* $\in \{R, I, L\}$. Pipes connect objects horizontally or vertically. Thus, a case can be represented by a set of vertices and a set of edges representing connected_to relations among these objects.

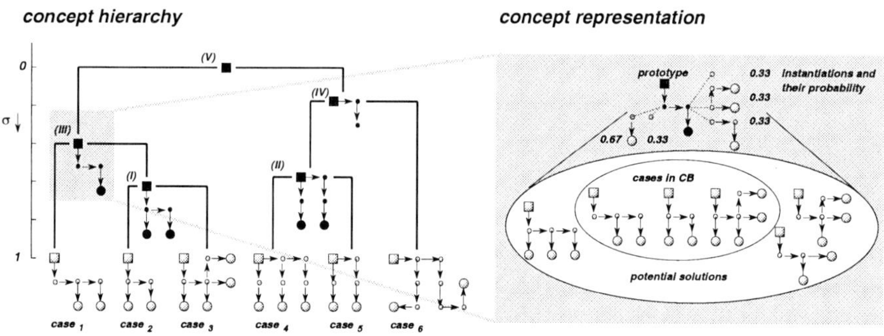

Fig. 8.7. Concept hierarchy and concept representation

Formally, a structurally represented *case* $c = (V^c, E^c)$ is a tree. A *case base* CB is a finite set of cases. A typical design *problem* provides the main access, the outlets, and perhaps some pipes; i.e., it is a forest. A *solution* of a problem contains the problem objects and relations and eventually adds intermediate vertices from past cases and provides the relations that connect all outlets to the main access.

Memory Organization. Memory Organization starts with a case base CB providing a significant number of cases as well as a structural similarity function σ.

To explain memory organization, some basic definitions will be given first. A *case class* CC is a non-empty subset of CB. The (unique) maximum common, connected subgraph of the cases in CC containing the root vertice is denoted by $mcs(CC) = (V^{mcs}, E^{mcs})$. The structural similarity[3] is defined as $|E^{mcs}|$ divided by the total number of edges in the cases of CC:

$$E\sigma(CC) = \frac{|E^{mcs}|}{|\bigcup_{c \in CC} E^c|} \in [0,1]$$

Given a case base and a similarity function σ, a *case class partition* CCP is a set of mutually disjoint, exhaustive case classes CC:

$$\begin{aligned} CCP \;=\{ \;& CC_i \mid \bigcup_i CC_i = CB \;\wedge \\ & \forall i \neq j (CC_i \cap CC_j = \emptyset) \;\wedge \\ & \forall i \neq j ((c_1, c_2 \in CC_i \wedge c_3 \in CC_j) \\ & \rightarrow \sigma(c_1, c_2) \geq \sigma(c_1, c_3) \wedge \sigma(c_1, c_2) \geq \sigma(c_2, c_3)) \\ \} \end{aligned}$$

A *case class hierarchy* CCH is the set of all partitions CCP of $CB = \{c_1, .., c_N\}$:

$$CCH = (CCP^0, CCP^1, ..., CCP^{n-1})$$

Memory organization starts with a set of cases $CB = \{c_1, .., c_N\}$ represented by trees. Nearest-neighbor-based, agglomerative, unsupervised conceptual clustering is applied to create a hierarchy of case classes grouping cases of similar structure. Clustering starts with a set of singleton vertices representing case classes, each containing a single case. The two most similar case classes CC_1 and CC_2 over the entire set are merged to form a new case class $CC = CC_1 \cup CC_2$ that covers both. This process is repeated for each of the remaining $N - 1$ case classes, where $N = |CB|$. Merging of case classes continues until a single, all-inclusive cluster remains. At termination, a uniform, binary hierarchy of case classes is left.

Subsequently, a concept description $K(CC)$ is assigned to each case class CC. The concept represents the $mcs(CC)$ (named prototype) of the cases in CC and a set of instantiations thereof, along with the probability of these

---

[3] Note that the structural similarity function is commutative and associative. Thus it may be applied to a pair of cases as well as to a set of cases.

instantiations. The probability of an instantiation corresponds to the number of its occurrences in the cases of CC divided by the total number of cases in CC. The *mcs* denotes the structure relevant for similarity comparisons and serves as an index in the case base. The instantiations (subtrees) denote possibilities for adaptation. The probabilities will direct the search through the space of alternative instantiations.

In such a way, large numbers of cases with many details can be reduced to a number of hierarchically organized concepts. The concrete cases, however, are stored to enable the dynamic reorganization and update of concepts.

Analogical Reasoning. Analogical Reasoning is based on concepts exclusively. Given a new problem, it is classified in the most applicable concept, i.e., the concept that shares as many relations as possible (high structural similarity) and provides instantiations that contain the problem objects that are not covered by the prototype (adaptability)[4]. Thus instead of retrieving one or a set of cases, the function classify maps a concept hierarchy $K(CCH)$ and a problem p into the most *applicable* concept $K(CC)$.

Next, the *mcs* of the most applicable concept is transferred and instantiated. Instantiations of high probability are preferred. Each solution connects all problem objects by using those objects and edges that show the highest probability in the concept applied. Instead of *adapting* one or more cases to solve the problem, the function instantiate maps the concept representation $K(CC)$ of a case class CC and the problem p into a set of adapted solutions $S_{CC,p}$. In general, there exist more than one applicable concept. The set of all solutions $S_{CB,p}$ of a CB for a problem p equals the union of solution sets $S_{CC,p}$.

Finally, the set of solutions may be ordered corresponding to a set of preference criteria: (1) maximal structural similarity of the solution and the concept applied, (2) maximal probability of edges transferred, and (3) minimal solution size.

If the solution was accepted by the user, its incorporation into an existing concept changes at least the probabilities of the instantiations. Given that the problem already contained relations, it might add new instantiations or even change the prototype itself. If the solution was not accepted, the case memory needs to be reorganized to incorporate the solution provided by the user.

Figure 8.7 (left) depicts the organization of cases into a concept hierarchy. N cases are represented by $2N-1$ case classes respective concepts $K(CC)$. Leaf vertices correspond to concrete cases and are represented by the cases themselves. Generalized concepts in the concept hierarchy are labeled (I) to (V) and are characterized by their *mcs* (prototype) denoted by black circles and line segments. The representation of concept no. (III) representing $case_1$ to $case_3$ is depicted on the right hand side of Figure 8.7. The instantiation of

[4] Note that the most similar concept may be too concrete to allow the generation of a solution.

its prototype results in $case_1$ to $case_3$ as well as combinations thereof. Given a new problem, the most applicable (i.e., most similar) concept containing all problem objects is determined in a top-down fashion. The set of problems that may be solved by concept no. (III) corresponds to the set of all subtrees of either concrete or combined cases, containing the root vertice.

The general approach of *Conceptual Analogy* has been fully implemented in SYN, a module of a highly interactive, adaptive design assistant system (Börner 1995b). While its compile and recompile functions are especially suited to support the geometrical layout of pipe systems the general approach to structural similarity assessment and adaptation is domain independent. See Börner and Faßauer (1995) as well as Börner (1997) for a more detailed description of the implementation.

8.6.5 Comparison

All three approaches, TOPO, MACS, and CA/SYN, apply structural similarity assessment and adaptation to retrieve and transfer case parts to solve new problems. However, the approaches differ in their focus on different parts of the CBR-scenario. In the following, the strengths and limitations of each approach and their domain specific and domain independent parts are discussed.

First of all, it must be recognized that the definitions of the compile and recompile functions strongly depend on the domain and task to support. The higher the required expressibility of structural case representations the more complex is the graph matching, i.e., the less efficient are retrieval and adaptation. The application of labeled graphs (TOPO) or trees (SYN) allows the inversion of the function compile to recompile. This can not be guaranteed for arbitrary graphs (MACS). Whereas the representation of cases by trees (SYN) guarantees unique *mcs*, this does not hold for graph representations, as in TOPO or MACS. Domain specific selection rules need to be defined or extensive user interaction is necessary to select the most suitable *mcs*. This may be advantageous during retrieval allowing the selection of different points of view on two graphs (the *mcs* and a problem) but may not be acceptable for efficient memory organization over huge case bases.

While TOPO performs no structural retrieval at all, MACS and SYN retrieve a set of cases from a dynamically organized case base. MACS uses a two-level case organization. The lower level contains the concrete cases grouped into classes of similar cases. The upper level contains graphs describing the *mcs* of classes of similar cases. It does a two stage retrieval selecting the case class of the most similar *representative* first and searching in its cases for the most similar concrete case(s). SYN uses a hierarchical memory organization, i.e., a case class hierarchy. Each case class is represented intentionally by a concept representing the unique *mcs*, instantiations thereof, as well as the *probabilities* of these instantiations. Given a new problem, the most applicable concept of the concept hierarchy is searched for.

In order to compare graph representations, MACS and TOPO need to apply graph matching algorithms (clique search and backtracking) that are known to be NP-complete. For this reason, TOPO uses the Fish & Shrink retrieval algorithm, reducing retrieval to the computationally expensive match between a selected case and a problem. MACS memory organization allows the reduction of the number of matches required to search through N cases to $2\sqrt{N}$ in the best case. SYN's restriction to represent cases by trees reduces expressibility but offers the advantage to match efficiently.

For adaptation, TOPO investigates the compatibility of object types and relation types of layouts. The frequency of relations in past layouts is exploited to come up with preferable positions for solution objects. MACS realizes a simple variant of case adaptation by adding all walks of the case which do not have an isomorphic mapping in the problem but begin and end with vertices of their *mcs*. CA/SYN concentrates on efficient structural case combination. Therefore, the approach integrates the formation of hierarchically organized concepts (i.e., concept hierarchies) and the application of these concepts during analogical reasoning to solve new problems. It is unique in its representation of concepts by the *mcs* and its *instantiations* plus *probabilities*. Its definition of *applicability* allows the efficient selection of the most similar concept that is neither too general not too concrete and guarantees the generation of a problem solution. The instantiation of its *mcs* is guided by the probabilities of these instantiations, resulting in a set of solutions that may be ordered corresponding to a set of preference criteria.

8.7 Structural Adaptation by Case Combination

EADOCS[5] is an interactive, multi-level, and hybrid expert system for aircraft panel structures (Netten et al. 1995; Netten 1997). The primary design objective is to find a feasible and optimal concept for a panel design.

The structure of a design defines the set of components, their configuration and parameter values. The configuration defines the set of design variables that can be retrieved and adapted. Parameter values should be assigned within the context of a configuration. Retrieval and adaptation of design structures should, therefore, be distinguished for configurations, components and parameters.

In many applications, specialist operators are only available for parameter adaptation. Other approaches are necessary to adapt configurations. The EADOCS system adapts the configuration, components, and parameters by combining cases.

---

[5] Expert Assisted Design of Composite Sandwich Panels

8.7.1 Required Functionality

EADOCS' task is to support the conceptual design phase. In this phase, a designer specifies the initial requirements, objectives, and preferences. The system suggests, evaluates and modifies alternative solutions for the configuration and discrete design parameters. Initial specifications are elaborated from EADOCS' conclusions or a designer's new input. The optimum panel concept is the starting point for more detailed (numerical) analysis and optimization.

Conceptual design is regarded as an innovative reasoning process for configuration and parametric design. Plans for designing components are not available. Only partial models for evaluating behavior are available.

EADOCS divides the iterative design process into four subsequent phases. Each phase solves a specific and more fine-grained iterative step that results in a set of sub-solutions. A sub-solution is an alternative starting point for the next phase. The level of detail, type of design decisions, and type of reasoning changes with each phase (Netten et al. 1995).

Modifying the R^4 CBR-cycle introduced by (Aamodt and Plaza 1994), Figure 8.8 depicts the four phases in bold. The first phase selects a set of prototype solutions and configures them qualitatively. In the second phase, case-based reasoning is applied to solve two tasks: Firstly, complete case solutions are retrieved to generate quantitative conceptual solutions. The second task is to adapt the retrieved concepts by integrating other case components. The third phase revises the parameters heuristically, while the fourth phase optimizes the concepts numerically.

The case base covers only a small part of the problem and design spaces, which is also biased by previous design intentions. It is unlikely that a case is completely similar to a new problem, and their behavior is not representative for the feasibility and optimality upon reuse of their solution (Netten and Vingerhoeds 1997). Additional information is required to guide retrieval.

EADOCS provides this information in the first phase in which the best solutions are selected and configured into a set of prototypes. In the second phase, it is assumed that the prototype defines the design space of feasible and optimal configurations from which conceptual solutions can be retrieved. If no case can be retrieved for the best prototype, the solution is relaxed to the next best prototype.

8.7.2 Sandwich Panel Structures

Thin-walled skin panels are applied as components of semi-monocoque aircraft structures. A skin alone cannot provide sufficient stiffness. Several types of panels can be configured to provide additional stiffness to the skin, such as a sandwich panel. A sandwich panel has a core of honeycomb or foam material, sandwiched between the skin and an additional inner skin. Figure 8.9 gives an example of a symmetrical sandwich panel with skin laminates of

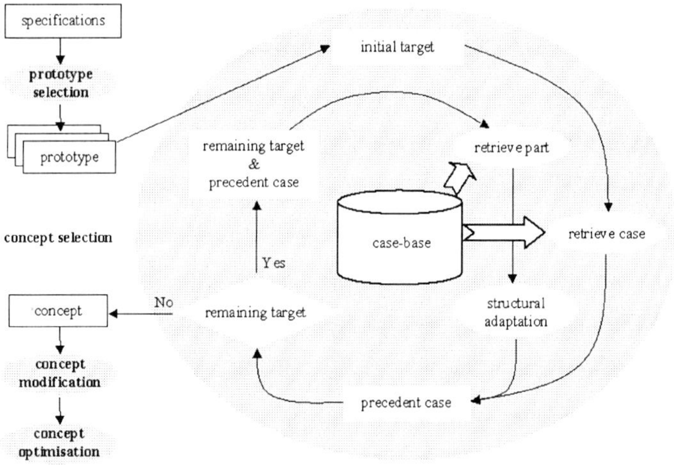

Fig. 8.8. EADOCS design process

three layers and a honeycomb core. The skins can be made out of light alloy sheet material or as composite laminates. A laminate is made out of several layers and a layer is made out of thin plies of fiber reinforced material.

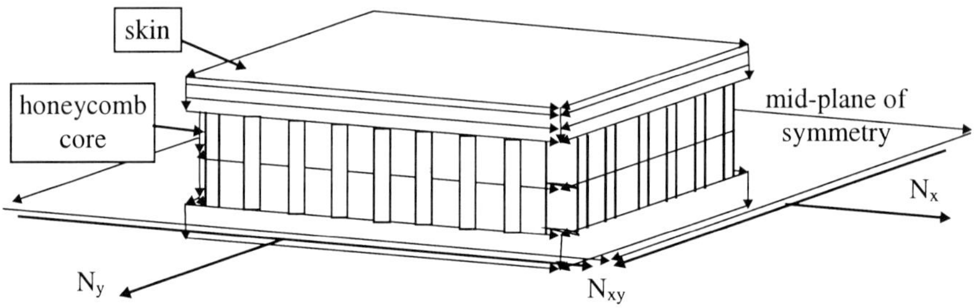

Fig. 8.9. Example of a sandwich panel

The configuration defines the type of panel and the lay-up of each laminate. A prototype is an abstract representation of a panel, and only defines the types of panel, material, and laminates a concept may be selected from. The concept defines all laminates in detail. The dimensions of the panel, core or stiffeners are continuous parameters. For each layer, discrete design parameters are defined for the type of fiber reinforced plastic (FRP) material, the number of plies, and the orientation of the plies.

A sandwich panel has one of the simplest panel configurations. Other types of panels can be configured, for example, with longitudinal stiffeners joined to the skin. Each stiffener is composed of one or more laminates.

The most important function of a panel is to carry aerodynamic and structural loads. A loading condition is defined as a potentially critical combination of normal and shear (N_{xy}) loads. A normal load is a combination of tension or compression loads in the longitudinal (N_x) and transverse (N_y) panel directions. Typically, several loading conditions are specified for the most severe operational conditions.

Behavior of panels is modeled in terms of stress, strain, strength, stiffness, cost, and weight. The strength is primarily a function of the strength, stress, and strain of individual plies. The stiffness is a function of the panel components and their dimensions. Behavior is analyzed with existing numerical techniques, which require a completely defined concept as input. Prototypical behavior is represented qualitatively as categories of behavior (Netten and Vingerhoeds 1997).

A designer specifies an initial problem by a set of loading conditions and panel dimensions. Objectives are defined for optimality and feasibility, while preferences may be defined for the prototype solutions. For feasibility, panel behavior should withstand each of the loading conditions. For optimality, the cost and/or weight of the panel should be minimized.

8.7.3 Cases and Case Retrieval

EADOCS has an object oriented data structure. Classes are defined at several levels of abstraction for function, behavior, and structure. A design case is an instance of a design problem with objects, or parts, for these classes. Figure 8.10 gives an example of a sandwich panel with a symmetric laminate of 4 skin layers.

All objects are stored in the case with their relations. The buckling behavior relates to the panel, while stress and strain behavior relate a loading condition to a specific layer. The ordering of layer objects defines the lay-up of a laminate and is defined by a layer number. Generic relations about configuration, such as the relation between a skin laminate and the core, are not defined in cases.

Cases are indexed on three levels. A case part is indexed by its features as an object of its class, while the class is indexed by its abstract classes. A case part is also indexed by its relation to other objects as a part of the case. The complex indexing hierarchy enables the retrieval of features, parts, and complete cases. The current implementation of EADOCS indexes features onto discrete values, which is sufficiently accurate when only a few cases can be retrieved.

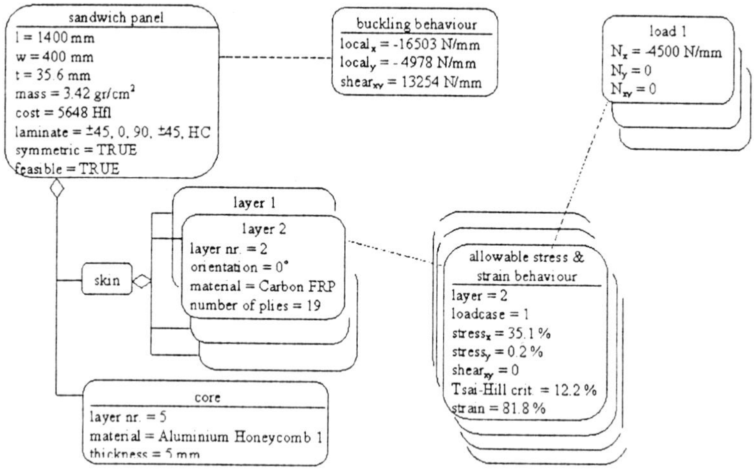

Fig. 8.10. Example of a sandwich panel case

The case base is consulted after selection of a prototype from phase 1 (see Figure 8.8). The initial target restricts retrieval to cases with the configuration of the selected prototype. The initial target for retrieval is defined by objects, or sub-targets, for the specifications and the selected prototype. Each sub-target is indexed in a similar way as its counterparts in the case base. The similarity is measured locally between case parts and sub-targets, and globally as the aggregate similarity of a case for the target.

8.7.4 Case Combination

One case is retrieved that best matches the initial target. Local similarities identify which initial sub-targets are satisfied by this precedent case. Repair of functional or behavioral requirements usually requires the adaptation of several components. Unfortunately, sub-targets for functional and behavioral requirements cannot be causally related to components. Specialist operations are available for the local adaptation of some layer parameters. These adaptations are only useful after adaptation of the laminate lay-ups. Additional information for configurational adaptations may be retrieved from the case base. Searching the case base again for the remaining sub-targets only will not reveal the necessary adaptations.

Predicting and adapting behavior for the remaining sub-targets is essentially different from retrieving a solution to the initial target. Here, it can be assumed that designs with a similar structure will behave similarly as well. Predictions and adaptations can be retrieved from cases with a structure similar to the precedent case. Combination of new components requires four steps:

1. A new target for retrieval is defined by the structure of the precedent case and the remaining sub-targets.
2. Cases are retrieved for the new target. For these cases:
   a) Behavior of the precedent case is predicted from cases with a similar structure.
   b) Adaptations can be retrieved from the differences in functionality, behavior, and structure of cases from 2a.

The assembly of components is defined in the structural model. This model is also applied for indexing and can now be searched for other components. The similarity of a new case to the new target identifies whether features or components should be substituted or inserted. Not all differences in step 2b should be retrieved for adaptation. Some of these differences are non-conservative adaptations; i.e., adaptations that violate the feasibility of previously satisfied requirements. Usually, a small set of allowable or conservative adaptations can be defined in conjunction with the modifications of phases 2a and 2b. In EADOCS, the number of plies in a layer is never reduced, and layer orientations and materials are never changed but inserted in a new layer.

The major advantage of this adaptation approach is that new structural solutions can be generated automatically. The operations for steps 1 and 2 are relatively simple, require little search and little domain knowledge. Their success depends primarily on the coverage of the case base; i.e., the existence of cases with similar structures that have been designed for different purposes. Experiments with EADOCS have shown that, even for a small case base, design improvements can be quite significant. A large number of possible loading conditions can be covered by only a few cases, and combination of these cases strongly increases coverage (Netten 1997). The retrieved structural adaptations are rudimentary but can be revised. Many such discrete adaptations, however, could not have been suggested from heuristics or numerical optimization routines (see also Bladel 1995).

8.8 Discussion and Summary

This chapter started with a general characterization of design tasks. Concentrating on *innovative* and *creative* design tasks, we gave an overview of applicable reasoning methods and case-based design systems. The domain of architectural design was used to illustrate the general problems that have to be solved in order to provide efficient design support. Finally, we presented approaches to complex case retrieval, to structural similarity assessment, and to structural adaptation.

To conclude, we contrast approaches for *compositional case adaptation* used for automating *routine design* or *configuration* tasks, as introduced in Chapter 6, with approaches for *structural adaptation* aiming at the interactive, assistant-like support of *innovative and creative design* tasks. Finally, the importance of adequate user interfaces and its influence on future research in CBD is discussed.

Compositional and structural case adaptation. Adaptation is central to CBR systems for configuration (i.e., routine design) as well as for innovative and creative design. It can work by assimilating parts of different cases to meet a new specification.

In configuration, a new specification is given by a well defined set of configurable components, a set of constraints that the final configuration solution must satisfy, and configuration operators that encode valid component configurations (cf. Section 6.4). The term *compositional adaptation* refers to the retrieval, adaptation, and subsequent composition of multiple cases (Redmond 1990; Sycara and Navinchandra 1991). Additional knowledge is employed to repair edges of solution chunks such that they work together as a whole.

Innovative and creative design tasks differ in that constraints or repair knowledge is not available in general. *Structural adaptation*, as introduced in Section 8.6, refers to the transfer and completion of the most specific common structure shared by a class of structurally similar cases. Exclusively, cases of high structural similarity are combined.

However, in both approaches adaptation is compositional rather than rule or operator based. Both approaches share the risk that locally optimal case components from different cases and, thus, different contexts will not produce globally optimal solutions when combined.

Adequate human-computer interfaces and future research in CBD. As discussed in Section 8.3, adequate user interfaces are an indispensable requirement to built effective assistance systems. Therefore, one major direction of research is appropriately designed human-computer interfaces that are easy to integrate into the workflow of designers.

In architectural design, CAD tools are very powerful in managing exact numbers and measurements. They provide less support during the abstract or *sketchy* phase at the beginning of a design process in which conceptual decisions are made and major constraints are established. Aiming at an efficient support of the early stages of design development, *Virtual Reality* techniques and fast computer graphics can offer new ways of human-computer interaction as well as efficient possibilities to support, e.g., architectural design. Multiple building partners at different locations can virtually enter the design and experience the space that gets created. Multimodal interaction directly in three-dimensional space, using two hands and audio, enables the user to formulate design ideas in a much more intuitive way. Using AI techniques, so called interface agents can be provided that are trained by each user to adapt to their individual preferences. They may support navigation and manipulation in 3D as well as retrieval, adaptation, and evaluation of design solutions.

A promising research result in this direction is the spatial modeling tool SCULPTOR (Kurmann 1995; Kurmann 1997). The tool and the agents (a *Navigator*, a *Sound Agent* and a *Cost Agent*, are implemented so far) that are connected with it allow direct, intuitive, and immersive access to three dimensional design models. Through interactive modeling in a virtual space, an easy way of generating and manipulating architectural models is enabled. SCULPTOR's connection to IDIOM (Smith et al. 1995; Smith et al. 1996), a tool that supports spatial configuration using previous designs in domains such as architectural design, circuit layout or urban planning, results in a design system that provides extensive design support via a highly interactive human-computer interface.

The design of intuitive and efficient human-computer interfaces will have strong implications on the knowledge representations used (they have to support graphical interaction as well as structural retrieval and adaptation) and the reasoning mechanisms applied to support design tasks.

Acknowledgments

The author thanks Jörg W. Schaaf for providing Section 8.5 and Bart Netten for composing Section 8.7. Carl-Helmut Coulon and Elisabeth-Ch. Tammer deserve thanks for commenting on Sections 8.6.2 and 8.6.3, respectively. Hans-Dieter Burkhard, Mario Lenz, Michael M. Richter, and Brigitte Bartsch-Spörl gave many critical comments and improvements to the chapter. Nonetheless, the paper reflects the authors personal view on case-based design research.

The research within the joint project FABEL was supported by the German Ministry for Research and Technology (BMBF) under contract no. 413-4001-01IW104. Project partners in FABEL have been German National Research Center of Computer Science (GMD), Sankt Augustin, BSR Consulting GmbH, München, Technical University of Dresden, HTWK Leipzig, University of Freiburg, and University of Karlsruhe.

9. CBR for Experimental Software Engineering

Klaus-Dieter Althoff, Andreas Birk, Christiane Gresse von Wangenheim, Carsten Tautz

9.1 Introduction

The objective of our work is to exploit the mutual interrelations between case-based reasoning and experimental software engineering (ESE) for the sake of both fields. In particular, we address the following topics:

- Presentation of a logical infrastructure of organizational learning in the software domain that makes use of principles, methods, and established practices from CBR.
- Utilization of CBR technology for implementing experience bases.
- Outlining of additional uses of CBR for ESE that go beyond infrastructures for organizational learning (i.e., data analysis, problem solving, etc.).
- Evolution of a methodology for developing CBR-based software systems based on software engineering methods and practices that are established in other application domains.

These topics are gradually developed throughout this chapter. We start with brief introductions to software engineering and ESE (Sections 9.2 and 9.3). Following this, we outline possible CBR support for ESE and give an overview of research related to both CBR and ESE (Sections 9.4 and 9.5). In the main part of this chapter, we describe the approach we take at the Fraunhofer Institute for Experimental Software Engineering in Kaiserslautern (Section 9.6). We also report on two case studies and give an outlook on work still to be done (Sections 9.7 and 9.8).

9.2 Software Engineering

Software engineering aims at providing technologies that can be used for developing software and for managing software development. This involves the definition, selection, tailoring, and integration of principles, methods, techniques, and tools, in order to achieve a software product that meets the desired quality, time, and cost requirements. For managing these requirements and for demonstrating that they actually have been achieved, analytical and empirical measures must be applied (Basili et al. 1994a; Rombach 1993).

We distinguish software engineering from programming and software development. *Programming* is the construction of a single coherent piece of software by one person who utilizes a previously determined approach. *Software development* differs from programming in that the software product is more complex and a group of people has to co-operate for constructing it following a previously defined process. This process can involve quite a large and integrated set of possibly complex technologies.

For our work, we have chosen the following definition of software engineering (Rombach and Verlage 1995):

Definition 9.2.1 (Software Engineering). Software engineering *is concerned with the definition, refinement, and evaluation of principles, methods, techniques, and tools to support:*

- *individual aspects of software development and maintenance (i.e., design, coding, verification, validation, etc.);*
- *planning of software development project (i.e., choosing appropriate methods, techniques, and tools and integrating them into project plans);*
- *performing development, project management, and quality assurance activities according to the plan;*
- *assessing the performance of the development, feeding back, and improving products, methods, techniques, and tools.*

□

IEEE's glossary of software engineering (1987) defines software engineering as *"the systematic approach to the development, operation, maintenance, and retirement of software"*. According to Boehm (1981), software engineering is *"the application of science and mathematics by which the capabilities of computer equipment are made useful to man via computer programs, procedures, and associated documentation"*. Zelkowitz (1978) emphasizes the scientific dimension of software engineering when defining that *"software engineering is the study of the principles and methodologies for developing and maintaining systems"*.

The main objects of interest within software engineering are principles, techniques, methods, tools, and technologies for developing software and managing software development. In the following, we briefly define these terms according to Basili et al. (1994a) and ISERN (1996).

A *principle* is a basic rule underlying software development and management. Principles are operationalized through techniques and methods.

A *technique* is a basic algorithm or set of steps to be followed in constructing or assessing the software. For instance, Jacobson's use cases are a technique for identifying system requirements during software construction (Jacobson et al. 1995). As another example, code reading by stepwise abstraction is a technique for assessing the code.

A *method* is an organized approach based upon applying some technique. A method has associated with it a technique, as well as a set of guidelines about how and when to apply the technique, when to stop applying it, when the technique is appropriate and how it can be evaluated. For instance, a method will have associated with it a set of entry and exit criteria and a set of management supports. Code inspection is a method based upon some reading technique, which has a well-defined set of entry and exit criteria as well as a set of management functions defined for how to manipulate the technique.

A *tool* is a computer-based implementation of a technique or method.

Technology is a generic term that covers techniques, methods, and tools.

A *software development process* is designed by integrating several techniques, methods, and tools (Basili et al. 1994a). This also involves the identification work-products, human and technical resources, and a strategy called lifecycle methodology that determines how the individual activities interact.

The *V-model* is a model of the work-products of software development and the interrelations of these products. It implies a framework of basic activities of software construction. Figure 9.1 depicts a common version of the V-model. For different development tasks (e.g., information system development, embedded systems development, expert system development) there exist variants of the basic model.

A *lifecycle model* is an integrated set of methods that covers the entire lifecycle of a software product. A lifecycle model determines the basic steps of software development and defines whether, and in which way, the product is constructed iteratively and incrementally. The basic lifecycle model is the waterfall model (Royce 1970). It is sequential, non-iterative, and non-incremental. Iterative and incremental approaches include the iterative enhancement model (Basili and Turner 1975), the spiral model (Boehm 1988), and prototyping models (von Mayrhauser 1990).

At present, a particular concern of software engineering is the improvement of software quality, development time, and development cost. This is due to the fact that software products often fail at satisfying these kinds of requirements. A root cause for this is the dramatic increase of software complexity and quality demands.

It is a widely shared understanding in the software engineering discipline that product quality (including development time and cost) should be improved by improving the software development practices. This so-called software process improvement is addressed through two general strategies: top-down and bottom-up improvement approaches (Thomas and McGarry 1994). Top-down approaches utilize capability frameworks and assessments of software development organizations and processes. Prominent among such approaches are the Software Engineering Institute's (SEI) Capability Maturity Model (CMM), Bootstrap, the ISO 9003 standard, and SPICE[1]. They address improvements based on a reference model of best practice software development and quality assurance. Software organizations and processes are

[1] Software Process Improvement and Capability Evaluation

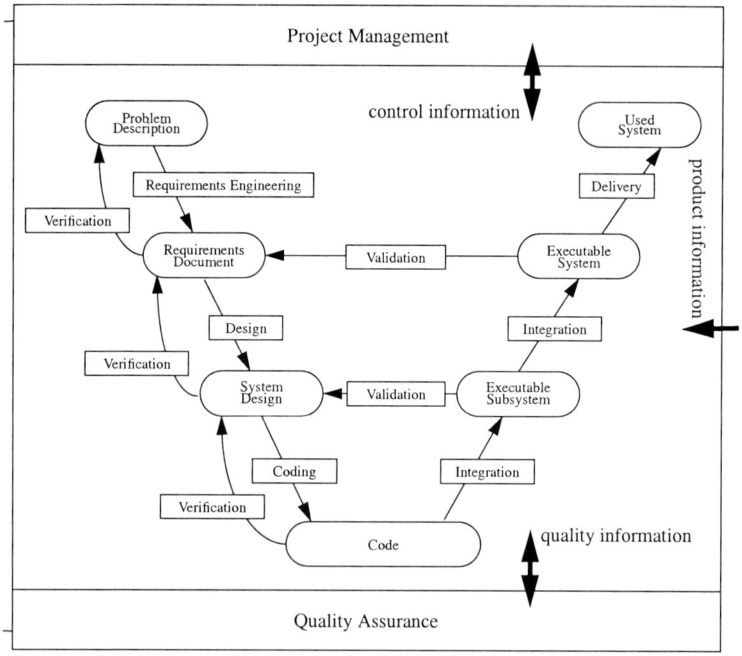

Fig. 9.1. The V-Model (from Rombach and Verlage (1995))

assessed against the reference model and their according capability is determined. Improvement actions are suggested based on the reference model in order to reach higher capability levels or better conformance with the model.

Bottom-up improvement approaches realize the principles of Total Quality Management (TQM, Ishikawa 1985) and implement an organizational learning strategy. They aim at continuous learning and reuse of learned experience. Prominent such approaches are Sheward and Deming's Plan-Do-Check-Act cycle (PDCA, Deming 1996) and the Quality Improvement Paradigm / Experience Factory approach (QIP/EF Basili et al. 1994a). They involve the identification of improvement needs and possibilities based on the specific goals and characteristics of software organizations. Therefore, bottom-up improvement approaches utilize analytical and empirical approaches such as statistical process control in mechanical engineering and goal-oriented measurement in software engineering (Basili et al. 1994b). The organizational learning strategy of bottom-up improvement approaches is shared by experimental software engineering, which is introduced in the following section. As we will see, both approaches have very much in common and show mutual interrelations with CBR.

9.3 Experimental Software Engineering

ESE is a branch of software engineering that addresses problems and research questions of software development and improvement by an experimental approach. It utilizes experiments and other kinds of empirical studies in order to enhance our knowledge about the software domain. ESE is built on the principle of continuous learning and reuse of experience which is defined through the Quality Improvement Paradigm / Experience Factory (QIP/EF) approach. Underlying ESE is the assumption that software engineering is a comparatively young discipline that still has to gain experiences and guidelines based on the application of software engineering techniques in various environments.

The QIP/EF approach provides a methodological framework and infrastructure technologies for capturing, capitalizing, and reusing software engineering experience. ESE applies this approach for developing an empirically justified body of knowledge about systematic software development and improvement. Subject of continuous learning and reuse in ESE are software products, processes, and technologies.

ESE can be characterized by a set of fundamental principles (Basili et al. 1994a) that provide a framework for systematic software development and improvement. This framework is made operational by techniques for capturing, capitalizing and storing, and making accessible as well as reusing experience.

The QIP is a six steps procedure for structuring software development and improvement activities. It involves three overall phases: planning, execution, and evaluation of the task. The planning phase is based on the explicit characterization (QIP1) of the initial situation, the identification of the goals to be achieved (QIP2), and the actual development of the plan (QIP3). The planning can benefit from the reuse of possibly existing artifacts that can facilitate the achievement of the goals and that can be identified based on the characterization of the initial situation. The plan then guides the systematic execution of the task (QIP4). The subsequent evaluation phase involves the analysis of the performed actions (QIP5) and the packaging of the lessons learned into reusable artifacts (QIP6). The evaluation allows to learn for similar tasks in the future. This is the key for institutionalizing organizational learning and continuous improvement. In summary, the six steps of the QIP are as shown in Figure 9.2.

The QIP implements two feedback cycles: the project feedback cycle (control cycle) and the corporate feedback cycle (capitalization cycle). Project feedback is provided to the ongoing project during the execution phase (QIP4). This demands for empirical techniques through which the actual course of the project can be monitored in order to identify and initiate immediately corrective actions when needed. Corporate feedback is provided to the organization (i.e., other ongoing and future projects of the organization). It provides analytical information about project performance at project completion time (e.g., cost and quality profiles) and accumulating reusable

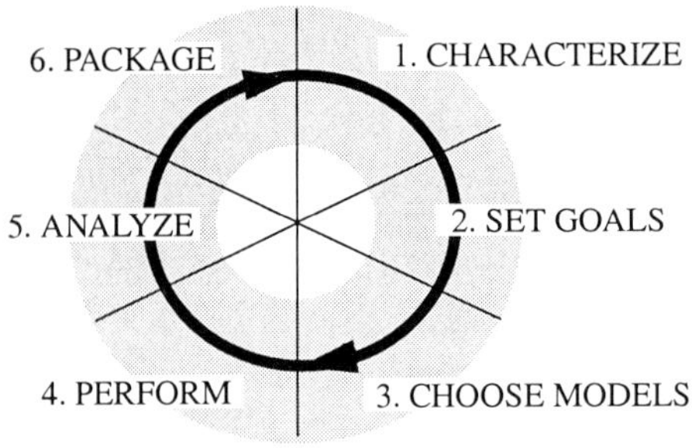

Fig. 9.2. Quality Improvement Paradigm (QIP)

experience in the form of software artifacts that are applicable to and useful for other projects.

The Experience Factory is a logical and/or physical organization that supports project developments by analyzing and synthesizing all kinds of experience, acting as a repository for such experience, and supplying that experience to various projects on demand. The experience factory complements the project organization (Basili et al. 1994a). The experience factory is mainly responsible for conducting the steps 5 and 6 of the QIP while steps 1 to 4 mainly concern the project organization (see Figure 9.3).

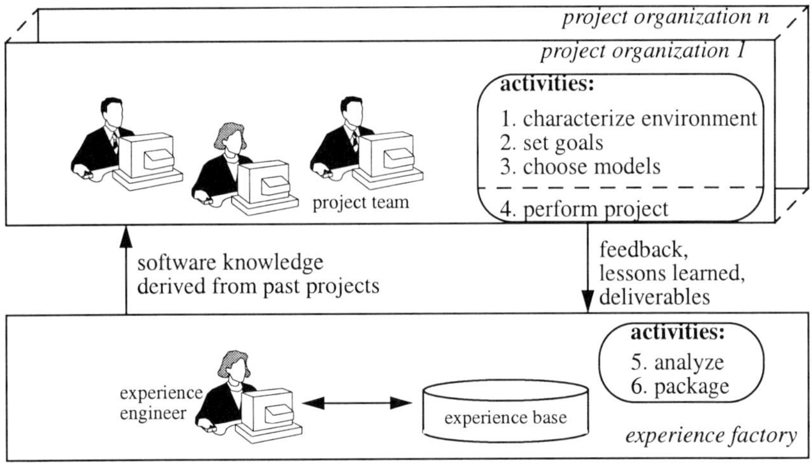

Fig. 9.3. The Experience Factory

For making the QIP/EF approach work effectively, the software organization needs to have three key competencies, also called key technologies, in place: goal-oriented measurement, explicit modeling, and comprehensive reuse.

Goal-oriented measurement provides the data and information needed for understanding, guiding, and changing the software processes of an organization within the course of an improvement program.

Explicit modeling of products, processes, quality, and other kinds of knowledge is the prerequisite for identifying, storing, and communicating the experience of a software organization.

Comprehensive reuse addresses the storing, retrieving, and tailoring of any relevant kind of experience and thus provides the basis for effectively making them available for software projects.

Throughout this chapter, we focus on explicit modeling and comprehensive reuse. We investigate how CBR is interrelated with explicit modeling, the QIP, and the experience factory. An analysis of these interrelations shows that both fields, CBR and ESE, can mutually benefit from each other.

9.4 CBR Support for Experimental Software Engineering

The main goal of ESE, to systematically and continuously learn from software engineering experiences, requires a technology that supports learning from experience in a very *flexible* and *open* way. We decided to explore CBR for this purpose. As suggested by Althoff and Aamodt (1996a), our approach is both top-down and bottom-up:

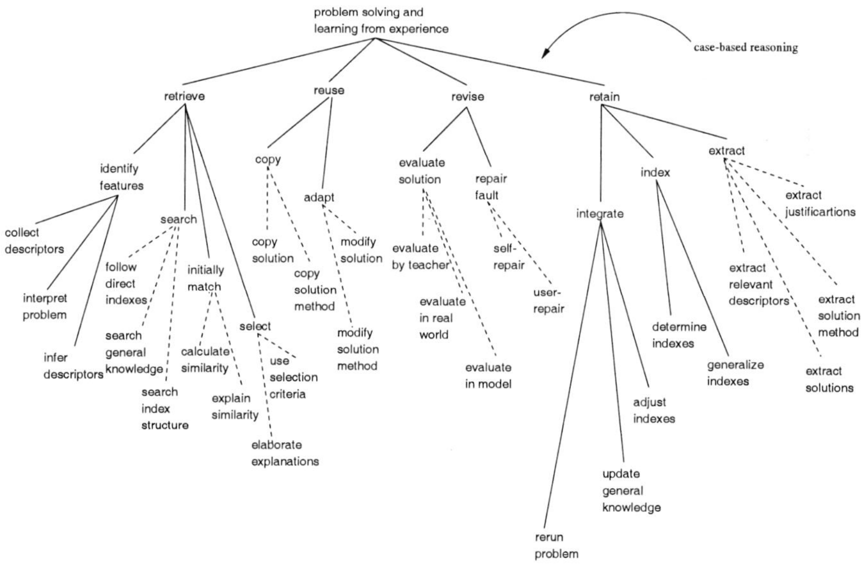

Fig. 9.4. The CBR task-method decomposition model (Aamodt and Plaza 1994)

Top-down approach: We operationalize existing models for software knowledge reuse using the CBR task- method decomposition model (Aamodt and Plaza 1994) (see Figure 9.4) and its extensions (Althoff and Aamodt 1996a; Althoff 1996). In Section 9.6, this approach is described in further detail.

Bottom-up approach: We realize concrete experience bases for reusing experiences about CBR applications and software inspections in different industries. This is detailed in Section 9.7.

Since it is needed later on, we now shortly introduce the task-method decomposition model shown in Figure 9.4. It further decomposes the tasks of the CBR cycle introduced in Chapter 1. The tasks have node names in bold letters, while methods are written in plain text. The links between task nodes (bold lines) are task decompositions, i.e., part-of relations. The links between tasks and methods (stippled lines) identify alternative methods applicable for solving a task. The top-level task is *problem solving and learning from experience* and the method to accomplish the task is a CBR method. This splits the top-level task into the four major CBR tasks corresponding to the CBR cycle. All four tasks are necessary in order to perform the top-level task. The *retrieve* task is, in turn, partitioned in the same manner (by a retrieval method) into the tasks *identify features*, *search* (to find a set of past cases), *initially match* (the relevant descriptors to past cases), and *select* (the most similar case). All task partitions in Figure 9.4 are considered complete, i.e., the set of subtasks of a task is intended to be sufficient to accomplish the task, at this level of description. The figure does not show any control structure over the subtasks. The actual control is specified as part of the problem-solving method. The actual retrieval method, for example (not explicitly indicated in the figure), specifies the sequence and loop-backs for the subtasks of *retrieve*. A method specifies the algorithm that identifies and controls the execution of subtasks, or solves the task directly, while accessing and utilizing the domain knowledge needed to do this. The methods shown in the figure are high-level method classes, from which one or more specific methods should be chosen. The method set, as shown, is incomplete; i.e., one of the methods indicated may be sufficient to solve the task, several methods may be combined, or there may be other methods that have not been mentioned.

9.5 State-of-the-Art

Research activities carried out in the scope of the CBR and ESE community, respectively, overlap in many aspects. While CBR lends itself to operationalize software knowledge reuse (Basili and Rombach 1991; Tautz and Althoff 1997a), ESE research results – especially technology transfer experiences – are important for extending current CBR approaches by organizational aspects (Basili et al. 1994a; Tautz and Althoff 1997b). In addition, both research areas have many goals in common (reuse of similar objects based on an incomplete problem description, learning from experience, adaptation/tailoring of objects to current needs, etc.) resulting in quite complex relationships between the approaches of the respective fields.

We decided to structure this overview according to a number of selected topics. To ease understanding, we tried to be constructive and ignored some *terminological differences*, e.g., whether a system uses CBR or analogy, or whether a retrieval component is based on *similarity*, a *pattern matching approach*, or CBR.

A large area of *overlapping* research activities in CBR and ESE is software reuse (Harandi and Bhansali 1989; Smyth and Cunningham 1992; Fouqué and Matwin 1993; Bergmann and Eisenecker 1995; Katalagarianos and Vassiliou 1995; Fernandez-Chamizo et al. 1996). Many approaches known from literature apply some kind of similarity based retrieval (Prieto-Daz and Freeman 1987; Ostertag et al. 1992; Gish et al. 1994) without directly referring to CBR. While CBR can be helpful in supporting comprehensive reuse on a very broad level (cf. Section 9.6, Althoff and Wilke 1997; Tautz and Althoff 1997b; Tautz and Althoff 1997c; Tautz and Althoff 1997a), an experience factory organization offers an organizational infrastructure necessary for operationalizing CBR systems in industrial environments (Tautz and Althoff 1997b). Currently, CBR is applied to introduce more flexibility in software reuse (Gómez 1997) and maintenance (Althoff et al. 1997), e.g., in combination with object-oriented techniques: (Talens et al. 1997; Gonzáles and Fernández 1997).

ESE approaches like software process modeling (Rombach and Verlage 1995), experience factory, meta models for requirements engineering (Jarke and Team 1996), etc. can contribute to the systematic development of CBR systems and applications. This is described in Bergmann et al. (1997a). Building a methodology for CBR system development (cf. Chapter 12, Kitano et al. 1993; Aamodt and Plaza 1994; Althoff and Aamodt 1996a; Althoff 1996; Curet and Jackson 1996) is very important for putting CBR into practice (cf. Chapter 11), e.g., in areas like software quality management (Kitano et al. 1992; Lees et al. 1996) or quality management in general (Althoff and Wess 1991; Pfeifer and Zenner 1996; Barr and Magaldi 1996; Adams et al. 1997). In the next section, we will describe how the methodology introduced by Althoff and Aamodt (Althoff and Aamodt 1996a; Althoff 1996) can be applied to operationalize software knowledge reuse within an experience factory approach.

Currently, CBR is applied in various ESE areas like capturing and formalizing best practices (Sary and Mackey 1995; Althoff and Bartsch-Spörl 1996; Henninger 1997; Bartsch-Spörl et al. 1997; Feldmann et al. 1997), effort prediction (Mukhopadhyay et al. 1992; Finnie et al. 1997), and requirements acquisition (Maiden 1991; Maiden and Sutcliffe 1992; Maiden and Rugg 1996;

Hsu and Chiu 1997). Applications of CBR to information system design are described in (Krampe and Lusti 1997; Czap 1997).

9.6 Our Approach

In the remainder of this chapter, we illustrate the application of CBR in ESE. As an example, we use the modeling of application domains of software engineering technologies for supporting the planning of software projects and improvement programs. A technology application domain describes the situations in which a technology can be applied successfully. By technologies we mean software engineering technologies such as lifecycle methodologies, design methods, testing and inspection techniques, compilers, or configuration management systems. Here, we only give an overview of technology domain analysis. More details can be found in Birk (1997).

In the following sections, we describe our approach with respect to case representation and acquisition, using cases for decision support, and maintaining a case base.

9.6.1 Case Representation

Successful application of a technology (e.g., reading by stepwise abstraction) means that using the technology for a particular task (e.g., code verification) leads to the achievement of a desired goal (e.g., highly reliable software). Whether a technology can be applied successfully depends on the characteristics of the context situation (e.g., programming language, amount of reuse, experience of developers, etc.).

Hence, a technology application should be described by referring to the overall task, the technology used, the goal of technology application, and the context, or domain, of technology application. Here, we are interested in more detail in the representation of technology domains. We refer to this as *technology domain models.* A technology domain model should be described in intuitive terms that make it easy for human decision makers to use them during decision support when selecting the appropriate technologies for a forthcoming project or improvement program. We represent such an intuitive domain model as a set of context characteristics, each containing a context factor (such as *experience of developers*) and an attribute value of that factor (e.g., *high*).

Figure 9.5 presents an example technology domain model. It contains the above described characterization of the technology application (technology, task, goal, and domain) where the domain is described through a set of intuitive domain characteristics.

Technology:	Reading by stepwise abstraction
Task:	Code verification
Goal:	High reliability of software product
Programming language:	C
Amount of reuse:	less than 40%
Experience of developers:	average
Size of project:	small (on-site)

Fig. 9.5. Case representation of exemplary intuitive domain model

9.6.2 Acquisition of Cases

Technology domain models are a kind of qualitative experience that can be gained from experienced software professionals using knowledge acquisition techniques. The knowledge acquisition should be backed up with theoretical analysis for identifying the present knowledge about the particular technology as it is reported in the literature. For instance, impacting factors on the success of using inspection techniques are reported in Fagan (1986). Such a theoretically grounded model allows for model-based knowledge acquisition using structured interviews and checklists. In addition, the information provided by the domain experts during knowledge acquisition should always be traced back to concrete projects in which the technology has been used. This is a first means for assuring validity of the knowledge acquisition results.

9.6.3 Using Cases for Decision Support

If a repository of domain models is available (i.e., a case base), how can it be used for supporting technology selection during project planning? In order to be valuable for project planning, such a repository should contain domain models for multiple technologies that share the same task and goal. A decision maker can then use this repository for selecting the technology whose application domain best meets the characteristics of the forthcoming project. Thus, the decision process contains the following steps:

1. Determine task and goal within the forthcoming project for which a technology should be retrieved from the repository. The pair of task and goal determines the set of factors through which the technology domain is represented.
2. Characterize the forthcoming project in terms of the relevant domain factors that have been determined in the previous step.
3. Perform similarity-based retrieval of those technologies whose domain models are sufficiently similar to the present project characteristics.

We are currently developing a decision support method with tool support that performs similarity-based retrieval based on technology domain models.

CBR is embedded into a multiple-attribute decision method (Mollogliasemi and Pet-Edwards 1997) that establishes an interactive decision process. Such an interactive decision process is desirable because of the qualitative nature of technology domains and the low probability of exact matches in similarity-based retrieval of cases. It allows decision makers to explore a filtered and prioritized set of alternative cases for making informed decisions during planning of software projects and improvement programs.

9.6.4 Maintaining a Case Base

In the preceding sections, we described how cases should be represented and how they can be of use for decision support. In order to make decision support effective, and allow continuous enhancement, case bases have to be maintained. The maintenance of case bases can be described using Aamodt's and Plaza's task-decomposition model (see Figure 9.4).

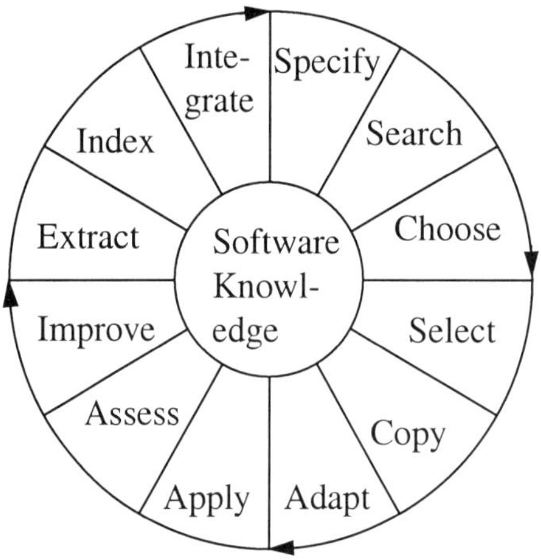

Fig. 9.6. Model Integrating Reuse And Case-based reasoning for Lots of software engineering Experiences (Miracle)

However, it must be tailored to the principles of ESE, which are described by the QIP presented in Section 9.3. The CBR task-method decomposition model and the QIP can be combined to a more general model we call Miracle[2]. It is shown in Figure 9.6. The task-method decomposition model has been extended by explicitly including the apply task resulting in a CBR process model. Except for this additional step, Miracle corresponds exactly to the tasks of the task-method decomposition model by Aamodt and Plaza (1994); only some of the names have been changed to reflect the needs of our application domain ESE (Specify instead of Identify features,

[2] Model Integrating Reuse And Case-based reasoning for Lots of software engineering Experiences

Choose instead of Initially match, Assess instead of Evaluate, Improve instead of Repair faults). MIRACLE can be mapped onto the QIP (Figure 9.7) and the task-method decomposition model as shown in Figure 9.8, and interpreted for project planning as described in Table 9.1.

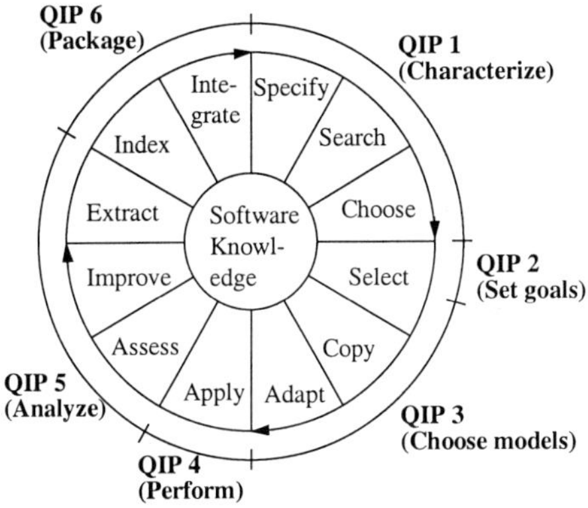

Fig. 9.7. Matching MIRACLE with the QIP

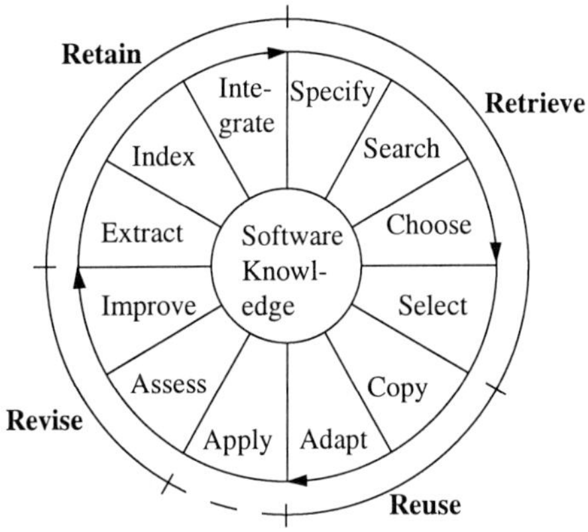

Fig. 9.8. Matching MIRACLE with the CBR task-method decomposition model

Since the CBR process model can be directly matched with MIRACLE, CBR methods and algorithms can be adapted to the needs of software knowledge reuse. Software knowledge reuse is essential for ESE as it allows to capture and retrieve the current state of the *corporate memory* (Henninger 1997; Barr and Magaldi 1996). Without a *corporate memory* no organizational learning across software projects can take place. This operationalizes QIP in the sense that the methods describe how the steps are to be performed technically (Althoff and Aamodt 1996a). In the following, we interpret MIRACLE using the methods described by Aamodt and Plaza (1994) and relate them to the domain of ESE. Where necessary, we complement the methods.

Table 9.1. Applying MIRACLE for Project Planning

Project Planning	MIRACLE
Specify project	Specify
Search for possibly relevant planning information	Search
Choose planning information which was used with projects similar to the one specified	Choose
1. Select suitable goals 2. Select most suitable models for the selected goals	Select
Copy most suitable models or create new ones	Copy
Modify models	Adapt
Perform project and collect data	Apply
Evaluate success of applying models based on collected data	Assess
Detect weaknesses and find out how models can be improved	Improve
Identify information items which must be stored (e.g., lessons learned)	Extract
Set up suitable characterization schemes for and relationships between the information items to be stored	Index
Update experience base	Integrate

Finding the Most Suitable Objects. Before reuse can actually take place, the most suitable objects have to be found. In the software domain, reuse is typically done by characterizing the needed objects using a predefined set of dimensions (features) and retrieving those objects having the most similar characterization to the one specified (Basili and Rombach 1991). A crucial aspect is that the retrieval mechanism must be able to cope with incomplete information, i.e., the characterization of the required objects may not be known in all details. CBR can cope with both aspects: similarity and incompleteness. This is accomplished by specifying the needed objects in as much detail as possible (step specify of MIRACLE), searching for potential objects (step search), choosing similar objects (step choose), and finally selecting the best suited objects (step select).

The specification step (which corresponds to the task identify features of the task-method decomposition model) itself can be refined into:

- Collecting feature values of the actual problem situation. Known feature values are entered into the retrieval system of the experience base.
- Interpreting the problem. Next, it has to be checked whether the feature values make sense within the context, e.g., looking for an algorithm which is minimal w.r.t. both time and space complexity does not make sense in general, because usually there is a tradeoff between the two. However, if similarity is computed based on the specified features, the features may be weighted differently resulting in a definition how the tradeoff should be treated. Another possibility is to disregard certain features.
- Inferring more feature values. If the needed objects cannot be specified completely (because of unknown feature values), additional feature values may be inferred by using a general knowledge model or by taking an

existing characterization from the experience base and disregarding those features which are irrelevant or unsuitable for the current problem.

After entering all known and inferable feature values, plausible candidates have to be retrieved (step search of MIRACLE). Once a set of plausible candidates is identified, it should be reduced to a smaller set of candidates which are similar to the one specified (step choose of MIRACLE). This is usually done by applying a *global* similarity measure, i.e., while the task search produces a set of candidates which are similar to those specified in some aspects (e.g., in terms of one feature), the step choose returns a set of candidates which are similar by taking into account all specified features. Finally, the best suited object is selected from the set (step select). Usually this requires a thorough analysis (of the objects returned by the step choose).

Copying and Adapting the Most Suitable Objects. As part of the selection step, the cost for modifying the most suitable object should be estimated. In order to be able to decide whether it is worthwhile to reuse the object, the cost for constructing the object from scratch should also be estimated. Based upon both estimations, the decision can be made whether to create a new object or to modify an existing one[3]. If a new object is created, a template (e.g., an outline for a text document) may be used. Thus, in both cases an object (most suitable object or template) is copied (step copy of MIRACLE) and adapted (step adapt).

There are two basic approaches for adaptation (Aamodt and Plaza 1994):

Transformational reuse: Based upon the differences between the retrieved object and the needed object, a set of transformation rules is defined, which will transform the retrieved object into the needed object.

Derivational reuse: In this case, the retrieved object will not be reused, but rather the development process[4] of the retrieved object. The needed object will be created using the development process associated with the retrieved object as guidance.

Applying the Adapted Objects. After constructing a suitable object, the object has to be validated. In case of a project plan (consisting of process models, technologies to be used, guidelines for documents to be created, measurement goals, etc.) this means the actual performance of the project. In addition to the applications in projects, there are less expensive ways to apply the objects (Aamodt and Plaza 1994):

Review by expert: An expert reviews the reused objects. The findings will be evaluated in the next step of MIRACLE (assess).

---

[3] This is a simplification of the real world. For instance, reuse is also a means for improving the reliability of software systems. Therefore, cost is not the only factor influencing the decision.

[4] The development process may either be the creation process if the retrieved object was created from scratch or the adaptation process if the retrieved object was adapted from some other object.

Test by model: A formal model may be used to determine the suitability of the objects. For instance, a project may be simulated using the project plan. Based on such simulations, the probability for completing the project on time can be determined.

The application and revision (detailed in the following section) of an object can be repeated; e.g., an expert can review an object, then the object is revised and applied in a real project, and then the object is revised again.

Revising the Reused Object. While applying a reused object, data should be collected which allows the evaluation of the success of the application (step assess of MIRACLE). If the application was a total success, the adapted object is characterized and can be stored as a new case. If the reused object was not applied in an optimal way, opportunity for learning from failure arises[5]. In principle, there are several possible reasons why the application did not work optimally[6]:

Wrong specification. The needed object was specified incorrectly. In this case, the step adapt was carried out correctly (presumably), but the adapted object (e.g., a lifecycle methodology) is not adequate for the project context.

Wrong application. The reused object was not applied as planned. For instance, a project may be planned perfectly, but the people working on the project do not follow the project plan (for whatever reason).

Wrong adaptation. Even if the needed object was specified correctly and the adapted object was applied as planned, the application may fail due to a fault in the adaptation step.

Of course, any combination of the above reasons may cause an application to fail partly or even totally. If the application did not work as expected, it is important to find out why; i.e.: Which of the above reasons were the cause? Why was the object specified incorrectly? Why did the project workers not follow the project plan? What exactly went wrong during the adaptation?). After assessing the application of the objects, they should be improved accordingly (step improve of MIRACLE).

Retaining the Objects. After the reused objects have been assessed (and possibly improved), the new insights become part of the software knowledge, i.e., the gained experience has to be stored. Since there is always something

[5] In the following, we are only concerned with applying the object successfully. However, it can also be of interest to evaluate the retrieval and reuse tasks. Typical questions could be: Was the most suitable candidate retrieved? Was the effort for adapting the most suitable candidate minimal? Was the estimated adaptation effort correct? If not, how can retrieval and reuse be improved?

[6] At this point, we hypothesize that the tasks retrieve and reuse have been performed satisfactorily, i.e., that the reuse task compensates for other deficiencies of the CBR systems such as wrong cases, wrong general knowledge, and wrong retrieval.

which can be learned from an application, the experience base should be updated regardless of whether the reused objects were applied successfully (in which case the increased reliability of the reused objects is noted) or not and regardless of how the original problem was solved (i.e., whether new objects were created or existing ones were modified).

Updating the experience base encompasses selecting the information to be stored, deciding how to represent it, how to index it for future retrieval, and how to integrate it into the already existing structure of the experience base.

There are several aspects to be considered when selecting the information to be stored (step extract in MIRACLE) (Aamodt and Plaza 1994):

- The reused object can either be stored as a new object, or an existing object within the experience base can be generalized/modified.
- Objects other than the one reused (e.g., rules describing which application process works under which conditions) should also be stored.
- Information related to the reused object (e.g., its characterization, assessment results, its development process) should also be stored. We call such a related set of information items including the object itself an experience package.

The last step is to integrate the new experience package. Integrating means that similar experience packages already existing in the experience base and the new experience package itself must be indexed in the same way. In addition, the general knowledge might have to be updated, e.g., if new relationships between different types of objects become important. The task retain is completed by testing the restructured experience base. If the test was not successful, the indexing structure or the general knowledge might have to be updated again. Otherwise the cycle of MIRACLE is complete, i.e., the experience base is ready for new queries.

9.7 Current Status

Parallel to the top-down approach presented so far, we are applying a bottom-up strategy by building specialized experience bases for our current needs focusing on the representation of cases for reusable objects, the definition of similarity measures, and the representation of the general knowledge. In addition, we use these prototypes for validating and refining MIRACLE for two types of objects: software tools and software development technologies.

In the area of software tools, we are concerned with suggesting the most appropriate tool for a given problem. For instance, a detailed review of five industrial CBR tools revealed that the optimal choice depends upon more than 200 features (Althoff et al. 1995a). This choice is even more complex when research systems are also included as candidates (Althoff 1996). This means that the choice does not only depend upon the problem at hand, but also on the context in which the problem is to be solved. It follows that the context must be part of the problem specification.

Currently, we are focusing on CBR systems (which solve a particular application problem, but can be adapted to similar application problems by the provider) and tools (which can be viewed as a development environment for CBR systems). About 50 features have been selected to *reflect* basic information about a CBR system and to allow CBR practitioners to describe their systems within a short period of time[7]. Both, CBR *applications*, i.e., applied CBR systems, as well as more generic CBR *tools*, covering a whole class of application problems, can be described using this feature subset. For instance, for a specified application problem one can search for a similar problem (i.e., an application problem solved with a specific CBR system) or a similar generic CBR tool (i.e., a CBR tool that in principle can deal with the problem). We used the CBR-Works system from TecInno (Kaiserslautern, Germany). The cases have been represented (and are available) in the Casuel common case and knowledge representation format (Casuel 1994). This system is accessible at http://www.iese.fhg.de/Competences/QPE/QE/metaCBR.html and offers a central experience base for CBR applications to the CBR community.

We hypothesize that the project is well worth the effort once a critical mass of CBR applications has been surveyed, because people considering a CBR application for solving their problem will be able to find a suitable CBR system or tool with almost no effort in comparison to today's situation where WWW search engines return a huge list of CBR web pages of unknown quality and unknown relevance to the application problem.

In the area of development technologies, we are concerned with learning how to tailor them for particular projects. The objective is to characterize a project in such a way that the experience base returns a technology tailored to the specific needs of the project. Currently, we are focusing on the inspection technique we are infusing into the software development of companies in various businesses. While performing the inspections in real-life projects we learned many lessons about successes, failures, and possible improvements. Inspections are used for improving the quality of software development documents. There are many ways in which an inspection can be conducted. For example, the document to be inspected can be presented by the author before the reading phase. Under certain conditions, it is useful to split the document into several pieces and inspect them separately. For each inspection, a meeting is conducted. In certain environments, an inspection meeting may result in unresolved issues. Further actions have to be defined to resolve such issues.

From these technology domain examples, it becomes evident that the creation or modification of an ideal inspection process is a non-trivial task. The idea is to capture the knowledge gained from applying inspections and reuse

[7] 50 questionnaires have been collected from 14 countries (Bartsch-Spörl et al. 1997).

this knowledge for similar projects. Over time, we will be able to formalize the knowledge; i.e., we will define a process which tells how to tailor a basic inspection process for the particular needs of a project. We hypothesize that we will produce a large number of lessons learned from different projects which cannot be handled manually and must be validated across projects and organizations.

9.8 Outlook

We have illustrated the application of case-based reasoning in experimental software engineering (ESE). As an example we used decision support for software engineering technology selection based on technology application domain models for supporting the planning of software projects and improvement programs.

We have built an integrated model called MIRACLE merging the QIP and the CBR task-method decomposition model, a refinement of the CBR cycle also introduced by Aamodt and Plaza (1994). MIRACLE details the QIP, since it was not described as detailed as the task-method decomposition model proposed in Aamodt and Plaza (1994). At the same time, MIRACLE extends the CBR task-method decomposition model by explicitly showing the application task. We used the methods described for the (sub)tasks in (Aamodt and Plaza 1994) to operationalize MIRACLE with respect to software knowledge reuse.

MIRACLE and decision support for technology selection, based on technology domain models, represent exemplary overlapping areas for CBR and ESE. Both fields share a lot of goals and can benefit from each other. One common goal is learning from experience; while CBR focuses on the automated support of learning from experience, the QIP and the experience factory approach explicitly include organizational aspects and, in this way, offer an approach for organizational learning. We believe that the experience factory concept offers a kind of infrastructure that is helpful for CBR applications not only in ESE, but in any kind of applications fielded in industrial or other business environments. Thus, an experience factory organization *operationalizes* a CBR system in industrial/business environments, while CBR offers computer based support on a very broad level.

An extension of the CBR cycle towards the inclusion of organizational issues helps to model *organizational processing of knowledge* in a very flexible way. In addition, CBR is a means to model experience based reasoning and acting of human problem solvers (at a certain level of abstraction). Thus, the key issue of optimizing the combination of *human and computer* can be addressed.

We believe that a CBR based experience factory or, vice versa, a CBR system embedded in an experience factory like infrastructure, will be the key factor for building corporate memories and effectively organizing the knowledge management of industrial or other kinds of business organizations.

10. CBR for Tutoring and Help Systems

Gerhard Weber, Thomas J. Schult

10.1 Introduction

Knowledge-based tutoring and help systems are designed to support learners and users individually. Such a capability stems from two so-called intelligent properties. Firstly, such a system is able to generate problem solutions automatically, based on its domain knowledge, without having to go back to inflexible, pre-compiled problem solutions (Self 1974). This allows the system to analyze complex and uncommon problem solutions, and to identify and explain errors. Secondly, representing the learners' knowledge acquisition processes and their current knowledge in so-called learner models allows the system to adapt to the learners' needs. Such learner models depend on representing the learners' knowledge about the respective domain and on describing their ability to solve problems in that domain. In existing tutoring systems, these intelligent properties involve, to varying degrees, automatic, cognitive diagnoses of activities and problem solutions offered by the learner. Results from these diagnoses are used for supporting learners and for giving advice in a communication process (Wenger 1987).

Learner models based on overlays (Carr and Goldstein 1977) identify the learner's performance as a subset of an expert's capabilities. They are adapted in their view of explaining solutions or errors from a learner to the point of view of the expert who planned or programmed the system (Ohlsson 1986). However, even models using bug libraries (e.g., the PROUST system, Johnson and Soloway 1987), or generative, runnable models (e.g, the program space approach, Ohlsson 1986), and the model-tracing method (Anderson et al. 1989) are limited in their ability to take into account the learners' intentions or their personal problem solving style.

Individualizing helping actions and tutorial activities will effectively depend on two issues: (a) individual information about how a particular learner solved tasks should be kept for a long while, and (b) this knowledge must be used in subsequent diagnoses and tutorial decisions. How much and how long information has to be stored is an open question up to now. These issues directly lead to what is called a case-based learning or reasoning system. However, not only cases gathered from a particular learner can be used by the system to tailor tutorial activities to the learner's needs. For example, pre-stored cases collected from experiences with other learners or those cases that are foreseen and valued as helpful by experienced human tutors will be useful in case-based tutoring and help systems.

In the following, we give a short overview of goals and techniques used in case-based tutoring and help systems, we refer to some different approaches of these case-based learning systems and, finally, we outline two systems developed in Germany in more detail.

10.2 General Aspects of Case-Based Tutoring and Help Systems

Though CBR techniques used in tutoring and help systems mostly support users and learners during the problem solving phase, they are not limited to these aspects. One can distinguish at least two different types of goals for CBR in tutoring and help systems. Firstly, case-based user modeling supports different types of adaptation techniques in computer applications. Secondly, case-based reasoning is used to support the learning process in teaching and learning systems. Such systems are often called case-based learning systems (CBL) or case-based teaching systems (CBT).

Case-based Adaptation: One prominent goal in software engineering is to provide interactive applications with adaptable and adaptive features. Adaptable features are well know and are used very often. They allow users to tailor a user interface or a sequence of subtasks to their specific needs or to their preferred behavior. These adaptable features are well suited to experienced users. On the other hand, novices often are not able to use these features appropriately because they are overloaded with learning to solve tasks and to use the interface. In this case, adaptable features may be helpful to assist the user. Case-based techniques can be used to adapt interface components to the user's needs (Specht and Weber 1996) and such adaptable systems can learn together with the user. In a broader sense, CBR systems that not only use pre-stored cases but also store new cases and, therefore, learn can be viewed as adaptable systems. For example, the planning system CHEF (Hammond 1990) is an adaptable system that, together with the user, learns to create new cooking receipts and adapts to how the user prefers to cook dishes.

Case-based Teaching: The main goal in case-based teaching and learning systems is to provide the learner with cases that are useful for him or her to understand new units of knowledge and to support problem solving. In static case-based teaching systems (e.g., Schank 1991), pre-stored cases that are provided by human instructors are used to give examples and to explain new topics that enable the learner to solve new problems in analogy to these cases. Other systems (e.g., McCalla and Greer 1986) use pre-stored cases to identify types of problem solutions and errors in order to tailor advice and feedback. In adaptive case-based teaching systems (e.g., Schult and Reimann 1995; Weber 1996), the system learns new cases while observing the learner during problem solving. These learned cases are used to show up individual remindings to similar problem situations that the learner already solved in his or her learning history.

The types of case-based reasoning methods used in tutoring and help systems differ with respect to the goals of theses systems. Systems that provide help based on well known pre-analyzed cases rely on a classification approach (e.g., McCalla and Greer 1986; Schult and Reimann 1995). Systems that support learning to solve problems use a problem solving approach to diagnose solutions to problems submitted by a learner and to identify the problem solving path the learner used in his or her solution (e.g., Weber 1996). Systems that support planning are based either on a problem solving approach (e.g., Weber 1996) or on a planning approach (e.g., case-based decision aiding, Kolodner 1991).

One can distinguish two different types of case representation in case-based tutoring and help systems. Most systems mentioned above store cases as a whole. These complete cases can be retrieved to show up examples or to give advice tailored to these specific cases. In the ELM approach (Weber 1996), cases are stored in forms of snippets (Kolodner 1993) that describe subgoals of problems and their solution within different contexts. These partial cases are used during the diagnostic process to trigger the selection of a problem solving path, in a similar way to the derivational analogy method used in PRODIGY (Veloso 1994).

10.3 Examples of Case-Based Tutoring and Help Systems

Case-based reasoning has been used in several tutoring and help systems developed during the past ten years. These systems encompass a wide range of applications including domains such as physics (Murray et al. 1990), biology (wild animals, Edelson 1991), business (Fergusson et al. 1992; Feifer and Allender 1994), chess (Schult and Reimann 1995), instructional planning (Du and McCalla 1991; Kolodner 1991), jurisprudence (Ashley and Aleven 1991), and programming (McCalla and Greer 1986; Weber and Möllenberg 1995; Weber and Specht 1997). Many of these systems have been reported only once and it seems that they have been not much more than promising ideas of how to use CBR in instructional and teaching contexts. However, some of these systems have been examined in extended empirical studies and even have been or are currently used in practice.

Two areas are of special interest to studies of problem solving and, in particular, to tutoring and help systems; programming and playing chess. Both areas are of special interest because there are no complete domain theories that cover all aspects of these domains. In traditional textbooks, both domains typically are introduced with the aid of many examples. This is especially true for chess books. Therefore, a case-based teaching system, like CACHET (see Section 10.6), seems to be well suited to support learning to play chess interactively (and not only via written, static examples).

The most successful tutoring and help systems have been developed in the domain of programming. These systems comprise the CMU-LISP tutor (Anderson et al. 1989), the LISP programming environments ELM-PE (Weber and Möllenberg 1995) and ELM-ART (Weber and Specht 1997), the intelligent LISP advisor SCENT (McCalla and Greer 1986), the intention-based program analyzer for PASCAL programs PROUST (Johnson 1986) and the PASCAL tutor BRIDGE (Bonar and Cunningham 1988).

Interestingly, the most recent systems (SCENT and the ELM-based systems ELM-PE and ELM-ART) use CBR methods. However, both approaches differ significantly. ELM is a case-based learning system, which aggregates cases from observing a particular student and using information from previous cases to trigger the diagnostic process. SCENT, in contrast, has cases pre-stored by the developer of the system, allowing for detailed advice tailored to a particular case on different granularity levels. Thus, both systems differ in that SCENT uses a categorization type CBR while ELM uses a problem solving type CBR.

Both, the systems based on the ELM approach and the CACHET system will be described in detail in separate sections later in this chapter.

10.4 Perspectives

The discussion of currently existing tutoring systems shows that many of the newest systems rely on CBR methodologies. This leads to the promising expectation that in future even more tutoring systems will use CBR.

Many of the current systems follow the CBT approach developed by Roger Schank and colleagues at the Institute of the Learning Sciences in Evanston. These teaching systems have a static case base with pre-compiled indexing mechanisms. This reduces their flexibility to adapt to the individual development of a single learner.

The systems described in this chapter demonstrate the advantages of CBR-based adaptation techniques. Showing the examples from the user's own learning history appears to be especially useful to beginners in a new domain. These cases remind the user of previous learning situations and of problem solutions that he or she worked at and solved before. Therefore, they easily can understand the meaning of the example. In case of new examples offered by the system, the user first has to understand this new example – which may be another difficult problem – and then he or she has to switch back to the actual task and has to map similarities. Apparently, this can be too complex to a beginner. On the other hand, specific new cases selected and presented by the system seem to be more appropriate to experienced users.

Besides using CBR in traditional tutoring systems, case-based techniques will emerge in on-line help systems that adapt to a single user. In the future, such adaptive help systems will not only rely on user characteristics obtained from some introductory questionnaire or on remembering the last selections a user made, but also will interpret, store, and use cases from the user's problem solving history (e.g., Specht and Weber 1996). These systems require fast computers with a lot of memory. But these requirements are fulfilled in current computer systems. In schools, universities, other institutions, and in companies the next generation of computers acquired will be powerful enough to use case-based adaptive features.

In on-line systems, however, it remains an open question, how larger case bases can be managed in such a way that adaptation can work in the background without disturbing the actual user actions and remain up to date at the same time. Therefore, the problem of forgetting in CBR systems will be a prominent research goal that, in the future, has to be investigated intensively.

10.5 ELM

The Episodic Learner Model (ELM) is a learning model that is used in the knowledge-based learning environments ELM-PE and ELM-ART. ELM is utilized in the diagnostic process to analyze users' solutions to problems or to partial solutions. That is, problem solutions not necessarily have to be complete to be analyzed. In the situation of complete solutions, the diagnosis looks for problem solving errors and returns explanation templates that can be used by an explanation module to present appropriate feedback to a particular user. In case of incomplete solutions, the diagnosis can identify whether the incomplete solution path principally will be correct and will give hints on which plans have to be followed to complete the problem solution as well as how this can be done. Actually, ELM is used to analyze solutions to programming problems in the programming language LISP. Additionally, ELM is the basis to retrieve examples and remindings that the learner may use to solve a new problem. Before we describe how ELM is used in the learning environments ELM-PE and ELM-ART, we first outline the architecture of ELM and describe how ELM is used in the diagnostic process at hand of an example. Then we introduce the explanation-based retrieval method (EBR). This retrieval method is able to find and to retrieve useful remindings from an individual episodic learner model.

ELM is a type of user or learner model that stores knowledge about the user (learner) in terms of a collection of episodes. In the sense of case-based learning, such episodes can be viewed as cases (Riesbeck and Schank 1989). To construct the learner model, the code produced by a learner is analyzed in terms of the domain knowledge and a task description (Figure 10.1). This cognitive diagnosis results in a derivation tree consisting of concepts and rules the learner might have used to solve the problem. These concepts and rules are instantiations of units from the knowledge base. The episodic learner model is built out of these instantiations and later generalizations based on them. To explain this form of episodic learner model, the knowledge representation and the diagnostic process will be described in some more detail.

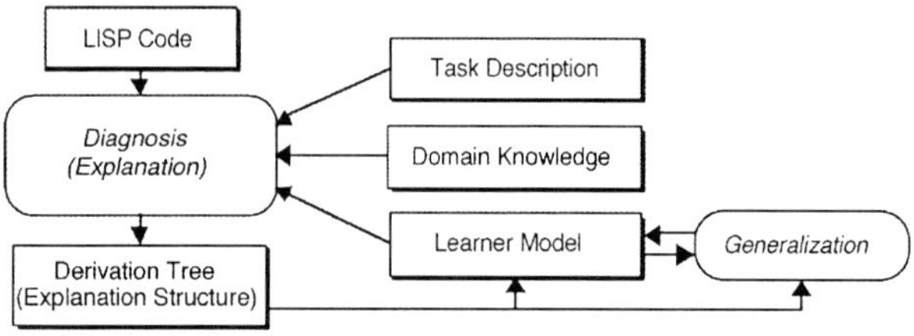

Fig. 10.1. The ELM Architecture

10.5.1 Representation of the Subject Domain

The domain knowledge is represented in a hybrid model which consists of concepts and rules in terms of hierarchically organized frames. Concepts comprise knowledge about the programming language LISP (concrete LISP procedures as well as superordinate semantic concepts) and schemata of common algorithmic and problem solving knowledge (e.g., recursion schemata). These concept frames contain information about plan transformations leading to semantically equivalent solutions and about rules describing different ways to more or less appropriately solve the goal stated by this concept. Additionally, there are bug rules describing errors observed by other students or buggy derivations of LISP-concepts which, for example, may result from confusion between semantically similar concepts.

10.5.2 The Diagnostic Process

In the application environment, students develop function definitions in a structured LISP-editor (Köhne and Weber 1987; Weber et al. 1996). Hence, the function code is at least syntactically correct. The cognitive analysis of the program code starts with a task description related to higher concepts, plans, and schemata in the knowledge base. Most concepts of the knowledge base have transformations describing semantically equivalent variations of this concept. For example, such transformations allow the altering of the order of clauses in a case decision or the sequence of arguments in a commutative function. The sequence of testing these transformations is determined by heuristic information. Usually, in the beginning, transformations used by most programmers are preferred, but, as individual information in the episodic student model grows, those transformations are preferred which the student has used in previous, comparable situations and which, therefore, are typical for him or her.

For every transformation, a set of rules is indexed by these concepts describing different ways to solve the goal stated by the concept. There are *good*, *bad*, and *buggy* rules explaining correct, correct but too complicated, and incorrect solutions of the actual goal or subgoal. The set of buggy rules is comparable to an error library in other intelligent tutoring systems (e.g., in the CMU LISP-tutor, Anderson et al. 1989). All rules within one category are checked. In this way, different explanations may be given as to how the code was constructed. Applying a rule results in comparing the current plan or subplan description to the corresponding part of the student's code. In the plan description, further concepts may be addressed. So, the cognitive diagnosis is called recursively until the coding of a function name, a parameter, or a constant is matched.

The cognitive diagnosis results in a derivation tree built from all concepts and rules identified to explain the student's solution. Figure 10.2 shows part of a derivation tree for the definition of the recursive function Simple-And. In this task, the programmer has to define a recursive predicate function that takes a list containing truth-values as its argument. The function has to test whether all elements of the list are of the truth-value `t`. In this case, the function should return `t`, otherwise it should return `nil`. The solution analyzed in this example was as follows:

```
(defun simple-and (li)
   (cond ((null li) t)
         ((null (car li)) nil)
         (t (simple-and (cdr li)))))
```

Information from the derivation tree can be used for two different purposes. First, identified *bad* and *buggy* rules may be used directly by a tutorial component to explain bugs and misconceptions, and second, the episodic student model will be updated.

All information captured in the derivation tree is integrated in terms of instances of their respective concepts and rules into the knowledge base. Special slots in these instances refer to the context in which these instances occurred (especially the current task). Other slots refer to type of transformations of concepts, and to argument bindings. For instance, for the concept `NULLTEST` in Figure 10.2, an episodic frame `nulltest.tg.4-1.2` is created containing slots for the current plan

```
(NULLTEST (FIRST-ELEMENT (PARAMETER ?LIST)))
```

for the rule Unary-Func-Rule that applied to solve this plan, and for the corresponding code `(null (car li))`. The set of all instances (plus further generalizations) constitutes the episodic student model. In subsequent analyses by the diagnostic component, these episodic instances can be used to trigger the selection of transformations and rules. This form of episodic student modeling is a combination of case-based reasoning (Hammond 1989a;

Hammond 1990; Kolodner 1984; Schank 1982) and explanation-based learning (Mitchell et al. 1986). One single event (or case) is interpreted with respect to the knowledge base and the student model. The result of this interpretation is integrated into the student model. So, it is a form of single-case learning as in explanation-based learning programs (DeJong 1988; Mitchell et al. 1986).

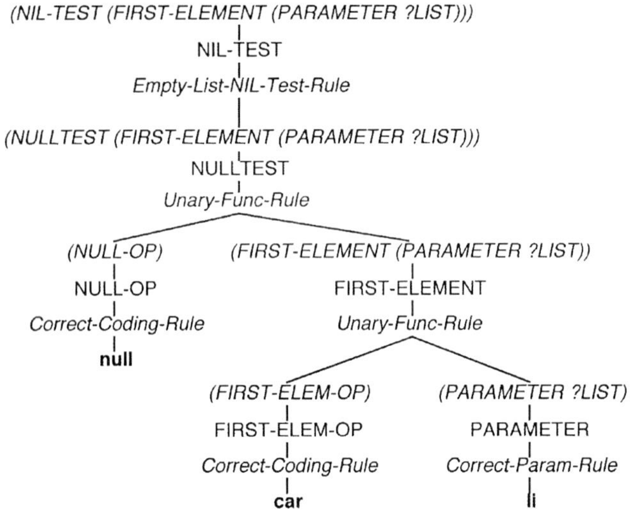

Fig. 10.2. Partial derivation tree explaining the code `(null (car li))` for the plan `(NIL-TEST (FIRST-ELEMENT (PARAMETER ?LIST)))` in task `Simple-And`. Legend: *ITALIC-CAPITALS*: plans, CAPITALS: concepts, *Italics*: rules, **bold**: LISP code.

One advantage of this form of episodic modeling is the possibility to generalize about episodic instances. During the student's learning history it happens that different instances in the student model are subsumed under the same frame of the knowledge base. These will differ in some aspects but they may coincide with respect to others (e.g., number and type of local parameters, subfunction call, etc). If there are several such correspondences between instances on the same hierarchy-level they will be generalized by some type of similarity-based generalization (Lebowitz 1986). With more and more knowledge about a particular learner, increasingly complex hierarchies of generalizations and instances are built under the concepts of the knowledge base. Figure 10.3 shows part of the concept hierarchy after inserting episodic frames for all examples from the first lesson on recursion, and for the analyzed solution from the `Simple-And` task. The entire set of episodic instances constitutes the episodic learner model.

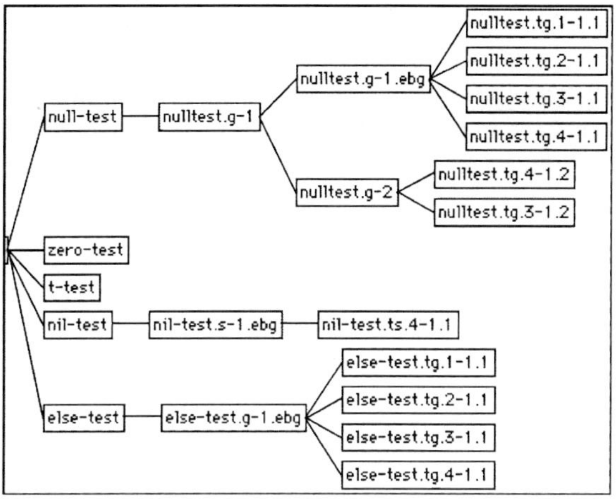

Fig. 10.3. Part of the concept hierarchy after inserting episodic frames for three examples from the learning materials and for task `Simple-And`.

The set of episodic frames of a particular episode constitutes a case in the case library, the episodic learner model. Each case is identified by an episode frame that indexes all other episodic frames contributing to the episode. Starting from the episode frame, the complete derivation tree can be reconstructed by scanning all episodic frames and re-establishing the old plan contexts and rules. That is, in ELM, cases are not stored as a whole but are divided into snippets (Kolodner 1993) that are stored with respect to the concepts in the system's knowledge base. Related notations of distributed cases can be found in DMAP (Riesbeck and Martin 1986) and in CELIA (Redmond 1990).

Information from episodic instances can be used in further diagnoses to reuse previous explanations or to prefer applying previously used rules if the current part of the code matches a solution to a similar plan stored in the episodic learner model. Using episodic information in ELM is a type of analogical replay using multiple cases in the sense of derivational analogy (Veloso 1994). This aspect of explanation-based diagnosis and of case-based learning in ELM is described in more detail in Weber (1996).

10.5.3 Explanation-Based Retrieval of Cases

An advantage of episodic modeling is its potential to predict code the programmers will produce as solutions to new programming tasks (Weber et al. 1993). These predictions can be used to search for examples and remindings that are useful for solving the new task.

Searching for a best analog to a given new programming problem works as follows. First, rules that are used by the diagnostic component to analyze program code can be used by a generation component to generate an expected solution to a new programming task (Weber et al. 1993). This results in an explanation structure of all concepts and rules used to generate the solution. Second, the resulting explanation is stored temporarily in the episodic learner model. Third, from computing the values of organizational similarity (Wolstencroft 1989) to other episodes (examples and remindings) stored with the user model, a best match can be found and offered to the learner as an example solution to a similar programming problem. Finally, the temporarily stored case is removed. The mechanism of retrieving useful examples from the episodic learner model is described in more detail in the next section.

10.5.4 The EBR Algorithm

When starting to work on a new lesson, the appropriate examples from the text materials are analyzed and the resulting derivation trees of these example-episodes are integrated into the individual learner model, as if they were solved by the learner. This reflects that the learner read and – hopefully – understood the exercises. In addition, it guarantees that examples are processed in the same way as solutions to exercises and that examples and remindings can be accessed by the same analogy mechanism.

On the basis of explanation structures, stored in distributed frames representing steps of the solution path, it is easy to retrieve previous problem solutions similar to the current problem. From the system's knowledge about the problem, a solution can be generated taking into account the individual case memory. On the basis of concepts and rules used to generate the new solution, the case memory can be probed for cases most similar to this solution. Concepts from the resulting explanation structure are inserted temporarily into the existing concept hierarchy of the episodic learner model. All episodic frames that are neighbors of the temporarily inserted frames contribute to computing weights for similar episodes. In Figure 10.3, for instance, the episodic frame `NULL-TEST.TG.4-1.1` (from Episode No. 4) is most similar to the episodic frames `NULL-TEST.TG.1-1.1`, `NULL-TEST.TG.2-1.1`, and `NULL-TEST.TG.3-1.1` (from Episodes No. 1, 2, and 3, respectively) and it is less similar to the episodic frame `NULL-TEST.TG.2-1.2` from the second episode. Spreading to other related concepts does not give any further discriminating information because all episodes have at least one episodic frame under the concept `NULL-TEST`. Therefore, this frame does not discriminate between previous episodes. The episodic frame `NOT.TG.4-1.1`, however, is only similar to the episodic frame `NOT.TG.3-1.1` (from Episode No. 3). This will give a high contribution to the similarity value for Episode No. 3. Spreading to semantically related concepts, such as other predicates (e.g., list predicates or arithmetic predicates) will give contributions to the similarity values for Episodes No. 1 and No. 2, but these values are much lower than the contribution from the directly related episodic frame `NOT.TG.3-1.1`. In the end, Episode No. 3 will be selected as most similar to Episode No. 4. Stored explanation structures are the basis for retrieving previous cases, so we call it *Explanation-Based Retrieval* (EBR).

This EBR method mainly computes organizational similarity. Episodic frames stored under a concept of the knowledge base are semantically similar because they belong to the same concept. This retrieval method reflects semantic similarity that plays the most prominent role in analogical retrieval (Thagard et al. 1990). However, because structural similarities play an important role in the generalization of episodic frames, structural consistencies are also considered (Forbus et al. 1995; Gentner 1983; Thagard et al. 1990). Pragmatic aspects are not considered directly in the current version of the EBR algorithm, but it would be easy to give special pragmatic weights to observed buggy rules and to poorly solved concepts, such that corresponding episodic frames from previous cases can dominate the retrieval of these episodes. Thus, tutorial goals could, in principle, impose pragmatic constraints on the retrieval process.

10.5.5 ELM-PE

The knowledge-based programming environment ELM-PE is designed to support novices who learn the programming language LISP (Weber and Möllenberg 1995). It has several features that are especially useful when learning to solve problems in a new, complex domain. Some of these features, relevant to the case-based ELM approach used in ELM-PE, will be sketched briefly in this section.

ALFRED - *a Syntax-driven Structure Editor.* In order to reduce syntax errors, coding function definitions is supported by a syntax-driven LISP-editor. In the program window of the structure editor, program code can be produced by filling in slots of LISP expressions. These patterns can be accessed from buttons in the function panel or by typing in the first part of a function call. Additionally, expressions can be typed in directly via keyboard or can be pasted from the buffer window. The buffer window displays the six most recent expressions from a kill ring. The user can apply filters on the buffer to display only atoms or lists or ask the system to display only those expressions that may be helpful in the current programming context (Brusilovsky et al. 1995). Programs developed in this structure editor can be analyzed even if they are not complete. In this case, the diagnosis module explains the next plan to follow and gives hints on how to code the function correctly.

Intelligent analysis of task solutions. Students can ask the system for help if they are not able to find an error in the code or if they simply want to know whether their solution is correct. To offer students a complete explanation of errors and suboptimal solutions and to explain which plans have to be followed to solve the task correctly, a *cognitive diagnosis* (as described above) was developed as a central *intelligent* component in the ELM programming environment. This diagnostic tool is based on the episodic learner model ELM (Weber 1996). The diagnosis results in an explanation of how the program code submitted to the cognitive diagnosis could have been produced by the learner. This explanation is the basis of the system's hints to the learner as to what part of the code is incorrect, which plans must be followed to solve subgoals during problem solving and possibly partial solutions in the context of the learner's solution. Explanations are stored in an individual, episodic learner model. They can be used as the basis for retrieving (Weber 1994) and explaining (Burow and Weber 1996) similar examples.

Example-based Programming. Examples of LISP-code can be displayed in a separate example window to support example-based learning. An example can be selected from examples discussed in the textbook of the LISP course as well as from the set of function definitions the student has coded already. Students can select examples by themselves or they can ask the system to provide an appropriate example or reminding. The example window has the same functionality as the program window of the structure editor, so LISP-expressions can be altered and parts of the code can be copied into the program window. The example-based programming technique used in ELM-PE is described in more detail in Brusilovsky and Weber (1996).

Example-based Explanation. Example code displayed in the example window can be explained by the explanation module. Example explanation is based on matching the interpretation of an expected solution to interpretations of solutions to previous problems that are stored in the episodic learner model. In this way, not only corresponding parts of code can be compared but also similarities between higher goals of the planning process will be explained. The method of example-based explanation is described in more detail in Burow and Weber (1996).

10.5.6 ELM-ART

The WWW-based introductory LISP course ELM-ART[1] is based on ELM-PE (described above). ELM-PE was limited due to the platform dependent implementation of the user interface and the large size of the application. Both limitations hindered a wider spread and usage of the system. Therefore, we decided to build a WWW-based version of ELM-PE that can be used both in intranets and in the Internet. The first step was to translate the texts of the printed materials into WWW-readable form (HTML-files) and to divide it into small subsections and text pages that are associated with concepts to be learned. These concepts are related to each other by describing the concepts' prerequisites and outcomes building up a conceptual network. All interactions of the learner with ELM-ART are recorded in an individual learner model. For each page visited, the corresponding unit of the conceptual network is marked accordingly. When presenting text pages in the WWW browser, links shown in section and subsection pages and in the overview are annotated according to a simple traffic lights metaphor, referring to information from

[1] ELM Adaptive Remote Tutor

the individual learner model (Schwarz et al. 1996). A red ball in front of the link indicates that the according section or text page is not ready to be learned because necessary prerequisites are not yet met. A green ball indicates that this page or section is ready and recommended to be learned and a yellow ball indicates that this link is ready to be visited but not especially recommended by the system.

ELM-ART enables direct interaction by providing live examples and intelligent diagnoses of problem solutions. All examples of function calls can be evaluated. When clicking on such a live example link, the evaluation of the function call is shown in an evaluator window similar to a listener in ordinary LISP environments. Users can type solutions to a programming problem into an editable window and then send it to the server. Evaluation and diagnosis of problem solutions are performed the same way as in ELM-PE. Therefore, the same feedback messages that have proven to be useful in ELM-PE can be sent back to the learner.

ELM-ART supports example-based programming. That is, it encourages students to re-use the code of previously analyzed examples when solving a new problem. The hypermedia form of the course and, especially, similarity links between examples help the learner to find the relevant examples from his or her previous experience. As an important feature, ELM-ART can predict the student way of solving a particular problem and find the most relevant example from the individual learning history. This kind of problem solving support is very important for students who have problems with finding relevant examples. Answering the help request, ELM-ART selects the most helpful examples, sorts them according to their relevance, and presents them to the student as an ordered list of hypertext links. The most relevant example is always presented first, but, if the student is not happy with this example for some reason, s/he can try the second and the following suggested examples. This feature is directly implemented from the most recent version of ELM-PE (Burow and Weber 1996).

ELM-ART has been implemented with the programmable WWW-server CL-HTTP[2] and can be accessed via the URL:

http://cogpsy.uni-trier.de:8000/TLServ.html

10.6 CACHET

10.6.1 Static and Dynamic Case-Based Teaching

Central to the standard static case-based teaching approach (Schank 1991) is a situation (problem case) the student has to act and solve problems in, e.g., a simulation environment. The problems presented to the learner are

[2] http://www.ai.mit.edu/projects/iiip/doc/cl-http/home-page.html

designed in a way that facilitates the diagnosis of a failure. Possible failures are classified by failure types, and each type is associated with a supporting case to help the student overcome the failure. Thus, if a description of a failure type matches the solution proposed by the learner, the respective supporting case is presented, otherwise the systems proceed by presenting the next problem.

The standard architecture described above has proven its effectiveness in several domains. Nevertheless, there are limitations. It is well suited to domain representations of low complexity with a small number of failure types and simple failure detection by pattern matching. More complex and open domains are likely not to be manageable in this way.

In the standard architecture, not only is the state space in a certain sense static and manageable, but also the case base. The quality of the tutoring system depends crucially on the cases the system designer delivered. There is no change in the case base over time and no influence of the learner concerning its content. In particular, the cases the learner deals with are forgotten, even though they are a valuable source for later reference and analogical reasoning, because the learner is familiar with them.

Furthermore, the designer has to take all future failure situations into consideration when equipping the case base with supporting cases. This may not be possible in complex domains, especially if one wants the supporting case to be very similar to the problem case in order to ease adaptation. Therefore, generating supporting cases on demand can be a valuable extension to the standard approach to case-based teaching.

The dynamic approach to case-based teaching is characterized by the feature that all problems are solved twice - by the learner as well as by the system. Thus, at the beginning of the interaction cycle, the teaching system presents the problem case to the learner and solves the problem itself without telling the solution. In contrast to the standard model tracing approach (Anderson et al. 1990) the solution of the system's domain expert - if different from the learner's solution - is not used for direct feedback. Instead, it serves as a means to index and retrieve supporting cases. An expert component capable of assessing and comparing solutions is part of this approach. If this component detects a major quality difference between the solution of the learner and that of the system, it looks for similar cases to support the learner. Thus, there is still the chance for the learners to find the solution themselves.

In contrast to static or dynamic case-based teaching, the model tracing approach is known as an established architecture often employed in tutoring systems. The learner's activities are compared with the results of an expert module solving the same problem, and the result of the comparison leads to feedback. Although the effectiveness of the model tracing approach has been proven in many domains, some researchers point out disadvantages. In some circumstances, it may suppress the learner's own debugging (Reiser et al.

1994) or multiple solution paths (Collins and Brown 1988). Additionally, model tracing combined with immediate feedback may interfere with students' own learning activities (Scardamalia et al. 1989) and can be regarded as too directive (Fox 1991). According to Ridgway (1988), model tracing may be especially useful for teaching well understood procedural skills.

Often the developer does not have the choice between a case-based and a model tracing learning environment. Since the model tracing approach depends on a very detailed model of the cognitive processes involved in task accomplishment, it is only suitable for domains for which cognitive psychology has produced such models. There are not – and will not be – many. In particular, in domains where formalizations are very hard to come up with, model tracing is not applicable. In contrast, case-based reasoning is especially suited to teaching domains with a lack of a complete and concise domain theory.

10.6.2 Dynamic Teaching in CACHET

CACHET[3] (Schult 1995; Schult and Reimann 1995) supports a fairly complex kind of case-based problem solving. The domain drawn upon is chess end games. This is a topic that is well suited to being communicated with the help of cases, as there is no complete domain theory of end games. Accordingly, all chess books teach by presenting annotated cases (and not much more). Playing chess successfully requires a mixture of general reasoning strategies (such as planning) and experience, a combination of which is required for successful problem solving in other areas as well.

The instructional situation is a combination of learning from examples and of exploratory learning. The relevant chess heuristics are not given to learners; they have to infer them from analyzing worked-out examples and from their own problem solving experiences (i.e., by playing the game). The computer helps learners to keep records of the relevant experiences and to structure this external memory of learning episodes in a way useful for later problem solving. In addition, the program can actively support students by providing cases automatically, thereby lowering the burden of searching for or generating situations, leaving more room to focus on adapting the former experience to the problem at hand.

When learning chess end games with CACHET, the learner initially watches worked-out examples of successful and effective end games. She is asked to elaborate what happens on the board (e.g., by identifying goals underlying the actions visible). Elaborations help to gain a richer mental encoding and, therefore, facilitate later retrieval and usage of the cases (Chi et al. 1989). After the worked-out examples, the learner is asked to solve problems on her own (i.e., to play end games). When playing, analogical

---

[3] Case-Based Chess Endgame Tutor

transfer of cases is supported extensively (see Reimann and Schult (1996), for a discussion from a psychological perspective).

An expert component capable of assessing and comparing solutions is part of this approach, and it is implemented in CACHET. A position evaluator recognizes moves that are suboptimal by analyzing structural features of the respective end game situation. In contrast to the model tracing approach, this diagnosis does not lead to direct interventions concerning strategical issues. Instead, a suboptimal behavior triggers the presentation of supporting cases, if available. This comprises situations previously encountered (e.g., in the worked-out examples) or situations generated to demonstrate possible severe consequences some moves ahead. Thus, there is still the chance for the learner to find out the solution herself.

After having found or generated a case, CACHET displays it in a second game board to the right of the current board and provides the student with the advice to inspect the similar situation on the second board before continuing her game (see Figure 10.4). The student can then reconsider the recent sub-optimal move or continue with her original plan. CACHET will not force the student to make a different move, but intervene when another suboptimal move has been identified.

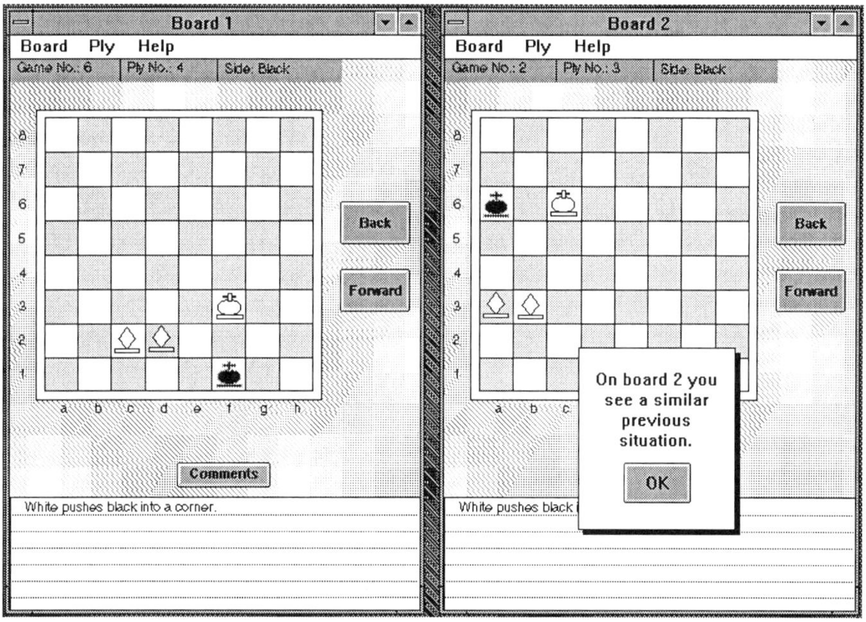

Fig. 10.4. Presentation of a reminding (right) when solving a problem (left)

CACHET realizes its instructional strategy utilizing three case libraries:

Pre-defined cases: Prototypical, informative games are analyzed off-line and entered into the case repertoire. However, specifying cases in advance means that the system is severely restricted in choosing a case that fits to the current learning situation.

For supporting learners, we realized two additional kinds of cases:

Cases generated on demand: This kind of case is useful if there are many constraints as to what a useful case for the current learning situation should look like. For instance, CACHET is able to generate a case (here: chess position as a subcase of a whole endgame case) illustrating an awkward, but possible constellation three moves ahead, and then the learner may react to this scenario.

Cases produced by the learners themselves: When students solve problems, they generate cases as a side effect. Self-generated cases of this kind were successfully employed as remindings in a simulation environment (Schult 1993). The tutoring dialog itself serves as a case memory that is exploited by a memory assistant that reminds the learner of previous problems similar to the current one. This mechanism is also included in CACHET's repertoire of interventions.

CACHET's tutorial strategy was extensively evaluated (Schult 1995). First, a computational experiment served to assess the position evaluator in CACHET. End game situations were given to the heuristic chess player in CACHET with CACHET playing the stronger side. It had to beat a commercial chess program (Fritz2, ELO 2280) in a nearly optimal way, and it did. When Fritz2 played the stronger side, it needed, on average, more than 20 percent more moves to reach a mate. Thus, CACHET's end game abilities are sufficient for the purpose of the teaching system. The heuristic chess player in CACHET serves two purposes; on the one hand it is the opponent of the learner playing end games, on the other hand it assesses the learner's actions and triggers tutorial interventions, e.g. the presentation of a supporting case.

Concerning the tutorial interventions, it turned out that reminding of cases as well as generating relevant cases leads to a significant increase in the problem solving capacity in the domain. However, there are no significant differences compared to standard model tracing interventions providing direct advice. But a tendency is observed towards a better performance of a learner studying cases generated on demand, when those cases illustrate the sort of problem the player would run if she had continued with her current move. Furthermore, direct advice was especially helpful to novices, whereas generated cases were more effective for advanced learners.

11. CBR in Medicine

Lothar Gierl, Mathias Bull, Rainer Schmidt

11.1 Medicine and Knowledge Based Systems

11.1.1 Specific Features of Medicine

Medicine differs from other knowledge domains by the interaction of research and practice. The objects are the patients - very complex organisms with high biological variance and a lot of interactive vital processes. The knowledge of these processes and their interactions is often weak. It mostly depends on a high number of sometimes even contradicting signs and symptoms. Furthermore, the individual vital processes are affected by changes of the environmental situations (e.g., new resistances, diseases or pathogens). To discover new medical knowledge, traditional research is based on disease case descriptions, case collections, and biostatistical case studies.

In contrast to other knowledge domains, clinical practice is characterized by a professional documentation of cases. Numerous case collections have been accumulated.

On the one hand, knowledge of special topics is often highly centralized. This means that only one person is an expert in this field, such as antibiotic therapy. On the other hand, medical knowledge in different clinics is distributed in specialists and knowledge sources such as patient oriented documents, medical journals, data bases, text work, etc.

Physicians are overwhelmed by the amount of data, even for one patient (e.g., hundreds of parameter values from clinical chemistry, dozens of images from radiology, sonography, etc., and dozens of textual documents). Physicians are usually confronted with contradicting information. For instance, laboratory parameters and clinical features may contradict. Moreover, they have to cope with vague data, e.g., complaints of a patient.

Clinicians mostly work under stress. This means, they have to choose rapidly from a large number of alternatives. For instance, they have to decide for an appropriate dosage of a selection of drugs in order to preserve a desired impact for a particular disease.

The process of decision making of a physician or a nurse is unique for the medical domain. It is strongly associated with the object of the decision, namely the patient. Figure 11.1 roughly depicts the general sequence of tasks of each encounter with a patient (Hadorn and Zöllner 1979). The feedback loops indicate this process as cyclical.

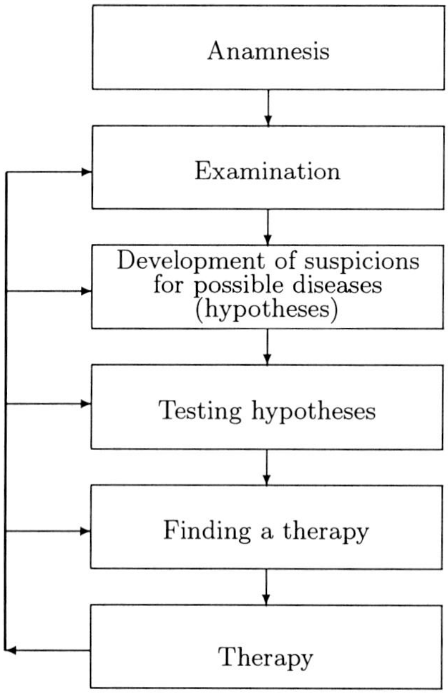

Fig. 11.1. Rough sequence of the general tasks of each encounter with a patient (Hadorn and Zöllner 1979)

We do not understand in detail how physicians decide. Experienced physicians especially are unable to describe precisely the first step of recognizing diseases which could explain the symptoms and signs of a patient. In certain situations, they obviously recall a prototype, a typical case, or a typical exception of a disease or therapy connected with a previous patient.

Empirical investigations give certain hints about the general problem solving strategies of physicians. These strategies have been observed as *symptom-centric* and *disease-centric* (Connelly and Johnson 1980). A combination of both strategies often forms the architecture of knowledge-based systems. The symptom-based strategy characterizes a direct association of symptoms and signs with diseases (hypotheses) (Clancey 1985). Physicians and knowledge-based systems use the following facts and knowledge in decision making:

- Symptoms of diseases, used as triggers to find hypotheses initially.
- Knowledge on increased risks for a patient associated with certain diseases, therapies, etc.
- Frequency of diseases derived from epidemiological studies.
- Frequency of diseases derived from individual experience.

Building on the identification of application classes by Waterman (1986) and Clancey (1985), we give, in this chapter, a compound overview of CBR systems in medicine. We address

- Diagnosis
- Classification
- Planning
  - therapy support
  - personal or material resources
- Prognosis
- Tutoring

11.1.2 The History of Knowledge-Based Systems in Medicine

Shortliffe (1976) presented his famous approach to formulate domain knowledge explicitly (diagnosis of infection diseases) and to use it in medical decision making. The paradigm of expert systems was born. It was the beginning of a bulk of research on knowledge-based systems aiming at the support of physicians in their daily work as clinicians and practitioners.

But all these systems produced only academic toy solutions. Systems for real world use in a medical setting have relied on traditional statistical methods of medical decision making (e.g., diagnosis of abdominal pain, de Dombal et al. 1972) since the work of Ledley and Lusted (1959) at the end of the 1950s.

It has not yet been possible, not even partially, to fulfill the hope of making the wide and rapidly growing medical knowledge available to physicians in the form of expert systems. Only a few of these systems have found their way into clinical application (approximately 20 worldwide). Miller and Masarie (1990) summarized over 10 years of experience with the development of the expert system INTERNIST-1, which, as a diagnostic consulting system, was supposed to cover the whole area of internal medicine. The attempt has failed to provide physicians with a system yielding a diagnosis with 65 to 75 percent certainty, as the sole result after a very time-consuming dialogue of between 30 and 90 minutes. The amount of details, the uniqueness of each singular case and the lack of complete and correct data make every result of this kind, except for a few classic examples, questionable. Miller summarizes his criticism of INTERNIST-1 (and other systems) as follows:

> *"The style of diagnostic consultation embodied in the* INTERNIST-1 *program was a 'Greek Oracle' model."*

11.1.3 Advantages of CBR in Medicine

Case-based reasoning is appropriate in medicine for some important reasons:

Cognitive Adequateness. Cased-based systems correspond to the incremental keeping in mind, abstraction and recognition of human knowledge in a natural manner. As another important aspect, we point out that physicians often use their case experiences from their clinical practice to treat a current case more efficiently, to diagnose similar exceptions, etc. Schank et al. (1994, p. 27) postulate that even the human creativity is an ability based on experiences.

Explicit Experience. CBR systems use less *clotted* knowledge(e.g., rules) but extend, replace, change, and forget knowledge by continuous integration of cases into the case base. Thus, each case-based system can adjust itself to the specific requirements of a clinic or a surgery.

Duality of Objective and Subjective Knowledge. In medicine, it is conventional to discover new knowledge by evaluating data through the use of clinical cases. Such knowledge is objective; it does not depend on the explorer. This knowledge, contained in textbooks, norms and proceedings, is not specific enough and often it is not accepted because of different views on medical problems or different opinions and experiences on diagnosis and therapy. Most often, the practice in expert systems is different. They usually use the subjective knowledge of one or more physicians. This knowledge is limited in time and space. Nevertheless, such knowledge is applicable because of its specifity and because it is rather accepted by physicians. Here is an obvious dilemma which is unsolvable by conventional expert systems. Objective, as well as time and space limited subjective knowledge, is often combined in medical knowledge-based systems without any reflection. For example, the expression *"the patient has a prerenal kidney failure with the probability of 50%"* includes the spatio-temporal statement about the event kidney failure and the objective statement about the anatomy of the urogenital tract. This dualism is embodied explicitly in a case-based system. Such a system contains cases, i.e., subjective knowledge and formal causal, generalized knowledge (from physiology, microbiology, anatomy, etc.) as objective knowledge. By the separation of objective and subjective knowledge, CBR leads to an objectivity and to a specificity of the knowledge base and solves the dilemma mentioned above.

Automatic Acquisition of Subjective Knowledge. The continuous integration of cases during the use of a CBR system leads to an incremental knowledge acquisition. Furthermore, the system is able to abstract knowledge by generalizing cases via case groups to prototypes.

System Integration. The use of data and medical patient records, which are already being collected by hospitals and practitioners and stored on machine readable mediums, allows an integration in existing clinical communication systems.

Our experience shows that case-based systems which combine knowledge acquisition as a machine learning process during the consultation process can give an important contribution to the solution of the knowledge acquisition problem. As an example, Goos and Schewe (1993) report a comparison of knowledge acquisition for a case-based system and a rule-based system. The building of the knowledge-base for the latter was achieved in 18 months and for the case-based system in 2 months. Furthermore, we are able to show that a knowledge-base generated from cases seen and documented in an outpatient clinic can produce a more accurate consultation than a knowledge-base compiled from case descriptions in international medical literature of the domain (dysmorphic syndromes, Gierl 1992a). A second aspect in assessing CBR systems in medicine is to evaluate them using real clinical data. A study in Haddad et al. (1997) using sensitivity and specificity shows a good performance of a CBR system for detecting coronary heart disease from myocardial scintigrams.

Moreover, knowledge-based approaches, in general, seem to be superior to competing methods. Molino et al. (1996) compared a hybrid system of prototypes and rules with a probabilistic system in the domain of diagnosing jaundice. Five experienced gastroenterologists provided the reference diagnosis. The knowledge-based program showed better performance than the probabilistic system. A study of Goos and Schewe (1993), however, which compared a case-based system with a rule-based system depicted a less optimistic picture.

Most evidence is given by the fact whether a CBR system is in clinical routine use or not. As far as we know only GS.52 (cf. Section 11.3.1) has been in use in a clinical setting since 1988.

11.2 CBR Systems in Medicine

Kolodner and Kolodner (1987) introduced a framework for using experience in clinical problem solving. Unfortunately it is a framework for their general CBR ideas, only supplemented by some fitting medical examples. This leads to the dilemma of CBR (and other methods) in the medical domain. Often, researchers build CBR systems using data from a medical domain. PROTOS (Bareiss 1989) uses the *exemplar* approach and stores prototypes and exemplars as more specialized prototypes. The medical domain is obscure. Such systems have no chance to be routinely used in a medical setting. They do not even contribute to an understanding of the role of CBR in medical decision making.

On the other hand, useful medical programs are sometimes implemented which are dominated by specific requirements of single care units. So, they lack in investigating knowledge processing methods. Only a few systems are sophisticated from both points of view.

11.2.1 Diagnosis

CASEY. CASEY (Koton 1988) is an expert system in the domain of heart failure diagnosis that combines case-based and rule-based reasoning techniques. The system uses three steps; a search for similar cases, a determination of differences and their evidences, and a transfer of the diagnoses of similar cases or – if the differences are too important – an attempt to explain and repair them. If no similar case can be found or if all repair attempts fail, CASEY uses the rule-based domain theory.

The most interesting aspect of CASEY is the attempt to use more general adaptation operators. For medical applications, some CBR researchers have entirely given up the claim to perform any adaptation at all (Macura and Macura 1995), others apply only very specialized operators. However, in CASEY not all adaptation problems could be solved.

FLORENCE. The FLORENCE system (Bradburn and Zeleznikow 1993) deals with health care planning in a broader sense; for nursing, which is a less specialized field. It fulfills all three basic planning tasks; diagnosis, prognosis, and prescription. Diagnosis is not used in the common medical sense as the identification of a disease but it seeks to answer the question *"What is the current health status of this patient?"* Rules concerning weighted health indicators are applied. The health status is determined as the score of the indicator weights.

Prognosis seeks to answer the question "How may the health status of this patient change in the future?" Here a case-based approach is used. The current patient is compared to a similar previous patient for whom the progression of the health status is known. Similar patients are searched for first concerning the overall status and subsequently concerning the individual health indicators. As the further development of a patient not only depends on his situation (current health status, basic and present diseases), but additionally on further treatments, several individual projections for different treatments are generated.

Prescription seeks to answer the question "How may the health status of this patient be improved?" The answer is given by utilizing general knowledge about likely effects of treatments and also by considering the outcome of using particular treatments in similar patients. That means it is a combination of a rule-based and a case-based approach. The best prognoses and their treatments are considered. As the treatments may come from different patients, they may be contrasting or forbidden to combine. Additionally, to deal with time and duration problem of treatments, rules about treatment constraints are applied.

MEDIC. The interesting aspect of MEDIC (Turner 1988) is not the medical application, but the memory organization. MEDIC is a schema-based diagnostic reasoner on the domain of pulmonology. Schemata represent the problem solver's knowledge. These are packets of procedural knowledge about how to achieve a goal or a set of goals (Figure 11.2 shows an example of a schema). The memory does not only consist of schemata, but additionally of diagnostic memory organization packets (similar to the memory organization packets (MOPs) of Schank (1982)) of individual cases of diagnosis and of scenes. A scene represents an instantiation of a schema in a particular case. This memory organization and retrieval allows a reasoner to find the most specific problem-solving procedures available.

```
Goal: interpret a finding of dyspnea
Patient: any patient
Findings: dyspnea
Preconditions: there is a finding of dyspnea
Actions:

  A1: action: ask how many stairs patient can climb
      goal: determine severity of dyspnea
      next:
            if patient can climb flight of stairs ⇒ A3
            else ⇒ A2
  A2: action: ask how far patient can walk
      goal: determine severity of dyspnea
      next: A3
  A3: action: estimate the severity of the dyspnea
      goal: determine severity of dyspnea
```

Fig. 11.2. A schema for interpreting a finding of dyspnea

PSIQ. Another example is PSIQ (Schwartz et al. 1997) which gives diagnostic and therapeutic advice in the domain of mental disorders. After a language treatment component has delivered ICD-10 categories from the patient's history and grouped them concerning different aspects, these categories can be used to search for similar cases which are shown to the user (including their diagnoses and treatments).

Image Interpretation. Grimnes and Aamodt (1996) are developing a prototype of an image interpretation system for computer tomography with a two layer CBR architecture. They want to use two case-based reasoners, one for a lower level segment identification and the other for a higher level interpretation and understanding of the image as a whole. The most sophisticated image understanding system is SCINA (Haddad et al. 1997) which derives an assessment concerning the presence of coronary artery disease from a scintigraphic image data set automatically. Each image consists of 6 planes, each plane is divided into 12 segments. For each segment, a value of the relative thallium activity obtained by polar map analysis is determined. The retrieval, which is performed by nearest neighbor match, considers these 72 integer values, those from segments of planes placed in the middle are weighted high, those from the edges are weighted low. As the case base comprises only 100 cases, an indexing mechanism is not necessary. However, it was implemented for testing. A problem specific adaptation process is based on the model of coronary circulation. SCINA is implemented in the CBR programming shell ESTEEM (King 1994). Tsukamoto (1993) reported convincing results (up to 97% sensitivity) evaluating a CBR system for CT diagnosis.

Further Diagnostic Systems. MERSY is a system for rural health care workers (Opiyo 1995). This system explicits the most convincing advantages of CBR, namely, the relocation of expertise. This is especially valuable in countries where health care workers are rare and perform with only modest skills. The knowledge-base can be automatically adapted to the special health care problems of a region by simply using the CBR system. The system by Evans (1996) on the same topic as GS.52 (see Section 11.3.1) – dysmorphic syndromes – is based on an incremental algorithm to generate a hierarchical network of generalized cases from prototypical signs of syndromes. Similar to COSYL (see below) Evan's algorithm focuses on the semantics of the two highest levels of the hierarchy. These are built from the trigger signs of a syndrome and from important but secondary signs. This sounds pragmatic, but it is necessary to avoid the building of artifacts a physician would assess as medical nonsense. Other diagnostic domains are bone healing (Seitz and Uhrmacher 1996), histopathology (Jaulent 1997), which uses a combination of surface and structural similarity to retrieve similar pathological cases, urology (Burkhard et al. 1996), which uses *Case Retrieval Nets* (cf. Section 3.4) as a mechanism for retrieval of similar previous cases, and MEDUSA (Fathi-Tortsagham and Meyer 1994) a hybrid system using cases, rules and fuzzy sets in the domain of diagnosing acute abdominal pain. Stamper et al. (1994) use the possibilities of CBR for explanation in medical diagnosis applied to a problem in gynaecology.

11.2.2 Classification

Image Retrieval. PROTOISIS (Kahn and Anderson 1994) uses a version of PROTOS (Bareiss 1989) to provide an intelligent retrieval for image studies. The features of a case are clinical indications and questions to be answered. A semantic network relates cases, features and imaging procedures to built explanations for user questions. Relations include "feature of", "causes", "has exemplar", "visualizes". PROTOISIS does not use a similarity measure or adaptation of former cases.

The goal of MACRAD (Macura and Macura 1995) is to provide a feature-coded image resource that allows the user to formulate image content-based queries when searching for reference images. As it is implemented in 4th Dimension™, a relational database management system, it provides multi-level access to data, uses some hierarchies for the indexing, applies a precise matching of constraints expressed in the query for the retrieval, but does no adaptation. Macura justifies the lack of adaptation with the statement that, in medical domains, the diagnostic judgment should remain the users responsibility. However, systems like PROTOISIS and MACRAD do not attempt any interpretation of images at all.

Classification for Structuring the Case Base. Research to structure the case base by prototypes was undertaken recently. Malek (1995) proposed a memory structure combining one level of prototypes, each of which represents a group of cases, with an incremental neural network. She applied this approach to the initial diagnosis of the cause of toxic comas and to neuropathy diagnosis (Malek and Rialle 1994). Bichindaritz (1994) developed a system called MNAOMIA for eating disorders whose memory consists of models, concepts, prototypes and cases. An object-oriented methodology is used for generalization / specialization between these different knowledge structures.

The knowledge-base in Malek and Rialle (1994) consists of a two-level structure. The first level comprises automatically generated prototypes which point to a set of similar cases, each associated with a prototype. Prototypes are unique cases from a sufficient number of cases of the same diagnosis. Atypical cases, which cannot be associated with any prototype, are stored as a special group. During an evaluation and correction phase, new prototypes can be generated or existing ones can be deleted. Cases can be shifted to the group of atypical cases. The physician, as evaluator, accepts or rejects diagnoses of cases and, thus, triggers the reorganization of the knowledge-base.

Prototype-based CBR systems are an appropriate answer to the problem of the large number of cases that, even for a small medical domain, a physician or a clinical ward encounters in a few years. The approach in Malek and Rialle (1994) has some resemblance to systems described in Schmidt et al. (1995).

Scientific Systems. CBR methods have also been used to implement knowledge based systems for scientific projects. In Wendel (1995) cases are experiments for simulating a neural network. Leng et al. (1993) investigate a two-level CBR system to predict protein secondary structures. Aaronson et al. (1993) derive a classification tree of eukariotic protein coding genes discovering knowledge in the GenBank nucleic acid sequence database.

11.2.3 Planning

Therapy Support. Compared to CBR systems for diagnosis, decision making in therapy attracted fewer researchers. Petersen et al. (1994) developed a system for postoperative pain therapy, Jurisica and Shapiro (1995) applied CBR methods to therapy a problem in gynaecology. ROENTGEN supports radiation therapy planning (Berger 1989).

Planning of Personal or Material Resources. The CAMP system is an experimental prototype for daily menu planning which meets individual, nutritional and personal preference requirements (Kovacic et al. 1992). The planning problems are similar to those of CHEF (Hammond 1986).

11.2.4 Tutoring

Education in medicine is largely based on confronting students with actual cases in clinics. In some countries, even in the first more theoretical-centric phase of the study, bedside teaching takes place. Theoretical and bedside teaching as well as textbooks use cases to explain medical problems. Therefore, CBR should be particularly suitable for knowledge-based instruction. Unfortunately, only a few systems have been published.

An early example of a tutorial system is PlanAlyzer (Beck et al. 1989). It is one of the early products of a tutorial system developed as part of the long term effort at Dartmouth College using computers in medical education. PlanAlyzer has been applied to anemia and coronary heart diseases. It has been evaluated in a controlled clinical study (Lyon et al. 1992). The result was that using PlanAlyzer significantly improves efficiency in studying special medical domains.

Another CBR System for instruction in Medicine is the Neurology Trainer (Puppe et al. 1995). It is based on the hybrid diagnostic shell D3 using rules and cases.

11.3 Real World CBR Applications in Medicine

11.3.1 GS.52: Simple Prototype Architecture for Diagnosis of Dysmorphic Syndromes

GS.52 (Gierl and Stengel-Rutkowski 1992; Gierl and Stengel-Rutkowski 1994) is a prototype-based expert system that has been routinely used in the children's hospital of the University of Munich for many years. It is a diagnostic support system for dysmorphic syndromes. Such a syndrome involves a non-random combination of different disorders. The major problems are the high variability of the syndromes (hundreds), the high number of case features (between 40 and 130) and the continuous modifications of the knowledge about dysmorphic syndromes.

Each syndrome is represented by a prototype that contains its typical features. The prototypes are acquired during an expert consultation session. A physician selects a new or an existing syndrome and typical cases for this syndrome. Subsequently, GS.52 determines the relevant features and their relative frequency (see Table 11.1).

The diagnostic support occurs by searching for the most adequate prototypes for a current case. A similarity value between each prototype and the current case is calculated and the prototypes are ranked according to these values.

GS.52 differs from typical CBR systems, because cases are clustered into prototypes which represent diagnoses and the retrieval searches among these prototypes. The adaptation consists of two examinations of the probable

Table 11.1. Portion of an example of a generated prototype. The numbers show the relative frequency in percentages the features occurred in the cases of the prototype

Heart murmur	30%	Depressed nasal bridge	23%
Diminished postnatal growth rate	77%	Anteverted nares	63%
Hypercalcaemia	30%	Prominent lips	17%
Prenatal onset	75%	Long philtrum	17%
Mild microcephaly	67%	Fullness of peri-orbital region	75%
Full cheeks	46%	Medial eyebrow flare	25%

prototypes; a plausibility check with general rules (constraints) and a check of evidences for specific syndromes (some syndromes are nearly a proof for or against some diagnoses).

In a study we have evaluated our system GS.52 by using 903 patients (a fraction of all cases) and 229 different prototypes of dysmorphic syndrome diseases which have been collected since 1987, in the Department for Paediatric Genetics at the University of Munich. The catalogue of signs used to describe cases comprises 823 entries. We applied sensitivity as a measure of diagnostic accuracy. We could confirm that prototypes are a solid basis for medical expert systems. However, the similarity measures which we investigated showed different results with regard to the number of cases available, prototypicality of disease prototypes, etc. Figure 11.3 displays the sensitivity expressed in the percentages of cases in which the consultation system detected the correct diagnosis. It comprises the cases with a concurrence between GS.52 and the proved diagnosis trisomy 21 (Downs disease). For all of these patients, a cytological investigation of their chromosomes has been conducted which serves as a reference for the assessment of diagnostic accuracy.

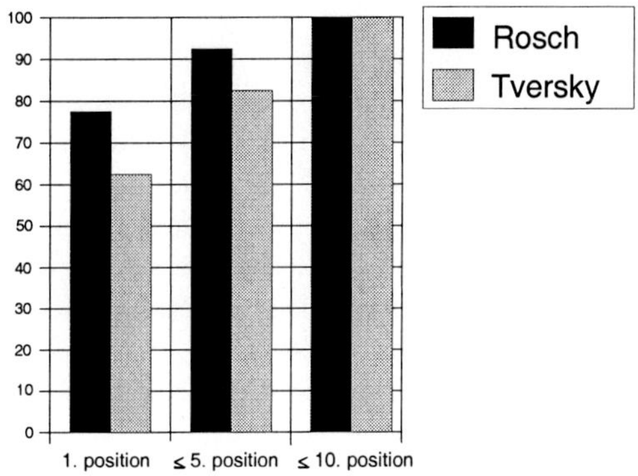

Fig. 11.3. Sensitivity of GS.52 using cases of trisomy 21 using the similarity measure of Rosch and Tversky, respectively (see page 293)

The consultation produces a list of suspicious syndromes. We defined that the system provides a correct diagnosis if the correct dysmorphic syndrome appeared on the first screen. This screen comprises the 10 most suspicious diagnoses. We count a situation as a failure of the system if it ranks the syndrome (trisomy 21) on the following screens. On the following screens the physician can not see the correct diagnosis at first sight. It could be possible that the physician selects a wrong diagnosis if the correct one is mixed up with many other possible diagnoses.

11.3.2 COSYL: Domain-Specific Levels in Prototype Hierarchy

Liver-Transplantation is a highly efficient therapy for well selected patients with an acute liver-failure or an end-stage chronic liver disease with poor spontaneous prognosis. However, low 2-year mortality rates enforce a search for the best treatment strategies. Furthermore, this strategy is very expensive and, therefore, requires a detailed cost/benefit analysis. Transplantations are limited to a restricted number of patients and only performed in specialized centers. Usually, the cases are well documented. This allows easy acquisition of an adequate knowledge-base. However, up to now, only limited experience with the use of artificial intelligence in this field has been gathered (Tusch and Gubernatis 1991).

In the Hospital of the University of Munich about 200 liver-transplanted patients with more than 700,000 data records have been documented. Since in many aspects the underlying pathophysiological concepts of relevant complications are not well understood and the amount of data is enormous, we decided to apply the method of case-based reasoning to design an expert system on this domain.

The outcome of liver-transplantation is highly influenced by the medical history of the transplant donor and recipient. Furthermore, surgical techniques and postoperative management of complications are of great importance. In this context, complications are defined as the diagnoses of diseases which are closely correlated to liver transplantation. Many of these complications influence each other. To avoid acute or chronic rejection immune-suppressive therapy is necessary. On the other hand, due to this suppression of the immune system, the occurrence of infectious diseases is markedly increased. These two types of complications are the most important ones during the immediate period after transplantation. Other typical complications are primary graft dysfunctions, impaired organ perfusion, side effects of necessary drugs, diseases of the biliary tree and recurrence of the underlying diseases (tumor, hepatitis B or C infection, etc.).

To evaluate the appropriate diagnostic and therapeutic strategy for these complications, it is important not only to register these diagnoses but also to determine the necessary examinations and their corresponding findings, as well as the applied drug therapy and their time course.

Our knowledge-based expert system, called COSYL[1], uses a data base of cases of liver transplanted patients (Swoboda et al. 1994). First of all, COSYL imports the data from this database, grades them according to postoperative

[1] CОnsiliar SYstem for Liver-transplanted patients

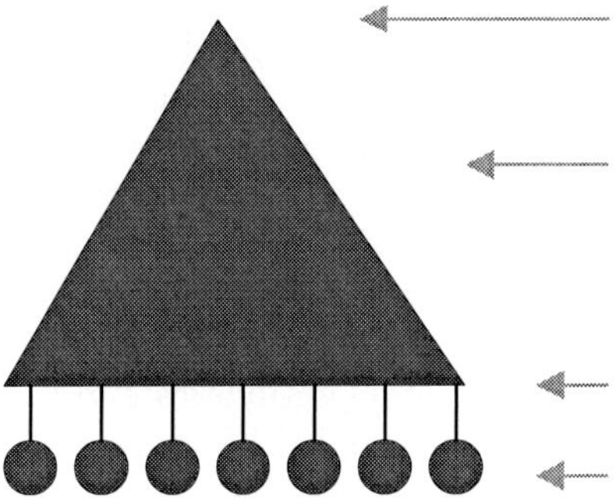

Fig. 11.4. Structure of the tree of complications. In this tree, the leaves correspond to the complications that appeared in a treatment group. Using this hierarchical approach, the time between the start of system and system-answer can be decreased, because for a current patient only the complications of his treatment group need to be compared.

complications and saves a pattern of data for every complication. When the system is consulted, it compares the pattern of the current patient with the saved patterns and displays the complication with the highest similarity.

COSYL imports the data of the patients and matches them with a tree of complications (Figure 11.4). For example, the patients data are matched with the reasons of transplantation and the number of possible retransplantations in the tree of complications.

The leaves of this tree contain a set of complications found in the corresponding treatment group. The benefit of the tree is that not all complications for every treatment group have to be compared, but only the specific ones for this group. In this way, the systems performance increases. For instance, only patients with tumor as reason for transplantation are prone to the risk of tumor recurrence. The structure of this data tree is defined in a declaration-list, which can be modified any time.

The next step is to sort according to the pattern of the complications. However, not every feature is necessary for each complication. Therefore, the declaration list contains an enumeration of features for each complication and a definition of these features (location in the database, etc.), For instance, the complication `acute rejection` has the features `course of GOT`, `course of GPT`, `histology of liver specimen`, and so on. The selection of features in the declaration list means application of medical knowledge. Only by defining the maximal number of features for every complication can the system work exclusively as a case-based system. The case-based concept combined with this technique of a variable declaration-list allows the system to work better and faster.

11.3.3 ICONS: Antibiotic Therapy Advice

ICONS is an antibiotics therapy adviser for intensive care patients who develop an infection as additional complication. The identification of the pathogen that causes the infection needs at least 24 hours in the laboratory. In contrast to normal patients, where physicians usually can wait for the results from the laboratory, intensive care patients need an immediate introduction of an appropriate antibiotics therapy. As the real pathogen is still unknown, a spectrum of probable pathogens has to be calculated. The aim of ICONS is to give rapid antibiotic therapy advice. Besides the expected pathogen spectrum, which has to be covered by the antibiotics, the current resistance situation, contra-indications of the patient against some antibiotics and the sphere of activity of the antibiotics have to be considered. CBR techniques are used to speed up the process of finding suitable antibiotics therapies and to update those parts of the knowledge-base that are modified frequently.

Antibiotics Selection Strategy. As ICONS is not a diagnostic system, we do not attempt to deduce evidence for the diagnosis of symptoms, frequencies and probabilities, but instead pursue a strategy (shown in Figure 11.5) that can be characterized as follows: Find all possible solutions and reduce them using the patient's contra-indications and the complete coverage of the calculated pathogen spectrum (establish-refine strategy). First, we distinguish among different groups of patients and affected organs to determine the calculated pathogen spectrum. A first list of antibiotics is generated by a susceptibility relation that returns, for each group of pathogens, all antibiotics which usually have therapeutic effects. This list contains those antibiotics that can control at least a part of the considered pathogen spectrum. We obtain a second list of antibiotics by reducing the first one by applying criteria such as the patient's contra-indications and the desired sphere of activity. Using the antibiotics of this second list, we apply general rules for the generation of sensible antibiotics combinations that subsequently have to be proved for their ability to cover the whole calculated spectrum.

Before the user chooses one therapy, they can investigate potential side effects of the antibiotics. Moreover, they may obtain information about the calculated spectrum and the daily costs of each suggested therapy. After the physician has chosen one therapy, ICONS computes the recommended dosage.

Adaptation of a Similar Case. The principal argument for CBR, that it is often faster to solve a new problem by modifying the solution of a similar case (Kolodner 1993), also applies to the process of finding adequate therapies. Considering the close relation concerning the group of patients and the affected organ, a similar case is retrieved from a hierarchical and generalizing memory structure containing prototypes as well as cases. As features the contra-indications and as methods a variation of the similarity measure of Tversky (1977) and the Hash-Tree-Retrieval-Algorithm of Stottler et al. (1989) are applied. Furthermore, a criterion for adaptability is used

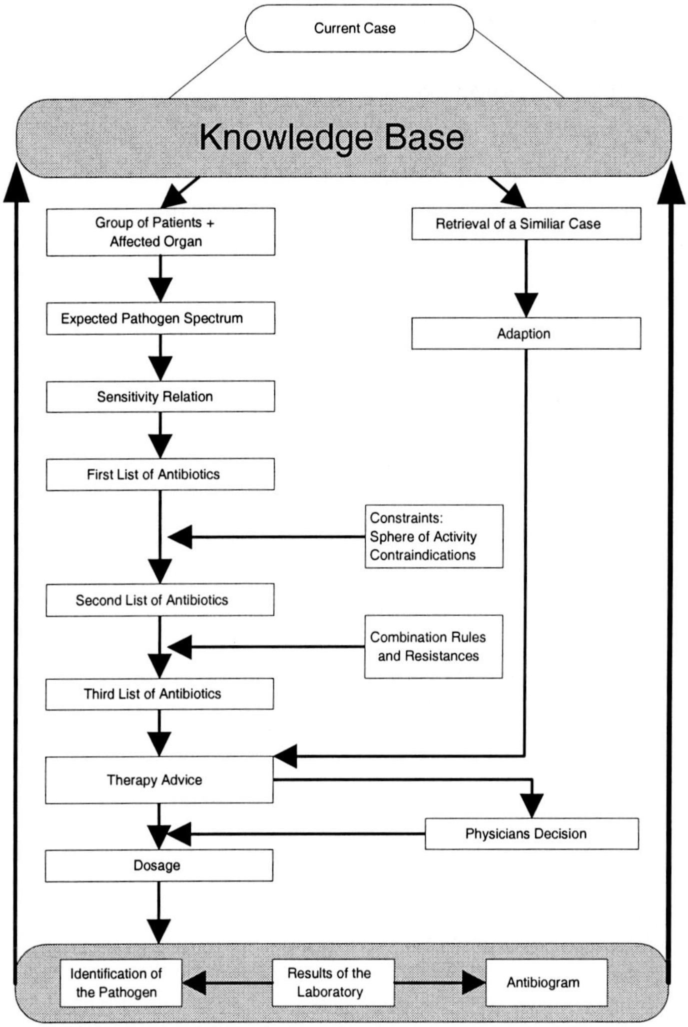

Fig. 11.5. ICONS process flowchart

during the retrieval, because similar cases with additional contra-indications in comparison to the current patient are not adaptable. The adaptation is performed by a solution transfer of the advisable therapies of a similar case and subsequently by a reduction concerning additional contra-indications of the current patient.

Adaptation to the Results of the Laboratory. Identifications of pathogens and sensitivity tests (antibiograms) made in the laboratory are used as control mechanisms. When the actual pathogen is identified, the calculated pathogen spectrum is replaced by this pathogen and the already started therapy has to be checked to see if it fits for the identified pathogen. The set of possible antibiotic therapies is reduced by the antibiogram to those antibiotics the pathogens are not resistant to.

The frequently changing parts of the knowledge-base are updated by an interpretation of the laboratory findings. This means that each theoretically determined pathogen spectrum is supplemented by the one that is empirically justified by the identifications of the pathogens. The information about resistances is correspondingly updated by the antibiograms. For both adaptations, those to the findings of current patients and those of parts of the knowledge-base, no retrieval but an evaluation or a statistical interpretation is performed.

11.3.4 ICONS: Abstraction of Data and Time to Prognose Kidney Function Courses in an Intensive Care Setting

As intensive care patients are often no longer able to maintain adequate fluid and electrolyte balances themselves, due to impaired organ functions and, above all, renal failures or medical treatments (e.g. parenteral nutrition of mechanically ventilated patients), physicians need objective criteria for the monitoring of the kidney function and to diagnose therapeutic interventions as necessary. Thus, at our intensive care unit, a renal function monitoring system, NIMON (Wenkebach et al. 1992), was developed that daily prints a renal report that consists of 13 measured and 33 calculated parameters of those patients to whom renal function monitoring is applied. However, the interpretation of all reported parameters is quite complex and needs special knowledge of the renal physiology.

Our aim was to develop a system that gives an automatic interpretation of the renal state to elicit impairments of the kidney function on time. In the domain of fluid and electrolyte balance, neither prototypical courses in ICU (Intensive Care Unit) settings are known nor exists complete knowledge about the kidney function. In particular, knowledge about the behavior of the various parameters over time is not yet incomplete. Therefore, we had to design our own method to deal with course analyses of multiple parameters without prototypical courses and without a complete domain theory.

The method consists of three main steps; two abstractions plus CBR retrieval. We took the idea of abstracting many parameters into one single parameter from RÉSUMÉ (Shahar and Musen 1993) where the course of this single parameter is analyzed by means of a complete domain theory. The comparison of parameter courses with well-known course pattern is performed in many medical knowledge-based systems (e.g. Haimowitz and Kohane 1993, VIE-VENT Miksch et al. 1995). As no such patterns are yet known for the kidney function, we use single courses and incrementally learned prototypes, instead of well-known course patterns, to compare with. We attempt to learn course patterns by structuring the case base by prototypes (see Section 11.4.1).

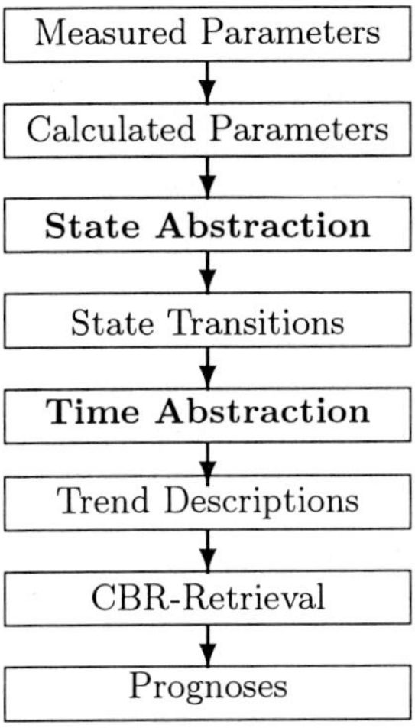

Fig. 11.6. General model of prognosis of the kidney function of patients in intensive care unit

Our procedure for interpretation of the kidney function corresponds to a general linear model (see Figure 11.6). Firstly, the monitoring system NIMON gets 13 measured parameters from the clinical chemistry and calculates 33 meaningful kidney function parameters. As the interpretation of all parameters is too complex, we decided to abstract them. For this data abstraction, we have defined states of the renal function which determine states of increasing severity, beginning with a normal renal function and ending with a renal failure. Based on these definitions, we ascertain the appropriate state of the kidney function per day. Only if this classification is not obvious, we present the states under consideration to the user, sorted according to their probability. The physician has to accept one of them. Based on the sequence of assessments of transitions of the state of a day to the state of the next day, we generate four different trends. These trends, which are temporal abstractions, describe courses of states. Subsequently, we use CBR retrieval methods (Tversky 1977; Anderson 1989; Smyth and Keane 1993; deSarbo 1992) to search for similar courses. We present the current course, in comparison to similar ones, to the user (see Figure 11.7). The course continuations of the similar courses serve as prognoses. As there may be too many different aspects between both patients, the adaptation of the similar to the current course is not done automatically. ICONS offers only diagnostic and prognostic support; the user has to decide about the relevance of all displayed information. When presenting a comparison of a current and a similar course, ICONS supplies the user with the ability to access additional renal syndromes and courses of single kidney function parameter values during the relevant time period.

Retrieval. The parameters of the trend descriptions are used to search for similar courses. As the aim is to develop an early warning system, a prognosis is needed. Since there are many different possible continuations for the

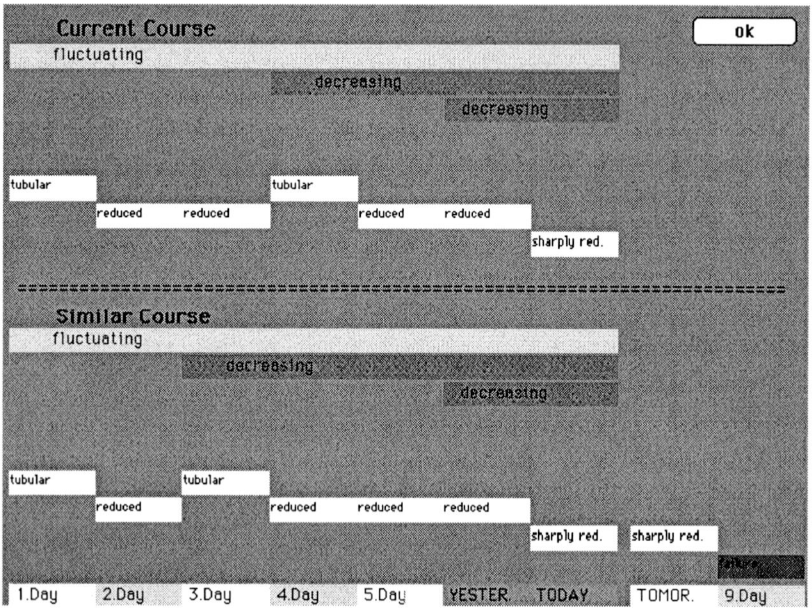

Fig. 11.7. Presentation of a current and a similar course of the kidney function

same previous course, it is necessary to search for similar courses and different projections. Therefore, we have divided the search space into nine parts corresponding to the possible continuation directions. Each direction forms its own part of the search space. During retrieval, these parts are searched separately and each part may provide at most one similar course. Before the main retrieval, we search for a prototype that matches most of the trend descriptions (see Section 11.4.1). Below this prototype, the main retrieval starts. It consists of two steps for each projection part. First, we search with an activation algorithm (Anderson 1989) concerning qualitative features. Subsequently, we check the retrieved cases with an adaptability criterion (Smyth and Keane 1993) that looks for sufficient similarity, since even the most similar course may differ from the current one significantly.

If several courses are selected in the same projection part, we use a sequential similarity measure concerning the quantitative features in a second step. It is a variation of TSCALE (deSarbo 1992) and goes back to Tversky (1977).

11.3.5 TeCoMED: Forecasting Epidemics of Infections Diseases

TECOMED[2] is an early warning system based on a network to discover health risks, to forecast temporal and spatial spread of epidemics, and to

[2] Tele-Consultation to Monitor Emerging Diseases

estimate the consequences of an epidemic according to the personnel load and costs of the public health service.

The crucial point of the analysis of the time-spatial pattern of diseases and pathogens is the reliability, the validity and, for an early warning system, the timeliness of the data. In Germany, the hospitals have to collect patient records on machine-readable mediums (§301 SGB V, §301-agreement on the transmission of medical data) and have to send these records to the health insurance companies. Moreover, both patient and general practitioner have to send the medical certificate within three days to the health insurance companies. We daily receive all these data as anonymous patient records via a net from the computing center of the general health insurance company "AOK Mecklenburg-Vorpommern". Furthermore, the public health office "Landeshygieneinstitut Mecklenburg-Vorpommern" sends weekly information about notifiable diseases and about pathogens identified by the microbiological laboratories.

The public health surveillance is a complex problem of multiparametric times courses of diseases, pathogens, resistances, health services etc. in a geographical region. Marshall (1991) discussed various methods for analysis of geographical distribution of diseases and points out that statistical methods are partially applicable to problems of disease clustering, either in time or in space, but not appropriate to examine the time-spatial dynamics of communicable diseases. Further, Marshall mentioned that there are observable time-spatial patterns of the spread of diseases which are too complicate to describe by means of statistics (see Marshall 1991, Section 5). Pyle (1986) compared the diffusion paths of influenza epidemics and found out that there exist similar epidemic waves according to the time-spatial dynamic. Nevertheless, there are successful applications that use case-based techniques for monitoring complex processes in time and space on other domains (see Cliff et al. 1986; Lekkas et al. 1994; Schmidt et al. 1996). Therefore we combine methods of statistics and case-based reasoning to cope with the problem of health surveillance.

For our project, we divided the considered geographical region into a finite number of disjoint geographical units. Here, we have chosen the ZIP-code districts because this dissection implicitly includes facts on the demography and the infrastructure. Further, we chose a reasonable period (e.g. one week) and divided the time scale in equidistant time steps. As a *scenario* we understand a concept which describes the public health situation and the load of the health service in the considered region during such a period. So, we are able to describe the course of any epidemic by a scenario sequence, since it keeps all information on the public health situation during a particular time interval.

Forecasting of a regional health situation means the prediction of a future scenario. The system retrieves all scenario sequences from the case base so that the differences between them and the current scenario sequence are minimal. Here, all epidemic scenario sequences are indexed by the diseases, by the outbreak locations and by the diffusion paths of the epidemics.

By using the retrieved sequences, the system adapts the scenario to a forecast scenario. Here, we use background knowledge about demographic structures, several statistical models of epidemics (see Marshall 1991) and the defined threshold values of epidemical levels which are based on the epidemiological studies. The resulting data will be stored in a case-based fashion and will be available for graphical presentation in the user interface. After a certain time period, we know what has really happened in a scenario. In comparing the forecast scenario with this scenario the system evaluates the forecast mechanism. If the difference of these scenarios is too large then the system has to learn this new scenario sequence or the inference mechanism must be changed. In the first case, the current scenario sequence is integrated in the case base. In the latter, an expert (e.g. epidemiologist, biostatistician) has to execute a working cycle with the system. This work cycle contains the modification of the threshold values and of the metrics, the visualization of the multiparametric data of the current scenario sequence and those in the case base and the forecasting of a scenario (as a simulation step). This cycle is executed until the difference of the current scenario and the forecast scenario is within a tolerance range. In the CBR framework of Aamodt and Plaza (1994) this is the revision step.

11.4 Special Techniques for Medical CBR Systems

11.4.1 The Importance of Prototypes

The systems in the previous section have one thing in common that distinguishes them from most CBR systems; they use prototypes as a form of knowledge representation that fills the gap between specific cases and general rules. Some cases are clustered and the most typical example for this cluster is called a prototype (Gierl and Stengel-Rutkowski 1992; Hampton 1993; Murphy 1993). Case-based knowledge allows the incremental change of the memory structure, from single cases via case groups to prototypes and eventually to a taxonomy of diseases or therapies in a medical domain. A *prototype* shows the essential signs and symptoms. Selz (1924, p. 368 ff) characterized it as a description of an entity where at least one component is undetermined. Intuitively speaking, a prototype can be thought of as the result of *laying together* and *fusing* of typical cases of a disease. In visualizing this idea, the research group of the department for pediatric genetic and prenatal diagnostic of the LMU has generated the *typical face* of a Williams-Beuren patient by superposing photos of such patients (see Figure 11.8).

The knowledge of physicians consists of general knowledge they have obtained from medical books plus their experiences connected with cases they have treated themselves or colleagues have told them about. Particularly in

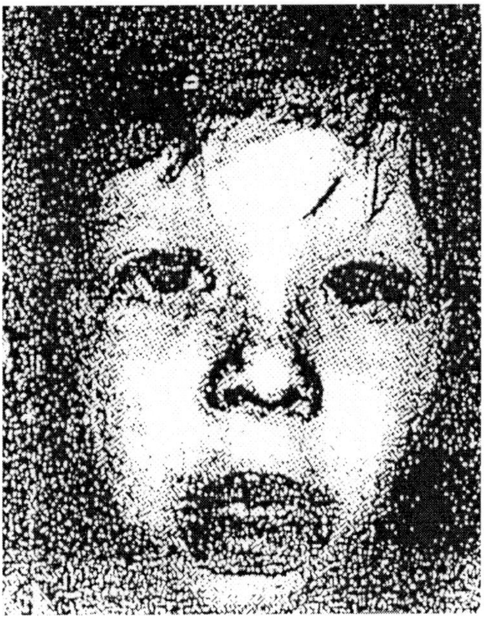

Fig. 11.8. The scheme of the Williams-Beuren-syndrome obtained by photographic superposing of case photos (The picture has been provided by Prof. Dr. S. Stengel-Rutkowski, University of Munich)

diagnostic tasks, the thoughts of physicians circle around typical cases. They consider the differences between a current patient and typical or known exceptional cases.

The main purpose of such generalized knowledge is to guide the retrieval process and sometimes to decrease the amount of memory requirements by erasing redundant cases. In domains with rather weak domain theories, another advantage of case-oriented techniques is their ability to learn from cases (Schmidt and Gierl 1996). Only gathering new cases may improve the system's ability to find suitable similar cases for current problems, but it does not elicit the intrinsic knowledge of the stored cases. To learn the knowledge contained in cases, a generalization process is necessary.

Tversky (1977) determined the similarity between a case C and a prototype P by adding up the number of shared features, subtracting the number of features of the prototype which the case does not share, and subtracting the number of features the case does not share with the prototype:

$$D(P,C) = \alpha \cdot f(P+C) - \beta \cdot f(C-P) - \gamma \cdot f(P-C) \tag{11.1}$$

Here, the coefficients $\alpha, \beta, \gamma > 0$ are scaling values. In contrast to this model, Rosch and Mervis (1975) ignored those case features which the prototype does not share:

$$P(F,k) = \frac{\sum_k g_m f(M(k)+F)}{\sum_{m(F)} f(M(k)+F) + \sum_{m(F)} f(M(k)-F)} \tag{11.2}$$

where k is the class, $m(F)$ are the signs of the case F, $g_m(k)$ is the weight of the sign $m(k)$, and $M(k)$ are the signs of the prototype of the disease k. Our experiment in GS.52 with both measures (see Chapter 11.3.1) indicates that the latter measure performs better than Tversky's.

The idea of considering the numbers of properties the case shares with members of contrasting concepts seems to have a limited suitability for open world domains like medicine. Especially for diagnostic applications, the ability to elicit new diagnoses (prototypes) is very important.

As ICONS performs a therapeutic task, the purpose of prototypes is to structure the case base and to guide the retrieval. In GS.52, prototypes are used in a typical medical diagnostic task. They correspond directly to the physician's sense of prototypes. As comparisons with single cases are unable to identify typical features, in this application, the use of prototypes is not only sensible but even necessary. In our early warning system, apart from guiding the retrieval and structuring the case base, prototypes serve yet another purpose. In a domain where the relevant kidney parameters are known but no knowledge about their temporal course behavior exists, we attempt to learn typical course patterns.

11.4.2 Multiparametric Time Course Abstraction

Time-stamped parameters, such as creatinine, calcium, pulse frequency, CO_2 saturation etc., are essential for diagnosis and therapy. Most often, more than one parameter has to be considered. Reasoning concerns, therefore, a very complex problem of multiparametric time courses. It is a problem each physician is confronted with. The more parameters have to be considered for decision making, the greater is the information overload of the physician. Post-operation care of transplanted patients requires the surveillance of up to 60 parameters in parallel over time. It is obvious that a knowledge-based system would be helpful in coping with this problem. Statistical methods, such as Box-Jenkins, are not able to detect and forecast, e.g., fluid disorders of patients of an intensive care unit. In analogy to the strategy of physicians to abstract multiparametric time-varying data to symbolic meta-parameters, such as *sharp ascending*, *alternating* etc., one approach is to abstract context-sensitive time course concerning data and time (see Section 11.3.4). The reasoning process uses a method which works on sequences of abstracted meta-parameters.

11.5 Future of CBR Systems in Medicine

The main obstacle in routinely utilizing expert systems within a clinical environment is the lack of integration (van der Lei et al. 1985). This is the lesson we learned from the different states of development of medical knowledge-based systems and their actual application. Integration covers several aspects and levels:

- integration in a special hardware and software system within a hospital;
- integration in the clinic organization;
- cognitive integration in order to fit the system to the particular ability of the physician and machine, such that the process of problem solving is best supported;
- adequate representation of knowledge combining different approaches;
- integration of problem solving and learning (El-Gamal et al. 1993).

To use CBR systems in hospitals in the future in a broad field, these problems must be solved.

11.5.1 Integration in a Medical Communication System

Using expert systems as stand-alone systems decreases their acceptance dramatically. They should be involved in the daily data exchange going on in a hospital, because they are part of a wealth of functions (Gierl et al. 1993). In some systems, physicians are daily forced to type in data of clinical chemistry for each patient. This procedure lasts about two hours. The same data have been printed via computer at the ward. Nobody understands why such a system needs the input of data already available in another system.

11.5.2 Integration in the Clinic Organization

Knowledge-based reasoning driven by intensive man/machine interaction designers of expert systems should not be the ultimate goal. Supply of daily activities in wards and central facilities is necessary. The problem, often overlooked by data processing professionals, is that medical activities are much more complicated, vague and information intensive than those in an industrial setting; formalizing medical decision making is hardly possible. Therefore, *simple* things like reports (Pohl and Trendelenburg 1988), drug orders, duty rosters (PEP, Gierl et al. 1993) etc. are, in many cases, the only domains which expert systems could support.

Expert systems are valuable if they fill the knowledge gap between activities in clinics. For example, PEP serves as an assistant in constructing a duty roster. Moreover, administration of personnel data, data entry for holidays and the coordination of these functions is of great importance in this system. DIACONS (Schneider et al. 1988) intends to combine documentation, long range monitoring and education. GS.52 integrates entry of patient data, database, research, diagnosis, reports and knowledge acquisition. Tusch and Gubernatis (1991) developed a system integrating database, reports, laboratory findings, statistical packages and reasoning supplying liver transplantations.

Change in medical practice and economic impact using expert systems has only been reported in few studies. In a prospective study, Schewe et al. (1988) have tried to assess how far such a system could be used in a rheumathologic outpatient facility considering duration of dialog, reaction of patients confronted with this system, reaction of physicians, results of consultation, etc.

11.5.3 Cognitive Integration

It is widely accepted that man's ability in processing visual events should be exploited in designing a user interface of an expert system. Unfortunately, many designers of expert systems assume that a screen useful for themselves, filled with windows for editing, debugging and controlling during software development, is what the target group of physicians would like to work with as well. The contrary holds; users are irritated when being confronted with a system opening windows in varying places or when having to search for the right window on a small strip on the screen. We have experienced that users like to navigate freely when running the expert system, but seeing the results of their former decisions at a glance. Explanation capabilities are of minor interest. In particular, the questions *why* and *how* do not improve overview. It is better to provide a set of small knowledge-based operations the physician can oversee. The architecture of such a system consists of pieces of knowledge sources processed by control knowledge (Gierl 1992b). For instance, the operations provided in GS.52 to the physician are search case, infer initial hypotheses, make a special case-based inference, insert syndrome in the list of hypotheses, delete syndrome in the list of hypotheses, use constraints, store case, etc.

One approach to cope with this problem is Minsky's central topic of a "Society of Mind" (Minsky 1986) – i.e., a society of interacting agents representing our mind. Each of these agents plays a special role learned during our lifetime. Neither do we understand this system as a whole, nor the agents of higher cognitive functions. Therefore, we should not try to model our cognitive abilities in a homogeneous way. Instead, we should specifically model only those agents which enhance accuracy, completeness and skillfulness of physicians.

The consequence is, we have to integrate meta-knowledge of the physician (knowledge over the world, common sense) with machine knowledge.

11.5.4 Further Tasks to Solve to Extend CBR Systems in a Broad Range of Medical Tasks

Although case-based reasoning is appropriate to solve the problem of multiple disorders, only sparse attempts have been made to cope with this problem. Multiple disorders are a daily problem in diagnosing and treatment. However, most systems focus on one disease. Methods have to be developed to support decisions on multiple disorders (Miller 1997).

In medical practice, data of patients are collected for different medical specialities. For instance, if a patient has a prostate disorder the urologist, the surgeon and the pathologist, all of whom are involved in the diagnosis and treatment have different views. Usually, knowledge-based systems provide a main view, e.g. the urologist view, which concerns a broad range of possible prostate related disorders requiring laboratory tests, possibly biopsy, sonography etc. In contrast, the pathologist is only interested in classification of the tissue and some information on the location the material is extracted from. Lindemann and Burkhard (1996) suggest to solve this problem using Case Retrieval Nets (cf. Section 3.4) as a flexible, open structure of information entities and weighted similarity links.

12. Methodology for Building CBR Applications

Ralph Bergmann and Klaus-Dieter Althoff

12.1 Introduction

As the previous chapters of this book have shown, case-based reasoning is a technology that has been successfully applied to a large range of different tasks. Through all the different CBR projects, both basic research projects as well as industrial development projects, lots of knowledge and experience about how to build a CBR application has been collected. Today, there is already an increasing number of successful companies developing industrial CBR applications. In former days, these companies could develop their early pioneering CBR applications in an ad-hoc manner. The highly-skilled CBR expert of the company was able to manage these projects and to provide the developers with the required expertise.

Today, the situation has changed. The market for CBR has started to increase significantly. Therefore, these companies have to face the fact that the market demands companies executing more and larger CBR projects than in these early days. It is required that they develop software that fulfills current quality standards. Consequently, contemporary IT companies can no longer sustain inefficient or ineffectual CBR application development. What is required is a *methodology for building CBR applications.* Such a methodology should make CBR application development a systematic engineering activity rather than an art known by a few experts (Shaw 1990; Gibbs 1994). A methodology usually combines a number of *methods* into a philosophy which address a number of phases of the software development life-cycle (e.g., Booch 1994, Chapter 1). It should give guidelines (recipes) about the activities that need to be performed in order to successfully develop a certain kind of product, that is, in our case, a CBR application.

The use of an appropriate methodology should provide significant quantifiable benefits in terms of

- *productivity*, e.g., reduce the risk of wasted efforts;
- *quality*, e.g., inclusion of quality deliverables;
- *communication*, a reference for both formal and informal communication between members of the development team;
- *management decision making*, i.e., providing a solid base for, e.g., planning, resource allocation, and monitoring.

Currently, there are several activities with the goal of establishing a methodology for building case-based reasoning applications. Contributions can be found in books on CBR (Kolodner 1993; Wess 1995) and in papers collecting the experience of people who have successfully developed CBR applications (Kitano and Shimazu 1996; Lewis 1995; Bartsch-Spörl 1996b; Curet and Jackson 1996); most valuable experience-based contributions arose from projects where methodology development was explicitly included as a project task, like INRECA (Althoff et al. 1995b; Johnston et al. 1996) or APPLICUS (Bartsch-Spörl 1996a; Bartsch-Spörl 1997).

In this chapter, we present a new methodology for building case-based reasoning systems which is based on the Esprit projects INRECA and INRECA-II, particularly on the experience gained by all of the project partners. While the main objective of the INRECA project was the development of the core CBR technology with methodology development being a minor issue, the major focus of the INRECA-II project is the development of a methodology for building and maintaining CBR applications in the area of diagnosis and decision support (Bergmann et al. 1997a; Bergmann et al. 1998).

The approach presented in this chapter covers the two major aspects that are important for CBR development to become an engineering activity. Firstly, it presents an analytic framework for describing and classifying CBR systems and applications. This is necessary to structure the large spectrum of different systems that have already been developed. Part II of this book gives a good impression of the variety of CBR applications ranging from analytic tasks, such as classification and diagnosis, to synthetic tasks, like design and planning. Any application developer must first analyze the particular application field to decide which type of CBR approach is most appropriate. The analytic framework described in Section 12.2 supports this analysis.

Secondly, the application developer must determine the specific development steps s/he has to follow in order to come to a CBR system of the desired kind. These development steps also depend very much on the particularities of the current client, like the existing organizational structure, existing IT environment, etc. Section 12.3 describes an experience-based approach to systematically develop a process model of how a particular CBR application should be built for a certain client. Finally, Section 12.4 concludes by stating future directions for about how the presented CBR methodology for building and maintaining CBR applications should evolve.

12.2 Analytic Framework for Developing CBR Systems

Over the last few years substantial progress has been made within the field of CBR. The problems we are facing have become more clearly identified, research results have led to improved methods for case retrieval as well as improved approaches to the harder problems of adaptation and learning (see, e.g., the collection of papers from ICCBR-95: Aamodt and Veloso 1995). In the course of this development, it has also become clear that a particular strength of CBR over most other methods is its inherent combination of problem solving with sustained learning through problem solving experience. This is, therefore, a particularly important topic of study, and an issue that has now become mature enough to be addressed in a more systematic way. To enable such an analysis of problem solving and learning, a unified framework for describing, analyzing, and comparing various types and aspects of CBR methods is needed.

Integration of learning and problem solving may, in general, start out from different goals, and be viewed from different perspectives. One example is *concept formation* as a goal, and the formation and utilization of operationalization criteria related to the problem solving task, as the perspective. Another example is *improved performance* as a goal, and the improvement of total problem solving speed - for computer and human together - as the perspective. A third example is *sustained learning*, i.e., continuous learning through problem solving experience, as a goal, and the impact of the application problem task on the learning method as a perspective. Many more examples may be given, and for each of them a particular area of overlap, an "intersection space" between machine learning (ML) and problem solving (PS) methods can be identified. Within this space, dependencies and other relations between specific ML and PS methods may be described and analyzed in a systematic way, provided we have a suitable means to structure the space.

In the following, we describe first steps towards the development of a framework and a methodology which defines and makes use of such a structure. Since we are studying CBR methods, the natural focus is on the third of the above goals: Sustained and (continuous) learning from each problem solving experience as a natural part of a problem solver's behavior. Within a broader perspective of integrated learning and problem solving, it is also natural to start a study of learning as close as possible to the source of learning, namely a concrete experience. Our work is related to some earlier suggestions for analytic CBR frameworks, such as the similarity-focused framework by Richter and Wess (1991), the analysis of systems for technical diagnosis by Althoff (1992), the comparison of knowledge-intensive CBR methods by Aamodt (1991), the analysis of CBR system architectures by Armengol and Plaza (1993), and the framework for systems comparison and evaluation as described by Auriol et al. (1994). Our framework extends these previous suggestions in several respects. It provides an explicit ontology of basic CBR task types, domain characterizations, and types of problem solving and learning methods. Further, it incorporates within this framework a methodology for combining a knowledge-level, top-down analysis with a bottom-up, case-driven one. In this section, we present the underlying view and the basic approach being taken, the main components of the framework and the accompanying methodology as well as some applications of the framework (one application has been described in Section 9.7). Examples of studies recently carried out and how they relate to the framework have been described by Althoff and Aamodt (1996b). A detailed description can be found in (Althoff 1996).

12.2.1 Basic Approach

Knowledge-Level Analysis. A potentially useful way to describe problem solving and learning behavior is in terms of the *goals* to be achieved, the *tasks* that need to be solved, the *methods* that will accomplish those tasks, and the *knowledge of the application domain* that those methods need. A description of a system along these lines is often referred to as a knowledge level description, and more recent research in knowledge acquisition (Steels 1990; Wielinga et al. 1993) has clearly demonstrated the usability of this approach. The original knowledge-level idea has undergone some modifications over the years, from Newell's highly intentional, purpose-oriented way of describing a system (Newell 1982), to a more structured and usable type of description. An incorporation of the CBR perspective into knowledge-level modeling is discussed by Aamodt (1995).

Adopting a knowledge-level perspective to the analysis of integrated PS-ML systems enables the description of methods and systems both from a general (intensional) and case-specific (extensional) perspective. A general description relates a method to descriptive terms and relationships within a general model of descriptive concepts - i.e., an ontology of task types, domain characteristics, and method types. Through a case-driven description, methods can be understood by relating them to already known methods within already described/implemented systems. For example, CBR is combined with rule- and model-based reasoning in the same way as in CREEK (Aamodt 1993); a decision tree is generated as in INRECA (cf. Chapter 3); the similarity measure is adapted as in PATDEX (Wess 1993); partial determination rules are generated and used like the so-called "shortcut rules" in MOLTKE (Althoff 1992); etc. After having developed/described a certain number of systems, we will be able to select/instantiate a system description at the knowledge level by a combined use of general and case-specific descriptors. What we are aiming at is an effective combination of top-down and bottom-up analysis and modeling methods, based on an integration of these two perspectives.

From an engineering point of view, this will enable a particular symbol-level architecture to be chosen, and/or a chosen architecture to be instantiated, based on a thorough understanding of the real world application task and its domain characteristics. However, a knowledge-level description in itself will not provide a language detailed enough to describe or analyze system designs, or to arrive at a symbol-level architecture specification. Our approach therefore incorporates a focusing perspective and an analytic "tool" to help in the more detailed description that guides the architectural specification based on a knowledge-level model.

Similarity as a Focusing Mechanism. The focus provided by this mechanism leads to a view of - in principle - all CBR methods as operations related to *similarity*, in one sense or another. That is, problem solving can be described as a process of initial assessment of similarity (case retrieval) followed by a more deliberate assessment of similarity (case adaptation), and learning (case extraction, case indexing, and possibly updates of general knowledge) can be described by relating it to later similarity assessment - i.e., to a pragmatic learning goal. Along with Richter and Wess (1991) we view similarity as an *a posteriori* criterion, and any attempt to assess similarity before a retrieved case has been found useful will only result in a hypothesized similarity assessment. Our retrieval methods should of course try to minimize the difference between the hypothesized similarity measure and the actual similarity determined after the attempt has been made to use the case. The general domain knowledge can then be seen as a means to reduce this uncertainty of the initial similarity assessment with respect to the final similarity assessment made after having evaluated the success of the (possibly modified) case in finding a solution to the input problem.

Tasks and Domain Characterizations. The types of application domains we address cover a wide spectrum, ranging from strong-theory domains with rather well-defined relationships between domain concepts (e.g., diagnosis of purely technical systems), to weak-theory and open domains with uncertain domain relationships (e.g., medical diagnosis). This is an important feature of the framework, since we particularly want to relate characteristics of the task (the *what-to-do*) and the knowledge on which performance of the task is based, to the methods (*how-to-do*'s) that enable the problem solver to accomplish the task by use of the knowledge. The starting point is always the real world setting in which the system is to operate. Medical diagnosis, for example, in a real world setting, is far away from a pure classification task. If a system shall cover the major tasks involved in practical diagnosis, it will have to include planning tasks (e.g., setting up and continuously revising an examination protocol), as well as prediction tasks (assessing the consequences of a treatment). The next section outlines the core components of the framework, with a focus on the knowledge-level description and analysis and the combined top-down and bottom-up oriented methodology. The incorporation of the similarity assessment mechanism is part of ongoing research.

12.2.2 Framework and Methodological Issues

Basic Framework Components. At the highest level of generality, a general CBR cycle may be described by four tasks (Aamodt and Plaza 1994): `Retrieve` the most similar case or cases, `reuse` the information and knowledge in that case to solve the problem, `revise` the proposed solution, and `retain` the parts of this experience likely to be useful for future problem solving. See Chapter 1, particularly Figure 1.2 on page 11. Note that these tasks are internal reasoning tasks, and different from the application problems tasks (diagnosis, planning, etc.) referred to earlier. Each of the the four CBR tasks involves a number of more specific sub-tasks. An initial description of a problem (top of the CBR cycle) defines a new case. In the retrieve task, this new case is used to find a matching case from the collection of previous cases. The retrieved case is combined with the input case - in the reuse task - into a solved case, i.e., a proposed solution to the initial problem. The revise task tests this solution for success, e.g., by applying it to the real-life environment or have it evaluated by a teacher, and repaired if failed. This task is important for learning, since the system needs a feedback of how successful its proposed solution actually was. Retain is the main learning task, where useful experience is retained for future reuse, by updating the case base and possibly also the general domain knowledge. As indicated in the figure, general knowledge usually plays a role in this cycle, by supporting the CBR processes. This support may range from very weak to very strong, depending on the type of CBR method. By general knowledge we mean general domain knowledge, as opposed to the specific domain knowledge embodied by cases. For example, in diagnosing a patient by retrieving and reusing the case of a previous patient, a model of anatomy together with causal relationships between pathological and other physiological states may constitute the general knowledge used by a CBR system. A set of rules may play the same role.

Knowledge-level analysis, as previously described, is a general approach to systems analysis. It is, therefore, applicable to the analysis of application tasks and domains - as manifested in the knowledge acquisition methodologies referred to earlier - as well as internal reasoning tasks of a problem solver and learner. In our framework, we therefore take a "task – method – domain knowledge" approach both to the analysis of real-world application tasks, and to the analysis of the CBR reasoning tasks themselves. The mapping between the two is as follows: a method from the application analysis (how to solve a technical diagnosis problem, or how to determine the next test to be done) either decomposes an application task into subtasks, or it solves the task directly. In both cases these *methods* set up *tasks* at the reasoning level (problem solving and learning from experience). In the following, we concentrate on the reasoning tasks.

The tasks from the CBR cycle are further decomposed in Figure 12.1[1]. The tasks are printed in bold letters, while methods are written in plain text. The links between task nodes (bold lines) are task decompositions, i.e., part-of relations. The links between tasks and methods (stippled lines) identify alternative methods applicable for solving a task. The top-level task is problem solving and learning from experience and the method to accomplish the task is

[1] In Chapter 9 the same CBR task-method decomposition has been used for the purpose of detailing selected models of software knowledge reuse.

a case- based reasoning method. This splits the top-level task into the four major CBR tasks of the CBR cycle. Each of the four tasks is necessary in order to perform the top-level task. The retrieve task is, in turn, partitioned in the same manner (by a retrieval method) into the tasks identify features, search (to find a set of past cases), initially match (the relevant descriptors to past cases), and select (the most similar case). All task partitions in the figure are considered complete, i.e., the set of subtasks of a task are intended to be sufficient to accomplish the task, at this level of description. The figure does not show any control structure over the subtasks. The actual control is specified as part of the problem-solving method. The actual retrieval method, for example (not explicitly indicated in the figure), specifies the sequence and loop-backs for the subtasks of retrieve. A method specifies the algorithm that identifies and controls the execution of subtasks, or solves the task directly, while accessing and utilizing the domain knowledge needed to do this. The methods shown in the figure are high level method classes, from which one or more specific methods should be chosen. The method set as shown is incomplete, i.e., one of the methods indicated may be sufficient to solve the

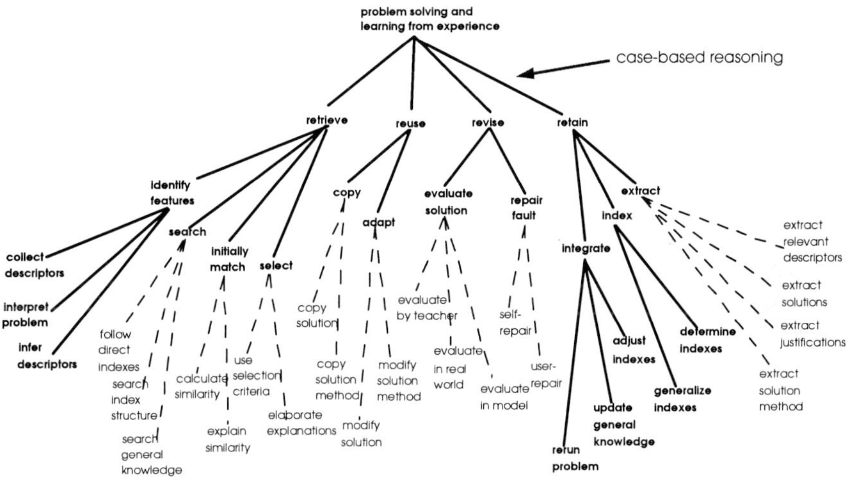

Fig. 12.1. Task-method decomposition of CBR

The above structure provides the basis for the analytic framework. It needs to be elaborated and described in more detail, characterizations of domain knowledge types need to be added, and dependencies between the various knowledge types need to be identified.

Methodology. As previously stated, the basic methodological approach is to combine a top-down oriented analysis of application tasks, domain knowledge descriptions, and methods with a bottom-up, case-driven method of studying existing systems. The aim is to arrive at a coherent framework and description language that specializes from the high-level analysis and generalizes from the example systems studied. The baseline of the approach is as follows. We *describe* CBR systems as well as domains and application tasks using two different kinds of criteria, namely criteria characterizing the domain and task at hand (domain/task criteria) and criteria describing the abilities and limitations of existing systems and system components (technical/ergonomic criteria). Examples for domain/task criteria are

Size: The size of a domain is characterized by the amount of different items representing the explicit knowledge.

Theory strength: The theory strength of a domain depends on the degree of certainty of the involved relationships.

Openness: The openness of a domain depends on its environmental dependencies.

Change over time: The change over time of a domain means that a domain is called static if there are no expected changes and it is called dynamic if it is clear that changes will appear in continuation.

Complexity: The complexity of a domain means the amount of different taxonomic relations.

On the other hand, *case and knowledge representation*, *similarity assessment*, *validation*, and *data acquisition and maintenance* exemplify important technical/ergonomic criteria. We analyze the underlying methods and domain/task characteristics by relating domain/task criteria with technical/ergonomic criteria. Figure 12.2 gives an example of how CBR systems can be labeled with domain criteria. Combining such a description with a more general kind of analysis based on the subtask structure of Figure 12.1 was shown to be useful for evaluating the final INRECA system (Althoff 1996).

From a software or knowledge engineering perspective, we try to arrive at non-functional system properties as a systematic means for (CBR) system development. Since we focus on CBR systems, we can define more precise criteria than we could for software systems in general. Additionally, we combine these system-oriented, more technical criteria with an analysis of application domains in which we have experience. On the one hand, feedback from applications can be systematically transformed in an evaluation based on domain and application task criteria. On the other hand, methods extracted from CBR-related systems and tools can be labeled with the results of the application of such criteria. Again, the aim is to close the gap between high level characterizations, on the one side, and concrete systems on the other side. General knowledge level analysis and case-driven analysis are merged in order to come up with application frameworks for particular types of systems, based on a common terminology and a unified model. Here technical/ergonomic criteria are combined with domain/task criteria. The intended use of this framework both for analysis and development of integrated

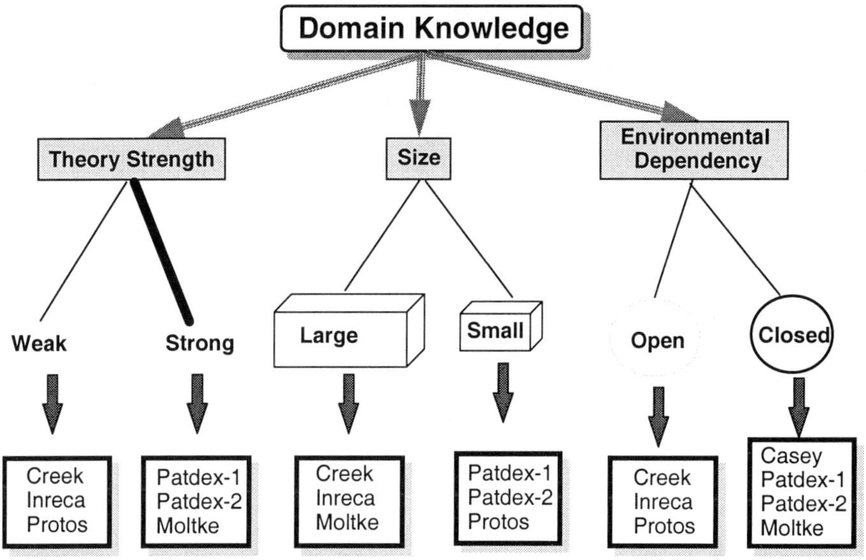

Fig. 12.2. An example of domain criteria related to existing systems (Casey: (Koton 1989); Creek: (Aamodt 1993); Inreca: (Althoff et al. 1998), see also Chapter 3; Moltke: (Althoff 1992; Althoff et al. 1990a); Patdex-1: (Stadler and Wess 1989; Richter and Wess 1991); Patdex-2: (Wess 1990; Althoff and Wess 1991); Protos: (Bareiss 1989))

problem solving and learning systems, can be described as providing answers to the following questions related to the evaluation of AI research (Cohen 1989):

- How is the CBR method to be evaluated an improvement, an alternative, or a complement to other methods? Does it account for more situations, or produce a wider variety of desired behavior, or is it more efficient in time or space, or does it model human behavior in a more useful way/detail?
- What are the underlying architectural assumptions? Are all design decisions justified? Does the method rely on other integrated methods? Does it subsume other methods?
- What is the scope of the method? How extendible is it? Will it scale up?
- Why does the method work? Under which conditions would it not work?
- What is the relationship between the class of task, of which the current task is an example, and the method used? Can this relationship be stated clearly enough to support a claim that the method is general to the class of task?

12.2.3 Applications of the Framework

Up to now, there are a number of applications of the introduced framework. The original application (within the Inreca Esprit project) was a comparison of commercially available CBR tools (Althoff et al. 1995a). The underlying goals for the Inreca project were achieving deeper insights for the development of the final Inreca system, finding a reasonable and realistic combination of research and application issues, and getting a more concrete estimation of what can be expected from CBR technology in the near and the far future. Based on this comparison, the framework was extended and used for the evaluation of the final Inreca system (Althoff 1996) consisting of a comparison with commercial tools, a comparison with a number of CBR-related research systems as well as an in-depth analysis of the system using the introduced framework. The application of the framework to the validation of CBR systems has been described by Althoff and Wilke (1997). Parts of the framework have been used for gathering information about existing CBR systems by means of two structured questionnaires (Meissonnier 1996) that have been collected from CBR system developers from 14 countries. An analysis of the collected information has been described by Bartsch-Spörl et al. (1997). Using the described framework enabled us to formally describe the collected questionnaires as cases and to build a CBR system for accessing the included information via similarity based retrieval (Meissonnier 1996). This will be made available via WWW (see Section 9.7 for further details including the URL).

12.3 Building CBR Applications for Analytic Tasks

When building a CBR application that should be used in the daily practice within an existing client organization a large variety of different kinds of processes have to be considered:

- the process of *project management* (cost and resource assessment, time schedules, project plans),
- the *analysis and re-organization of the environment* (e.g., a department) in which the CBR system should be introduced, and of course,
- the process of *technical product development* and *maintenance*: particularly tool selection, customer-specific software development, and domain modeling.

All these processes must be defined and tailored according to the needs and circumstances of the current client. This is an activity that requires a lot of practical experience. Although this experience is available in the minds of experienced application developers, it is usually not collected and stored systematically. This creates serious problems, e.g., in case of staff departures or when the companies grow and new staff must be trained. The approach presented here addresses this problem in the line of the experience-based construction of software. It combines two recent approaches from software engineering: the *experience factory* (see below) and *software process modeling* (Rombach and Verlage 1995). The approach to a CBR development methodology is itself very "CBR-like". In a nutshell, it captures previous experience from CBR development and stores it in a so-called experience base (a term from the experience factory approach). The entities being stored in the experience base are software process models, or fragments of it, such as processes (managerial, organizational, and technical), products being produced or consumed by the different processes, and methods that can be executed to realize a process. Although this approach is applicable to any kind of CBR development experience, the CBR applications covered so far are analytic tasks only. The current experience base was built by analyzing several successful industrial applications developed by or in cooperation with the INRECA-II consortium partners. Since, at the date of printing this book, this project is still on-going, further refinements of this approach are very likely and further experience will be entered into the experience base.

12.3.1 Experience Factory

We now briefly introduce the experience factory idea (Basili et al. 1994a; see also Section 9.3). This approach is motivated by the observation that any successful business requires a combination of technical and managerial solutions which includes a well-defined set of product needs to satisfy the customer, assist the developer in accomplishing those needs and create competencies for future business; a well-defined set of processes to accomplish what needs to be accomplished, to control development, and to improve overall business; a closed-loop process that supports learning and feedback. The key technologies for supporting these requirements include: modeling, measurement, the reuse of processes, products, and other forms of knowledge relevant to the (software) business. An experience factory is a logical and/or physical organization that supports project developments by analyzing and synthesizing all kinds of experience, acting as a repository for such experience, and supplying that experience to various projects on demand (see Figure 12.3). An experience factory packages experience by building informal, formal, or schematic models and measures of various software processes, products, and other forms of knowledge via people, documents, and automated support. The main product of an experience factory is an *experience base*. The content and the structure of an experience base varies based upon the kind of experience clustered in the base. See Chapter 9 of this book for a more detailed discussion of the experience factory approach, the associated Quality Improvement Paradigm, related work from software engineering as well as relationships to CBR.

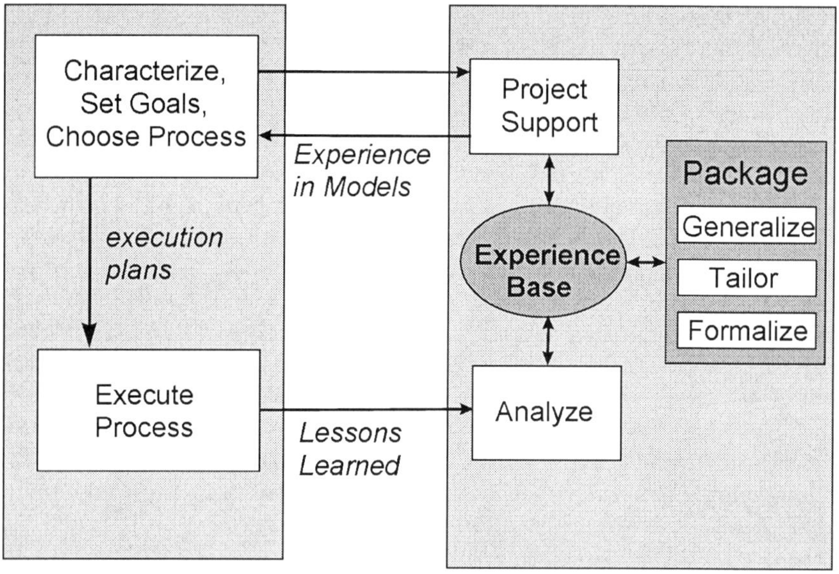

Fig. 12.3. The Experience Factory approach (Basili et al. 1994a)

12.3.2 Software Process Modeling

Software process modeling is an approach that is highly important in the context of the experience factory approach. Software process models describe the engineering of a product, e.g., the software that has to be produced. Unlike early approaches in software engineering, the software development is not considered to follow a single fixed process model with a closed set of predefined steps. A tailored process model particularly suited for the current project must be developed in advance. Software process models include *technical* software engineering *processes* (like requirements engineering, design of the system to be built, coding, etc.), *managerial* software engineering *processes* (like management of product related documentation, project management, quality assurance, etc.), and *organizational processes* (covering those parts of the business process in which the software system will be embedded and that need to be changed in order to make best use of the new software system). From time to time, such a model must be refined or changed during the execution of the project if the real world software development process and the model do not match any longer. Several formalisms and languages have been already developed for representing process models. One such language currently being developed at the University of Kaiserslautern is called MILOS (Dellen et al. 1997a). In MILOS, a process model is defined in terms of *processes, methods, products, goals,* and *resources* (see Figure 12.4). Within our approach to software process modeling, we adopt the terminology and the concepts from this language to formalize process models for developing CBR applications. Other representation languages often contain similar concepts, but use different terms.

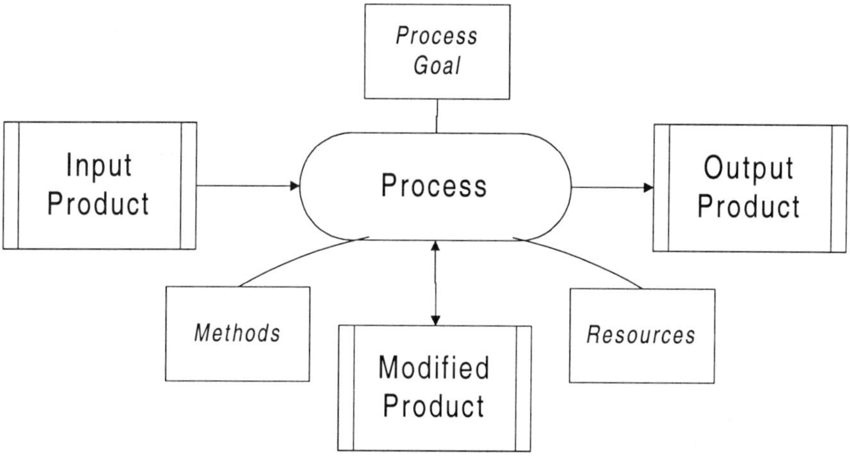

Fig. 12.4. Graphical notation for representing process models

Generic Processes. A process is a basic step that has to be carried out in a software development project. Each process is defined as an instance of a certain *generic process*. A generic process describes a class of processes by defining the following properties:

- A particular *goal* of such a step specifies *what* has to be achieved.
- A set of different alternative *methods* that can be used to implement the step. Such a method specifies one particular way of carrying out the process, i.e., one way of how to reach the goal of the process.
- *Input, output,* and *modified products* that describe which products are required at the beginning, which products must be delivered at the end of the step, and which products are changed during enactment.
- A set of *resources* (agents or tools) that are required to perform the step. Here the necessary qualifications or specifications are defined that an agent or a tool must have so that he can be assigned to the process.

Methods. Methods contain a detailed specification of a particular way of reaching the goal of a process. A method can be either *simple* or *complex*. While a simple method provides only a description of what to do to reach the goal of the associated process, a complex method specifies a set of subprocesses, a set of intermediate products (called *by-products*), and the flow of products between the subprocesses. This allows the definition of very flexible process models in a hierarchical manner, since very different process refinements can be described by utilizing alternative subprocess models.

Generic Product. The main goal of processes is to create or modify products. Products include the executable software system as well as the documentation like design documents or user manuals. Products are modeled by *generic product descriptions*, which declare certain properties that all products of a certain kind must have. For example, a generic product can be a domain definition in the CASUEL case representation language. Additionally, a product can be decomposed into several subproducts, e.g. the definition of attribute types, object classes, cases, and similarity measures.

Resources. Resources are entities necessary to perform the tasks. Resources can be either *agents* or *tools*. Agents are models for humans or teams (e.g. managers, domain experts, designers, or programmers), which can be designated to perform a processes. The most relevant properties of agents are their qualifications. Tools (e.g., a modeling tool, a CBR tool, or a GUI builder) are used to support the enactment of a process and can be described by a specification. Therefore, by using the required qualifications and specifications defined in the generic process, it is possible to determine available agents and tools which can be assigned to a certain process.

12.3.3 The Experience Base for Developing Analytic CBR Applications

In our CBR methodology, software process models are used to represent the CBR development experience that is stored in the experience base. Software processes that must be represented can be either very abstract, i.e., they can just represent some very coarse development steps such as: domain model definition, similarity measure definition, case acquisition. But they can also be very detailed and specific for a particular project, such as: analyze data from Company X's product database, select relevant product specification parameters, etc. The software process modeling approach allows to construct such a hierarchically organized set of process models. Abstract processes can be described by complex methods which are themselves a set of more detailed processes. We make use of this property to structure the experience base.

The experience base is organized on three levels of abstraction: a *common generic level* at the top, a *cookbook-level* in the middle, and a *specific project level* at the bottom (see Figure 12.5).

Common Generic Descriptions. At this level, processes, products, and methods are collected that are common for a large spectrum of different CBR applications. These descriptions are the basic building blocks of the methodology. The documented processes usually appear during the development of most CBR applications. The documented methods are very general and widely applicable and give general guidance of how the respective processes can be enacted. At this common level, processes are not necessarily connected to a complete product flow that describes the development of a complete CBR application. They can be isolated entities that can be combined in the context of a particular application or application class.

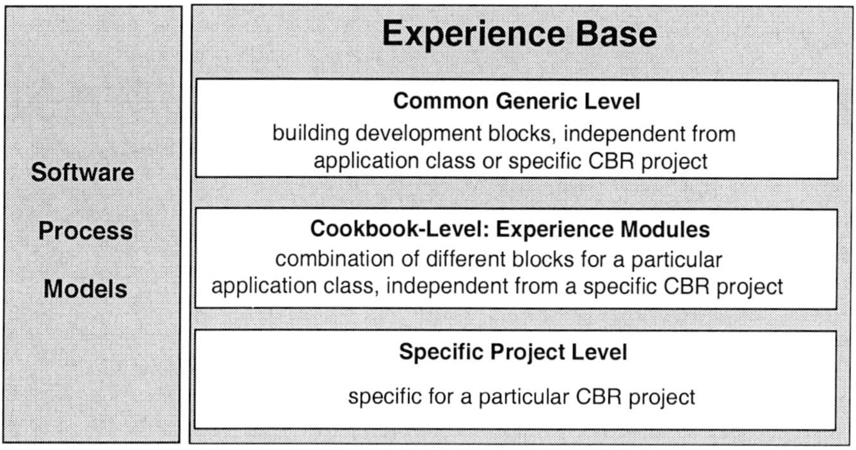

Fig. 12.5. Structure of the Experience Base

Cookbook-Level. Experience Modules. At this level, processes, products, and methods are tailored for a particular class of applications (e.g., help desk, technical maintenance, product catalog). For each application class, the cookbook-level contains a so-called experience module. Such an *experience module* is a kind of recipe describing how an application of that kind should be developed and/or maintained. Thereby, process models contained in such a module provide specific guidance for the development of a CBR application of this application class. Usually, these items are more concrete versions of items described at the common level. Unlike processes at the common level, all processes which are relevant for an application class are connected and build a product flow from which a specific project plan can be developed.

Specific Project Level. The specific project level describes experience in the context of a single particular project that had already been carried out in the past. It contains project specific information such as the particular processes that were carried out, the effort that was spent for these processes, the products that have been produced and methods that have been selected to actually perform the processes and the people that had been involved in executing the particular processes. It is a complete documentation of the project which is today more and more required anyway to guarantee quality standards required by industrial clients.

12.3.4 Documentation of the Experience Base

Processes, products, methods, agents, and tools being stored in the experience base are documented using a set of different *types of sheets*. A sheet is a particular form that is designed to document one of the items. It contains several predefined fields to be filled as well as links to other sheets. We

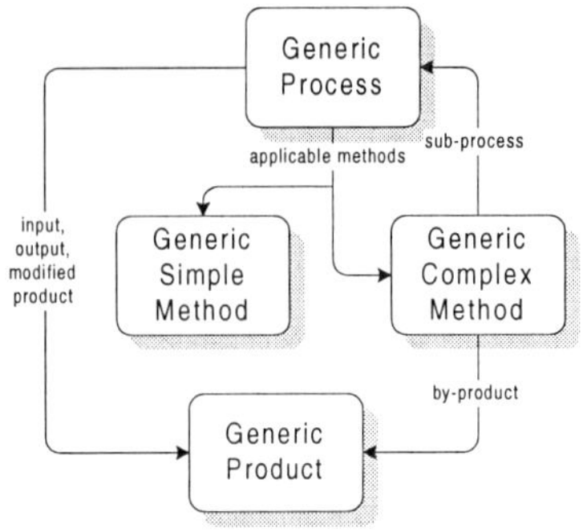

Fig. 12.6. Overview of generic description sheets

have developed four types of sheets (for products, processes, simple methods, and complex methods) for documenting generic processes that occur on the top and the middle layer of the experience base and six types of sheets (four sheets for products, processes, simple methods, and complex methods, and two additional sheets for tool and agent descriptions) for documenting specific processes for the specific project level of the experience base. Figure 12.6 shows the four generic description sheets. One kind of sheet is used to describe generic processes. Generic process sheets contain references to the respective input, output, and modified products of the process. Each product is documented by a separate generic product description sheet. Each process description sheet also contains links to one or several generic methods. A generic method can either be a generic *simple* method (which is elementary and does not contain any references to other description sheets) or it can be a generic complex method. Such a generic complex method connects several subprocesses (each of which is again documented as a separate generic process description) which may exchange some by-products (documented as separate generic product descriptions). Figure 12.7 gives an example of a sheet that documents generic complex methods for defining similarity measures.

As part of the INRECA-II project, a particular methodology tool was implemented by Interactive Multimedia Systems which supports the management of the experience base and the different modules it consists of (see Figure 12.8). It supports the filling of the different sheets, checks consistency, and creates the required links. It exports the experience base as HTML network in which each sheet becomes a separate HTML page that includes links to the related pages. Therefore, it is possible to investigate the experience base via intranet/internet using a standard Web browser.

12.3.5 Current Experience at the Common Generic Level

A large number of processes are involved in a CBR project. As introduced, we distinguish between the technical processes (getting the CBR system to work in context), the organizational processes (ensuring that the relationships be-

Generic Complex Methods Description Sheet			
Project:	**Version:** 1.0	**Date:** 07.04.97	**Context:** TP
Author: Armin Stahl			
Method Name: similarity construction method			

Product Flow Diagram:

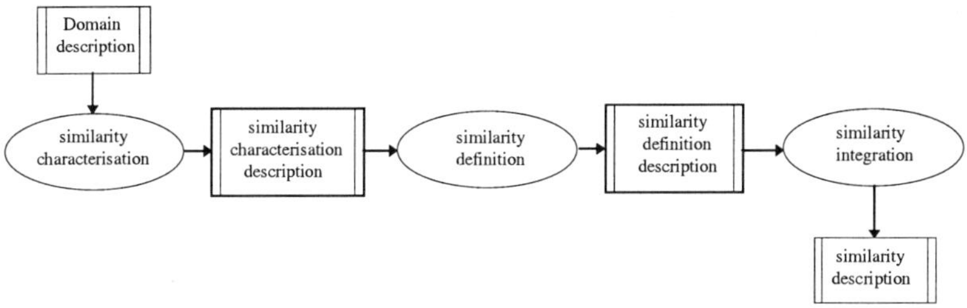

Subprocesses	
Name	**Generic Process**
similarity characterisation	similarity characterisation process
similarity definition	similarity definition process
similarity integration	similarity integration process

By-Products	
Name	**Generic Product**
similarity characterisation description	similarity characterisation description document
similarity definition description	similarity definition description document

Remarks: In the first subprocess the CBR consultant and the domain expert must characterise the similarity measures for every simple attribute of the domain model. This means that they find out general properties of the similarity measures. In the second subprocess these properties are used to define the concrete similarity measures. In the last step the similarity measures of all simple attributes must be combined to a complex similarity measure for the domain model.

Fig. 12.7. Generic complex method description sheet for constructing similarity measures

tween the users of the system and their working environment are adapted to take advantage of the power of the system), and the management of the associated process of change (or the project). However, this distinction does not imply that these different kinds of processes can be considered independently. There is in fact a lot of interaction between them. Altogether, the common generic level currently consists of a network of about 150 description sheets. Fig. 12.9 gives an overview of the processes and the products that they exchange. Only the top-level processes and products are shown in this figure. For most of these top-level processes, refinements have been defined through subprocesses which are combined in the context of complex methods or subproducts. Here, we only give an overview of top-level processes we

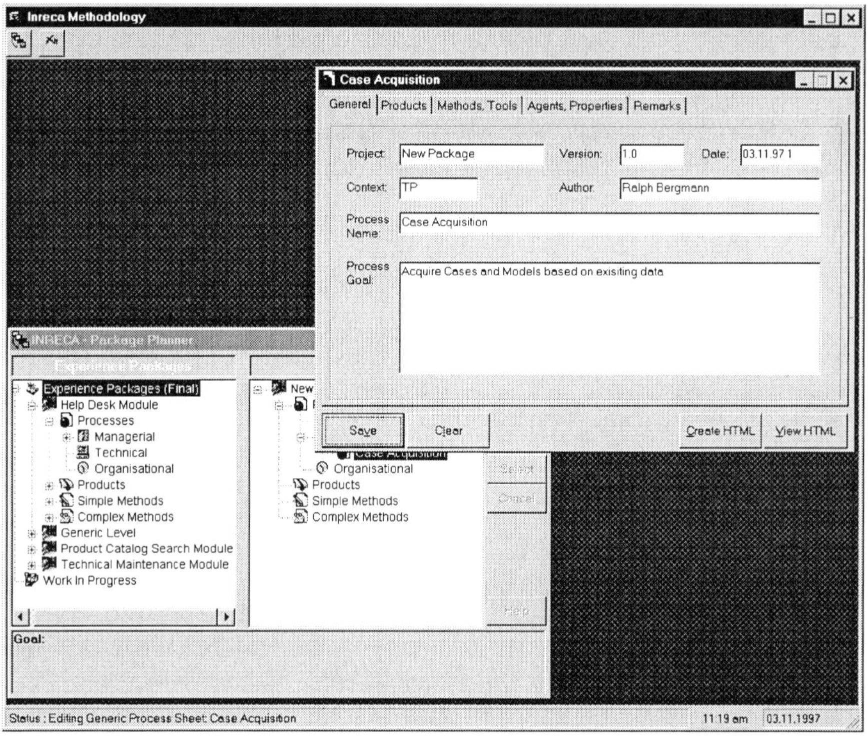

Fig. 12.8. INRECA-II methodology tool (Image provided by the courtesy of IMS)

have identified. At this top-level, the processes look very much like processes that might occur in any IT project. While this is in fact true for some of the processes or subprocesses (e.g. some of the managerial processes are standard IT processes) most of them are described at the lower levels in a way that is particularly tailored for CBR application development. In the following we give a brief overview of all the top-level processes and there interactions, before explaining them in some more detail.

A CBR project starts with a statement of a client's problem. In the *top-level start-up* process (managerial) a first vision document is created, which preliminary defines the mission of the project. The following *goal definition* process (managerial) is executed in strong interaction with the *preliminary organizational analysis* process (organizational). The organizational problems (that should be addressed by introducing the CBR system) and the respective problem owners are identified. Additionally, a basic goal checklist for the project is created. Based on this goal check list and the general project vision, a *feasibility study* (technical) should be carried out. Depending on the results of this study, it must be decided whether

– to continue the project as planned,

– to revise the main project goals,
– to stop the project.

Thereafter, the *identification of the high-level processes* (managerial) leads to a set of technical and organizational processes that should be addressed within the project. The methodology experience module should be consulted during this process since it gives valuable advice on the processes that are relevant. Additionally, a *detailed analysis of the organization* (organizational process) can be carried out in order to revise and refine the set of organizational processes that should be addressed and to identify possible project teams. Then, the project leader should *plan and schedule the technical and organizational processes* (managerial) and produce an overall project plan. Here, again the experience module should be consulted in order to build on concrete experience from other, similar CBR projects. The resulting project plan is then enacted and monitored during the technical process of *software development for case-based reasoning* and the *organizational development* of the environment into which the CBR system will be introduced. The resulting software implementation and the newly established responsibilities and workflow in the organization will then be *implemented and evaluated.*

Typically, a CBR project requires several development cycles, each of which results in a prototype application that is evaluated by the end-user. The evaluation feedback states whether a new development cycle must be considered or whether a satisfying solution is reached already. At this point, the first living application being in real use has been reached. During the lifetime of this application, some *maintenance* (technical process) will be required during which the application will be modified.

Please note that a separate *monitor & review* process (managerial) is introduced. This process controls the enactment of the software and organizational development. This process does not have a formal output. It also uses the evaluation feedback from the implemented application to allow the project leader to decide whether a new development cycle should be considered to further improve the current system or the organizational structure.

Managerial Processes. This subsection is primarily concerned with the management of the process of development and implementation of the system in its context, but it also touches the other two aspects where necessary given that they are impossible to separate. Managing a CBR project (or any AI project in general) differs from managing other IT projects to the extent that the associated concepts of the CBR technology are mostly previously unknown to the users. Therefore, there must be more than usual emphasis on early awareness training, and user-participation in the successive iterations of the prototyping process.

Top-Level Start-up. During the top-level start-up process, client and the top-management of the consulting firm agree on a terms of reference, which specifies the problem or opportunity to be addressed. During this process, the

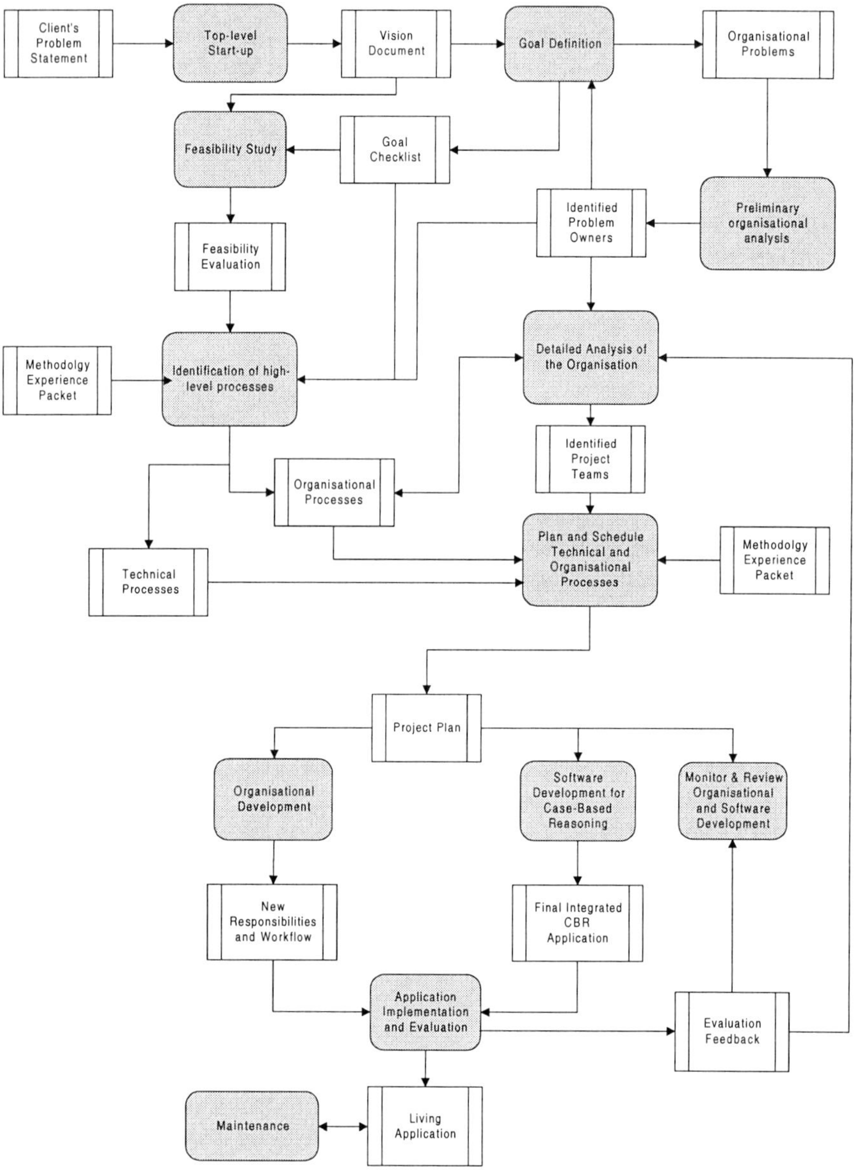

Fig. 12.9. Interaction between top-level processes involved in a CBR project. The grey and white boxes denote processes and products, respectively.

project leader is also identified. This person should have the time and motivation to ensure that the project is a success, and should also have some ownership of the project results. The leader then helps to define the overall project vision stated in the vision document in close interactive consultation with the client and the consultant- firm's management. It is also the duty of the leader to set up a system for monitoring the implementation of the project.

Goal Definition. The first process after start-up is to define the project goal. The vision of what life will be like when the project is completed has to be written down. At this stage, it is appropriate to introduce a high-level abstract concept of a 'case', from which case-based reasoning can be developed, and to identify what will be different about the people, their tasks, the technology and organization when the project is finished. This description should also elaborate any associated or dependent goals, in a goal checklist. These goals should be agreed amongst all participants in the project, and by anybody affected by the outcomes of the project. When this has been done, it becomes possible to define the high-level processes which support the performance of scheduled technical and organizational tasks during the whole project.

Identification of High-Level Processes. Even though it is difficult to define precisely each project process in detail, it is possible first to produce a lot of high-level processes that have to be enacted in order to achieve the project goal. As described, the processes can usefully be subdivided into technical and organizational categories. For each process the project planner should check the resource requirements, input- and output products and the dependencies between processes. The determination of the relevant processes should be done based on existing CBR building experience. For this purpose, the project leader should have access to the experience base of CBR methodology (see section 12.3.8).

Plan and Schedule Processes. During the detailed planning of the technical and organization processes, a couple of important aspects must be considered by the project leader. S/he must

- ensure that the immediate objectives of each project phase is embedded in strategic objectives of the overall project.
- ensure that in the design of the system there is provision for the participative interactive re-design of the work-practices of those using it.
- ensure that when the developed system is implemented, there is timely provision for the necessary level of training in its use by all who interact with it.
- ensure that the implemented system is evaluated critically, with a view to future improvements, identification of possible weaknesses etc., bearing in mind that development is an ongoing process.

Monitoring and Review of Organizational and Software Development. There is no difference in monitoring and reviewing the development processes compared to the management of standard IT projects. The implementation of the project plan in the organizational and software development processes must be monitored by the project leader. He must ensure, that the important project milestones can be reached in time. He must control the overall quality of the development process and of the deliverables. Based on the feedback from the evaluation of the application he finally has to decide whether a new organizational or technical development cycle should be considered.

Technical Processes: Software Development. The technical processes described in the subsection are general processes, i.e., such processes that we expect to be a part of most CBR application development projects. A number of the technical processes appear in usual software development projects, too. An example is the GUI development process. Such processes can be handled by standard methods. However, we emphasize on the CBR specific aspects.

Feasibility Study. The feasibility study consists of a cost/benefit analysis and should deliver an estimation of the commercial success potential of the intended CBR application. A simple mock-up of the intended application should be developed as a means to further clarify the goals and the vision of the project as well as a means to convince the customer to believe in the success of the project. Figure 12.10 gives a brief overview of the subprocesses involved in the feasibility study.

- Cost/Benefit Analysis
- Application Mock-up Development
  - GUI Mock-up Development
  - Case-Base Mock-up Development
  - Retrieval Mock-up Development
  - Integration Mock-up Development

Fig. 12.10. Sub-Processes occurring in the Feasibility Study Process

Software Development for Case-Based Reasoning. This is the technical top-level process during which the CBR application itself is developed. A CBR application development process in general is a usual software development process with mostly standard ingredients on its top-level. This includes a large number of different subprocesses listed hierarchically in Figure 12.11. Each of these processes is described in detail in the experience base.

Maintenance Process. The maintenance process relies heavily on the successful installation of organizational structures that support this process. One important organizational aspect is the installation of a board of users and domain experts that review the case data regularly and that decides what changes and updates to perform. From the technical point of view it should be aspired that updates of the system should be executed by an application

- GUI Development
  - GUI Requirements Analysis
  - GUI Design
  - GUI Programming
  - GUI Manual Writing
  - GUI Acceptance Testing
- CBR Engine Development
  - CBR Retrieval Requirements Analysis
  - CBR Engine Design
  - CBR Engine Implementation
  - CBR Engine Test
- Case Base Development
  - Case Base Requirements Analysis
  - Descriptive Model Development
  - Similarity Development
    - Similarity Characterization
    - Similarity Definition
    - Similarity Integration
  - Case Acquisition
    - Develop Case Collection Forms
    - Collect Case Data
    - Evaluate Selected Good Cases
    - Case Entry into the Case Base
- System Integration
  - Integration Requirements Analysis
  - Integration Design
  - Integration Implementation
  - Integration Test

Fig. 12.11. Sub-Processes occurring in the Software Development Process

administrator of the user organization in order to ensure some independence from the consulting company. The application should therefore provide means for easy updating of the case base and simple modifications of the domain model. However, more drastic changes of the system (e.g. restructuring of the domain model) should only be performed by or in cooperation with a CBR consultant. Figure 12.12 gives an overview of the maintenance processes identified so far.

- Change Selection
- Model Maintenance
- Case Base Maintenance
- Application Update

Fig. 12.12. Sub-Processes occurring in the Maintenance Process

Organizational Processes. In analyzing the existing organization's structure and related procedures, there is a preliminary scoping of the environment of the project. This includes a listing of the perceived problems and opportunities at the human and organizational levels.

Preliminary Organizational Analysis. In the preliminary organizational analysis process the first step is to identify the boundaries of the socio-technical system of which the perceived problems or opportunities are currently or potentially dealt with by introducing a CBR system. Once this has been identified, it can be regarded as being a 'production' unit embedded in a larger organization. We need to enact this preliminary organizational analysis in strong interaction with the managerial goal definition process. Bearing this in mind, we go on to analyze the processes embedded in the socio-technical unit, and to assess the impact of the technological change on the process management. This naturally leads to a synthesis in which the processes are re-organized in the context of the new technology.

Detailed Analysis of the Organization. The design of the CBR system will be the result of an iterative process involving all the people in the existing organization who are involved with the cases, the collective of stake-holders who own the material which will end up in the case- file, and who are potential users of the results of the system.

It is useful, having identified the problems and/or opportunities, to set up one or more working groups focused on them, to address the questions (a) how is this problem handled elsewhere and (b) how does the present situation compare with other CBR applications? The group should consider the processes, the people, the technologies and the structure within the socio-technical unit which deals with the cases. In this way they can begin to tease out the implications for the organization.

Organizational Development. The basic processes that must be addressed during the organizational development are the

- adaptation of the structure of the organization, including
- the structuring of the maintenance process for the CBR application,
- the training of the maintenance personal, and
- the training of the users of the system.

12.3.6 Current Experience at the Cookbook Level

We draw on the cookbook metaphor in the following sense: like a cookbook that contains a collection of recipes each of which leads to a particular dish, the cookbook-level of the methodology contains a collection of experience modules each of which combines selected generic processes in order to realize a particular kind of CBR application. Till the end of the INRECA-II project, we intend to have three modules for: *Parametric Search in Product-Bases, Complex Help Desk, and Technical Maintenance.*

The most advanced module currently is the parametric search module. The basic action is a search by a potential client, or a sales person in the presence of a client, in a product-base or catalogue. Typically, the set of all available products can be divided into several product categories each of which might contain some hundred products. Each product can be characterized (or even exactly specified) by a set of parameters. Typically each product might be characterized by some dozen parameters. The client specifies a need by specifying constraints on certain product parameters, and the search comes up with something approximating to it. Such a service can be provided for example on a CD-ROM or on the World-Wide-Web.

To summarize the catalogue search application class in the form of a checklist, we can say that:

– a catalogue of products must exist, each of which can be characterized by a number of qualitative (real or integer values) or quantitative parameters (symbols).
– the list of products subdivides into a number of subsets (product categories), in each of which the products share a common structure of parameters.
– a sufficient number of products must exist to make the task of searching for a product with a desired set of parametric values onerous.
– a group of potential users of the products must exist who are in a position to specify the parametric profile of the product that they need, making use of expert knowledge.

12.3.7 Current Experience at the Specific Level

At the specific project level, the experience from five projects from the industrial INRECA-II partners is captured and stored in about 350 sheets. These projects are documented using the software process modeling approach after the projects were finished. These projects provide the basis for developing experience modules at the cookbook-level through generalization.

12.3.8 Using and Maintaining the Experience Base

When a new CBR project is being planned, the relevant experience from the experience base must be selected and reused. The experience modules of the cookbook-level are particularly useful for building a new application that directly falls into one of the covered application classes. We consider the experience modules to be the most valuable knowledge of the methodology. Therefore, we suggest to start the "retrieval" [2] by investigating the cookbook-level and only using the common generic level as fall-back. Furthermore, it is important to maintain the experience base, i.e., to make sure that new experience is entered if required. For using and maintaining the experience base we propose the following procedure:

[2] Up to now, this retrieval is not supported by a tool, but through an index schema. However, support for retrieval (e.g., a CBR approach) is considered important for the future.

1. Identify whether the new application to be realized falls into an application class that is covered by an experience module of the cookbook. If this is the case then goto step 2a; else goto step 3.
2a. Analyze the generic processes, products, and methods that are proposed for this application class.
2b. Select the most similar particular application from the specific project level related to this module and analyze the specific description sheets in the context of the current application.
2c. Develop a new project plan and workflow for the new application based on the information selected in steps 2a and 2b. Goto step 4.
3. Develop a new project plan and workflow for the new application by selecting and combining some of the generic processes, products, and methods from the common generic level; make these descriptions more concrete and modify them if necessary.
4. Execute the project by enacting the project plan. Record the experience during the enactment of this project.
5. Decide whether the new project contains new valuable information that should be stored in the experience base. If this is the case, goto step 6, else stop.
6. Document the project using the specific description sheets and enter them into the specific project level of the experience base (supported by the methodology tool).
7. If possible, create a new experience module by generalizing the particular application (together with other similar applications) to an application class and generalize the specific descriptions into generic descriptions. Add the new to the current cookbook (supported by the methodology tool).
8. If new generic processes, methods, or products could be identified that are of a more general interest, i.e., relevant for more than the application class identified in step 7, then add them to the common generic level (supported by the methodology tool).

12.4 Conclusion

In this chapter, we have presented a methodology for building CBR applications. First, this methodology consists of an analytic framework for describing different kinds of CBR approaches. It provides an explicit ontology of basic CBR task types, domain characterizations, and types of problem solving and learning methods. Further, it incorporates within this framework a methodology for combining a knowledge-level, top-down analysis with a bottom-up, case-driven one. Second, the presented methodology consists of a systematic way to identify the main steps required to build a CBR application, based on collected experience stored as CBR specific software process models. We gave an overview of the main processes involved in building a CBR application for an analytic task, including managerial, organizational, and technical processes.

Up to now, this methodology is supported by two tools:

- A CBR system for retrieving descriptions of CBR approaches, CBR systems, and CBR applications. This retrieval system (implemented by the Fraunhofer Institute for Experimental Software Engineering in cooperation with TecInno) is currently be made available via WWW.
- The INRECA-II methodology tool (implemented by Interactive Multimedia Systems) which supports the management of the experience base and the different modules it consists of (see Figure 12.8). Thereby, this tool currently supports step 6 and partially the steps 7 and 8 from Section 12.3.8.

The development of a methodology is an ongoing task which is not finished yet. Future work should address the following two major points: Firstly, the scope the of the methodology must be enlarged as new kinds of applications are being developed. That is, more kinds of analytic applications must be covered, but in the long-term also synthetic applications should be included. Therefore, the experience base must grow further. More specific experience from successful CBR projects must be collected and generalized into new experience modules (cookbook recipes). New processes at the generic level must be identified.

Secondly, further tool support is required to make the methodology easier to use. Based on our current experience with the methodology, tools are necessary that also support steps 1 to 5 from Section 12.3.8. Particularly, a tool is required that allows to access process models from the experience base more efficiently, either by a flexible navigation approach or by a retrieval system (support of steps 1 to 2b). The application of case-based reasoning to this retrieval task would certainly be a new challenging CBR application itself.

Further, an integration with existing project planning and workflow management tools is desirable. This would allow to select certain processes from the experience base and to combine and tailor them according to the current application being developed (support of steps 2c to 4). A first case study that shows the appropriateness of the flexible workflow management system CoMoKit (Dellen et al. 1997b) for representing and enacting a process model of a CBR application development project has been performed (Bergmann et al. 1997b).

Acknowledgments

Parts of the work described in this chapter have been funded by the European Commission:

Inreca: Esprit Project P6322. Partners: Acknosoft (prime contractor, France), TecInno (Germany), Interactive Multimedia Systems (Ireland), University of Kaiserslautern (Germany)

Inreca-II: Esprit Project P22196. Information & Knowledge Reengineering for Reasoning from Cases. Partners: Acknosoft (prime contractor, France), Daimler Benz AG (Germany), TecInno (Germany), Interactive Multimedia Systems (Ireland), University of Kaiserslautern (Germany)

Applicus: Esprit Trial Application P20824. Partners: Acknosoft (prime contractor, France), BSR Consulting (Germany), Sepro Robotique (France)

13. Related Areas

Gerd Kamp, Steffen Lange, Christoph Globig

13.1 Introduction

As already mentioned in the introduction of this book, case-based reasoning has its origins in cognitive science and artificial intelligence:

- Cognitive science was looking for a model of human problem solving.
- Artificial Intelligence was searching for means to overcome the shortcomings of rule-based expert system for generic and effective problem solving methods.

Because of that interdisciplinary tradition and the generality of the approach, case-based reasoning found widespread use in a great variety of application domains. The previous chapters gave an impressive demonstration of this fact. We have seen the integration of many different techniques and methods with the case-based reasoning approach. It has become clear that CBR is a generic methodology for building knowledge-based systems, rather than an isolated technique that is capable of solving only very specific tasks.

Because of its integrative nature, it is not surprising that most publications that cover the topic of CBR extensively, contain a chapter (or a section) concerning the relations between CBR and various other disciplines.

The previous chapters focused on the use of CBR for specific applications. In this very last chapter, we will step back and take a look at the relations between CBR and various neighboring disciplines from an application-independent point of view.

Obviously, we have to restrict ourselves to a selection of related areas. Our focus is on aspects concerning the relations to other fields in computer science and artificial intelligence, the relationship to cognitive science must be neglected, but is covered excellently in other publications (e.g. Kolodner 1993).

For each of the related areas we consider, we are especially interested in the following two aspects:

- Uses of techniques from related areas within CBR.
- Influences of CBR in related areas.

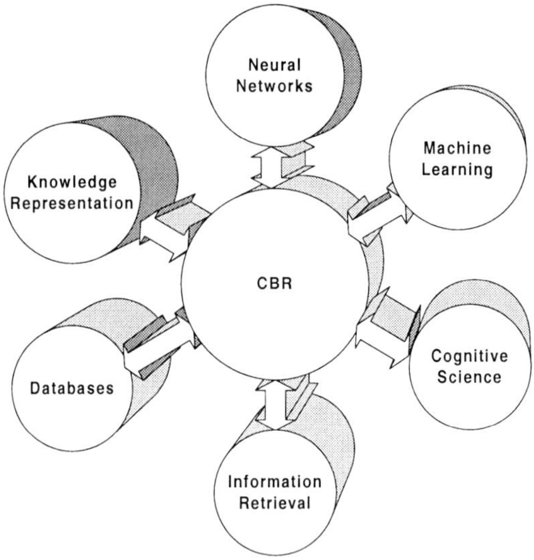

Fig. 13.1. CBR and (selected) related areas

Even within computer science and artificial intelligence, we have to select some areas, and are not able to give an exhaustive overview. The areas of interest are described below.

Due to the explosive growth of the Internet and especially WWW, the topic of *intelligent retrieval of information* has made it to the front-pages of daily newspapers and caught the eye of a very broad audience. Web-based intranets that allow the content-oriented retrieval of information are predicted to become the backbone of corporate-wide information systems. Simultaneously, they are used to establish the presence of the company on the Internet serving as the interface to its customers.

Since intelligent retrieval is one of the key aspects of CBR, there is a big window of opportunity for case-based reasoning in this area. Hence, within computer science we focus on areas related to this topic. Obviously, *information retrieval* is of great interest. *Databases*, especially newer tendencies such as *vague retrieval* and *multi-dimensional access methods*, is the second area whose relationship to CBR is presented.

We also look at *knowledge representation* techniques from the perspective of intelligent retrieval. In this area, we focus on *description logics*. Description logics are a formalism from artificial intelligence, that, due to their formal semantics and their powerful inferences, have caught the interest of researchers in case-based reasoning as well as information retrieval and databases.

Another area from artificial intelligence we investigate is *machine learning*. Here, we focus on *case-based learning*. After presenting a formal framework for case-based learning the topics of representability and learnability within that framework are discussed.

13.2 CBR and Information Retrieval

Although case-based reasoning (Aamodt and Plaza 1994; Kolodner 1993; Slade 1991) and Information Retrieval (IR) (Rijsbergen 1979; Salton and McGill 1983; Frakes and Baeza-Yates 1992; Fuhr 1993b; Schäuble 1993) have a great deal in common and are often used for similar tasks, there are relatively few systems and publications dedicated to the integration of the two techniques. The first scientific event focusing on this topic was the 1993 AAAI Spring Symposium on case-based reasoning and information retrieval (CBR-AAAI-WS 1993). This symposium had the goal to explore the opportunities for technology sharing. Since then, a number of activities between the two fields have been started, e.g., the invited talks of noted IR researchers at CBR Workshops and conferences.

13.2.1 Similarities and Differences – Common Perceptions

Similarities. Most people agree that CBR and IR pursue the same basic approach, and can be regarded to follow similar goals. The main similarities are:

Retrieval of relevant information. CBR and IR both focus on retrieving *relevant* information from a set of collected data.

Easy database querying. Both allow easy and flexible database querying.

Approximating relevance by similarity. Both fields approximate the relevance of the data entities w.r.t. the query by computing the similarity of the respective entities to the query. Hence, they deliver a collection of *inexact matches* as the retrieval result.

Differences. Nevertheless, CBR and IR are regarded as two different fields by the vast majority of people. This viewpoint is often substantiated by setting out the following major differences between CBR and IR:

Data Type. CBR and IR operate over different data types. Whereas IR methods mainly operate on textual data, traditional CBR methods operate on vectors of several basic data types, mainly numbers, intervals, dates, symbols and strings. Recently, CBR researchers also addressed textual data as shown in Chapter 5.

Amount of Data. IR methods can handle amounts of data much larger than those manageable by CBR. CBR Systems often operate on a few hundred cases. Systems capable of handling some thousand cases are the exception. In contrast to this, IR can search hundreds of thousands, and up to millions of documents, which consume gigabytes of memory.

Use of knowledge. IR systems operate without using knowledge about the user's problem solving task. They provide a generic indexing and retrieval engine operating on textual data. This generic, knowledge agnostic method, can be used for a wide scope of tasks, but has its limitations in accuracy of the retrieval with respect to the queries. CBR systems use knowledge of the problem-solving process to build effective case indices to improve the accuracy.

Evaluation Techniques. The information retrieval community has a strong tradition of evaluating its techniques. There is a well developed experimental methodology, based on standardized test collections and evaluation criteria such as precision and recall (Rijsbergen 1979). New proposed methods are evaluated with this methodology this, in CBR every system works with its own data, new methods and procedures are tested with this specific data. Therefore, a comparison of different systems is difficult.

Adaption. IR is only concerned about the retrieval of information, whereas a major part of case-based reasoning is the adaption of the retrieved cases. However, the bigger part of the commercially available case-based systems do not employ any adaption of the retrieved cases.

13.2.2 Current Forms of Integration

At present, mainly two forms of integration between CBR and IR can be found. The first one more or less perpetuates the distinctions from above. The second form of integration is a first attempt to overcome these distinctions and limitations.

Coarse Integration – CBR for IR focusing. One approach is a coarse integration of CBR and IR, where CBR is used to drive IR. Not surprisingly, it is proposed in the areas where the user must have access to large corpora of texts in addition to a set of cases; help-desk systems (Barletta 1993) and law (Rissland and Daniels 1995; Daniels and Rissland 1997). In this scenario, there are different CBR and IR modules dedicated to, for example, the technical documentation and the diagnostic episodes. One suggested way of using the system would be that a user interacts first with the CBR module in order to come up with a good idea and starting point for a search within the IR system. Hence, the information provided by the case-based reasoner is used to formulate a better query to the IR system and to provide better overall results.

Fine Integration – Providing a text data type in CBR systems. Often a finer integration of CBR and IR is needed. In nearly every application area, some kind of textual attributes of the cases have to be represented. The best way to do so is to provide an additional data type for texts (Kamp 1993). This data type extends the set of data types normally provided by CBR systems, such as symbol sets and numbers; that is, it provides the mechanisms developed in IR for free-form text retrieval, e.g., *n-grams* or *inverted files*[1].

[1] We cannot go into details concerning these IR techniques, and refer the reader to the respective IR literature, e.g., Rijsbergen 1979; Frakes and Baeza-Yates 1992, etc. Chapter 5 also contains a brief discussion of these techniques.

The retrieval functions of CBR then operate on this basic data type in the same way as they operate on numbers or intervals. Obviously this technique can be extended to other data types now handled by IR techniques, such as audio and images.

13.2.3 Recent Developments - IR and CBR come closer

The latter type of integration is a first indication of the fact that the distinction between the two fields is not that strict as the differences set out in Section 13.2.1 may suggest. It is an indicator for a process that brings the two fields closer together. Over the last couple of years, the way people (not only scientists) access and search for information has been revolutionized. Information is at the fingertips of everyone, the people suffer now from information overload instead of having problems getting access to the information. In sync with this revolution, both the information itself and the interaction model have changed and pose new challenges to IR and CBR:

Structured multimedia documents. Most textual documents nowadays are written on computers, using text processors and stored in descriptive formats such as RTF, LaTeX, SGML and HTML. Hence, a description of the structure is already contained in the original document, it is at least easily accessible. In addition, these documents contain pictures, graphs etc. Web pages take this multimedia aspect to the extreme but are in no way special.

Automatically generated documents. More and more documents are generated automatically from databases. Moreover, these documents are often generated on demand as the result to queries to this databases.

Interactive Systems. Users want to be in control of the retrieval process. Retrieval is no longer a process of submitting a query, waiting, and collecting the results. Users want to refine their query on the fly, follow hyperlinks within the retrieved documents, etc.

Semantic Retrieval. The techniques developed so far are often not sufficient to fulfill the needs of todays users, especially experts. They want retrieval by content using the available knowledge, not only retrieval based on syntactic criteria such as n-grams and inverted files.

IR and CBR have reacted to these new challenges in a number of ways that actually bring the two fields closer together:

IR systems operate on other data types than text. Whereas textual data is the natural data type of information retrieval, several systems support other data types such as *numbers.* Additionally the techniques developed for text retrieval were successfully transformed to handle multimedia data types such as *sound* and *pictures* (Glavitsch and Schäuble 1992; Glavitsch et al. 1994; Mittendorf et al. 1995). Another data type developed within IR are *proper names* (Pfeifer et al. 1995b). Here, techniques like *Soundex* and Phonix cope with the problem of finding similar sounding names.

IR systems operate on semi-structured and structured data. To accommodate the change in the original document format towards structured documents, more and more IR systems are operating on semi-structured and structured documents (e.g., Shoens et al. 1993; Wilkinson 1994). One area that traditionally operates on semi-structured data is that of bibliographic retrieval. There are two variants of systems operating on structured data.

1. A number of systems, such as freeWais-sf (Pfeifer et al. 1995a) and Harvest (Brown et al. 1995) first parse textual documents, or better, documents available in some markup language like SGML or HTML in order to gather the structural information. Then, these systems index the documents w.r.t. the gathered structural information. These kind of systems most often are restricted to simple attribute-value vector representations of the document, allowing only for textual, and maybe numerical attributes.
2. On the other hand there is the sub-area of fact retrieval that integrates IR techniques with databases (Motro 1988; Fuhr 1990; Fuhr 1992). These systems more or less operate directly on the structures of the database.

IR and CBR systems make use of available knowledge. In IR as well as in CBR there is rising interest in using knowledge to enhance the retrieval result. Traditionally, there is the subfield of "intelligent IR" that employs AI techniques for IR. This interest in knowledge-intensive methods was boosted in the late 80's by van Rijsbergen and his introduction of the logical model of IR (Rijsbergen 1986; Chiaramella and Chevallet 1992; Sebastiani 1995). In this model, the relevance of the documents w.r.t. to a query is determined as an implication $d \rightarrow q$ in some logic. Hence, the transition from "traditional IR" to "intelligent IR" can be characterized as the transition from index terms to concepts and from matching to inference:

> "*... to design the next generation of IR systems, we will need to have a formal semantics for documents and queries. This semantic representation will interact with other types of knowledge in a controlled way, and this way is inference!*" (van Rijsbergen, SIGIR89)

Right now, knowledge is employed in various forms in IR. Thesauri (esp. the WordNet thesaurus) are used as simple semantic nets (Kazman and Kominek 1997). Conceptual graphs (Kheirbek and Chiaramella 1995), (Probabilistic) Datalog (Fuhr 1995a; Fuhr 1995b) as well as frames and scripts have all been and are used within IR.

The logical model of IR is seen by a large fraction of IR researchers as one of the main themes within future IR research[2], especially in the area of multimedia information retrieval. Besides Datalog and probabilistic extensions of it (Fuhr 1995b), several other logic formalisms are considered, such

[2] At least that was the consensus at the 1995 European Summer School on Information Retrieval.

as the Dempster-Shafer theory of evidence in conjunction with situation theory (Lalmas 1997), and logical imaging (Crestani and Rijsbergen 1995), a concept based on conditional logic is another approach.

However, the most active approach to incorporate knowledge into the retrieval process are description logics (Fuhr 1993b; Meghini et al. 1993; Sebastiani 1994; Sebastiani 1995; FERMI 1996). The previous chapters have shown that there is an increased interest in CBR on object-oriented case representations and other knowledge-intensive methods of CBR. Not surprisingly, description logics are also the central approach to incorporate knowledge within CBR We will have a closer look at description logics in the Section 13.4.

IR and CBR actively integrate techniques developed in the other area. We have already seen how IR techniques are integrated into existing CBR systems. However, CBR techniques are also used within IR systems. For example, CBR is used for the guidance of user sessions in (Tißen 1991; Tien 1993). In these systems, old sessions of the user interacting with the retrieval system are stored as cases and used to guide the current retrieval session.

CBR systems operate on larger collections. Whereas older CBR systems often relied on linear search for finding the best cases in the case library, technologies developed recently allow for much larger case-bases. For example, Wess (1995) reports a case-base with 16,000 cases realized with INRECA, Case Retrieval Nets (cf. Section 3.4) are used by Lenz and Burkhard (1996a) to provide access to the last minute offers – approx. 200,000 cases – of a major German tour operator. More recently, Case Retrieval Nets have been used to directly operate on textual documents by parsing these documents for certain keywords and interpreting these as information entities of the Case Retrieval Net (cf. Section 5.7.1, Lenz and Burkhard 1997b). Kitano et al. (1992), Shimazu et al. (1993), and Kitano and Shimazu (1996) realize case-based systems on top of corporate-wide data-bases.

Towards an evaluation methodology for interactive IR systems. Our last observation is a negative one. With the advent of interactive IR systems the evaluation of IR systems also has to cope with several methodological problems. Recall and precision measures loose some of their importance in advanced IR systems that provide links between information units and which offer navigation and browsing facilities. In such systems, a query might just serve to find some suitable starting points for exploring the information space in search for useful information. Moreover, the link between traditional measures of effectiveness and optimal retrieval is not clear in these contexts and will have to be re-examined. IR has reacted by starting the ESPRIT project MIRA to come up with an evaluation methodology that takes these changes into account.

13.2.4 Summary

CBR and IR are often considered as two areas of computer science that share some basic ideas and goals, such as the retrieval of relevant information, but use different technologies to achieve these goals. We claim that, although this is true as long as standard (or should we say legacy) systems are considered, in the long run, both fields will more and more move towards each other. As long as only the retrieval step is considered, the borders between both areas will be blurred and there will be a large overlap in the intelligent retrieval techniques that are used in both fields. In our opinion, in a few years, labeling a certain system or method as a CBR or an IR system will be largely a question of preference than of technical differences between the two fields.

13.3 CBR and Databases

Generally, databases and case-based reasoning are differentiated in the following way:

> *"Database systems are designed to do exact matching between queries and stored information, while the goal of CBR is to retrieve a 'most similar' case or set of similar cases. The most similar cases may include conflicts with some of the attributes that were specified in the retrieval query. In CBR, whether a particular case should be retrieved depends not only on the case itself, but whether there are better competitors."* (Leake 1996, Chapter 1)

However, similarly to the relation between CBR and IR, this difference is only true as long as "traditional" relational database management systems are considered. Moreover, this comparison focuses on the retrieval result and neglects other main differences between the two fields. A number of differences, such as transactions, recovery, etc., can be ignored for the moment, but the following two aspects are relevant for the retrieval:

- Firstly, databases operate on data sets that are orders of magnitude larger than the case bases of CBR. Hence, the retrieval and access methods include the management of secondary storage.
- Secondly, the access methods are fully dynamic, i.e., insertion and deletion of data items can be arbitrarily intermixed with queries, without performance loss.

CBR today mostly ignores these topics, but they are of paramount importance if larger case bases should be supported. In this section, we first briefly review current forms of integration between the two fields. We then have a look at two sub-areas of current database research that are concerned with "non-standard" databases and are closely related to case-based reasoning.

Firstly, we present different approaches for handling imprecise and vague information in databases. Secondly, we review multi-dimensional access methods that were developed within database research over the last couple of years. These access methods pay attention to the above aspects and, as we will see, are very well suited to implement CBR systems. Up to now, CBR has paid very little attention to these access models, only *k*d-trees have been considered (Wess et al. 1993a; Wess 1995).

13.3.1 Using Databases as a CBR Backend

The most prominent current use of database techniques within CBR is to use database management systems (DBMS)[3] as a backend for the CBR system. Two different forms can be distinguished (see Wess 1995):

DBMS as a persistent case store. Here, databases are only used as a persistent store for the cases. The cases are stored within a database, they are bulk loaded while starting the CBR system. The index structures are computed and stored in main memory, they contain only pointers to the cases stored in the database. Throughout the CBR session, these index structures are used for the retrieval and, if necessary, the original cases are retrieved from the database.

Actually, the CBR-ANSWERS system described in Section 5.5 makes use of a database this way.

Realizing a CBR system with database means. In this scenario, the database system plays an active role. The CBR system is realized with database means. If relational systems are used, the similarity based retrieval is performed by generating tables encoding the similarity measures as well as the appropriate SQL-queries (Kitano et al. 1992; Shimazu et al. 1993; Kitano and Shimazu 1996). The difficulties then are the generation of adequate queries and the integration of this query generation within a typical CBR architecture.

The situation is different when object-oriented database management systems (OODMBS) are used. Since most object-oriented databases are lacking a descriptive query language, they are tightly coupled with a programming language or they provide their own. Ironically, this conceptual deficit of OODBMS makes it easier to realize CBR systems, since the retrieval process can be directly realized in the programming language of the database. An example of this approach has been given by Öchsner and Wess (1992).

13.3.2 Incompleteness/Vagueness in Databases

Handling of incomplete and vague data is closely intertwined with case-based reasoning. However, also within database research there is a growing interest

[3] Most often relational database systems (RDBMS), but also object-oriented ones (OODBMS) are used in newer systems.

in handling of incomplete and vague data. This research originated from the topic of missing attribute values in relational database management systems. An excellent overview of the various methods to cope with incompleteness and vagueness in data bases, as well as artificial intelligence, is given in Parsons (1996). Due to space constraints, we are only able to note some interesting facts:

Use of Dempster-Shafer Theory. A number of database researches suggested to use the Dempster-Shafer theory of evidence in order to cope with this problem (e.g. Lee 1992; Bell et al. 1996). This is especially interesting since there is a general understanding in artificial intelligence that Dempster's rule is computationally too expensive (Orponen 1990). However, it is argued that it is only exponentially complex in the worst case, and linear algorithms for special cases are devised. The result of Richter (1994) concerning the relation between the Hamming distance and Dempster-Shafer theory is, therefore, an interesting link between the two fields.

Probabilistic Datalog. Another interesting approach is to use a probabilistic version of Datalog (Fuhr 1990; Fuhr 1993a; Fuhr 1995b; Fuhr 1995a) for modeling the retrieval of incomplete data. This technique has been developed in the area of information retrieval, an indicator that all three areas are moving into one direction as far as the intelligent retrieval of information is concerned.

Approaches based on similarity measures. The approach most similar to traditional CBR techniques is the one pursued in Motro (1988). It presents an extension to the relational data model by so-called *data metrics.* These data metrics are nothing else than distance measures defined over the various attributes, combined by using a weighted Euclidean distance. The retrieval itself delivers a ranking on the retrieved tuples. All in all, this can be classified as a classical CBR approach.

13.3.3 Multi-dimensional Access Methods

Traditional database management systems (DBMS) normally use some variation of the B^+-tree for single-attribute indexing. However, today various applications need to deal with multi-attribute, i.e., multidimensional, data; Geographic informations systems (GIS) operating on spatial objects (either 2D or 3D) is the oldest and most established application area. Newer application areas include multimedia databases (images, audio, video), time series, string and DNA databases, as well as data mining and online analytical processing (OLAP). These application areas typically operate on higher dimensional data (typically $10 < d < 100$)[4]. To efficiently handle multi-attribute data, one needs multidimensional access methods.

[4] Within this picture, information retrieval tasks can be (and are) modeled as string databases with a typical dimensionality $10^4 < d < 10^6$. E.g., trigrams over a 27 character alphabet (26 case-insensitive alphabetic chars plus 'other')

The main problem in designing multi-dimensional access methods is that there exists no total ordering among spatial objects that preserves spatial proximity. Hence there is no easy and obvious way to extend the well understood and efficient one-dimensional access methods from traditional databases in order to handle multidimensional data.

Over the last two decades, research in spatial and multi-dimensional database systems has resulted in a wealth of access methods. In this section, we investigate to what extent these access methods can be and have been used for case-based reasoning. Due to space limitations, we can only give a very brief introduction to the various access models. We refer the reader to the excellent overviews of Gaede and Günther (1996) and Güting (1994) for an in depth analysis of the various methods.

Query types. We first present the scope of queries that is typically supported by multidimensional access methods:

Exact match queries. Given a query object find all the objects in the database with the same geometry.

Range queries. There are several variants of range queries. The *window query* finds all objects in the database that share at least one point with the query object, a d-dimensional interval. The *point query* is a specialization of this query type, where the query interval is reduced to a point in d-dimensional space. Additional variants are the *enclosure query*, the *containment query* and the *intersection query*. These operate on arbitrary input regions as query items and return the objects that are either fully enclosing, are fully contained, or have an non-empty intersection with the query item.

Nearest-neighbor queries. These are the well known nearest neighbor queries that, given a query item, find the item that is closest or most similar to the query item. Variants are *k-nearest neighbor queries* that find the k elements closest to a query, and *fixed-radius-near-neighbor queries* that retrieve all objects with a distance of at most r from the query item.

Obviously, all these query types can be used for case-based reasoning. Most prominently, the nearest-neighbor queries can be directly used to determine the most similar cases. However, there are also uses of the range and exact match queries, e.g. in the preselection step of a case-based reasoner. These are also of use when expert users want to be in control of the retrieval (Kamp et al. 1996).

The different multidimensional access methods vary in the query and object types they support. In particular, one has to distinguish access models that operate only on point data and access models operating on data with spatial extent.

---

results in $d = 19683$, vector-space models based on terms typically are in the range $100000 < d < 500000$.

Point access methods. The most prominent access method for point data is the kd-tree, developed by Bentley in the 1970s (Bentley 1975; Friedman et al. 1977; Bentley 1979). It is more or less a straightforward generalization of a binary decision tree to d dimensions. Most importantly, algorithms for nearest-neighbor search were devised (Fukunaga and Narendra 1975; Friedman et al. 1977). In principle, it is a quite static data structure working on internal memory, so it is not optimal with respect to these two important aspects. Later, various extensions, such as the *adaptive* kd-tree (Bentley and Friedman 1979) and the *k-d-b-tree* (Robinson 1981), an extension of the kd-tree that operates on secondary memory, were proposed.

The basic kd-tree was adopted in case-based reasoning (Öchsner and Wess 1992; Wess et al. 1993a; Goos 1994) and further optimized for the needs of CBR by Wess (1995). Optimizations include dynamic bounding boxes for speeding up nearest-neighbor queries and the extension to unordered attributes (see also the description of the INRECA project in Chapter 3). However, as far as we know, neither one of the kd-tree extensions, nor any of the following access methods has been considered for use within CBR.

Other tree based access models for point data include the *hB-Tree* and its extension the *hB$^{\Pi}$-Tree* (Evangelidis et al. 1997), as well as the *LSD-Tree* (Henrich et al. 1989). The latter is interesting because it is an extension of the adaptive kd-tree that used a special split strategy and balances the external path length using a clever paging algorithm.

It has been noted that most of the multidimensional access models were originally spatial access models, designed for two or three dimensional data (Lin et al. 1994). In principle, they can be scaled to arbitrary dimensions, but there is a severe performance loss with most of the models. Since CBR normally deals with problems having a dimensionality between 10 and a few hundred, the question arises if the generalized spatial access models are really best of breed. Most notably, the nearest-neighbor search algorithm given by Friedman et al. (1977) does almost as much work as linear scanning for $d > 9$. The *TV-Tree* presented in Lin et al. (1994) is designed to work with high-dimensionality data, using varying length feature vectors. This method most definitely is of interest for CBR.

A second class of point-based access models is based on hashing methods rather than tree structures. Prominent examples are the *Grid-File* (Nievergelt et al. 1984) and the *BANG-File* (Freeston 1987).

Spatial access models. It is often argued, or implicitly assumed, that cases are points in d-dimensional space and the retrieval process is built upon this assumption. In our experience, this assumption is wrong. Most often, cases are incompletely described; the values of certain attributes are unknown, or only vague.

CBR systems try to cope with this problem by only considering known attributes, introducing a special value *unknown*, or using qualitative scales. All these approaches have certain flaws. For example, in Wess (1995) *unknown* is introduced as a special value and hence can be used for attributes. However, it is impossible to restrict the values of an attribute to be in a certain interval. Moreover, the indexing structure is not symmetric. Since the developed architecture was devised for classification tasks, the classification result is always unknown in the query item. Hence, the classification attribute is not used when building then index structure, it is treated specially. It is not possible to use the index structure for answering queries of the form: "All the cases having a certain classification x".

Another way to cope with this problem is to model cases as objects with a spatial extent. Hence, multidimensional access methods for objects with spatial extent are of interest for CBR. Most of the access models so far approximate spatial objects using their minimum bounding rectangles, i.e. d-dimensional intervals.

Using this approximation, spatial objects in d dimensions can be represented as points in $2d$-space and then the point access methods from above can be used. Unfortunately, this approach has several disadvantages. Firstly, the formulation of point and range queries is usually much more complicated than in the original space. Secondly, the distribution in dual space may be highly non-uniform, even though the original data is uniformly distributed. Thirdly, images of objects that are close in the original space may be arbitrarily far apart in dual space. Fourthly, and most important, more complex queries, such as distance based queries, may not be expressible at all.

On the other hand, there are various multidimensional access methods that operate directly on the spatial data. The most prominent ones are the *R-Tree* (Guttman 1984) and its variants. However, spatial extensions of the kd-tree, such as the *extended* kd-tree and the *SKD-Tree*, are also proposed. The latter contains mechanism similar to the dynamic bounding boxes proposed by Wess (1995) in his extensions for CBR.

All these access models still operate with ortho-rectangular objects. However, often intervals are not a good approximation of the data objects enclosed[5]. Polyhedral Tree Structures like the *Cell Tree* (Günter 1989) and the *BV-Tree* (Freeston 1995; Freeston 1996) facilitate searches on data objects with arbitrary shapes, especially polyhedra.

13.3.4 Integration via Extensible Databases

Until recently, all these multidimensional access models were mainly of academic interest, only few of them were deployed in commercial database servers. However, the world has radically changed in the last years. Due to applications like inter- and intranets, OLAP, etc., most database vendors are working on extensible database servers right now. These so called object-relational database management systems (ORDBMS) can be extended

[5] See Kamp (1996) for an example from case-based diagnosis where this is the case.

to incorporate multidimensional data types like spatial information, texts, etc. Informix and Oracle are already providing such universal servers. Multidimensional access structures for geographic information systems as well as for multimedia data and texts are already available. Up to now, there are no extension modules (e.g., *data blades*, *data cartridges*, or whatever the database vendor calls them) available for doing case-based retrieval.

We think that this is a big, if not the greatest, opportunity for the developers of CBR systems. However, in order to do so successfully commercially[6], a lot of research lies ahead.

Firstly, and most important, the case-based reasoning techniques have to be scaled up to handle large case-bases that are stored on secondary memory. One way to do so, is to host CBR techniques on top of multi-dimensional access structures. Hence, the various multi-dimensional access methods have to be carefully analyzed w.r.t. their relevance and usefulness for CBR and the methods must be chosen. The presentation of the various multi-dimensional access methods in the previous section only gives some hints. The following questions must be answered in detail:

- Does the access method support the dimensionality of CBR?
- Does the access method support the right kind of data? What are the implicit assumptions on the data type?
- How can the supported query types be used for CBR?
- Can missing query types, e.g. nearest-neighbor, be integrated/implemented? If so, how efficient?

The existing access methods must then gradually evolve to access methods optimized for doing case-based retrieval.

Secondly, solutions must be implemented and tested on real-world data. Evaluation methods must be devised. Standard benchmarks (both for testing the quality of the retrieval as well as the performance) must be agreed upon. This is an area where CBR lags behind information retrieval and databases.

13.3.5 Summary

Besides hosting CBR technology on top of relational databases, as is done today, there are two areas within database research that are relevant to CBR. Firstly, there are several approaches to handle incomplete and vague data within data bases that should be worth looking at. One interesting thing to note is the use of the Dempster-Shafer Theory of evidence within these approaches, as well as in some approaches to information retrieval. Secondly (and this is in our opinion the most promising area for a tight and fruitful integration of CBR techniques with databases) there are multi-dimensional access models. A wealth of access models have been defined, all of which may

[6] At least in the long run. It is, of course, possible to do a quick port of some existing technology, but this will be suboptimal.

be applicable for CBR. Up to now, only kd-trees have been investigated and used by CBR. However, since their introduction twenty years ago, a lot of progress has been made, and may be of interest to CBR.

13.4 CBR and Knowledge Representation

As we have seen in Section 13.2.3, there is a trend in IR as well as in CBR to integrate more knowledge into the systems. Most of the current state-of-the-art CBR systems, at least the non-commercial ones, are object-oriented and allow structural domain knowledge to be represented.

We have also seen that description logics play a major role in IR and CBR when the formal semantics of the retrieval and automatic semantic indexing are considered. On the other hand, description logics[7] are a knowledge representation scheme that combines strict semantic and powerful inferences with an object-oriented representation of the knowledge (Brachman and Schmolze 1985). Therefore, description logics can be viewed as a powerful extension of object-oriented representations.

Hence, it is not surprising that description logics are the major topic of research w.r.t. the integration of object-oriented databases and knowledge representation schemes (see for example (Beneventano and Bergamaschi 1997) and the various proceedings of the KRDB workshops (Baader et al. 1995; Baader et al. 1996)) and one of the major topics in knowledge representation in general.

Within case-based reasoning, description logics are used for various applications including law (Ashley and Aleven 1993), planning (Köhler 1994; Napoli et al. 1996), service support (Kamp 1994; Kamp et al. 1996; Kamp 1996), software reuse (Fernandez-Chamizo et al. 1996), and retrieval of bibliographic data (Kamp 1997). However, most of the developed techniques are independent of the application area. In this section, we briefly discuss the reasons for using description logics in CBR, present the basics of description logics and sketch their use for intelligent, similarity-based retrieval.

13.4.1 Description Logics

Description logics (DL) have a long tradition (originating from the KL-ONE system, Brachman and Schmolze 1985) in organizing information with a powerful representation scheme, clearly defined model-theoretic semantics and powerful inferences based on that semantic. In short, they can be used to overcome the following shortcomings of object-oriented representations:

---

[7] Finally, the researchers working in the field have settled on the term *description logics*. Earlier, description logics where know as *terminological logics*, *KL-ONE like languages*, etc.

No seamless integration of knowledge. Whereas it is possible to integrate device knowledge into object-oriented systems, it is not clear how the integration of physical laws and models of behavior could be done in a uniform way.

No declarative semantics. In a number of application areas, especially when the users are experts, the numerical similarity values delivered by most case-based systems have too little explanatory value; their semantics are not transparent to the users.

No automatic semantic indexing. Whereas the syntactical indexing of cases (e.g., assigning a bucket in a kd-tree, Wess 1995) could be done automatically; a semantic index, such as the membership of an object to a certain class, must be assigned by the user (Kamp 1993).

Basics. Description logics consist of two parts; a so called Terminological Box (TBox) containing terminological knowledge and an Assertional Box (ABox) containing assertional knowledge. Since we can not elaborate on the basics of description logics, we only give a brief introduction in the following and refer the reader to the relevant literature (e.g. Baader et al. 1992) for a more detailed introduction:

Definition 13.4.1 (TBox). Concept terms *allow for a structured (object-oriented) representation of a relatively large fragment of first order-logic. Starting with primitive concept and role terms, new concept terms can be constructed from others by a set of concept forming operators. There are mainly three categories of such operators (Hanschke 1996):*

- Boolean operators *(e.g. (and C_1 ...), (or C_1 ...), (not C_1))*
- Role Forming operators *(e.g. composition of roles (compose r_1 r_2)).*
- Operators on Role Fillers *(e.g. quantification (some r C), (exists r C)).*

Terminological axioms *in the form (define-concept CN C) associate a concept name CN with a concept term C and are used to define the relevant concepts of an application. Terminological axioms are therefore an extension to the class definitions of an object-oriented CBR approach. A* TBox *($\mathcal{T}$) is a finite set of terminological axioms.* □

Definition 13.4.2 (ABox). *Concrete objects are* instances *(individuals, objects) of concepts. A new instance o can be introduced into the ABox via (define-distinct-individual o), and assertions α concerning the membership of an instance o to a concept C, or about existing relations (functions) between two objects o_1 and o_2 can be made through (state (instance o C)) or (state (related o_1 o_2 r)), respectively. The set of assertions constitutes the* ABox *$\mathcal{A}$.* □

What distinguishes a description logic approach to CBR from pure object-oriented ones, is that one is able to formally define a declarative model-theoretic semantics for the T- and ABox constructs by means of an interpretation function $^{\mathcal{I}}$, e.g. (and C_1 C_2)$^{\mathcal{I}} = C_1^{\mathcal{I}} \cap C_2^{\mathcal{I}}$. These semantics allow a formal definition of a number of powerful inferences to be given, providing "intelligent" (semantic) access to information, that is independent of the syntax.

Definition 13.4.3 (Inferences). *In our context, the following* inference services *are of particular interest:*

- Consistency Test. *The consistency test checks if an ABox (w.r.t. a TBox) is consistent (i.e. it has a model):* $\mathcal{A}^{\mathcal{I}} \neq \emptyset$.
- Concept Classification. *Concept Classification is a TBox inference service that calculates the* subsumption hierarchy, *i.e., the subconcept-superconcept relationships between concepts. A concept* C_1 subsumes *another concept* C_2 *iff. for* C_2 *there exists also a model for* C_1 *(i.e.* $C_1^{\mathcal{I}} \supseteq C_2^{\mathcal{I}}$*).*
- Object Classification. *Object classification is an ABox inference service that determines, given an object o of the ABox, the set of most specific concepts* $\overline{C}(o) = \{C_1, \ldots, C_n\}$ *that this object belongs to, i.e.* $\overline{C}(o) = \{C_i \in \mathcal{T} \mid \{\mathcal{A} \cup \neg(o : C_i)\}^{\mathcal{I}} = \emptyset \wedge C_i \text{ minimal in } \mathcal{T} \text{ w.r.t. subsumption}\}$.
- Weak object classification. *Weak object classification, in contrast, delivers the set* $\underline{C}(o)$ *of the most general concepts the object may be specialized to if new information is added, i.e.,* $\underline{C}(o) = \{C_i \in \mathcal{T} \mid \{\mathcal{A} \cup (o : C_i)\}^{\mathcal{I}} \neq \emptyset \wedge C_i \text{ maximal in } \mathcal{T} \text{ w.r.t. subsumption}\}$.
- Retrieval. *Retrieval is dual to the object classification problem. Given an concept term C, the set of TBox objects (instances)* $\overline{O}(C) = \{o_1, \ldots, o_m\}$ *that are members of C, is returned.*
- Weak retrieval. *Weak retrieval returns the set of objects* $\underline{O}(C) = \{o_1, \ldots, o_m\}$ *which are possible members of the concept.*

□

Recent work in the area of DL focused on determining the computational properties of different description languages (i.e. sets of concept terms). Since all the above inference services are defined based on the consistency test of an ABox, it is sufficient to find an algorithm for this problem. It has been shown that there exist sound and complete algorithms to determine the consistency of an ABox for a number of description languages. These algorithms are inspired by the tableaux calculus. However, only a few available systems, such as KRIS (Baader and Hollunder 1990) and TAXON, are based on this technique. Most systems (e.g., LOOM (MacGregor 1991) and CLASSIC (Patel-Schneider et al. 1991)) use incomplete structural subsumption algorithms instead; and, since they do not reduce subsumption to the consistency test of an ABox, a number of the other inferences are unavailable. This is a fact that one has to keep in mind when reading articles about CBR and description logics.

13.4.2 Intelligent Retrieval Based on Description Logics

All of the above inference services can be used for similarity-based retrieval:

- Object classification is the method of choice if one wants to use the system in the traditional CBR way; i.e. a new case should be solved by looking for similar cases.
- Concept classification and retrieval can be used to implement a database like service where the user poses queries against the case base and retrieves the matching elements.

Methods based on object classification. Object classification maintains a dynamic index of the ABox objects $o_j \in \mathcal{A}$ with respect to the TBox concepts $C_k \in \mathcal{T}$. Hence, the indices (i.e., the most specific concepts a certain object belongs to) can be used as the base for all kind of similarity measures. The method proceeds as follows:

1. Add assertions. New assertions (e.g., parameter restrictions) about an object o_j trigger automatically a reclassification and, therefore, a reindexing of o_j and all the objects connected to it.
2. Retrieve the indices. Either the strong $I'(o_j) = \overline{C}(o_j)$, or the weak variant $I''(o_j) = \underline{C}(o_j)$ of object classification, or a combination of both $I'''(o_j) = (\overline{C}(o_j), \underline{C}(o_j))$ are used.
3. Determine similar objects. Based on the indices provided by the last step, the various well-known similarity measures can be used:
   a) Identical indices. The most simple, pure relational similarity measure returns all the objects as similar that have the same set of indices as the query object. Let $I^* \in \{I', I'', I'''\}$ and $\aleph_M$ be the characteristic function of M. Then, $sim_{I^*}(o_l, o_k) = \aleph_{I^*(o_l)=I^*(o_k)}(o_k)$.
   Due to the inferences drawn by the classification process, even this simple similarity measure is sufficient for most purposes.
   b) Various association measures. Alternatively, all the various similarity measures developed in IR and CBR (Rijsbergen 1979; Tversky 1977; Bayer et al. 1992) operating on index sets or index vectors, respectively, can be used. For example, the simple matching coefficient, the Jaccard coefficient, the Dice coefficient, the contrast rule, the cosine measure; virtually all the techniques known.
   c) Graph Distance between the index sets. Moreover, since the indices, e.g. concepts are arranged in a directed acyclic graph, the structure of this graph can be taken into account, and the respective measures can be used.
4. Display the similar objects.

Methods Based on Retrieval and Concept Classification. Retrieval and concept classification are useful for a more database-like use of the case base, i.e., query answering. The inference service that is most obvious to use is the retrieval service. Methods based on it work as follows:

1. Query formulation. Since the query language and the concept description language are identical, an arbitrary concept term C_q can be used as query formulation.

2. Calling the retrieval inference. Compute the sets $I'(C_q) = \overline{O}(C_q)$, $I''(C_q) = \underline{O}(C_q)$ resp. $I'''(C_q) = (\overline{O}(C_q), \underline{O}(C_q))$.
3. Display the matching instances.

Alternatively, concept classification can be used, to approximate the results of the retrieval step, or better, to provide approximate retrieval. The method works as follows:

1. Preprocessing. For each $C_j \in \mathcal{T}$, call the retrieval $O(C_j)$ and index the returned instances. Use either strong $I'(C_j) = \overline{O}(C_j)$, weak retrieval $I''(C_j) = \underline{O}(C_j)$ or a combination of both $I'''(C_j) = (\overline{O}(C_j), \underline{O}(C_j))$ as an index.
2. Query formulation. Formulate the query as a concept description.
3. Compute the indices. Use the concept classification C_q to determine its position in the concept hierarchy, i.e. calculate the sets of its direct upper neighbors $\overline{\mathsf{C_q}} = \{\overline{C_{q_1}}, \ldots, \overline{C_{q_n}}\}$ and direct lower neighbors $\underline{\mathsf{C_q}} = \{\underline{C_{q_1}}, \ldots, \underline{C_{q_m}}\}$. Use these sets as indices.
4. Compute the instances to be retrieved. As in the object classification method above, use the indices as the base for computing similarity measures.
5. Display the result.

13.4.3 Incorporating Base Types

One major shortcoming of description logics is that, initially, description logics operated only on the *abstract domain*. In order to refer to concrete values of attributes, such as a force F or a name n, one needs access to base types such as numbers, symbol sets and strings. However, traditionally, this was only possible in description logic systems based on structural subsumption algorithms such as LOOM and CLASSIC. However, their integration of base types was most often ad hoc, and the semantic were unclear.

Baader and Hanschke (1991) and Hanschke (1996) have devised a general method, *concrete domains*, to incorporate base types into description logics without losing soundness and completeness of the inferences. This extension of description logics not only overcomes the deficiency of description logics w.r.t. object-oriented representations, it also allows for the inclusion of background knowledge, such as physical laws, etc. Kamp (1996) and Kamp (1997) discuss admissible concrete domains in the context of different application scenarios.

13.4.4 Summary

Description Logics are a knowledge representation method that has been considered in IR, CBR, and DBMS and hence, can be used to integrate aspects from all these fields. Based on a model-theoretic semantics, they provide a powerful object-oriented representation, together with a set of powerful inferences, that allow for the automatic indexing of instances and classes. On top of these indexing services, traditional similarity measures can be implemented, but, due to the quality of the indices, often simple similarity measures, such as the simple matching coefficient, are sufficient. Concrete domains allow for the integration of primitive data types, such as numbers and strings, without losing soundness and completeness of the inferences. They can also be used to represent and use background knowledge. All in all, description logics are a viable base for building knowledge intensive case-based reasoning applications in a broad spectrum of domains.

13.5 Intelligent Retrieval – Summary and Outlook

The previous sections are best summarized as follows:

> Conceptually, CBR, IR, and DBMS are coming closer together, meeting each other in order to provide the intelligent retrieval techniques over complex, structured data that is needed to realize the applications of tomorrow.

Integrated retrieval methods, combining relational databases, with multidimensional access structures (for geographic information systems, as well as for multimedia data) and IR methods for text retrieval are already available in extensible object-relational databases. Up to now, there are no extension modules available for doing case-based retrieval. Building such a module based on the right multidimensional access structure is, in our opinion, a great opportunity, and should be one focus of future research within CBR.

Another topic of future research within intelligent retrieval is the integration of domain and background knowledge to enhance the semantic of the retrieval. This could be done by considering and integrating techniques from knowledge representation. One approach that was pursued simultaneously and independent within IR, CBR and DB is the use of description logics, a technique that automatically computes semantic indexes of classes, as well as instances, but also is computationally very expensive. In this area, further research includes finding guidelines for finding the right tradeoff between expressiveness and complexity for different application scenarios, the search for approximations, etc.

13.6 Case-Based Reasoning and Learning

In the introduction of this book, the case-based reasoning paradigm is illustrated by a methodological cycle consisting of the main activities retrieve, reuse, revise, and retain. An important phase in this cycle is the retain phase in which the system may be modified as a result of its usage and success in the past. In principal, there are the following options to adapt the system's behavior; new cases may be collected within the case base and/or the similarity concept in use may be tuned. From a certain perspective, the process of changing a system in response to its environment is *learning*. The naturalness of this approach is one of the advantages of the case-based reasoning paradigm.

There are two ways to discuss the relation between case-based reasoning and machine learning; one can analyze the strengths and weaknesses of the above mentioned approach to modify the system's behavior, subsequently called *case-based learning*; or one can suggest ways of combining case-based reasoning and classical machine learning techniques and point out benefits of such combinations. In this section, we focus our attention on the first aspect and show that case-based learning is also a quite powerful approach to improve the behavior of a case-based reasoning system. The second aspect has been addressed in Chapter 3 where the combination of CBR and induction has been explored.

13.6.1 A Formal Framework for Case-Based Learning

Not every change of a CBR-system is a reasonable one. Thus, there is some need to specify the intended learning behavior. In doing so, we borrow some notions from one of the most thoroughly studied areas in machine learning, namely, concept learning (cf. Dietterich and Michalski 1983; Osherson et al. 1986). Here, a learning system is considered to be a computer program that maps *evidence* on a target concept into *hypotheses* about it. Of special interest are scenarios in which the sequence of hypotheses *stabilizes* to an *accurate* and *finite* description of the target concept. Clearly, in this case, some form of learning must have taken place.

Subsequently, we discuss the following scenario: A learning system (or learning algorithm, synonymously) receives evidence about a target concept in the form of labeled examples. The labels indicate whether the corresponding example is a member or a non-member of the target concept, thereby using the labels '+' and '−', respectively. The learning system processes more and more labeled examples and generates, in every learning stage, a hypothesis. Learning systems differ in the way they build and represent their hypotheses. For instance, an ordinary learning system may generate a finite set of rules, a neural net, a decision tree, or any computer program that implements a decision function as its actual hypothesis. In contrast, a case-based learning system (case-based learner, for short) is constraint to represent its actual hypothesis in a case-based fashion; i.e., it has to output a case-based classifier consisting of a finite subset of the set of examples seen so far (the case base) and a similarity measure. We say that a learning system has successfully learned if, after only finitely many learning stages, it comes up with a correct description of the target concept that will be maintained in every subsequent learning stage.

Clearly, it is a rather useless task to design learning systems that are able to learn exactly one concept. Consequently, one is highly interested in learning systems that are suited to learn every concept of a class of concepts. For instance, it seems to be of practical interest to have learning systems that are able to learn every concept that is expressible as a monomial, a decision list or a DNF.

In the formal framework presented above, case-based learners are just ordinary learning systems that are designed to learn every concept from a given concept class. Additionally, case-based learners are requested to output case-based classifiers as their hypotheses. Now, the following questions immediately arise. Firstly, one has to investigate representability issues, since a case-based learner can only stabilize on a correct guess provided that every concept c in the concept class is case-based representable; i.e., there exists a case-based classifier that correctly describes c. Secondly, appropriate techniques have to be elaborated that allow a case-based learner to construct corresponding case-based classifiers. Finally, it seems to be of particular interest to compare the learning capabilities of case-based learners with the capabilities of ordinary learning systems. The latter yields general insight into the pros and cons of case-based learning.

13.6.2 Representability

The answers to the questions posed above heavily depend on the class of concepts to be learned. In order to achieve insight that are of interest within a broader perspective, we investigate the case-based learnability and, prior to this, the case-based representability of indexable concept classes.

Let $\mathcal{X}$ be any set, called the learning domain. Let $\mathcal{C}$ be any subset of the power set of $\mathcal{X}$, and let $c \in \mathcal{C}$; then we refer to $\mathcal{C}$ and c as a concept class and a concept, respectively. A class of concepts $\mathcal{C}$ is said to be an indexable concept classes provided there are an effective enumeration $c_0, c_1, c_2, \ldots$ of all and only the concepts in $\mathcal{C}$ and a recursive predicate p such that, for all $j \in \mathbb{N}$ and all $x \in \mathcal{X}$, $p(x) = 1$ if and only if $x \in c_j$.

For illustration, let us refer to some prominent examples of indexable concept classes. Firstly, let $\mathcal{X}$ be the set of all strings over any finite alphabet of symbols. Then, it follows that the set of all context sensitive languages, context free languages, and regular languages form indexable concept classes. Secondly, let $\mathcal{X}_\backslash$ be the set of all n-bit boolean vectors, and let $\mathcal{X} = \bigcup \mathcal{X}_\backslash$ be the underlying learning domain. Then, it follows that the set of all concepts expressible as a monomial, a DNF, and a decision list form indexable concept classes.

As already mentioned, a case-based classifier is a pair consisting of a finite case base and a similarity measure. Since case-based classifiers should be used to represent concepts, some discussion of the underlying semantics is required. Let $\mathcal{X}$ be a learning domain, let CB be a case base[8], i.e., CB is any finite subset of $\mathcal{X} \times \{+,-\}$. Let σ be a similarity concept, i.e., σ is a recursive function that assigns to any two elements $x, y \in \mathcal{X}$ their similarity, a rational number between 0 and 1. Then it follows that the concept represented by (CB, σ) is the set of all $w \in \mathcal{X}$ meeting the following requirement; there is a positive case $(u,+)$ in CB such that u is more similar to w than every negative case $(v,-)$ belonging to CB, i.e., $\sigma(u,w) > \sigma(v,w)$. Intuitively, w belongs to the represented concept, if all of its nearest neighbors in CB have the label '+.'

Next, let us summarize some of the basic results concerning case-based representability of indexable concept classes. Firstly, given a (recursive) concept c, one can easily define a similarity measure that allows to represent c using a singleton case base and, thus, every indexable concept class is case-based representable. However, from a practical point of view it is more desirable to have universal similarity measures that can be used to represent any concept of a given concept class. If such a measure has been fixed, it becomes much easier to represent each concept of the class in a case-based manner. Now, it suffices to select cases that are appropriate to sit in the case base. Surprisingly, the latter approach really works. Given any indexable concept class $\mathcal{C}$, one can define a similarity measure σ guaranteeing that, for every concept $c \in \mathcal{C}$, there is case base CB_c such that the concept represented by (CB_c, σ) equals c. Moreover, it is sufficient to put at most two cases into the case base provided that $\mathcal{X}$ is an infinite learning domain and, therefore, the concept itself or its complement is infinite.[9]

Finally, let us point to a problem of higher granularity. In some applications, the used similarity concept σ is defined via some underlying distance measure Δ and, therefore, σ inherits some of the properties Δ has. For instance, the similarity measure is necessarily symmetric[10] if it is defined via a metric. Theoretically, it is imaginable that similarity measures having such seemingly natural properties are less expressive. Interestingly, this phenomenon can really be observed. On the fairly concrete level of indexable concept classes, it has been shown that certain concept classes are case-based representable by non-symmetric similarity measures only (cf. Jantke and Lange (1995) for the corresponding details).

13.6.3 Learnability

It is known that, given any indexable concept class $\mathcal{C}$, one can design an ordinary learning algorithm that learns $\mathcal{C}$ from positive and negative examples

---

[8] Naturally, CB should be conflict-free, i.e., for any $x \in \mathcal{X}$, it should not contain $(x,+)$ together with $(x,-)$.

[9] In finite learning domains, the situation is much more complicated (cf. Globig and Lange (1996) for a more comprehensive discussion).

[10] A similarity measure σ is called symmetric, if $\sigma(v,w) = \sigma(w,v)$ for all v, w.

(cf. Gold 1967). Although the algorithm proposed in Gold (1967) is completely different from a case-based learning algorithm, it proves the existence of powerful learning systems. As we will see, one can be equally successful in designing case-based learners.

Firstly, we investigate the capabilities of the most restricted type of case-based learners. Learning algorithms of this type are not allowed to modify the similarity concept in use. Thus, the similarity measure is *a priori* fixed and the learning task reduces to the task of collecting appropriate cases. Surprisingly enough, this simple approach really works, if the learner is allowed to delete cases that have been temporarily stored in the case base; this assumption usually holds (cf. Globig and Lange 1994).

In some case-based systems, as for instance in INRECA (Wess 1995; Wilke and Bergmann 1996a) and PATDEX (Althoff et al. 1990b), the used similarity concepts are also modified during their life-cycles. A comparatively simple and well known approach to model this aspect is based on the idea of assigning weights to the cases sitting in the case base (cf. Cost and Salzberg 1993). Instead of modifying the underlying similarity measure σ itself, the assigned weights will be tuned, only. Thereby, cases that are of higher relevance for the concept to be represented get higher weights. More specifically, a weight α_w is assigned to each case (w, b) sitting in the case base. Thus, the value $\alpha_w \cdot \sigma(w, u)$ (instead of $\sigma(w, u)$ in the standard approach above) represents the similarity between (w, b) and a given $u \in \mathcal{X}$. Note that this approach may result in non-symmetric similarity concepts, even if the underlying similarity measure σ is symmetric. Case-based learners that implement the idea to learn by collecting cases and tuning weights are powerful in the sense that, given any indexable concept class, one can design a case-based learner of that type being able to learn the whole class (cf. Globig et al. 1997). Interestingly, these learners do not need the flexibility to delete cases from their actual case bases, in the overall learning process.

13.7 Summary

Having its origins in cognitive science and computer science, CBR is traditionally interdisciplinary. CBR borrows a number of techniques from other fields in AI and computer science in general; at the same time, these fields more and more use new ideas that originated in CBR.

In this chapter, we have restricted ourselves to a few selected areas related to CBR. We focused on connections to other areas in computer science and artificial intelligence, especially intelligent retrieval aspects and learning techniques. We argued that, concerning the intelligent retrieval of information, the areas of IR, Databases, Knowledge Representation, and CBR are moving in the same direction, and have already reached some kind of intersection in the area of intelligent retrieval of information from data. With respect to learning, we have discussed under which circumstances certain concepts are learnable using a case-based learner.

A. Glossary[1]

Abstraction: Reduction of the level of detail in the description of a case. Abstract cases are used for the organization of the case base and for similarity assessment (cases are considered as similar if they lead to the same abstraction).

Adaptation: Adjusting a retrieved case to fit the given problem situation. It is a consequence of the underlying principle of CBR ("similar problems have similar solutions") that there does not necessarily exist an exact match between a query and the retrieved cases. Simple adaptation processes concern the proportional adjustment of parameters (e.g. price for 5 persons instead of 4), while more complex ones can include the recombination of solutions from several cases (e.g. for planning).

Analogical reasoning: Analogical reasoning is commonly used for the transfer across different domains with special emphasis put to structural dependencies (e.g. the flow of water, of electrons, of heat). In contrast, CBR is usually concerned with the transfer of problem solutions within one domain. Nevertheless, the techniques for the transfer have common characteristics.

Application areas: CBR can be applied to a wide range of tasks, e.g.

- *Classification:* Each case consists of a problem description given as a set of symptoms, a class the case belongs to, and possibly an explanation. Given a new situation with a set of associated symptoms, the goal is to determine the class of that problem situation.
- *Configuration:* Configuration is the construction of an artifact from known parts taking into account the known interrelationships between these parts. In contrast to design, configuration can be modeled as a closed-world problem where classical AI problem solving methods are applicable.
- *Diagnosis:* A case represents observed symptoms of a specific problem situation, e.g., a malfunction in some technical device. The goal is to find the reason for that malfunction and possibly to suggest methods for repairing it. In contrast to classification, usually not all symptoms

[1] Further explanations can be found throughout the book. Please, use the index to locate these.

required for establishing the diagnosis are known at the beginning but have to be derived in a diagnostic process.

Decision support: As in diagnostic applications, a case represents a specific problem situation. However, there is generally no pre-selected element called a *diagnosis*. Rather, each case may be reused in a variety of situations. Hence, each component of a case may potentially play the role of a diagnosis.

Design: Design is the construction of an artifact from parts that my be either known and given or just newly created for this particular artifact. Depending on the degree of creativity involved we distinguish between routine design, innovative design and creative design. CBR is particularly interesting for innovative design tasks where classical AI problem solving methods are not applicable.

Planning: Planning in general consists of the construction of some course of actions to achieve a specified set of goals, starting form an initial situation. While the classical planning process consists mainly of a search through the space of possible sets of operators to solve a given problem, new problems are solved by reusing and combining plans or portions of old plans in case-based planning.

Attribute-Value pair: In the simplest form, a case can be represented as a flat set of attribute-value pairs (↗ attribute vector, feature vector) where every such pair encodes the value of a certain attribute for that case.

Attribute Vector: Special form of a case (or problem) description by encoding the values for a fixed set of attributes (e.g. symptoms for diagnosis). It may permit the application of classical methods from statistics, classification etc., with similarity measures related to distances.

Background knowledge: Cases need interpretations in their domains, especially for similarity assessment and for adaptation. All formalisms of knowledge representation may be useful, but especially terminological systems are widely investigated for CBR.

Case: A case represents the description of a specific episode. It combines facts from different concepts only because of their common occurrence in that episode. It is not necessary (but useful) to have an explanation of that common occurrence.

In a simple standard form, a case consists of two parts: problem description and solution. If the problem description of a case is similar to a given problem, then its solution part is a candidate for the solution of the new problem (may be after an appropriate adaptation).

Cases (especially problem descriptions) must provide means (e.g. indexes) for retrieval, and they must be comparable with respect to similarity to a query (new problem). (↗ Case representation)

Case base: The set of all cases; if equipped with a particular memory structure, this is referred to as ↗ cases memory.

Case-based reasoning: The underlying principle of CBR is expressed by the common life idea that "similar problems have similar solutions". CBR tries to model the acting by experience. Therefore, it needs to maintain a memory of experiences (case memory), the process of reminding (retrieval), the intelligent use of experiences (adaptation) and the update of experiences (learning). (↗ CBR cycle)
CBR can be applied in different domains and under different intentions. Cases can, for example, be used to detect regularities, and to cover the exceptions from these regularities, respectively. It may therefore be related to and may use methods from information retrieval, data bases, statistics, machine learning. Commercial CBR tools can give support for standard applications,
Primary ↗ application areas are those fields where case knowledge plays an important role (e.g., diagnostics, teaching, law, ...). But CBR techniques could be applied in further areas, too (e.g., information gathering for vague queries).

Case completion: A more general view to the *process* of CBR-problem solving, in contrast to viewing cases as fixed entities with a clear distinction between a problem part and a solution part. A new case appears with incomplete and vague information, and the process of problem solving is characterized by collecting new information until a satisfactory level is reached. The contents of the completed case depends on decisions during the problem solving steps (as, for example, in ↗ design).
CBR can guide this process (e.g., with proposals for test and repair in diagnosis) by comparison with more complete cases from the past.

Case memory: The set of all cases organized using a specific memory structure. This structure must support the retrieval (e.g. using indexes). Special attention to the similarity conditions can considerably improve the efficiency (fast access to the most similar cases).

Case representation: The way a single case encodes the knowledge about a specific situation. This can be done in a variety of ways, e.g. using a flat, structured, or object-oriented representation. Also, cases may contain multi-media information.
The representation in the ↗case memory may use only special indexes etc. from the cases for an efficient retrieval, while the cases may be stored in a special database. The case memory implements the access to the complete cases from this data base via related links.

Case Retrieval Net (CRN): Specific form of a ↗ case memory allowing for a flexible and efficient case ↗ retrieval. CRNs implement retrieval by performing ↗ case completion.

CBR cycle: Following the R^4 model, the CBR cycle consists of the following steps:
1) Retrieve: the best matching case(s) from memory;
2) Reuse: the information stored in these case(s);

3) Revise: the solution derived to fit the current situation;
4) Retain: knowledge obtained from that problem solving episode for future usage.

Classification: ↗ Application areas

Closed world assumption (CWA): Special treatment of unknown, missing, or unspecified information: The CWA supposes that only the given information can be true (like in a data base).

Configuration: ↗ Application areas

Constraint: In general, a form of knowledge representation expressing required relationships between objects. In CBR used to express a requirement which a case, a value, a solution etc. must fulfill in order to be applicable for a certain problem situation.

Contextual knowledge: Knowledge about the circumstances in which a case has been observed. Usually, contextual information is not directly part of the case but represented in additional structures.

Database: A widely used method to organize data and to provide access to it. Common are relational and, more recently, object-oriented databases. Databases provide methods for storing huge amount of data, recovery, handling of parallel transactions, and for querying the database using a fairly simple query language such as SQL. In contrast to CBR, however, databases can not cope with the notion of similarity — entries in the database are either identical or different.

Decision support: ↗ Application areas

Decision tree: A specific structure used in particular for classification tasks: Each node of the tree represents a test for a special attribute. The outcome of the tests indicate which subtree to follow for the next tests until the result (a class) is obtained at a leave of the tree. Special techniques are used to construct efficient decision trees. Problems arise for missing values in a test: They require the consideration of all related subtrees.

Design: ↗ Application areas

Diagnosis: ↗ Application areas

Distance: Distances are used as a reverse notion to similarity. Especially in metric spaces (of feature vectors), the notion of neighborhood provides a special similarity measure (e.g., used in *nearest neighbor* approaches, in statistics, classification ...). In this sense, distances (e.g., Euclidean, Manhattan, etc.) are used as reversed similarities.

Domain: Characteristics of a particular application area. These influence all design decision when building a CBR system – from case representation to retrieval and adaptation.

Domain model: Explicit knowledge about an application area that can support CBR. According to the strength of the domain model one may distinguish:

Closed domain: An application area is considered to be a closed domain if the available domain model that can support CBR is fairly strong.

In this case, problems may well be solved using other inference mechanisms. CBR is mainly used as an alternative way of reasoning, for the representation of highly specific exceptions, or for a kind of *short-cuts*.

Open domain: Application areas with only a very weak domain model. CBR will be the primary inference mechanism because of lack of generalized knowledge (rules, models etc.).

Episodic knowledge: An episode is a snapshot of a specific (problem solving) situation. Episodic knowledge is a set of such episodes. Cases can be considered as one way to represent episodic knowledge.

Experience: Knowledge gathered from long-term activities in a special field, from experiencing a wide variety of situations. This type of knowledge clearly distinguishes experts from good novices who mainly have acquired textbook knowledge. CBR attempts to utilize experiences encoded as cases.

Explanation: Besides the actual problem description and the solution, cases often also contain explanations, i.e. causal connections between the initial problem situation, the solution and the observed outcome. This information may be particularly helpful for reusing cases.

Feature vector: ↗ attribute vector

General knowledge: Knowledge about a particular domain which is not directly associated to specific cases, such as general laws, models of devices etc.

Hybrid techniques: Commonly the combination of different techniques, here the combination of CBR with other (usually stronger) techniques. As far as e.g. model knowledge or rule knowledge is available and tractable, this knowledge should preferably be used. Under such conditions, case knowledge can be used to cover the exceptions (the complex knowledge of experts). Machine learning techniques can be used to extract further rules from a case base.

Other techniques may be also used for the representation of ↗ background knowledge.

Indexing: Selection of features that tend to predict solutions and outcomes of cases. Indexes can be used to construct a case memory and to access cases efficiently.

Induction: In the machine learning sense used for hypothizing rules from examples (cases). It provides the replacement of a related cluster of cases by a rule. ↗ Hybrid systems can use cases as far as they do not support a rule (especially exceptional cases), and rules for "standard situations“.

Information retrieval: Research and application area concerned with accessing documents related to a given topic. Like CBR, information retrieval applies approximative methods to assess the relevancy of documents. In contrast to CBR, plain text documents have to be searched and the amount of data is usually much larger than in CBR systems (cf. Section 13.2).

Integration of approaches: CBR draws much of its power from an easy integration with other reasoning paradigms, such as induction, *k*d-trees, information retrieval, databases, etc. (↗ hybrid techniques).

Knowledge: In general, "data with implicit or explicit information about their use for solving problems" (Puppe 1993).

Knowledge representation: Formal framework for encoding the knowledge, including the methods which are used for interpreting the knowledge.

Machine Learning: Subfield of AI that studies the automated acquisition and discovery of domain-specific knowledge for improving problem solving capabilities.
With the retain phase, CBR explicitly includes a stage where learning should occur. Compared to Machine Learning, however, the emphasis in CBR is on problem solving and learning is considered a *byproduct* – whereas Machine Learning focuses on the learning but does not deal with the application of the acquired knowledge.

Model: (Formal) description of a domain containing the structure and the function. It can provide a powerful inference mechanism as far as available and tractable. CBR is often used when model knowledge cannot be used to such an extend. But model knowledge may be needed for CBR reasoners as ↗ background knowledge.

Planning: ↗ Application areas

Retrieval: ↗ CBR cycle

Reuse: ↗ CBR cycle

Revise: ↗ CBR cycle

Retain: ↗ CBR cycle

Rule: A rule describes interrelations between concepts. Thus, it can be considered as the abstraction from cases (which describe interrelations between concrete objects in a concrete episode). Thus, rules provide inferences for standard situations, while cases can be used in the absence of rules.
It was an observation of early expert system development, that knowledge acquisition from experts failed to discover rules, but could collect cases. The knowledge about special cases constitutes the skills of experts.
Rules can be extracted from cases by ↗ induction. Both can be used in ↗ hybrid systems. CBR systems can make use of rules in the ↗ background knowledge.

Similarity: Similarity is a key notion of CBR as already expressed in the fundamental principle of CBR: "similar problems have similar solutions". A deeper analysis identifies the presentation of *useful* proposals from past experiences as the central point of CBR. In this light, similarity (of problem descriptions) is only a vehicle to find useful cases (solutions): Similarity has to be defined in an appropriate way depending on the intended use of the cases. Higher similarity should express higher importance for reminding.

Similarity is used in CBR as the similarity between a query (new problem) and a case from the case memory. In particular, one can distinguish between:

- *Surface similarity:* To assess similarity of objects, only "syntactic" features common to these objects are considered.
- *Structural similarity:* To assess similarity of objects, structures common to these objects are considered, such as relations between the corresponding components.

With respect to the implementation of similarity measures, similarity of cases is often computed on the basis of similarity of the case's features:

- *Local similarity:* Similarity concerns a single feature only.
- *Global similarity:* Similarity of cases is determined based on a holistic view of the cases.

The global similarity of two cases may be computed as the

- combination from their local similarities w.r.t. special attributes (e.g., as a weighted sum of feature similarities), or by
- their relative positions in a (terminological) hierarchy (e.g., by abstraction), or by
- explanation of the common ground and the differences.

In metric (feature) spaces, similarity can be introduced as a reverse notion to ↗ distance.

References

AAAI, 1983. *Proceedings of the 3rd Annual National Conference on Artificial Intelligence AAAI-83*, Washington, D.C., USA, August 1983. AAAI, Morgan Kaufmann Publishers.

AAAI, 1986. *Proceedings of the 5th Annual National Conference on Artificial Intelligence AAAI-86*, Philadelphia, Pennsylvania, USA. AAAI, Morgan Kaufmann Publishers.

AAAI, 1990. *Proceedings of the Annual National Conference on Artificial Intelligence AAAI-90*, Boston, Massachusetts, USA. AAAI, Morgan Kaufmann Publishers.

AAAI, 1991. *Proceedings of the Annual National Conference on Artificial Intelligence AAAI-91*, Annaheim, California, USA. AAAI, Morgan Kaufmann Publishers.

AAAI, 1994. *Proceedings of the Annual National Conference on Artificial Intelligence AAAI-94*. AAAI, Morgan Kaufmann Publishers.

AAMODT, A., 1991. *A Knowledge-Intensive, Integrated Approach to Problem Solving and Sustained Learning*. Ph.D. thesis, University of Trondheim.

AAMODT, A., 1993. Explanation-Driven Cased Based Reasoning. In (Wess, Althoff, and Richter 1993b), pages 274 – 288.

AAMODT, A., 1995. Knowledge Acquisition and learning by experience the role of case-specific knowledge. In Kodratoff and Tecuci, editors, *Machine Learning and Knowledge Acquisition - Integrated Approaches*, pages 197–245. Academic Press.

AAMODT, A. and PLAZA, E., 1994. Case-based reasoning: foundational issues, methodological variations, and system approaches. *AI Communications*, 7(1):39–59.

AAMODT, A. and VELOSO, M., editors, 1995. *Case-Based Reasoning Research and Development, Proceedings ICCBR-95*, Lecture Notes in Artificial Intelligence, 1010. Springer Verlag. ISBN 3-540-60598-3.

AARONSON, J. S., HAAS, J., and OVERTON, C., 1993. Knowledge Discovery in GenBank. In *International Conference on Intelligent Systems for Molekular Biology (ISMB)*, pages 251–259.

AARTS, R. J. and J. ROUSU, J., 1996. Towards CBR for Bioprocess Planning. In (Smith and Faltings 1996), pages 16–27.

ADAMS, D. A., IRGENS, C., LEES, B., and MACARTHUR, E., 1997. Using case outcome to integrate customer feedback into the quality function deployment process. In (Bergmann and Wilke 1997), pages 1–9.

AHA, D. W., 1991. Case-Based Learning Algorithms. In (Bareiss 1991), pages 147 – 158.

AHA, D. W., KIBLER, D., and ALBERT, M. K., 1991. Instance-Based Learning Algorithms. *Machine Learning*, 6:37–66.

AID, 1992. *Case-Based Design Systems*, A Workshop of AID-92. AID, Carnegie Mellon University, Pittsburgh, USA.

AIPS, 1994. *Proceedings of the 2nd Int. Conference on AI Planning Systems (AIPS-94)*. AIPS.

ALEVEN, V. and ASHLEY, K. D., 1996. How Different is Different? In (Smith and Faltings 1996), pages 1–15.

ALLEN, J. F., 1984. Towards a general theory of action and time. *Artificial Intelligence*, 23(2):123–154.

ALTHOFF, K.-D., 1992. *Eine fallbasierte Lernkomponente als integrierter Bestandteil der* MOLTKE-*Werkbank zur Diagnose technischer Systeme*. Ph.D. thesis, Dept. of Computer Science, University of Kaiserslautern, Germany.

ALTHOFF, K.-D., 1996. The INRECA case study. Postdoctoral thesis, University of Kaiserslautern.

ALTHOFF, K.-D. and AAMODT, A., 1996a. Relating case-based problem solving and learning methods to task and domain characteristics: Towards an analytic framework. *AI Communications*, 9(3):109–116.

ALTHOFF, K.-D. and AAMODT, A., 1996b. Zur Analyse fallbasierter Problemlöse- und Lernmethoden in Abhängigkeit von Charakteristika gegebener Aufganstellungen und Anwendungsdomänen. *Künstliche Intelligenz, Themenheft Fallbasiertes Schließen*, 10(1):10–15.

ALTHOFF, K.-D., AURIOL, E., BARLETTA, R., and MANAGO, M., 1995a. *A Review of Industrial Case-Based Reasoning Tools*. AI Intelligence, Oxford. ISBN 1-898804-01-X.

ALTHOFF, K.-D. and BARTSCH-SPÖRL, B., 1996. Decision support for case-based applications. *Wirtschaftsinformatik, Schwerpunktheft Fallbasierte Entscheidungsunterstützung*, 38(1):8–16.

ALTHOFF, K.-D., BERGMANN, R., WESS, S., MANAGO, M., AURIOL, E., LARICHEV, O. I., BOLOTOV, A., ZHURAVLEV, Y. I., and GUROV, S. I., 1998. Integration of Induction and Case-Based Reasoning for Decision Support Tasks in Medical Domains: The INRECA Approach. *To appear in: AI in Medicine Journal*.

ALTHOFF, K.-D., MAURER, F., and REHBOLD, R., 1990a. Multiple Knowlegde Acquisition Strategies in MOLTKE. In B. Wielinga, J. Boose, B. Gaines, G. Schreiber, and M. van Someren, editors, *Proceedings of the 4th European Knowledge Acquisition Workshop EKAW'90*. IOS, Amsterdam.

ALTHOFF, K.-D., MAURER, F., and WESS, S., 1990b. Case-Based Reasoning and Adaptive Learning in the MOLTKE 3 Workbench for Technical Diagnosis. SEKI-Report SR-91-05 (SFB), Dept. of Computer Science, University of Kaiserslautern, Germany.

ALTHOFF, K.-D., RICHTER, M. M., and WILKE, W., 1997. Case-Based Reasoning: A New Technology for Experienced Based Construction of Knowledge Systems. Technical report, University of Berkeley / Center for LSA, University of Kaiserslautern.

ALTHOFF, K.-D. and WESS, S., 1991. Case-Based Knowledge Acquisition, Learning and Problem Solving for Diagnostic Real World Tasks. In *Proceedings of the 5th European Knowledge Acquisition Workshop EKAW'91*.

ALTHOFF, K.-D., WESS, S., BARTSCH-SPÖRL, B., and JANETZKO, D., editors, 1992. *Ähnlichkeit von Fällen in Systemen des fallbasierten Schließens*, University of Kaiserslautern. SEKI Working Paper SWP-92-11.

ALTHOFF, K.-D., WESS, S., WEIS, K.-H., AURIOL, E., BERGMANN, R., HOLZ, H., JOHNSTON, R., MANAGO, M., MEISSONNIER, A.AND PRIEBISCH, C., R., T., and W., W., 1995b. An evaluation of the final integrated system. Technical report, Esprit Project INRECA Deliverable D6.

ALTHOFF, K.-D. and WILKE, W., 1997. Potential uses of case-based reasoning in experienced based construction of software systems and business process support. In (Bergmann and Wilke 1997), pages 31–38.

ANALOG DEVICES, 1995. The Board of Analog Devices. Analog Devices Annual Report.

ANDERSON, J. R., 1988. A Spreading Activation Theory of Memory. In A. M. Collins and E. E. Smith, editors, *Readings in Cognitive Science*, chapter 2.4, pages 137–145. Morgan Kaufmann.

ANDERSON, J. R., 1989. A Theory of the Origins of Human Knowledge. *Artificial Intelligence*, 40(1–3):313–351. Special Volume on Machine Learning.

ANDERSON, J. R., BOYLE, C. F., CORBETT, A. T., and LEWIS, M. W., 1990. Cognitive modeling and intelligent tutoring. *Artificial Intelligence*, 42(1):7–49.

ANDERSON, J. R., CONRAD, F. G., and CORBETT, A. T., 1989. Skill acquisition and the LISP tutor. *Cognitive Science*, 13:467–505.

ARMENGOL, E. and PLAZA, E., 1993. A Knowledge Level Model of Case-Based Reasoning. In (Wess, Althoff, and Richter 1993b), pages 53 – 64.

ASHLEY, K. D. and ALEVEN, V., 1991. A Computational Approach to Explaining Case-Based Concepts of Relevance in a Tutorial Context. In (Bareiss 1991), pages 257 – 268.

ASHLEY, K. D. and ALEVEN, V., 1993. A Logical Representation for Relevance Criteria. In (Wess, Althoff, and Richter 1993b), pages 338 – 352.

AURIOL, E., ALTHOFF, K.-D., WESS, S., and DITTRICH, S., 1994. Integrating Induction and Case-Based Reasoning: Methodological Approach and First Evaluations. In (Keane, Haton, and Manago 1994), pages 18–32.

AURIOL, E., WESS, S., MANAGO, M., ALTHOFF, K.-D., and TRAPHÖNER, R., 1995. INRECA: A seamlessly integrated system based on inductive inference and case-based reasoning. In (Aamodt and Veloso 1995), pages 371–380. ISBN 3-540-60598-3.

BAADER, F., BUCHHEIT, M., JEUSFELD, M. A., and NUTT, W., editors, 1995. *Reasoning about structured objects – Knowledge Representation meets Databases, Proceedings of the 2nd Workshop*, volume 1 of *CEUR Workshop Proceedings*, Bielefeld, Germany.

BAADER, F., BUCHHEIT, M., JEUSFELD, M. A., and NUTT, W., editors, 1996. *Knowledge Representation meets Databases, Proceedings of the 3rd Workshop*, volume 4 of *CEUR Workshop Proceedings*, Budapest, Hungary.

BAADER, F., BÜRCKERT, H., HOLLUNDER, B., LAUX, A., and NUTT, W., 1992. Terminologische Logiken. *KI*, 6(3):23–33.

BAADER, F. and HANSCHKE, P., 1991. A Scheme for Integrating Concrete Domains into Concept Languages. In (Mylopoulos and Reiter 1991), pages 452–457.

BAADER, F. and HOLLUNDER, B., 1990. KRIS: Knowledge Representation and Inference System – System Description. Technical Memo TM-90-03, DFKI.

BABEL, L. and TINHOFER, G., 1990. A branch and bound algorithm for the maximum clique problem. *ZOR – Methods and Models of Operations-Research*, 34:207–217.

BAIN, W. M., 1986. A Case-Based Reasoning System for Subjective Assessment. In (AAAI 1986), pages 523–527.

BAJCSY, R., editor, 1993. *Proceedings of the 13th International Conference on Artificial Intelligence IJCAI-89*.

BARBER, J., BHATTA, S., GOEL, A., JACOBSON, M., PEARCE, M., PENBERTHY, L., SHANKAR, M., SIMPSON, R., and STROULIA, E., 1992.

AskJef: Integration of case-based and multimedia technologies for interface design support. In J. S. Gero, editor, *AI in Design'92*, pages 457–475. Kluwer Academic Publishers, Dordrecht.

BAREISS, R., 1989. *Exemplar-Based Knowledge Acquisition: A unified Approach to Concept Representation, Classification and Learning*. Academic Press.

BAREISS, R., editor, 1991. *Proceedings: Case-Based Reasoning Workshop*. Morgan Kaufmann Publishers.

BARLETTA, R., 1993. Case-based reasoning and information retrieval: Opportunities for technology sharing. *IEEE Expert*, 8(6):2–4.

BARLETTA, R. and HENNESSY, D., 1989. Case Adaptation in Autoclave Layout Design. In (Hammond 1989b), pages 203 – 207.

BARR, J. M. and MAGALDI, R. V., 1996. Corporate Knowledge Management for the Millenium. In (Smith and Faltings 1996), pages 487–496.

BARRETT, A. and WELD, D., 1994. Partial-order planning: Evaluating possible efficiency gains. *Artificial Intelligence*, 67(1):71–112.

BARROW, H. G. and BURSTALL, R. M., 1976. Subgraph isomorphism relational structures and maximal cliques. *Information Processing Letters*, 4:83–84.

BARTLETT, R., 1932. *Remembering: A study in experimental and social psychology*. Cambridge University Press, London.

BARTSCH-SPÖRL, B., 1996a. How to introduce case-based reasoning in customer support. Technical report, Esprit Project APPLICUS Deliverable D3.

BARTSCH-SPÖRL, B., 1996b. How to make CBR systems work in practice. In (Burkhard and Lenz 1996), pages 36–42.

BARTSCH-SPÖRL, B., 1997. How to introduce CBR applications in customer support. In (Bergmann and Wilke 1997).

BARTSCH-SPÖRL, B., ALTHOFF, K.-D., and MEISSONNIER, A., 1997. Reasoning About Case-Based Reasoning Systems. In P. Mertens and H. Voss, editors, *4th German Conference on Expert Systems*, pages 115–128. infix Verlag, Sankt Augustin, Germany. Proceedings in Artificial Intelligence 6.

BARTSCH-SPÖRL, B. and TAMMER, E.-C., 1994. Graph-based approach to structural similarity. In A. Voß, editor, *Similarity Concepts and Retrieval Methods*, volume 13 of *Fabel-Reports*, pages 45–58. GMD, Sankt Augustin.

BASILI, V. R., CALDIERA, G., and ROMBACH, H. D., 1994a. Experience Factory. In J. J. Marciniak, editor, *Encyclopedia of Software Engineering, volume 1*, pages 469–476. John Wiley & Sons.

BASILI, V. R., CALDIERA, G., and ROMBACH, H. D., 1994b. Goal Question Metric Paradigm. In J. J. Marciniak, editor, *Encyclopedia of Software Engineering, volume 1*, pages 528–532. John Wiley & Sons.

BASILI, V. R. and ROMBACH, H. D., 1991. Support for comprehensive reuse. *IEEE Software Engineering Journal*, 6(5):303–316.

BASILI, V. R. and TURNER, A. J., 1975. Iterative Enhancement: A practical technique for software development. *IEEE Transactions on Software Engineering*, 4(1).

BAUDIN, M., MANAGO, M., ALTHOFF, K.-D., TRAPHÖNER, R., and SEAN, B., 1996. The legacy of INRECA - 27/5/92 - 27/11/95. INRECA deliverable d28, Esprit Project 6322.

BAYER, M., HERBIG, B., and WESS, S., 1992. Ähnlichkeit und Ähnlichkeitsmaße. In *Fallbasiertes Schließen - Eine Übersicht, Vol.1*, SEKI Working Paper SWP-92-08 8, pages 135–153. Universität Kaiserslautern.

BEAM, C. and SEGEV, A., 1996. Electronic Catalogs and Negotiations. CITM Working Paper 96-WP-1016, Fisher Center for Information Technology and Managment, University of California, Berkely. Available at http://haas.berkly.edu/ citm/nego-proj.html.

BEAM, C. and SEGEV, A., 1997. Automated Negotiations: A Survey of the State of the Art. CITM Working Paper, Fisher Center for Information Technology and Managment, University of California, Berkely.

BECK, J. R., O'DONNEL, J. F., HIRAI, F., SIMMONS, J. J., HEALY, J. C., and LYON, H. C. J., 1989. Computer-based Exercises in Anemia Diagnosis, (PlanAlyzer). *Meth. Inf. Med*, 28:364–369.

BELL, D. A., GUAN, J. W., and LEE, S. K., 1996. Generalized union and project operations for pooling uncertain and imprecise information. *Data & Knowledge Engineering*, 18:89–117.

BENEVENTANO, D. and BERGAMASCHI, S., 1997. Incoherence and subsumption for recursive views and queries in obejct-oriented data models. *Data & Knowledge Engineering*, 21:217–252.

BENTLEY, J. L., 1975. Multidimensional binary search trees used for associative searching. *Communications of the ACM*, 18(9):509–517.

BENTLEY, J. L., 1979. Multidimensional binary search in database applications. *IEEE Transactions on Software Engineering*, 4(5):333–340.

BENTLEY, J. L. and FRIEDMAN, J. H., 1979. Data structures for range searching. *ACM Computing Surveys*, 11(4):397–409.

BERGER, J., 1989. Roentgen: A Case-Based Approach to Radiation Therapy Planning. In (Hammond 1989b), pages 218 – 223.

BERGMANN, R., 1996. *Effizientes Problemlösen durch flexible Wiederverwendung von Fällen auf verschiedenen Abstraktionsebenen.*

Ph.D. thesis, Universität Kaiserslautern. Available as DISKI 138, infix Verlag.

BERGMANN, R., BREEN, S., GÖKER, M., MANAGO, M., SCHUMACHER, J., STAHL, A., TARTARIN, E., WESS, S., and WILKE, W., 1998. The INRECA-II Methodology for Building and Maintaining CBR Applications. In (Gierl and Lenz 1998).

BERGMANN, R. and EISENECKER, U., 1995. Case-based reasoning for supporting reuse of object-oriented software: A case study (in German). In (Richter and Maurer 1995), pages 152–169. Proceedings in Artificial Intelligence 2.

BERGMANN, R., PEWS, G., and WILKE, W., 1993. Explanation-Based Similarity: A Unifiying Approach for Integrating Domain Knowledge into Case-Based Reasoning for Diagnosis and Planning Tasks. In (Wess, Althoff, and Richter 1993b), pages 182–196.

BERGMANN, R. and WILKE, W., 1995a. Building and refining abstract planning cases by change of representation language. *Journal of Artificial Intelligence Research*, 3:53–118.

BERGMANN, R. and WILKE, W., 1995b. Learning abstract planning cases. In N. Lavrač and S. Wrobel, editors, *Machine Learning: ECML-95, 8th European Conference on Machine Learning, Heraclion, Greece, April 1995*, number 912 in Lecture Notes in Artificial Intelligence, pages 55–76. Springer, Berlin. ISBN 3-540-59286-5.

BERGMANN, R. and WILKE, W., 1996. On the role of abstraction in case-based reasoning. In (Smith and Faltings 1996), pages 28–43.

BERGMANN, R. and WILKE, W., editors, 1997. *5th German Workshop on CBR — Foundations, Systems, and Applications —*, Report LSA-97-01E, Kaiserslautern. University of Kaiserslautern.

BERGMANN, R., WILKE, W., ALTHOFF, K.-D., JOHNSTON, R., and BREEN, S., 1997a. Ingredients for developing a case-based reasoning methodology. In (Bergmann and Wilke 1997), pages 49–58.

BERGMANN, R., WILKE, W., and SCHUMACHER, J., 1997b. Using software process modeling for building a case-based reasoning methodology: Basic approach and case study. In (Leake and Plaza 1997), pages 509–518. ISBN 3-540-63233-6.

BHAT, R. R., 1995. An agent approach to case adaptation. In *ICMAS '95, Proceedings of the First International Conference on Multi Agent Systems*.

BHATTA, S., 1995. *Model-based analogy in innovative device design*. Ph.D. thesis, Georgia Institute of Technology, College of Computing, Atlanta, GA.

BICHINDARITZ, I., 1994. A Case-Based Reasoning System Using a Control Case-Base. In A. G. Cohn, editor, *Proceedings 11th European Conference on Artificial Intelligence ECAI'94*. John Wiley and Sons.

BIRK, A., 1997. Modeling the application domains of software engineering technologies. Techn. report 014.97/e, Fraunhofer IESE, Kaiserslautern, Germany.

BLADEL, P. G., 1995. *Design of Fibre Reinforced Composite Panels for Aerospace Applications*. Ph.D. thesis, Faculty of Aerospace Engineering, Delft University of Technology.

BOEHM, B. W., 1981. *Software Engineering Economics*. Prentice-Hall, Englewood Cliffs, NJ.

BOEHM, B. W., 1988. A spiral model of software development and enhancement. *IEEE Communications*, 21(5):61–72.

BONAR, J. and CUNNINGHAM, R., 1988. BRIDGE: An intelligent tutor for thinking about programming. In J. Self, editor, *Artificial intelligence and human learning: Intelligent computer-aided instruction*, pages 391–409. Chapman & Hall, London.

BOOCH, G., 1991. *Object Oriented Desing with Applications*. Benjamin/Cummings.

BOOCH, G., 1994. *Object-Oriented Design with Applications*. Benjamin/Cummings.

BÖRNER, K., 1993. Structural similarity as guidance in case-based design. In (Wess, Althoff, and Richter 1993b), pages 197–208.

BÖRNER, K., 1995a. Conceptual analogy. In D. W. Aha and A. Ram, editors, *AAAI 1995 Fall Symposium Series: Adaptation of Knowledge for Reuse*, pages 5–11. November 10-12, Boston, MA.

BÖRNER, K., 1995b. Interactive, adaptive, computer aided design. In M. Tan and R. Teh, editors, *The Global Design Studio – Proceedings of the 6th International Conference on Computer-Aided Architectural Design Futures*, pages 627–634. Centre for Advanced Studies in Architecture, National University of Singapore, Singapore.

BÖRNER, K., 1995c. Modules for design support. Fabel-Report 35, Gesellschaft für Mathematik und Datenverarbeitung mbH (GMD), Sankt Augustin.

BÖRNER, K., 1997. *Konzeptbildende Analogie: Integration von Conceptual Clustering und Analogem Schließen zur effizienten Unterstützung von Entwurfsaufgaben*. Ph.D. thesis, Universität Kaiserslautern. Available as DISKI 177, infix Verlag.

BÖRNER, K. and FASSAUER, R., 1995. Analogical layout design (Syn*). In K. Börner, editor, *Modules for Design Support*, volume 35 of *Fabel-Report*, pages 59–68. GMD, Sankt Augustin.

BÖRNER, K., JANTKE, K. P., SCHÖNHERR, S., and TAMMER, E.-C., 1993. Lernszenarien im fallbasierten Schließen. Fabel-Report 14, GMD, Sankt Augustin.

BÖRNER, K., PIPPIG, E., TAMMER, E.-C., and COULON, C.-H., 1996. Structural similarity and adaptation. In (Smith and Faltings 1996), pages 58–75.

BRACHMAN, R. J. and SCHMOLZE, J. G., 1985. An overview of the KL-ONE knowledge representation system. *Cognitive Science*, 9(2):171–216.

BRADBURN, C. and ZELEZNIKOW, J., 1993. The Application of Case Based Reasoning to the Tasks of Health Care Planning. In (Wess, Althoff, and Richter 1993b), pages 365 – 378.

BREWKA, G., HABEL, C., and NEBEL, B., editors, 1997. *KI-97: Advances in Artificial Intelligence*, Lecture Notes in Artificial Intelligence, 1303. Springer Verlag.

BRON, C. and KERBOSCH, J., 1973. Finding all cliques in an undirected graph. *Communications of the ACM*, 16:575–577.

BROWN, C. M., DANZIG, P. B., HARDY, D. R., MANBER, U., and SCHWARTZ, M. F., 1995. The Harvest information discovery and access system. *Computer Networks and ISDN Systems*, 28(1-2):119–126.

BROWN, D. and CHANDRASEKARAN, B., 1985. Expert Systems for a class of mechanical design activity. In J. Gero, editor, *Knowledge Engineering in Computer-Aided Design*. Amsterdam: North Holland.

BROWN, M. G., 1993. An Under-Lying Memory Model to Support Case Retrieval. In (Wess, Althoff, and Richter 1993b), pages 132–143.

BROWN, M. G., 1994. *A memory model for case retrieval by activation passing*. Ph.D. thesis, University of Manchester, Manchester, England.

BRÜNINGHAUS, S. and ASHLEY, K. D., 1997. Using Machine Learning for Assigning Indices to Textual Cases. In (Leake and Plaza 1997), pages 303–312. ISBN 3-540-63233-6.

BRUSILOVSKY, P., SPECHT, M., and WEBER, G., 1995. Towards adaptive learning environments. In F. Huber-Waäschle, H. Schauer, and P. Widmayer, editors, *Herausforderungen eines globalen Informationsverbundes für die Informatik: GISI-95*, pages 322–329. Springer Verlag, Berlin.

BRUSILOVSKY, P. and WEBER, G., 1996. Collaborative example selection in an intelligent example-based programming environments. In D. C. Edelson and E. A. Domeshek, editors, *Proceedings of the International Conference on Learning Sciences, ICLS-96*, pages 357–362. AACE, Evanston, IL, USA.

BUNDY, A., VAN HARMELEN, F., HESKETH, J., and SMAILL, A., 1991. Experiments with proof plans for induction. *Journal of Automated Reasoning*, 7:303–324.

BURKE, R., HAMMOND, K., KULYUKIN, V., LYTINEN, S., TOMURO, N., and SCHOENBERG, S., 1997a. Natural Language Proessing in the FAQ Finder System: Results and Prospects. In *Working Notes AAAI Spring Symposium NLP for the WWW*. Stanford University, CA.

BURKE, R., HAMMOND, K., KULYUKIN, V., LYTINEN, S., TOMURO, N., and SCHOENBERG, S., 1997b. Question Answering from Frequently Asked Question Files. *AI Magazine*, 18(2):57–66.

BURKHARD, H.-D., 1995a. Case Retrieval Nets. Techn. report, Humboldt University, Berlin.

BURKHARD, H.-D., 1995b. Case Retrieval Nets and Cognitive Modelling. Techn. report, Humboldt University, Berlin. Extended abstract in Workshop "From AI to Cognitive Science, and Back". In L. Dreschler-Fischer, S. Pribbenow (Eds.): KI-95 Activities: Workshops, Posters, Demos. Gesellschaft für Informatik, 1995, pp.53-54.

BURKHARD, H.-D., 1995c. Case Retrieval Nets and Cognitive Modelling (Extended Abstract). In L. Dreschler-Fischer and S. Pribbenow, editors, *KI-95 Activities: Workshops, Posters, Demos*, pages 53–54. Gesellschaft für Informatik, Bonn.

BURKHARD, H.-D., 1997. Cases, Information, and Agents. In P. Kandzia and M. Klusch, editors, *Cooperative Information Agents: Proceedings First Int. Workshop CIA'97*, volume 1202 of *Lecture Notes in Artificial Intelligence*, pages 64–79. Springer Verlag, Berlin.

BURKHARD, H.-D., 1998. Information Gathering for Vague Queries Using Case Retrieval Nets. In I. Balderjahn, R. Mathar, and S. Martin, editors, *Classification, Data Analysis, and Data Highways*, Studies in Classification, Data Analysis, and Knowledge Organization, pages 345–354. Springer Verlag, Berlin.

BURKHARD, H.-D. and LENZ, M., editors, 1996. *4th German Workshop on CBR — System Development and Evaluation —*, Informatik-Berichte, Berlin. Humboldt University.

BURKHARD, H.-D., LINDEMANN, G., LOENING, S. A., and NEYMEYER, J., 1996. Remembering the Unexpected Cases - CBR for Experts in Urology. In *Proceedings ECAI-96-WS Intelligent Data Analysis in Medicine and Pharmacology*, pages 11–14.

BUROW, R. and WEBER, G., 1996. Example explanation in learning environments. In C. Frasson, G. Gauthier, and A. Lesgold, editors, *Intelligent Tutoring Systems - Proceedings of the Third International Conference, ITS '96*, pages 457–465. Springer Verlag, Berlin.

BYLANDER, T., 1991. Complexity results for planning. In (Mylopoulos and Reiter 1991), pages 274–279.

CARBONELL, J. G., 1983a. Derivational Analogy and Its Role in Problem Solving. In (AAAI 1983).

CARBONELL, J. G., 1983b. Learning by Analogy: Formulating and Generalizing Plans from Past Experience. In R. Michalski, J. G. Carbonell, and T. Mitchell, editors, *Machine Learning: An Artificial Intelligence Approach*, volume 1. Tioga, Palo Alto, California.

CARBONELL, J. G., 1986. Derivational analogy: a theory of reconstructive problem solving and expertise acquisition. In R. Michalski, J. Carbonnel, and T. Mitchell, editors, *Machine Learning: an Artificial Intelligence Approach*, volume 2, pages 371–392. Morgan Kaufmann, Los Altos, CA. ISBN 0-934613-00-1.

CARBONELL, J. G., KNOBLOCK, C. A., and MINTON, S., 1991. Prodigy: An integrated architecture for planning and learning. In K. VanLehn, editor, *Architectures for Intelligence*, pages 241–278. Lawrence Erlbaum Associates, Publishers.

CARR, B. and GOLDSTEIN, I., 1977. Overlays: A theory of modelling for computer aided instruction. AI Memo 406, MIT AI Laboratory, Cambridge, MA.

Casuel, 1994. CASUEL: A Common Case Representation Language. ESPRIT Project 6322 Deliverable D1, University of Kaiserslautern, Kaiserslautern.

CBR-AAAI-WS, 1993. *Working Notes AAAI Spring Symposium Series – Symposium Cased-Based Reasoning and Information Retrieval – Exploring the opportunities for Technology Sharing*, Menlo Park, CA. AAAI, AAAI Press.

CHAVEZ, A. and MAES, P., 1996. Kasbah: An Agent Marketplace for Buying and Selling Goods. In *Proceedings of the First International Conference on the Practical Application of Intelligent Agents and Multi-Agent Technology*. London, U.K.

CHI, M. T. H., BASSOK, M., M, L., REIMANN, P., and GLASER, R., 1989. Self-explanations: How students study and use examples in learning to solve problems. *Cognitive Science*, 13:145–182.

CHIARAMELLA, Y. and CHEVALLET, J. P., 1992. About Retrieval Models and Logic. *The Computer Journal*, 35(3):233–243.

CLANCEY, W. J., 1985. Heuristic Classification. *Artificial Intelligence*, 27(3):289–350.

CLIFF, A. D., HAGGETT, P., and ORD, J. K., 1986. *Spatial Aspects of Influenza Epidemies*. Pion Limited, London.

COHEN, P. R., 1989. Evaluation and Case-Based Reasoning. In (Hammond 1989b), pages 168–172.

COLLINS, A. and BROWN, J. S., 1988. The computer as a tool for learning through reflection. In H. Mandl and A. Lesgold, editors, *Learning issues for intelligent tutoring systems*, pages 1–18. Springer Verlag, New York.

COLLINS, A. M. and LOFTUS, E. F., 1988. A Spreading Activation Theory of Semantic Processing. In A. M. Collins and E. E. Smith, editors, *Readings in Cognitive Science*, chapter 2.3, pages 126–136. Morgan Kaufmann.

CONNELLY, D. P. and JOHNSON, P. E., 1980. The Medical Problem Solving Process. *Human Pathology*, 11:412–419.

COST, S. and SALZBERG, S., 1993. A Weighted Nearest Neighbor Algorithm for Learning with Symbolic Features. *Machine Learning*, 10(1):56–78.

COULON, C.-H., 1995. Automatic indexing, retrieval and reuse of topologies in complex designs. In P. J. Pahl and H. Werner, editors, *Proceeding of the Sixth International Conference on Computing in Civil and Building Engineering*, pages 749–754. Balkema, Rotterdam, Berlin.

COYNE, R., 1988. *Logic models of design*. Pitman Publishing.

COYNE, R. D., ROSENMAN, M. A., RADFORD, A. D., BALACHANDRAN, M., and GERO, J. S., 1988. *Knowledge-based design systems*. Addison-Wesley, Reading, MA.

COYNE, R. D., ROSENMAN, M. A., RADFORD, A. D., and GERO, J. S., 1987. Innovation and creativity in knowledge-based CAD. In J. S. Gero, editor, *Expert Systems in Computer-Aided Design*, pages 435–465. North-Holland, Amsterdam.

CRESTANI, F. and RIJSBERGEN, K. v., 1995. Probability Kinematics in Information Retrieval: A case study. In *Proc. SIGIR 95*. ACM Press, Seattle, WA.

CUNIS, R., GÜNTHER, A., and STRECKER, H., 1991. *Das PLAKON-Buch*. Number 266 in Informatik Fachberichte. Springer, Berlin.

CUNNINGHAM, P. and SLATTERY, S., 1993. Knowledge Engineering Requirements in Derivational Analogy. In (Wess, Althoff, and Richter 1993b), pages 234–245.

CURET, O. and JACKSON, M., 1996. Towards a methodology for case-based systems. In *Expert Systems 96: Proceedings of the 16th annual workshop of the British Computer Science Society*.

CZAP, H., 1997. CBR as a Mean for Developing Adaptive Business Systems. In (Bergmann and Wilke 1997), pages 75–84.

DANIELS, J. J. and RISSLAND, E. L., 1997. What You Saw Is What You Want: Using Cases to Seed Information. In (Leake and Plaza 1997), pages 325–336. ISBN 3-540-63233-6.

DASARATHY, B., 1990. *Nearest Neighbor Norms: NN Pattern Classification Techniques*. IEEE Computer Society Press.

de Dombal, F., D, L., Horrocks, J., Staniland, J., and McCann, A., 1972. Computer-aided diagnosis of acute abdominal pain. *British Med J*, 2:9–13.

DeJong, G., 1988. An introduction to explanation-based learning. In H. E. Shrobe, editor, *Exploring artificial intelligence*, pages 45–81. Morgan Kaufmann Publishers, San Mateo, CA.

Dellen, B., Maurer, F., and Jürgen Muench, M. V., 1997a. Enriching Software Process Support by Knowledge-based Techniques. *Int. Journal of Software Engineering and Knowledge Engineering*, 7(2):185–215.

Dellen, B., Pews, G., and Maurer, F., 1997b. Knowledge Based Techniques to Increase the Flexibility of Workflow Management. *Data & Knowledge Engineering Journal.*

Deming, W. E., 1996. *Out of the Crisis*. MIT Press, Cambridge.

deSarbo, W. S., 1992. TSCALE: A new multidemensional scaling procedure based on Tversky's contrast model. *Psychometrika*, 57:43–69.

Dietterich, T. G. and Michalski, R. S., 1983. A comparative review of selected methods for learning from examples. In R. S. Michalski, J. G. Carbonell, and T. M. Mitchell, editors, *Machine Learning: An Artificial Intelligence Approach*, volume I, chapter 3. Morgan Kaufmann, Los Altos, California.

Domeshek, E. A. and Kolodner, J. L., 1992. A case-based design aid for architecture. In J. S. Gero, editor, *Artificial Intelligence in Design '92*, pages 497–516. AID, Kluwer Academic Publishers, Dordrecht, Pittsburgh.

Domeshek, E. A. and Kolodner, J. L., 1997. The designer's muse. In (Maher and Pu 1997), pages 11–38. ISBN 0-8058-2313-1.

Doyle, J., 1979. A Truth Maintenance System. *Artificial Intelligence*, 12(3):231–272.

Drabble, B., editor, 1996. *Proceedings of the 3rd Int. Conference on AI Planning Systems (AIPS-96)*. AAAI-Press.

Du, Z. and McCalla, G., 1991. CBMIP - A case-based mathematics instructional planner. In L. Birnbaum, editor, *Proceedings of The International Conference on the Learning Sciences*, pages 122–129. AACE, Charlottesville, VA.

Edelson, D. C., 1991. Why Do Cheetahs Run Fast? Responsive Questioning in a Case-Based Teaching System. In L. Birnbaum, editor, *Proceedings of The International Conference on the Learning Sciences*, pages 138–144. AACE, Charlottesville, VA.

El-Gamal, S., Rafeh, M., and Eissa, I., 1993. Case-based reasoning algorithm applied in a medical acquisition tool. *Medical Informatics*, 18:149–162.

ENZINGER, A., PUPPE, F., and STRUBE, G., 1994. Problemlösen ohne Suchen? *KI*, 8(1):73–81.

ETZIONI, O., 1993. Acquiring search-control knowledge via static analysis. *Artificial Intelligence*, 62(2):255–301.

ETZIONI, O. and WELD, D., 1994. A Softbot-Based Interface to the Internet. *Comm. of ACM*, 37(7):72–76.

EVANGELIDIS, G., LOMET, D., and SALZBERG, B., 1997. The hB^{Π}-Tree: A multi-attribute index supporting concurrency, recovery and node consolidation. *The VLDB Journal*, 6:1–25.

EVANS, C. D., 1996. A case-based assistant for diagnosis and avalying of dysmorphic syndromes. In *Yearbook of Medical Informatics*, pages 473–483. Schattauer-Verlag, Stuttgart.

FAGAN, M. E., 1986. Advances in software inspections. *IEEE Transactions on Softare Engineering*, 12(7):744–751.

FALTINGS, B. and WEIGEL, R., 1994. Constraint-based knowledge representation for configuration systems. Technical Report Technical Report TR-94-95, EPFL Lausanne CH.

FATHI-TORTSAGHAM, M. and MEYER, D., 1994. MEDUSA: A Fuzzy Expert System for Medical Diagnosis of Acute Abdominal Pain. *Meth. Inf. Med*, 33:522–529.

FEIFER, R. and ALLENDER, L., 1994. It's not how multi the media, it's how the media is used. In T. Ottmann and I. Tomek, editors, *Proceedings of ED-MEDIA '94*, pages 197–202. AACE, Charlottesville, VA.

FELDMANN, R. L., MÜNCH, J., and VORWIEGER, S., 1997. Ein Schema zur experimentspezifischen Ablage von Software Engineering Erfahrungen. Technical report, SFB 501, Department of Computer Science, University of Kaiserslautern.

FERGUSSON, W., BAREISS, R., BIRNBAUM, L., and OSGOOD, R., 1992. ASK systems: An approach to the realization of story-based teachers. *Journal of the Learning Sciences*, 2:95–134.

FERMI, 1996. A Logic for Information Retrieval (Deliverable D2, FERMI Work Part 1). FERMI Report 96-2, Rome, Italy.

FERNANDEZ-CHAMIZO, C., GONZALEZ-CALERO, P. A., GOMEZ-ALBARRAN, M., and HERNANDEZ-YANEZ, L., 1996. Supporting Object Reuse Through Case-Based Reasoning. In (Smith and Faltings 1996), pages 135–149.

FIKES, R. E. and NILSSON, N. J., 1971. STRIPS: A new approach to the application of theorem proving to problem solving. *Artificial Intelligence*, 2:189–208.

FINNIE, G. R., WITTIG, G. W., and DESHARNAIS, J. M., 1997. Estimating Software Development Effort with Case-Based Reasoning. In (Leake and Plaza 1997), pages 13–22. ISBN 3-540-63233-6.

FISHER, G., MCCALL, R., and MORCH, A., 1989. Design environments for constructive and argumentative design. In *Human Factors in Computing Systems Conference*, pages 269–275. ACM Press, New York.

FLEMMING, U., ZEYNO, A., COYNE, R., and SNYDER, J., 1997. Case-based design in a software environment that supports the early phases. In (Maher and Pu 1997), pages 61–86. ISBN 0-8058-2313-1.

FORBUS, K. D., GENTNER, D., and LAW, K., 1995. MAC/FAC: A Model of Similarity-Based Retrieval. *Cognitive Science*, 19:144–205.

FOUQUÉ, G. and MATWIN, S., 1993. A case-based approach to software reuse. *Journal of Intelligent Information Systems*, 2(2):165–197.

FOX, B. A., 1991. Cognitive and interactional aspects of correction in tutoring. In P. Goodyear, editor, *Teaching knowledge and intelligent tutoring*, pages 149–172. Ablex, Norwood, NJ.

FRAKES, W. B. and BAEZA-YATES, R., 1992. *Information Retrieval: Data Structures and Algorithms*. Prentice-Hall, Englewood Cliffs, NJ.

FRANCIS, A. G. and RAM, A., 1993. The Utility Problem in Case-Based Reasoning. In D. B. Leake, editor, *Case-Based Reasoning: Papers from the 1993 Workshop*, Technical Report WS-93-01, page 168. AAAI, Menlo Park, CA.

FRANCIS, A. G. J. and RAM, A., 1995. A Domain-Independent Algorithm for Multi-Plan Adaptation and Merging in Least-Commitment Planning. In D. Aha and A. Rahm, editors, *AAAI Fall Symposium: Adaptation of Knowledge Reuse*. AAAI Press, Menlo Park, CA.

FREESTON, M., 1987. The BANG file: A New Kind of Grid File. In U. Dayal and I. Traiger, editors, *Proceedings of the ACM SIGMOD Annual Conference*, pages 260–269. ACM Press, San Francisco, CA.

FREESTON, M., 1995. A general solution of the n-dimensional B-tree problem. *ACM SIGMOD Record*, 24(2):80–91.

FREESTON, M., 1996. The Application of Multi-Dimensional Indexing Methods to Constraints. In G. Kuper and M. Wallace, editors, *Constraint Databases and Applications. Proceedings ESPRIT WG CONTESSA Workshop*, volume 1034 of *Lecture Notes in Computer Science*, pages 102–119. Springer Verlag, Friedrichshafen, Germany.

FRIEDMAN, J. H., BENTLEY, J. L., and FINKEL, R. A., 1977. An algorithm for finding best matches in logarithmic expected time. *ACM Transactions Math. Software*, 3:209–226.

FU, K. S., 1974. *Syntactic Methods in Pattern Recognition*. Academic Press, New York. ISBN 0-12-269568-7.

FU, K.-S. and BHARGAVA, B. K., 1973. Tree systems for syntactic pattern recognition. *IEEE Transactions on Computers*, C-22(12):1087–1099.

FUHR, N., 1989. Models for Retrieval with Probabilistic Indexing. *Information Processing and Management*, 25:55–72.

FUHR, N., 1990. A Probabilistic Framework for Vague Queries and Imprecise Information in Databases. In *Proc. VLDB90*, pages 696–707. Brisbane, Australia.

FUHR, N., 1992. Integration of Probabilistic Fact and Text Retrieval. In *Proc. of the 15th Annual International SIGIR Forum*, pages 211–222. Denmark.

FUHR, N., 1993a. A Probabilistic Relational Model for the Integration of IR and Databases. In E. R. R. Korfhage and P. Willett, editors, *Proceedings of the Sixteenth Annual International ACM SIGIR Conference on Research and Development in Information Retrieval*, pages 309–317.

FUHR, N., 1993b. Information Retrieval. Skriptum zur Vorlesung im SS 1993.

FUHR, N., 1995a. Modelling Hypermedia Retrieval in Datalog. In R. Kuhlen and M. Rittberger, editors, *Hypertext - Information Retrieval - Multimedia, Proceedings HIM'95*, pages 163–174. UVK - Universitätsverlag Konstanz, Konstanz, Germany.

FUHR, N., 1995b. Probabilistic Datalog – A Logic for Powerful Retrieval Methods. In *SIGIR95*.

FUKUNAGA, K. and NARENDRA, P. M., 1975. A Branch and Bound Algorithm for Computing k-Nearest Neighbors. *IEEE Transactions on Computers*, 24:750–753.

GAEDE, V. and GÜNTHER, O., 1996. Constraint-Based Query Optimization and Processing. In G. Kuper and M. Wallace, editors, *Constraint Databases and Applications. Proc ESPRIT WG CONTESSA Workshop*, volume 1034 of *Lecture Notes in Computer Science*, pages 84–101. Springer Verlag, Friedrichshafen, Germany.

GEBHARDT, F., VOSS, A., GRÄTHER, W., and SCHMIDT-BELZ, B., 1997. *Reasoning with Complex Cases*, volume 393 of *International Series in Engineering and Computer Science*. Kluwer Academic Publishers, Boston. ISBN 0-7923-9882-3.

GENTNER, D., 1983. Structure-mapping: A theorectical framework for Analogy. *Cognitive Science*, 7:155–170.

GENTNER, D. and FORBUS, K. D., 1991. MAC/FAC: A Model of Similarity-Based Retrieval. In *Proceedings of the 13th Annual Conference of the Cognitive Science Society*, pages 504–509.

GERO, J. S., 1990. Design Prototypes: A knowledge representation schema for design. *The AI Magazine*, 11:26–36.

GERO, J. S. and SUDWEEKS, F., editors, 1994. *Artificial Intelligence in Design '94*. Kluwer Academic Publishers, Dordrecht.

GIBBS, W. W., 1994. Software's chronic crisis. *Scientific American*, pages 86–95.

GIERL, L., 1992a. Klassifikation mit prototypischen Merkmalsmustern zur Entscheidungsfindung in Expertensystemen für die Medizin. Habilitationsarbeit, Universität München.

GIERL, L., 1992b. Prototypen als fallorientiertes medizinisches Wissen in Diagnose und Wissensakquisition. In (Althoff, Wess, Bartsch-Spörl, and Janetzko 1992).

GIERL, L. and LENZ, M., editors, 1998. *Proceedings 6th German Workshop on Case-Based Reasoning*, IMIB Series Vol. 7, Rostock. Inst. fuer Medizinische Informatik und Biometrie, University of Rostock.

GIERL, L., POLLWEIN, B., HEYDE, G., and KURT, H., 1993. Knowledge-based Duty Rosters for Physicians. *Medical Informatics*, 18:355–366.

GIERL, L. and STENGEL-RUTKOWSKI, S., 1992. Prototypes as a Core Representation of Medical Knowledge in Diagnosis and Knowledge Acquisition. In Lun et al, editor, *MEDINFO 92*, pages 1088–1094. Elsevier.

GIERL, L. and STENGEL-RUTKOWSKI, S., 1994. Integrating Consultation and Semi-automatic Knowledge Acquisition in a Prototype-based Architecture: Experiences with Dysmorphic Syndromes. *Artifical Intelligence in Medicine*, 6:29–49.

GILBOA, I. and SCHMEIDLER, D., 1995. Case-Based Decision Theory. *Quarterly Journal of Economics*, 110:605–639.

GISH, J. W., HUFF, K. E., and THOMSON, R., 1994. The GTE environment - Supporting understanding and adaptation in software reuse. In W. Schäfer, R. Prieto-Diaz, and M. Matsumoto, editors, *Software reusability*, pages 140–149. Ellis Horwood Ltd., Chichster, UK.

GLAVITSCH, U. and SCHÄUBLE, P., 1992. A System for Retrieving Speech Documents. In *Proc. of the 15th Annual International SIGIR Forum*, pages 168–176. Denmark.

GLAVITSCH, U., SCHÄUBLE, P., and WECHSLER, M., 1994. Metadata for Integrating Speech Documents in a Text Retrieval System. *SIGMOD Record*, 23(4):57–63.

GLOBIG, C., JANTKE, K. P., LANGE, S., and SAKAKIBARA, Y., 1997. On case-based learnability of languages. *New Generation Computing*, 15(1):59–83.

GLOBIG, C. and LANGE, S., 1994. On Case-Based Representability and Learnability of Languages. In S. Arikawa and K. P. Jantke, editors, *Proceedings of the 4th International Workshop on Analogical and Inductive Inference (AII '94)*, number 872 in LNAI, pages 106–121. Springer–Verlag.

GLOBIG, C. and LANGE, S., 1996. Case-based representability of boolean functions. In (Wahlster 1996), pages 117–121.

GOEL, A., BHATTA, S., and STROULIA, E., 1997. KRITIK: An early case-based design system. In (Maher and Pu 1997), pages 87–132. ISBN 0-8058-2313-1.

GOEL, A. K., 1989. *Integration of Case-Based Reasoning and Model-Based Reasoning for Adaptive Design Problem Solving*. Ph.D. thesis, Department of Computer and Information Sciences, The Ohio State University.

GOEL, A. K. and CHANDRASEKARAN, B., 1989. Use of Device Models in Adaption of Design Cases. In (Hammond 1989b), pages 100–109.

GOLD, E. M., 1967. Language identification in the limit. *Information and Control*, 10:447–474.

GÓMEZ, H., 1997. A cognitive approach to software reuse applying case-based reasoning to mutant cases. In *Proceedings of the 9th International Conference on Software Engineering and Knowledge Engineering*. Madrid, Spain.

GONZÁLES, P. A. and FERNÁNDEZ, C., 1997. A knowledge-based approach to support software reuse in object-oriented libraries. In *Proceedings of the 9th International Conference on Software Engineering and Knowledge Engineering*. Madrid, Spain.

GONZALEZ, R. C. and THOMASON, M. G., 1978. *Syntactic Pattern Recognition: an Introduction*. Addison-Wesley, Reading, MA. ISBN 0-201-02931-6.

GOOS, K., 1994. Preselection strategies for case based classification. In B. Nebel and L. Dreschler-Fischer, editors, *KI-94: Advances in Artificial Intelligence*, number 861 in Lecture Notes in Artificial Intelligence, pages 28–38. Springer, Berlin.

GOOS, K., 1996. *Fallbasiertes Klassifizieren: Methoden, Integration und Evaluation*. Number 127 in Dissertationen zur Künstlichen Intelligenz. infix, Sankt Augustin. ISBN 3-89601-127-8. Zugleich: Würzburg, Universität, Diss. 1995.

GOOS, K. and SCHEWE, S., 1993. Case Based Reasoning in Clinical Evaluation. In S. Andreassen, R. Engelbrecht, and J. Wyatt, editors, *Artificial Intelligence in Medicine*, pages 445–448. IOS Press.

GÖRZ, G. and HÖLLDOBLER, S., editors, 1996. *KI-96: Advances in Artificial Intelligence*, Lecture Notes in Artificial Intelligence, 1137. Springer Verlag.

GRIMNES, M. and AAMODT, A., 1996. A Two Layer Case-Based Reasoning Architecture for Medical Image Understanding. In (Smith and Faltings 1996), pages 164–178.

GÜNTER, A., editor, 1995. *Wissensbasiertes Konfigurieren Ergebnisse aus dem Project PROKON*. infix Verlag.

GÜNTER, O., 1989. The Design of the Cell Tree: An Object-Oriented Index Structure for Geometric Databases. In *Proceedings 5th Int. Conf on Data Engineering*, pages 598–605. IEEE, Los Angeles, CA.

GÜTING, R. H., 1994. An Introduction to Spatial Database Systems. *VLDB Journal*, 3:357–399.

GUTTMAN, A., 1984. R-Trees: A Dynamic Index Structure For Spatial Searching. In B. Yormack, editor, *Proceedings ACM SIGMOD 84*, pages 47–57. ACM, Boston, MA.

HADDAD, M., ADLASSNIG, K. P., and PORENTA, G., 1997. Feasibility analysis of a case-based reasoning system for automated detection of coronary heart disease from myocardial scintigrams. *Artifical Intelligence in Medicine*, 9:61–78.

HADORN, W. and ZÖLLNER, N., 1979. *Vom Symptom zur Diagnose*. Birkhäuser Verlag, Basel.

HAIMOWITZ, I. J. and KOHANE, I. S., 1993. Automated Trend Detection with Alternate Temporal Hypotheses. In (Bajcsy 1993), pages 146–151.

HAMMOND, K. J., 1986. CHEF: A Model of Case-Based Planning. In (AAAI 1986), pages 267–271.

HAMMOND, K. J., 1989a. *Case-Based Planning: Viewing Planning as a Memory Task*. Academic Press, Boston, Massachusetts.

HAMMOND, K. J., editor, 1989b. *Proceedings: Case-Based Reasoning Workshop*. Morgan Kaufmann Publishers.

HAMMOND, K. J., 1990. Case-Based Planning: a Framework for Planning from Experience. *Cognitive Science*, 14(3):385–443.

HAMPTON, J., 1993. Prototype Models. In van Mechelen et al, editor, *Categories and Concepts*, pages 67–95. Academic Press, London.

HANSCHKE, P., 1996. *A Declarative Integration of Terminological, Constraint-Based, Data-driven, and Goal-directed Reasoning*, volume 122 of *Dissertationen zur künstlichen Intelligenz*. infix, Sankt Augustin, Germany.

HARANDI, M. T. and BHANSALI, S., 1989. Program Derivation using analogy. In (IJCAI 1989), pages 389–394.

HAYES-ROTH, F., WATERMAN, D. A., and LENAT, D. B., 1983. *Building Expert Systems*. Addison-Wesley, New York. ISBN 0-201-10686-8.

HECKERMAN, D., 1991. *Probabilistic similarity networks*. MIT Press, Cambridge.

HEIDER, R., 1996. Troubleshooting CFM 56-3 Engines for Boeing 737 Using CBR and Data Mining. In (Smith and Faltings 1996), pages 512–518.

HEIDER, R., AURIOL, E., TARTARIN, E., and MANAGO, M., 1997. Improving the quality of case bases for building better decision support systems. In (Bergmann and Wilke 1997), pages 85–100.

HENNESSY, D. and HINKLE, D., 1991. Initial Results from Clavier: A Case-Based Autoclave Loading Assistent. In (Bareiss 1991), pages 225 – 232.

HENNINGER, S., 1997. Capturing and Formalizing Best Practices in a Software Development Organization. In *Proceedings of the 9th International Conference on Software Engineering and Knowledge Engineering*. Madrid, Spain.

HENRICH, A., SIX, H.-W., and WIDMAYER, P., 1989. The LSD tree: Spatial access to multidimensional point and non-point objects. In *Proceedings VLDB89*, pages 45–53. Amsterdam, Netherlands.

HINRICHS, T. and KOLODNER, J. L., 1991. The Roles of Adaption in Case-Based Design. In (Bareiss 1991).

HINRICHS, T. R., 1992a. *Problem Solving in Open Worlds: a Case Study in Design*. Lawrence Erlbaum Associates, Hillsdale, NJ.

HINRICHS, T. R., 1992b. Using Case-Based Reasoning for Plausible Design Tasks. In (AID 1992), pages 33 – 41.

HOLTE, R. C., MKADMI, T., ZIMMER, R. M., and MACDONALD, A. J., 1995. Speeding up problem solving by abstraction: A graph-oriented approach. Technical report, University of Ottawa, Ontario, Canada.

HOVESTADT, L. and SCHMIDT-BELZ, B., 1995. PM5 – a model of building design. In B. Schmidt-Belz, editor, *Scenario of FABEL Prototype 3 Supporting Architectural Design*, volume 40 of *Fabel-Report*. GMD, Sankt Augustin.

HSU, C.-I. and CHIU, C., 1997. Case-Based Modeling for System Requirements Engineering. Technical report, National Central University, Yuan Ze Institute of Technology.

HUA, K., SMITH, I., and FALTINGS, B., 1993. Exploring case-based design: CADRE. *Artificial Intelligence for Engineering Design, Analysis and Manufacturing (AI EDAM)*, 7(2):135–144.

HUTTER, D., 1994. Synthesis of Induction Orderings for Existence Proofs. In A. Bundy, editor, *Proceedings of 12th International Conference on Automated Deduction (CADE-12)*, Lecture Notes in Artificial Intelligence 814, pages 29–41. Springer.

IEEE, 1987. Software Engineering Standards: Glossary on Software Engineering Terminology.

IJCAI, 1989. *Proceedings of the 11th International Conference on Artificial Intelligence IJCAI-89*, Detroit, Michigan, USA. IJCAI.

ISERN, 1996. ISERN Glossary. http://wwwagse.informatik.uni-kl.de/ISERN/isern.html.

ISHIKAWA, K., 1985. *What Is Total Quality Control? The Japanese Way*. Prentice Hall.

JACOBSON, I., CHRISTERSON, M., JONSSON, P., and OEVERGAARD, G., 1995. *Object-oriented software engineering*. ACM Press.

JANETZKO, D., BÖRNER, K., JÄSCHKE, O., and STRUBE, G., 1994. Task-oriented knowledge acquisition and reasoning for design support systems. In *Proceedings of the First European Conference on Cognitive Science in Industry*, pages 153–184. Centre de Recherche Public Centre Universitaire, Luxembourg, Luxembourg.

JANTKE, K. P., 1994. Nonstandard concepts of similarity in case-based reasoning. In H.-H. Bock, W. Lenski, and M. M. Richter, editors, *Information Systems and Data Analysis: Prospects – Foundations – Applications, Proceedings of the 17th Annual Conference of the GfKl, Univ. of Kaiserslautern, 1993*, pages 28–43. Springer, Berlin, Kaiserslautern.

JANTKE, K. P. and LANGE, S., 1995. Case-based representation and learning of pattern languages. *Theoretical Computer Science*, 137:25–51.

JARKE, M. and TEAM, N., 1996. Meta Models for Requirements Engineering. In B. R. Gaines and M. Musen, editors, *Proceedings 10th Knowledge Acquisition for Knowledge-Based Systems Workshop*. Banff.

JAULENT, M. C., 1997. A Case-Based Reasoning Method for Computer-Assisted Diagnosis in Histopathology. In Keravnon et al, editor, *AIME-97*, pages 239–242.

JOHNSON, W. L., 1986. *Intention-based diagnosis of novice programming errors*. Pitman, London.

JOHNSON, W. L. and SOLOWAY, E., 1987. PROUST: An automatic debugger for Pascal programs. In S. Kearsley, editor, *Artificial intelligence and instruction. Applications and methods*, pages 47–689. Addison-Wesley, Reading, MA.

JOHNSTON, R., BREEN, S., and MANAGO, M., 1996. Methodology for developing CBR applications. Technical report, Esprit Project INRECA Deliverable D30.

JURISICA, I. and SHAPIRO, H., 1995. Case-based reasoning system applied on an advisor for IVF practitioners. In *Proceedings 1st Conference of the American Society for Reproduction Medicine*. Seattle.

KAHN, C. E. J. and ANDERSON, G. M., 1994. Case-based reasoning and imaging procedure selection. *Investigative Radiology*, 29:643–647.

KAMBHAMPATI, S., 1994. Exploiting Causal Structure to Control Retrieval and Refitting during Plan Reuse. *Computational Intelligence*, 10(2):213–244.

KAMBHAMPATI, S., IHRIG, L., and SRIVASTAVA, B., 1996. A Candidate Set Based Analysis of Subgoal Interactions in Conjunctive Goal Planning. In (Drabble 1996), pages 125–133.

KAMP, G., 1993. Integrating Semantic Structure and Technical Documentation in Case-Based Service Support Systems. In (Wess, Althoff, and Richter 1993b), pages 392–403.

KAMP, G., 1994. On the Use of CBR in Corporate Service and Support. In (Keane, Haton, and Manago 1994), pages 175–183.

KAMP, G., 1996. Using Description Logics for Knowledge Intensive Case-based Reasoning. In (Smith and Faltings 1996), pages 204–218.

KAMP, G., 1997. On the Admissibility of Concrete Domains for CBR based on Description Logics. In (Leake and Plaza 1997), pages 223–234. ISBN 3-540-63233-6.

KAMP, G., PIRK, P., and BURKHARD, H.-D., 1996. FALLDATEN: Case-Based Reasoning for the Diagnosis of Technical Devices. In (Görz and Hölldobler 1996), pages 149–161.

KATALAGARIANOS, P. and VASSILIOU, Y., 1995. On the reuse of software: A case-based approach employing a repository. *Automated Software Engineering*, 2:55–86.

KAZMAN, R. and KOMINEK, J., 1997. Supporting the Retrieval Process in Multimedia Information Systems. In R. H. Sprague, editor, *Proceedings 30th Hawaiian International Conference on System Sciences*. Computer Science Press, Wailea, HA.

KEANE, M. T., HATON, J. P., and MANAGO, M., editors, 1994. *Second European Workshop on Case-Based Reasoning (EWCBR-94)*. AcknoSoft Press.

KHEIRBEK, A. and CHIARAMELLA, Y., 1995. Integrating Hypermedia and Information Retrieval with Conceptual Graphs Formalism. In R. Kuhlen and M. Rittberger, editors, *Hypertext - Information Retrieval - Multimedia, Proceedings HIM'95*, pages 47–60. UVK - Universitätsverlag Konstanz, Konstanz, Germany.

KING, J., 1994. ESTEEM Enabling Solutions Through Experience Modeling. Technical report, Estem Software Inc., USA.

KITANO, H., SHIBATA, A., and SHIMAZU, H., 1993. Case-Method: A Methodology for Building Large-Scale Case-Based Systems. In *Proceedings AAAI-93*.

KITANO, H., SHIBATA, A., SHIMAZU, H., KAJIHARA, J., and SATO, A., 1992. Building Large-Scale Corporate-Wide Case-Based Systems: Integration of organizational and machine Executable Algorithms. In *Proceedings of the AAAI-92*.

KITANO, H. and SHIMAZU, H., 1996. The Experience-Sharing Architecture: A Case Study in Corporate-Wide Case-Based Software Quality Control. In (Leake 1996), chapter 13, page 420. ISBN 0-262-62110-X.

KNOBLOCK, C., 1996. Building a Planner for Information Gathering: A Report from the Trenches. In (Drabble 1996), pages 134–141.

KÖHLER, J., 1994. An Application of Terminological Logics to Case-based Reasoning. In *Principles of Knowledge Representation and Reasoning -Proceedings of the 5th International Conference*. Bonn, Germany.

KÖHLER, J., 1996. Planning from Second Principles. *Artificial Intelligence*, 87(1–2):145–186.

KÖHNE, A. and WEBER, G., 1987. STRUEDI: a LISP-structure editor for novice programmers. In H. J. Bullinger and B. Schackel, editors, *Human-Computer Interaction*, pages 125–129. North-Holland, Amsterdam.

KOLBE, T. and WALTHER, C., 1995. Second-Order Matching modulo Evaluation – A Technique for Reusing Proofs. In (Mellish 1995).

KOLODNER, J. L., 1980. *Retrieval and Organizational Strategies in Conceptual Memory*. Ph.D. thesis, Yale University.

KOLODNER, J. L., 1983. Maintaining Organization in a Dynamic Long-Term Memory. *Cognitive Science*, 7:243–280.

KOLODNER, J. L., 1984. *Retrieval and Organizational Strategies in Conceptual Memory*. Lawrence Erlbaum, Hillsdale, New Jersey.

KOLODNER, J. L., editor, 1988. *Proceedings Case-Based Reasoning Workshop*. Morgan Kaufmann Publishers.

KOLODNER, J. L., 1991. Improving Human Decision Making through Case-Based Decision Aiding. *AI Magazine*, 91(2):52–68.

KOLODNER, J. L., 1993. *Case-Based Reasoning*. Morgan Kaufmann, San Mateo.

KOLODNER, J. L. and KOLODNER, R. M., 1987. Using Experience in Clinical Problem Solving: Introduction and Framework. *IEEE Transactions on Systems, Man and Cybernetics*, 17:420–430.

KOTON, P., 1988. Reasoning about Evidence in Causal Explanation. In (Kolodner 1988), pages 260–170.

KOTON, P., 1989. Evaluating Case-Based Problem Solving. In (Hammond 1989b), pages 173–175.

KOVACIC, K., STERLING, L., PETOT, G., ERNST, G., and YANG, N., 1992. Towards an Intelligent Nutrition Manager. In *Proceedings ACM/SIGAPP Symposium on Computer Applications*, pages 1293–96. ACM Press.

Krampe, D. and Lusti, M., 1997. Case-based reasoning for information system design. In (Leake and Plaza 1997), pages 63–73. ISBN 3-540-63233-6.

Kratz, N., 1991. *Architektur eines wissensbasierten Systems zur Unterstützung der Konzeptionsphase in der Konstruktion.* Ph.D. thesis, University of Kaiserslautern.

Kunze, M., 1997. Das ExperienceBook. Studienarbeit, Dept. of Computer Science, Humboldt University, Berlin, Germany.

Kurmann, D., 1995. Sculptor - A Tool for Intuitive Architectural Design. In M. Tan and R. Teh, editors, *CAAD Futures 95: Proceedings of the 6th International Conference on Computer-Aided Architectural Design Futures*, volume 1. Singapore.

Kurmann, D., 1997. Sculptor.
http://caad.arch.ethz.ch/ kurmann/sculptor.

Lalmas, M., 1997. Dempster-Shafer's Theory of Evidence Applied to Structured Documents: Modelling Uncertainty. In *Proc. SIGIR 97*. ACM Press.

Leake, D. B., 1996. *Case-Based Reasoning: Experiences, Lessons, and Future Directions.* AAAI Press, Menlo Park, CA. ISBN 0-262-62110-X.

Leake, D. B. and Plaza, E., editors, 1997. *Case-Based Reasoning Research and Development, Proceedings ICCBR-97*, Lecture Notes in Artificial Intelligence, 1266. Springer Verlag. ISBN 3-540-63233-6.

Lebowitz, M., 1986. Integrated learning: controlling explanation. *Cognitive Science*, 10:219–240.

Ledley, R. J. and Lusted, L. B., 1959. Reasoning Foundations of Medical Diagnosis. *Science*, 130:9–21.

Lee, S. K., 1992. An Extended Relational Database Model for Uncertain And Imprecise Information. In *Proceedings VLDB92*, pages 211–220. Vancouver, Canada.

Lees, B., Hamza, M., and C, I., 1996. Applying case-based reasoning to software quality management. In (Burkhard and Lenz 1996), pages 162–169.

Lekkas, G. P., Arouris, N. M., and Viras, L. L., 1994. Case-Based Reasoning in Environmental Monitoring Applications. *Applied Artificial Intelligence*, 8:349–376.

Leng, B., Buchanan, B. G., and Nicholas, H. B., 1993. Protein secondary structure prediction using two-level Case-based Reasoning. In *International Conference on Intelligent Systems for Molekular Biology (ISMB)*, pages 3–11.

Lenz, M., 1994. Case-Based Reasoning for Holiday Planning. In W. Schertler, B. Schmid, A. M. Tjoa, and H. Werthner, editors, *Infor-*

mation and Communications Technologies in Tourism, pages 126–132. Springer Verlag.

LENZ, M., 1995. Lazy Induction Triggered by CBR. In A. Aamodt and J. Komorowski, editors, *SCAI'95: Proceedings 5th Scandinavian Conference on AI*, Frontiers in Artificial Intelligence and Applications, pages 61–70. IOS Press, Trondheim.

LENZ, M., 1996a. Case Retrieval Nets Applied to Large Case Bases. In (Burkhard and Lenz 1996), pages 111–118.

LENZ, M., 1996b. IMTAS: Intelligent Multimedia Travel Agent System. In S. Klein, B. Schmid, A. M. Tjoa, and H. Werthner, editors, *Information and Communications Technologies in Tourism*, pages 11–17. Springer Verlag, Wien, New York.

LENZ, M., 1998. Textual CBR and Information Retrieval – A Comparison. In (Gierl and Lenz 1998).

LENZ, M. and BURKHARD, H.-D., 1996a. Case Retrieval Nets: Basic Ideas and Extensions. In (Görz and Hölldobler 1996), pages 227–239.

LENZ, M. and BURKHARD, H.-D., 1996b. Lazy Propagation in Case Retrieval Nets. In (Wahlster 1996), pages 127–131.

LENZ, M. and BURKHARD, H.-D., 1997a. Applying CBR for Document Retrieval. In Y. Nakatani, editor, *Proceedings Workshop Practical Use of CBR at IJCAI-97*, pages 75–86.

LENZ, M. and BURKHARD, H.-D., 1997b. CBR for Document Retrieval - The FALLQ Project. In (Leake and Plaza 1997), pages 84–93. ISBN 3-540-63233-6.

LENZ, M., BURKHARD, H.-D., and BRÜCKNER, S., 1996a. Applying Case Retrieval Nets to Diagnostic Tasks in Technical Domains. In (Smith and Faltings 1996), pages 219–233.

LENZ, M., BURKHARD, H.-D., PIRK, P., AURIOL, E., and MANAGO, M., 1996b. CBR for Diagnosis and Decision Support. *AI Communications*, 9(3):138–146.

LENZ, M., HÜBNER, A., and KUNZE, M., 1998. Question Answering with Textual CBR. In *Proceedings FQAS-98. accepted.*

LENZ, M. and LADEWIG, H., 1996. Fallbasierte Unterstützung bei der Immobilienbewertung. *Wirtschaftsinformatik, Schwerpunktheft Fallbasierte Entscheidungsunterstützung*, 38(1):39–42.

LEWIS, D. D. and SPARCK JONES, K., 1996. Natural Language Processing for Information Retrieval. *Communications of the ACM*, 39(1):92–101.

LEWIS, L., 1995. *Managing computer networks: A case-based reasoning approach.* Artech House Publishers, London.

LIEBER, J. and NAPOLI, A., 1996. Using Classification in Case-Based Reasoning. In (Wahlster 1996), pages 132–136.

LIN, K. I., JAGADISH, H. V., and FALOUTSOS, C., 1994. The TV-Tree: An Index Structure for High-Dimensional Data. *VLDB Journal*, 3:517–542.

LINDEMANN, G. and BURKHARD, H.-D., 1996. Representation of Medical Knowledge via Case Retrieval Nets. In L. Czaja, P. Starke, H.-D. Burkhard, and M. Lenz, editors, *Proceedings Workshop Concurrency, Specification & Programming*.

LYON, H., SOLTANIANZAHED, H., HOHNLOSER, J., BELL, J. R., O'DONNEL, J. F., HIRAI, F., SHULTZ, E. K., WIGTON, R. S., ÜBERLA, K., EITEL, F., MANDL, H., and BECK, J. R., 1992. Significant Efficiency Finding from Research on Computer-based Interactive Medical Education Programs for Teaching Clinical Reasoning. In L. et al, editor, *MEDINFO 92*, pages 1088–1094. Elsevier.

MACGREGOR, R., 1991. The Evolving Technology of Classification-based Knowledge Representation Systems. In *Principles of Semantic Networks*. Morgan Kaufmann.

MACURA, R. T. and MACURA, K. J., 1995. MacRad: Radiology Image Resource with a Case-Based Retrieval System. In (Aamodt and Veloso 1995), pages 43–54. ISBN 3-540-60598-3.

MAHER, M. L., BALACHANDRAN, M. B., and ZHANG, D. M., 1996. *Case-Based Reasoning in Design*. Lawrence Erlbaum Associates, Mahwah, NJ. ISBN 0-8058-1832-4.

MAHER, M. L. and GOMEZ DE SILVA GARZA, A., 1997. AI in Design: Case-Based Reasoning in Design. *IEEE Expert*, 12(2).

MAHER, M. L. and PU, P., editors, 1997. *Issues and Applications of Case Based Reasoning in Design*. Lawrence Erlbaum Associates, Mahwah, NJ. ISBN 0-8058-2313-1.

MAHER, M. L. and ZHANG, D. M., 1991. CADSYN: Using case and decomposition knowledge for design synthesis. In J. S. Gero, editor, *Artificial Intelligence in Design*, pages 137–150. Butterworth Heinemann, Oxford.

MAHER, M. L. and ZHANG, D. M., 1993. CADSYN: A Case-Based Design Process Model. *Artificial Intelligence for Engineering Design, Analysis, and Manufacturing*, 7(2):97–110.

MAIDEN, N., 1991. Analogy as a paradigm for specification reuse. *Software Engineering Journal*, 6(1):3–16.

MAIDEN, N. and RUGG, G., 1996. ACRE: Selecting methods for requirements acquisition. *IEEE Software Engineering Journal*, 11(3):183–192.

MAIDEN, N. and SUTCLIFFE, A. G., 1992. Exploiting reusable specifications through analogy. *Communications of the ACM*, 35(4):55–64.

MALEK, M., 1995. A Connectionist Indexing System for CBR Systems. In (Aamodt and Veloso 1995). ISBN 3-540-60598-3.

MALEK, M. and RIALLE, V., 1994. A Case-Based Reasoning System Applied to Neuropathy Diagnosis. In (Keane, Haton, and Manago 1994).

MANAGO, M. and AURIOL, E., 1996. Mining for OR. *ORMS Today*, 23(1).

MARSHALL, R. J., 1991. A Review of the Statistical Analysis of Spatial Patterns of Disease. *J. R. Statist. Soc. A*, 154(3):421–441.

MCALLESTER, D. and ROSENBLITT, D., 1991. Systematic nonlinear planning. In (AAAI 1991), pages 634–639.

MCCALLA, G. I. and GREER, J. E., 1986. Two and one-half approaches to helping novices learn recursion. In E. Lemut, B. du Boulay, and G. Dettori, editors, *Cognitive models and intelligent environments for learning programming*, pages 185–197. Springer Verlag, Berlin.

MCDERMOTT, J., 1982. R1: A rule based configurer of computer systems. *Artificial Intelligence*, 19(1):39–88.

MEGHINI, C., SEBASTIANI, F., STRACCIA, U., and THANOS, C., 1993. A Model of Information Retrieval based on a Terminological Logic. In E. R. R. Korfhage and P. Willett, editors, *SIGIR93*, pages 298–307. ACM Press, Pittsburgh, PA.

MEISSONNIER, A., 1996. *Ein fallbasiertes Informationssystem für fallbasierte Anwendungen und Systeme auf der Basis von Inreca.* Diploma thesis, University of Kaiserslautern.

MELIS, E., 1994. How Mathematicians Prove Theorems. In *Proceedings of the Annual Conference of the Cognitive Science Society*, pages 624–628. Atlanta, Georgia U.S.A.

MELIS, E., 1995. A Model of Analogy-Driven Proof-Plan Construction. In (Mellish 1995), pages 182–189.

MELIS, E., 1997. Solution-Relevant Abstractions Constrain Retrieval and Adaptation. In (Leake and Plaza 1997). ISBN 3-540-63233-6.

MELIS, E. and WHITTLE, J., 1997a. Analogy as a Control Strategy in Theorem Proving. In *Proceedings of the 10th Florida International AI Conference (FLAIRS-97)*. Also published as DAI Research Paper 840, University of Edinburgh, Dept. of AI.

MELIS, E. and WHITTLE, J., 1997b. Analogy in Inductive Theorem Proving. In (Brewka, Habel, and Nebel 1997).

MELLISH, C. S., editor, 1995. *Proceedings of the 14th International Conference on Artificial Intelligence IJCAI-95*.

MIKSCH, S., HORN, W., POPOW, C., and PAKY, F., 1995. Therapy Planning Using Qualitative Trend Descriptions. In P. Barahona, M. Stefanelli, and J. Wyatt, editors, *Proceedings of the 5th Conference on Artificial Intelligence in Medicine Europe (AIME-95)*, Lecture Notes in Artificial Intelligence, 934, pages 197–208. Springer Verlag.

MILLER, R. A., 1997. A Heuristic Approach to the Multiple Diagnoses Problem. In K. et al, editor, *AIME-97*, pages 187–198.

MILLER, R. A. and MASARIE, F. E., 1990. The Demise of the "Greek Oracle" Model for Medical Diagnostic Systems. *Meth. Inf. Med*, 29:1–2.

MINSKY, M., 1986. *The Society of Mind*. Simon and Schuster, New York.

MITCHELL, T., MAHADEVAN, L., and STEINBERG, L., 1985. LEAP: A learning apprentice for VLSI design. In M. Kaufmann, editor, *Proceedings of the International Conference on Artificial Intelligence (IJCAI-85)*, pages 573–580.

MITCHELL, T. M., KELLAR, R. M., and KEDAR-CABELLI, S. T., 1986. Explanation-Based Generalization: A Unifying View. *Machine Learning*, 1:47–80.

MITTAL, S. and FALKENHAINER, B., 1990. Dynamic constraint satisfaction problems. In (AAAI 1990), pages 25–32.

MITTENDORF, E., SCHÄUBLE, P., and SHERIDAN, P., 1995. Applying Probabilistic Term Weighting to OCR Text in the Case of a Large Alphabetic Library Catalogue. In *Proc. SIGIR 95*. Seattle, WA.

MOLINO, G., MOLINO, F., FURIA, D., BAR, F., BATTISTA, S., and CAPPOLLO, N., 1996. Computer-Aided Diagnosis in Jamdice: Comparision of Knowledge-based and Probabilitstic Approaches. *Meth. Inf. Med*, 35:41–51.

MOLLOGHASEMI, M. and PET-EDWARDS, J., 1997. *Making multiple-objective decisions*. IEEE Computer Society Press, Washington, DC.

MORGENSTERN, K., 1993. *Anpassung im Bauentwurf mittels aktiver autonomer Objekte*. Master's thesis, Universität Bonn.

MOTRO, A., 1988. VAGUE: A User Interface to Relational Databases that Permits Vague Queries. *ACM Transactions on Office Information Systems*, 6(3):187–214. ESSIR Hintergrund Chiamarella.

MUÑOZ-AVILA, H., PAULOKAT, J., and WESS, S., 1994. Controlling a nonlinear hierarchical planner using case replay. In (Keane, Haton, and Manago 1994), pages 266–279.

MUÑOZ-AVILA, H. and WEBERSKIRCH, F., 1996. Planning for Manufacturing Workpieces by Storing, Indexing and Replaying Planning Decisions. In (Drabble 1996).

MUKHOPADHYAY, T., VICINANZA, S. S., and PRIETULA, M. J., 1992. Examining the Feasability of a Case-Based Reasoning Model for Software Effort Estimation. *MIS Quarterly*, 16(2):155–171.

MUÑOZ-AVILA, H. and HÜLLEN, J., 1995. Retrieving Relevant Cases by Using Goal Dependencies. In (Aamodt and Veloso 1995). ISBN 3-540-60598-3.

MUÑOZ-AVILA, H. and WEBERSKIRCH, F., 1996a. Planning for Manufacturing Workpieces by Storing, Indexing and Replaying Planning Decisions. In (Drabble 1996).

MUÑOZ-AVILA, H. and WEBERSKIRCH, F., 1996b. A Specification of the Domain of Process Planning: Properties, Problems and Solutions. Technical Report LSA-96-10E, Centre for Learning Systems and Applications, University of Kaiserslautern, Germany.

MURPHY, G., 1993. Theories and Concept Formation. In van Mechelen et al, editor, *Categories and Concepts*, pages 97–197. Academic Press, London.

MURPHY, P. M. and AHA, D. W., 1992. *UCI Repository of Machine Learning Databases and Domain Theories*. University of California, Irvine, CA.

MURRAY, T., SCHULTZ, K., BROWN, D., and CLEMENT, J., 1990. An analogy-based computer tutor for remediating physics misconceptions. *Interactive Learning Environments*, 1:79–101.

MYLOPOULOS, J. and REITER, R., editors, 1991. *Proceedings of the 12th International Conference on Artificial Intelligence IJCAI-91*.

NAPOLI, A., LIEBER, J., and CURIEN, R., 1996. Classification-Based Problem Solving in Case-Based Reasoning. In (Smith and Faltings 1996), pages 295–308.

NARASHIMAN, S., SYCARA, K., and NAVIN-CHANDRA, D., 1997. Representation and synthesis of non-monotonic meachanical devices. In (Maher and Pu 1997), pages 187–220. ISBN 0-8058-2313-1.

NAVINCHANDRA, D., 1988. Case-Based Reasoning in CYCLOPS, A Design Problem Solver. In (Kolodner 1988), pages 286–301.

NETTEN, B. D., 1997. *Knowledge-based conceptual design: An application to reinforced composite sandwich panels*. Ph.D. thesis, Faculty of Technical Mathematics and Informatics, Delft University of Technology.

NETTEN, B. D. and VINGERHOEDS, R. A., 1997. EADOCS: Conceptual design in three phases - An application to fibre reinforced composite panels. *Engineering Applications of Artificial Intelligence*, 10(2):129–138.

NETTEN, B. D., VINGERHOEDS, R. A., and KOPPELAAR, H., 1995. Expert assisted conceptual design: an application to fibre reinforced composite panels. In R. Oxman, M. Bax, and H. Achten, editors, *Design Research in the Netherlands*, pages 125–139. Faculty of Architecture, Planning, and Building Design Science, Eindhoven University, Eindhoven.

NEWELL, A., 1982. The knowledge level. *Artificial Intelligence*, 18:87–127.

NIEVERGELT, J., HINTERBERGER, H., and SEVCIK, K. C., 1984. The Grid File: An Adaptable, Symmetric Multikey File Structure. *ACM Transactions on Database Systems*, 9:38–71.

ÖCHSNER, H. and WESS, S., 1992. Ähnlichkeitsbasiertes Retrieval von Fallbeispielen durch assoziative Suche in einem mehrdimensionalen Datenraum. In (Althoff, Wess, Bartsch-Spörl, and Janetzko 1992).

OHLSSON, S., 1986. Some principles of intelligent tutoring. *Instructional Science*, 14:293–326.

OPIYO, E. T. O., 1995. Case-Based Reasoning for Expertise Relocation in Support of Rural Health Workers in Developing Countries. In (Aamodt and Veloso 1995), pages 77–87. ISBN 3-540-60598-3.

ORPONEN, P., 1990. Dempster's Rule of Combination is #P-complete. *Artificial Intelligence*, 44(1–2):245–253.

OSHERSON, D. N., STOB, M., and WEINSTEIN, S., 1986. *Systems That Learn*. MIT Press, Cambridge, MA.

OSTERTAG, E., HENDLER, J., PRIETO-DAZ, R., and BRAUN, C., 1992. Computing similarity in a reuse library system: An AI-based approach. *ACM Transactions on Software Engineering and Methodology*, 1(3):205–228.

PANTLEON, T., 1997. Use of CBR for CAD/CAM - Support at Mercedes-Benz. Unicom Seminar on Intelligent Decisions from Databases: CBR and Data Mining: Putting the Technology to Use.

PARSONS, S., 1996. Current Approaches to Handling Imperfect Information in Data and Knowledge Bases. *IEEE Transactions on Knowledge and Data Engineering*, 8(3):353–372.

PATEL-SCHNEIDER, P., MCGUINESS, D., BRACHMAN, R., RESNICK, L., and BORGIDA, A., 1991. The CLASSIC Knowledge Representation System: Guiding Principles and Implementation Rational. *SIGART Bulletin*, 2(3):1108–113.

PAULOKAT, J., 1995. Entscheidungsorientierte Rechtfertigungsverwaltung zur Unterstützung des Konfigurationsprozesses in IDAX. In (Richter and Maurer 1995). Proceedings in Artificial Intelligence 2.

PAULOKAT, J., PRAEGER, R., and WESS, S., 1992. CABPLAN – fallbasierte Arbeitsplanung. In T. Messer and A. Winklhofer, editors, *Beiträge zum 6. Workshop Planen und Konfigurieren*, number 166 in FR-1992-001, page 169. Forwiss, Germany.

PEARCE, M., GOEL, A. K., KOLODNER, J. L., ZIMRING, C., SENTOSA, L., and BILLINGTON, R., 1992. Case-based design support: A case study in architectural design. *IEEE Expert*, pages 14–20.

PEARL, J., 1988. *Probabilistic reasoning in intelligent systems: Networks of plausible inference*. Morgan Kaufmann, San Mateo.

PETERSEN, J., KOCHS, E., and KOCHS, H.-D., 1994. Expertensysteme in der Medizin: Einsatzmöglichkeiten in der Anästhesie. *Anästhesiologie, Intensivmedizin, Notfallmedizin, Schmerztherapie*, 29:74–89.

PETRIE, C., 1991. *Planning and Replanning with Reason Maintenance*. Ph.D. thesis, University of Texas at Austin, Computer Science Dept.

PFEIFER, T. and ZENNER, T., 1996. Using experience during failure analysis - the application of case-based techniques (in German). In J. Grob and J. Spiekermann, editors, *Workshop at the 3rd German Conference on Expert Systems*, pages V1–V12.

PFEIFER, U., FUHR, N., and HUYNH, T., 1995a. Searching structured documents with the enhanced retrieval functionality of freeWAIS-sf and SFGate. *Computer Networks and ISDN Systems*, 27(6):1027–1036.

PFEIFER, U., POERSCH, T., and FUHR, N., 1995b. Searching Proper Names in Databases. In R. Kuhlen and M. Rittberger, editors, *Hypertext - Information Retrieval - Multimedia, Proceedings HIM'95*, pages 259–275. UVK - Universitätsverlag Konstanz, Konstanz, Germany.

POHL, B. and TRENDELENBURG, C., 1988. Pro.M.D. - Diagnostic Expert System Shell for Clinical Chemistry Test Result Interpretation. *Meth. Inf. Med*, 27:111–117.

PRIETO-DAZ, R. and FREEMAN, P., 1987. Classifying software for reusability. *IEEE Software*, 4(1):6–16.

PUPPE, F., 1993. *Systematic Introduction to Expert Systems*. Springer Verlag.

PUPPE, F., REINHARDT, B., and POECK, K., 1995. Generated Critic in the Knowledge Based Neurology Trainer. In *AIME-95*, pages 427–428.

PURVIS, L. and PU, P., 1995. Adaptation using constraint satisfaction techniques. In (Aamodt and Veloso 1995), pages 289–300. ISBN 3-540-60598-3.

PURVIS, L. and PU, P., 1996. An Approach to Case Combination. In *Proceedings of the Adaptation in Case Based Reasoning Workshop of the European Conference on Artificial Intelligence (ECAI96)*. Budapest, Hungary.

PYLE, G. F., 1986. *The Diffusion of Influenza*. Rowman & Littlefield, Totowa NJ.

QUINLAN, J. R., 1983. Learning Efficient Classification Procedures and their Application to Chess End Games. In R. S. Michalski, J. G. Carbonell, and T. M. Mitchell, editors, *Machine Learning: An Artificial Intelligence Approach*. Morgan Kaufmann, Redwood City CA.

REDMOND, M., 1990. Distributed Cases for Case-Based Reasoning; Facilitating Use of Multiple Cases. In (AAAI 1990), pages 304–309.

REIMANN, P. and SCHULT, T. J., 1996. Turning examples into cases: Acquiring knowledge structures for analogical problem solving. *Educational Psychologist*, 31:123–132.

REISER, B. J., COPEN, W. A., RANNEY, M., HAMID, A., and KIMBERG, D. J., 1994. Cognitive and motivational consequences of tutoring and discovery learning. Report no. 54, The Institute for the Learning Sciences, Northwestern University.

RICHTER, M. M., 1992a. Classification and Learning of Similarity Measures. In Opitz, Lausen, and Klar, editors, *Studies in Clasification, Data Analysis and Knowledge Organisation (Proceedings der Jahrestagung der Gesellschaft für Klassifikation)*. Springer Verlag.

RICHTER, M. M., 1992b. *Prinzipien der Künstlichen Intelligenz*. B. G. Teubner, Stuttgart, Germany.

RICHTER, M. M., 1994. On the Notion of Similarity in Case-Basd reasoning. In G. d. Riccia, editor, *Proceedings Invitational Workshop on Uncertainty Reasoning*. Udine, Italy.

RICHTER, M. M., 1995. The Knowledge Contained in Similarity Measures. Invited Talk at ICCBR-95. http://wwwagr.informatik.uni-kl.de/~lsa/CBR/Richtericcbr95remarks.html.

RICHTER, M. M. and MAURER, F., editors, 1995. *3rd German Conference on Expert Systems*, Sankt Augustin, Germany. infix Verlag. Proceedings in Artificial Intelligence 2.

RICHTER, M. M. and WESS, S., 1991. Similarity, Uncertainty and Case-Based Reasoning in PATDEX. In R. Boyer, editor, *Automated Reasoning*, pages 249–265. Kluwer. Essays in Honour of Woody Bledsoe.

RIDGWAY, J., 1988. Of course ICAI is impossible ... worse though, it might be seditious. In J. Self, editor, *Artificial intelligence and human learning: Intelligent computer-aided instruction*, pages 28–48. Chapman & Hall, London.

RIESBECK, C. K. and MARTIN, C. E., 1986. Direct memory access parsing. In J. L. Kolodner and C. K. Riesbeck, editors, *Experience, memory, and reasoning*, pages 209–226. Lawrence Erlbaum Associates, Hillsdale, NJ.

RIESBECK, C. K. and SCHANK, R. C., 1989. *Inside Case-Based Reasoning*. Lawrence Erlbaum Associates, Hillsdale, NJ. ISBN 0-89859-767-6.

RIJSBERGEN, C. J. v., 1979. *Information Retrieval*. Butterworth-Heinemann, London, second edition.

RIJSBERGEN, C. J. v., 1986. A new theoretical framework for information retrieval. In *Proc. of the ACM SIGIR86*, pages 194–200. ACM Press, Pisa, Italy.

RILOFF, E. and LEHNERT, W., 1994. Information Extraction as a Basis for High-Precision Text Classification. *ACM Transactions on Information Systems*, 12(3):296–333.

RISSLAND, E. L. and DANIELS, J. J., 1995. Using CBR to drive IR. In (Mellish 1995), pages 400–407.

ROBINSON, J. T., 1981. The K-D-B-Tree: A Search Structurre for Large Multidimensional Indexes. In Y. E. Lien, editor, *Proceedings ACM SIGMOD 81*, pages 10–18. ACM Press, Ann Arbor, MI.

ROMBACH, H. D., 1993. Software-Qualität und Qualitätssicherung. *Informatik-Spektrum*, 16:267–272.

ROMBACH, H. D. and VERLAGE, M., 1995. Directions in Software Process Research. In M. V. Zelkowitz, editor, *Advances in Computers, Vol. 41*, pages 1–61. Academic Press.

ROSCH, E. and MERVIS, C. B., 1975. Family resemblances: studies in the structure of categories. *Cognitive Psychologie*, 7:573–605.

ROUSU, J. and AARTS, R. J., 1996. Adaptation Cost as a Criterion for Solution Evaluation. In (Smith and Faltings 1996), pages 354–361.

ROYCE, W., 1970. Managing the development of large software systems: Concepts and techniques. In *Proceedings WESCON*.

RUMELHART, D. E., MCCLELLAND, J. L., and THE PDP RESEARCH GROUP, 1986. *Parallel Distributed Processing: Explorations in the Microstructure of Cognition. Volume 1: Foundations*. MIT Press, Cambridge.

RUSSELL, S. and NORVIG, P., 1995. *Artificial Intelligence: A modern approach.* Prentice-Hall, Englewood Cliffs, New Jersey. ISBN 0-13-360124-2.

SACERDOTI, E., 1974. Planning in a hierarchy of abstraction spaces. *Artificial Intelligence*, 5:115–135.

SALTON, G. and MCGILL, M., 1983. *Introduction to Modern Information Retrieval.* McGraw-Hill, New York. ISBN 0-07-054484-0.

SALTON, G., WONG, A., and YANG, C. S., 1975. A Vector Space Model for Automatic Indexing. *Communications of the ACM*, 18:613–620.

SARY, C. and MACKEY, W., 1995. A Case-Based Reasoning Approach for the Access and Reuse of Lessons Learned. In *Proceedings 5th Annual International Symposium of the International Council on Systems Engineering*, page 249.

SCARDAMALIA, M., BEREITER, C., MCLEAN, R. S., SWALLOW, J., and WOODRUFF, E., 1989. Computer-supported intentional learning environments. *Journal of Educational Computing Research*, 5:51–68.

SCHAAF, J., 1998. *Über die Suche nach situationsgerechten Fällen im fallbasierten Schließen.* DISKI 179, Universität Kaiserslautern.

SCHANK, R. C., 1982. *Dynamic Memory: A Theory of Learning in Computers and People*. Cambridge University Press, New York.

SCHANK, R. C., 1991. Case-based teaching: Four experiences in educational software design. Report no. 7, The Institute for the Learning Sciences, Northwestern University, Evanston, IL.

SCHANK, R. C., KASS, A., and RIESBECK, C. K., 1994. *Inside Explanation-based Reasoning*. Lawrence Earlbaum.

SCHÄUBLE, P., 1993. A Tutorial on Information Retrieval. In *Proceedings of the 1993 Workshop on CBR*. Freiburg, Germany.

SCHEWE, S., SCHERRMANN, W., and GIERL, L., 1988. Evaluation and Measuring of Benefit of an Expert System for Differential Diagnosis in Rheumatology. In R. et al, editor, *Expert Systems and Decision Support in Medicine*, pages 351–354.

SCHMIDT, R., BOSCHER, L., HEINDL, B., SCHMID, G., POLLWEIN, B., and GIERL, L., 1995. Adaptation and Abstraction in a Case-Based Antibiotics Therapy Adviser. In P. Barahona, M. Stefanelli, and J. Wyatt, editors, *Proceedings of the 5th Conference on Artificial Intelligence in Medicine Europe (AIME-95)*, Lecture Notes in Artificial Intelligence, 934, pages 209–217. Springer Verlag.

SCHMIDT, R. and GIERL, L., 1996. The Roles of Prototypes in Medical Case-Based Reasoning Systems. In (Burkhard and Lenz 1996), pages 207–216.

SCHMIDT, R., HEINDL, B., POLLWEIN, B., and GIERL, L., 1996. Abstractions of Data and Time for Multiparametric Time Course Prognoses. In (Smith and Faltings 1996), pages 376–391.

SCHNEIDER, J., PIWERNETZ, K., ENGELBRECHT, R., and RENNER, R., 1988. DIACONS - Consultation System to Assist the Management of Diabetes. In Rienhoff et al, editor, *Expert Systems and Decision Support in Medicine*, pages 44–49.

SCHULT, T. J., 1993. Tutorial remindings in a physics simulation environment. In P. Brna, S. Ohlsson, and H. Pain, editors, *Proceedings of the World Conference on Artificial Intelligence in Education*. AACE, Charlottesville, VA.

SCHULT, T. J., 1995. *Ein dynamisches fallbasiertes Lehrsystem*. Ph.D. thesis, Universität Hamburg, Fakultät für Informatik.

SCHULT, T. J. and REIMANN, P., 1995. Dynamic case-based tutoring: A cognitive science approach. In J. Greer, editor, *Proceedings of the 7th World Conference on Artificial Intelligence in Education*, pages 154–161. AACE, Charlottesville, VA.

SCHUMACHER, J., WILKE, W., , and SMITH, B., 1998. Domain Independent Adaptation using Configuration Techniques. In (Gierl and Lenz 1998).

SCHWARTZ, A. B., BARCIA, R. M., MARTINS, A., and WEBER-LEE, R., 1997. PSIQ - A CBR Approach to the Mental Health Area. In (Bergmann and Wilke 1997), pages 217–224.

SCHWARZ, E., BRUSILOVSKY, P., and WEBER, G., 1996. World-wide intelligent textbooks. In P. Carlson and F. Makedon, editors, *Proceedings of ED-TELEKOM 96 - World Conference on Educational Telecommunications*, pages 302–307. AACE, Charlottesville, VA.

SEBASTIANI, F., 1994. A Probabilistic Terminological Logic for Modelling Information Retrieval;. In *Proc. of the ACM SIGIR-94*.

SEBASTIANI, F., 1995. A Note on Logic and Information Retrieval. In *Proc. MIRO Workshop*. Glasgow, Scotland.

SEITZ, A. and UHRMACHER, A., 1996. Cases versus Model-Based Knowledge - An Application in the Area of Bone Healing. In (Burkhard and Lenz 1996), pages 178–185.

SELF, J., 1974. Student models in computer-aided instruction. *International Journal of Man-Machine Studies*, 6:261–276.

SELZ, O., 1924. *Die Gesetze der produktiven und reproduktiven Geistestätigkeit*. Bonn.

SHAHAR, Y. and MUSEN, M. A., 1993. RÉSUMÉ: A Temporal-Abstraction System for Patient Monitoring. *Computers and Biomedical Research*, 26:255–273.

SHANNON, C. E., 1948. *The mathematical theory of communication*. University of Illinois Press, Urbana.

SHAW, M., 1990. Prospects for an engineering discipline of software. *IEEE Software*, 7:15–24.

SHIMAZU, H., KITANO, H., and SHIBATA, A., 1993. Retrieving Cases from Relational Data-Bases: Another Stride Towards Corporate-Wide Case-Based Systems. In (Bajcsy 1993), pages 909–914.

SHOENS, K., LUNIEWSKI, A., SCHWARZ, P., STAMOS, J., and THAMOS, J., 1993. The Rufus System: Information Organization for Semi-Structured Data. In *Proceedings of the 19th VLDB Conference*, pages 97–107. Dublin, Ireland.

SHORTLIFFE, E. H., 1976. *Computer-Based Medical Consultation: MYCIN*. Elsevier, New York.

SLADE, S., 1991. Case-based reasoning: a research paradigm. *AI Magazine*, 12(1):42–55.

SMITH, I. and FALTINGS, B., editors, 1996. *Advances in Case-Based Reasoning*, Lecture Notes in Artificial Intelligence, 1186. Springer Verlag.

SMITH, I., LOTTAZ, C., and FALTINGS, B., 1995. Spatial composition using cases: IDIOM. In (Aamodt and Veloso 1995), pages 88–97. ISBN 3-540-60598-3.

SMITH, I., STALKER, R., and CLAUDIO, L., 1996. Creating design objects from cases for interactive spatial composition. In J. Gero and F. Sudweeks, editors, *Artificial Intelligence in Design '96*, pages 97–116. Kluwer Academic Publishers.

SMYTH, B. and CUNNINGHAM, P., 1992. Déjà Vu: a hierarchical case-based reasoning system for software design. In B. Neumann, editor, *ECAI 92: 10th European Conference on Artificial Intelligence, August 1992, Vienna*, pages 587–589. Wiley, Chichester. ISBN 0-471-93608-1.

SMYTH, B. and KEANE, M. T., 1993. Retrieving Adaptable Cases: The Role of Adaptation Knowledge in Case Retrieval. In (Wess, Althoff, and Richter 1993b), pages 209–220.

SMYTH, B. and KEANE, M. T., 1995. Remembering to Forget. In (Mellish 1995), pages 377–382.

SMYTH, B. and KEANE, M. T., 1996. Using Adaptation Knowledge to Retrieve and Adapt Design Cases. *Journal of Knowledge Based Systems*, 9:127–135.

SOMMER, C., 1993. *MoKon - Ein Ansatz zur wissensbasierten Konfiguration von Variantenerzeugnissen*. Ph.D. thesis, infix Verlag.

SPECHT, M. and WEBER, G., 1996. Episodic adaptation in learning environments. In P. Brna, A. Paiva, and J. Self, editors, *Proceedings of the European Conference on Artificial Intelligence in Education*, pages 171–176.

STADLER, M. and WESS, S., 1989. *PATDEX: Konzept und Implementierung eines fallbasierten, analogieorientierten Inferenzmechanismus zur Diagnose eines CNC-Bearbeitungszentrums*. Project thesis, University of Kaiserslautern.

STAMPER, R., TODD, B. S., and MACPHERSEN, P., 1994. Case-based explanation for medical diagnostic programs, with an example from gynaecology. *Meth. Inf. Med*, 33:205–213.

STANFILL, C. and WALTZ, D., 1986. Toward memory-based reasoning. *Communications of the ACM*, 29(12):1213–1228.

STEELS, L., 1990. Components of expertise. *AI Magazine*, 11(2):29–49.

STOTTLER, R. H., HENKE, A. L., and KING, J. A., 1989. Rapid Retrieval Algorithms for Case-Based Reasoning. In (IJCAI 1989), pages 233–237.

SUN, R., 1995. Robust reasoning: integrating rule-based and similarity-based reasoning. *Artificial Intelligence*, 75(2):241–295.

SWOBODA, W., ZWIEBEL, F. M., SPITZ, R., and GIERL, L., 1994. A case-based consultation system for postoperative management of liver-transplanted patients. In P. Barahona, M. Veloso, and J. Bryant, editors, *Medical Informatics Europe, Proceedings of the 12th International*

Congress of the European Federation for Medical Informatics, pages 191–195.

SYCARA, K., 1988. Using Case-Based Reasoning for Plan Adaptation and Repair. In (Kolodner 1988), pages 425–434.

SYCARA, K. and NAVINCHANDRA, D., 1991. Influences: A Thematic Abstraction for the Creative Reuse of Multiple Cases. In (Bareiss 1991), pages 133–144.

SYCARA, K., NAVINCHANDRA, D., GUTTAL, R., KONING, J., and NARASIMHAN, S., 1992. CADET: a case-based synthesis tool for engineering design. *International Journal of Expert Systems*, 4:157–188.

TALENS, G., BOULANGER, D., DEDUM, I., and COMMEAU, S., 1997. A proposal of retrieval and classification method for a case library reuse. In *Proceedings of the 9th International Conference on Software Engineering and Knowledge Engineering*. Madrid, Spain.

TAMBE, M. and NEWELL, A., 1988. Some chunks are expensive. In *Proceedings of the 5th International Conference on Machine Learning*, pages 451–458.

TAMMER, E.-C., STEINHÖFEL, K., SCHÖNHERR, S., and MATUSCHEK, D., 1995. Anwendung des Konzeptes der Strukturellen Ähnlichkeit zum Fallvergleich mittels Term- und Graph-Repräsentationen. Fabel-Report 38, GMD, Sankt Augustin.

TANK, W., 1991. *Modellierung von Expertise über Konfigurationsaufgaben*. Ph.D. thesis, TU Berlin, infix Verlag.

TAUTZ, C. and ALTHOFF, K.-D., 1997a. Operationalizing the Reuse of Software Knowledge Using Case-Based Reasoning. Techn. Report 017.97/E, Fraunhofer IESE, Kaiserslautern, Germany.

TAUTZ, C. and ALTHOFF, K.-D., 1997b. Using case-based reasoning for reusing software knowledge. Techn. Report 004.97/E, Fraunhofer IESE, Kaiserslautern, Germany.

TAUTZ, C. and ALTHOFF, K.-D., 1997c. Using case-based reasoning for reusing software knowledge. In (Leake and Plaza 1997), pages 156–165. ISBN 3-540-63233-6.

THAGARD, P. and HOLYOAK, K. J., 1989. Why Indexing is the Wrong Way to Think About Analog Retrieval. In (Hammond 1989b), pages 36–40.

THAGARD, P., HOLYOAK, K. J., NELSON, G., and GOCHFELD, D., 1990. Analog Retrieval by Constraint Satisfaction. *Artificial Intelligence*, 46(3):259–310.

THOMAS, M. and MCGARRY, F., 1994. Top-Down vs. Bottom-Up Process Improvement. *IEEE Software*, 11(4).

TIEN, A., 1993. How to Use Cases for Information Seeking Processes. In *Proceedings 1993 AAAI Spring Symposium: Case-Based Reasoning and Information Retrieval – Exploring the Oportunities for Technology Sharing*, pages 120–127. AAAI Press, Stanford, CA.

TISSEN, A., 1991. A Case-based Architecture for a Dialogue Manager for Information-Seeking Processes. In A. Bookstein, editor, *Proceedings SIGIR 91*, pages 152–161. ACM Press, New York, NY.

TSATSOULIS, C. and ALEXANDER, P., 1997. Integrating cases, subcases, and generic prototypes for design. In (Maher and Pu 1997), pages 261–300. ISBN 0-8058-2313-1.

TSUKAMOTO, N., 1993. Supporting System for CT diagnosis to previous cases. *Nippon Acta Radiologica*, 53:45–55.

TURNER, R., 1988. Organizing and Using Schematic Knowledge for Medical Diagnosis. In (Kolodner 1988), pages 435–446.

TURTLE, H. R., 1991. *Inference Networks for Document Retrieval.* Ph.D. thesis, University of Massachusetts Amherst, USA.

TURTLE, H. R. and CROFT, B. W., 1990. Inference Networks for Document Retrieval. In J. L. Vidick, editor, *Proc. of the ACM SIGIR-90*.

TUSCH, G. and GUBERNATIS, G., 1991. Patient matching: A decision support system for liver transplantation. In P. R. Dalmonte, N. D. Imperio, and G. Giuliani Piccari, editors, *Imaging and computing in gastroenterology*, pages 153–158. Springer Verlag.

TVERSKY, A., 1977. Features of Similarity. *Psychological Review*, 84:327–352.

VAN DER LEI, J., KWA, H. Y., HASMAN, A., and WAAGE, M., 1985. IDEA - Integrating Expert Systems with Applications. In *Proceedings of Medical Informatics Europe*, pages 158–162.

VELOSO, M. M., 1994. *Planning and Learning by Analogical Reasoning.* Number 886 in Lecture Notes in Computer Science. Springer, Berlin. ISBN 3-540-58811-6.

VELOSO, M. M. and BLYTHE, J., 1994. Linkability: Examining causal link commitments in partial-order planning. In (AIPS 1994).

VON MAYRHAUSER, A., 1990. *Software Engineering: Methods and Management.* Academic Press, San Diego, CA.

VOSS, A., 1994. Similarity concepts and retrieval methods. Fabel-Report 13, Gesellschaft für Mathematik und Datenverarbeitung mbH (GMD), Sankt Augustin.

VOSS, A., 1997. Case design specialists in FABEL. In M. L. Maher and P. Pu, editors, *Issues and Applications of Case Based Reasoning to Design*, pages 301–338. Lawrence Erlbaum Associates, Mahwah, NJ.

WAHLSTER, W., editor, 1996. *Proceedings 12th European Conference on Artificial Intelligence ECAI-96*. John Wiley and Sons.

WALDINGER, R., 1977. Achieving several goals simultaneously. *Machine Intelligence*, 8:94–136.

WATERMAN, D. A., 1986. *A Guide to Expert Systems*. Addison-Wesley, Reading. ISBN 0201083132.

WEBER, G., 1994. Examples and remindings in a case-based help system. In (Keane, Haton, and Manago 1994), pages 165–177.

WEBER, G., 1996. Episodic learner modeling. *Cognitive Science*, 20:195–236.

WEBER, G., BÖGELSACK, A., and WENDER, K. F., 1993. When can individual student models beuseful? In G. Strube and K. F. Wender, editors, *The cognitive psychology of knowledge*, pages 263–284. Elsevier, Amsterdam.

WEBER, G., BRUSILOVSKY, P., SPECHT, M., and STEINLE, F., 1996. ELM-PE: An intelligent learning environment for programming. ITS '96 System Demonstrations.

WEBER, G. and MÖLLENBERG, A., 1995. ELM programming environment: A tutoring system for LISP beginners. In K. F. Wender, F. Schmalhofer, and H.-D. Böcker, editors, *Cognition and computer programming*, pages 373–408. Ablex, Norwood, NJ.

WEBER, G. and SPECHT, M., 1997. User modeling and adaptive navigation support in WWW-based tutoring systems. In A. Jameson, C. Paris, and C. Tasso, editors, *User Modeling: Proceedings of the Sixth International Conference*, pages 289–300. Springer Verlag, Vienna.

WEBERSKIRCH, F., 1995. Combining SNLP-like Planning and Dependency-Maintenance. Technical Report LSA-95-10E, Centre for Learning Systems and Applications, University of Kaiserslautern, Germany.

WENDEL, O., 1995. MOBIS - wissensbasiertes Experimentiersystem zur Simualtion biologischer neuronaler Netze. *KI*, 9(3):59–64.

WENGER, A., 1987. *Artificial intelligence and tutoring systems: computational and cognitive approaches to the communication of knowledge*. Morgan Kaufmann Publishers, Los Altos, CA.

WENKEBACH, U., POLLWEIN, B., and FINSTERER, U., 1992. Visualization of large datasets in intensive care. In *Proceedings Annual Symposium Computer Applications Medical Care*, pages 18–22.

WESS, S., 1990. *PATDEX/2: ein System zum adaptiven, fallfokussierenden Lernen in technischen Diagnosesituationen*. Diploma thesis, University of Kaiserslautern.

WESS, S., 1993. PATDEX – Ein Ansatz zur wissensbasierten und inkrementellen Verbesserung von Ähnlichkeitsbewertungen in der fallbasierten Diagnostik. In F. Puppe and Guenter, editors, *Proceedings XPS-93*. Springer-Verlag, Hamburg.

WESS, S., 1995. *Fallbasiertes Problemlösen in wissensbasierten Systemen zur Entscheidungsunterstützung und Diagnostik*. Ph.D. thesis, Universität Kaiserslautern. Available as DISKI 126, infix Verlag.

WESS, S., ALTHOFF, K.-D., and DERWAND, G., 1993a. Using kd-Trees to Improve the Retrieval Step in Case-Based Reasoning. In (Wess, Althoff, and Richter 1993b), pages 167–181.

WESS, S., ALTHOFF, K.-D., and RICHTER, M. M., editors, 1993b. *Topics in Case-Based Reasoning. Proceedings of the First European Workshop on Case-Based Reasoning (EWCBR-93)*, Lecture Notes in Artificial Intelligence, 837. Springer Verlag.

WHITTLE, J., 1995. Analogy in *CL^AM*. Technical Report MSc.thesis, University of Edinburgh, Dept. of AI, Edinburgh.

WIELINGA, B. J., VAN DE VELDE, W., SCHREIBER, G., and AKKERMANS, H., 1993. Towards a unification of knowledge modeling approaches. In K. . S. David, editor, *Second Generation Expert Systems*, pages 299–335. Springer.

WILKE, W., 1997. Case-Based Reasoning and Electronic Commerce. Invited Talk at ICCBR-97.

WILKE, W. and BERGMANN, R., 1996a. Considering decision cost during learning of feature weights. In (Smith and Faltings 1996), pages 460–472.

WILKE, W. and BERGMANN, R., 1996b. Incremental Adaptation with the INRECA-System. In *ECAI 1996 Workshop on Adaptation in Case-Based Reasoning*. http://wwwagr.informatik.uni-kl.de/~bergmann/adapt-quest.html.

WILKE, W., VOLLRATH, I., ALTHOFF, K.-D., and BERGMANN, R., 1997. A Framework for Learning Adaptation Knowledge Based on Knowledge Light Approaches. In (Bergmann and Wilke 1997), pages 235–242.

WILKINSON, R., 1994. Effective Retrieval of Structured Documents. In *SIGIR'94*.

WOLSTENCROFT, J., 1989. Restructuring, reminding, repair: What's missing from models of analogy. *AI Communications*, 2:58–71.

WOLVERTON, M., 1995. An Investigation of Marker-Passing Algorithms for Analogue Retrieval. In (Aamodt and Veloso 1995), pages 359–370. ISBN 3-540-60598-3.

WOLVERTON, M. and HAYES-ROTH, B., 1994. Retrieving semantically distant analogies with knowledge-directed spreading activation. In (AAAI 1994), pages 56–61.

ZELKOWITZ, M. V., 1978. Perspectives on Software Engineering. *ACM Computing Surveys*, 10(2).

Index

Springer and the environment

At Springer we firmly believe that an international science publisher has a special obligation to the environment, and our corporate policies consistently reflect this conviction.

We also expect our business partners – paper mills, printers, packaging manufacturers, etc. – to commit themselves to using materials and production processes that do not harm the environment. The paper in this book is made from low- or no-chlorine pulp and is acid free, in conformance with international standards for paper permanency.

Springer